FREEDOM TO DIE

Also by Derek Humphry

Euthanasia
Jean's Way
Let Me Die Before I Wake
The Right to Die (with Ann Wickett)
Final Exit
Dying with Dignity
Lawful Exit

General
Because They're Black
Passports and Politics
Police Power and Black People
False Messiah (with David Tindall)
The Cricket Conspiracy

FREEDOM TO DIE

People, Politics, and the Right-to-Die Movement

Derek Humphry and Mary Clement

St. Martin's Press

New York

Library of Congress Cataloging-in-Publication Data

Humphry, Derek
Freedom to die : people, politics, and the right-to-die movement /
Derek Humphry and Mary Clement.—1st ed.
p.   cm.
Includes index.
ISBN 0-312-19415-3
1. Right to die—United States—Public opinion.   2. Right to die—
Law and legislation—United States.   3. Public opinion—United
States.   I. Clement, Mary.   II. Title.
R726.H844   1998
179.7—dc21   98-21127
                                                CIP

First Edition: October 1998

10   9   8   7   6   5   4   3   2   1

There is one thing stronger than all the
armies of the world: and that is an idea
whose time has come.

—Victor Hugo

Contents

FREEDOM TO DIE

Prologue

Velma Howard, age seventy-six, knew that her life was coming to an end. Lou Gehrig's disease was taking away the use of her limbs one by one. Eventually it would affect her throat, and she would be in danger of choking on her own saliva. This elderly, respectable, Middle American and her husband decided on rational suicide. Her decision resulted in an emotional ordeal for her family, and a legal muddle typical of the mess in which America's laws on assisted death exist.

Velma and Bernard A. Howard were the "sweet old couple on the block" of their community in Belleville, Illinois. She had been a kindergarten schoolteacher. He had served as staff sergeant in the Marine Corps during World War II. They were married on December 8, 1945, and Bernard worked with the Department of Defense for twenty-five years until his retirement. Their two grown sons now lived elsewhere, but children in the neighborhood all knew that the Howards always opened their door to trick-or-treaters at Halloween. The day of their fiftieth wedding anniversary, young neighbors knocked on the door with a bunch of carnations. "I can honestly say that I never met two nicer people in my life," another neighbor told the local newspaper. The Howards attended church regularly, enjoyed themselves at senior citizens' clubs, and went square dancing until Velma was taken ill.

With her left arm useless and her legs weakening, Velma began to think about an accelerated death. The pain from the neuromuscular disease, a degenerative condition known medically as amyotrophic lateral sclerosis (ALS), was increasing. But, most of all, she did not want to linger for months in a steady decline, dragging down her husband at the same time. Velma read books on the subject of ending her suffering, talked on the telephone long-distance with a right-to-die group, and discussed her plan with close friends and immediate family. Unable to write clearly, Velma made a three-minute audiotape outlining her reasons for deciding to die now rather than wait. On the tape she accepted full responsibility for her action, stressing that no one else should be blamed.

One son was a businessman in Plano, Texas; the other a judge in Lenexa, Kansas. Always considerate of others, Velma resolved that they would all drive to a central point—Joplin, Missouri—and celebrate the golden wedding anniversary. The next day she would die. Velma had not taken into account that Joplin (population 40,961) is famous as "the Buckle of the Bible Belt."

The elder Howards checked into Room 305 of the Days Inn in Joplin, and on Saturday they celebrated with their two sons, Bernard junior and Stephen, reminiscing about the past but saying little about the future. Everyone present knew what would happen the next day and was in agreement with Velma's wishes.

On Sunday, when she was ready to die, the three men helped Velma, and by all accounts her death was swift and peaceful. Then one of the sons informed the motel staff, who called the police. What happened next illustrates the strange attitudes toward rational suicide of the terminally ill in Missouri—or in any other state, for that matter.

It was an easy case for Newton County police and the prosecutors because all three Howards made statements explaining exactly what happened. An immediate autopsy confirmed the presence of narcotics in the body. A few days later Joplin's police chief, David Neibur, typified police bafflement about these suicides, describing the case as "very bizarre."

Suicide is not a felony in Missouri—or in any other American state. Velma had committed no crime. But in 1984 the Missouri legislature had passed a one-line law (565.023.1[2], RSMo) stating that anybody *assisting* in suicide (or self-murder) was committing a Class B felony, punishable by five to fifteen years' imprisonment. In twelve years nobody in the state had been tried or even investigated for the offense; thus there was no case law available for review.

At the time nobody in the United States had been jailed for assisted suicide, although in 1996 in New York City George Delury pleaded guilty to assisting his wife's suicide and received six months' imprisonment. Since his conviction was the result of a plea bargain, there could be no appeal to clarify the law. Many legal observers believe that if he had fought the case, a jury would have acquitted him. Dr. Jack Kevorkian has been acquitted three times in jury trials in Michigan. In 1998 John Bement of Buffalo, New York, was convicted by a jury and given two weeks' imprisonment, plus probation, for aiding the suicide of his wife who had ALS.

How Velma Howard died is vividly described in the actual complaint sheet produced shortly afterward in court, when two of the three men were accused. (Stephen Howard was never charged with any offense, apparently because his physical involvement was found to have been minor.)

In the exact words of the prosecuting attorney's complaint, Bernard A. Howard, seventy-six, was charged with a Class B felony:

The defendant knowingly assisted Velma Howard in the commission of self-murder by providing for Velma Howard orange juice used by her in filling a recipe for death outlined in a book containing instructions on self-murder, by reducing the temperature of the room in which Velma Howard committed self-murder as called for in the book, by providing Velma Howard rubbers [sic] bands which Velma Howard used to affix a plastic bag over her head, thus cutting off the supply of air to her body and by arranging chairs and items used by Velma Howard to commit self-murder into such proximity as to give Velma Howard access to such items, to wit: a container of orange juice laced with sleeping powder and alcohol, a container of food substance containing a narcotic, a plastic bag, a rubber band ligature, and a springform pan, all used by Velma Howard in the commission of self-murder.

The charge sheet against her son, Bernard A. Howard, Jr., age forty-nine, read much the same, with additions that also accused him of "reading from a book containing instructions on self-murder and by helping Velma Howard into a position in which she was in immediate proximity to several items which were used by Velma Howard to commit self-murder." The book was *Final Exit*.

It was almost certainly the first time in history that anybody in the United States had been charged with reading a book, redolent of religious persecutions in medieval times. Could turning down the heat and moving chairs around also be a crime? The Howards had not provided the drugs because Velma had her own supply of Dalmane. The case promised to be a field day for lawyers and judges if it ever got to court.

Early in the proceedings the older man decided to plead guilty, but his son announced that he would prefer a trial. Both were granted bail.

The case attracted extensive media attention throughout Missouri, causing the county prosecutor, Greg Bridges, to call a press conference a month later. At this meeting Bridges revealed to reporters some of his doubts and fears about the case. "There are no other cases like this, there's no precedent to be guided by," he said. He was not unsympathetic to what happened but had to obey the law. Whereupon he read out the astonishing charges concerning, among other things, reading a certain book and altering the thermostat.

A reporter bluntly asked the prosecutor if this wasn't really a moral issue.

"This case doesn't have anything to do with whether it's right or wrong to commit suicide," replied Bridges. "It just happens to be illegal in Missouri to help somebody to do so." He added that he suspected there had been no previous prosecutions because "some people are hesitant to prosecute it [on account] of the emotional issues involved."

Prosecutor Bridges later told a local newspaper that after filing the charges he had received hate mail and been called names.

As the case was being prepared for trial, two influential high courts in the United States, the Ninth and Second Circuit Courts of Appeals, ruled that states could not ban assisted suicide for a competent terminally ill person. The rulings did not technically affect Missouri, which is in the Eighth Circuit. But immediately Bridges, who never seemed aggressive in his prosecution of the Howards, saw these rulings as a way out of his dilemma.

"I'll sit on the case for one year to see if something develops," Bridges announced. "To go blindly ahead, prosecute them, and maybe have the law overturned wouldn't be fair to the family. We should wait for a determination from a higher court."

Subsequently the attorney generals of Washington and New York States appealed the lower courts' decisions to the U.S. Supreme Court. The high court overturned the Ninth and Second Circuit Courts of Appeals, and bans on physician-assisted suicide (PAS) remained constitutional. Bridges could easily have prosecuted the Howards, since the Missouri felony law was firmly in place. He chose not to do so. When the case came up for review the following year, all charges were dropped.

This case exemplifies the discretion given prosecutors as well as the ambivalence they often feel when deciding how to handle cases of this kind. The Howards were solid citizens, unanimous in their decision; there was no hint of impropriety. In short they were decent people, trying to handle a difficult situation in a cautious and dignified manner. Many see an assisted dying as an action of compassion and love. But not everyone agrees— especially not leaders of the Roman Catholic Church and the National Right to Life Committee, which can bring enormous pressure to bear. Prosecutors, with no legal precedent to follow, may be torn with doubts and fears over the political, ethical, and judicial practicalities of pressing for a conviction. They also know that, as with the Howards, after all the grieving family's anguish and expense, any court proceedings usually come to naught in the end.

Introduction

The right to choose an assisted death has swiftly overtaken abortion as America's most contentious social issue. Indeed, activists and the media call it "the ultimate civil liberty." Some 60 to 75 percent of the general public supports the right to die.[1] The establishment—government, churches, the American Medical Association, those powerful, exclusive groups that control or influence society—however, is adamantly and vocally opposed. Nevertheless, the public is winning the debate.

Every so often a new social issue arises that shifts the paradigm of certainty, splintering the conventional wisdom of the social order. Such is the story of the right-to-die movement, rooted in the evolving concept that a dignified death is preferable to an intolerable life. Like other civil rights, this controversial issue did not suddenly arrive with the morning paper. It grew out of cultural and economic changes, unmet needs, and shifting priorities, which percolated relatively unnoticed until the pressure built to such a degree that it spilled over into mainstream America and became part of public policy.

Why, at the end of the twentieth century, has the right-to-die movement finally become part of the mainstream debate? Why have Oregonians now legalized physician-assisted suicide, overturning centuries of prohibition? Why did the U.S. Supreme Court feel compelled to address issues it clearly wanted to avoid? The answers lie in the tremendous advances of technology, the rights culture of the 1960s, the decline of the doctor-patient relationship, the medical profession's poor handling of end-of-life care, and the AIDS epidemic.

In answering the question Why Now? this book begins with the case of Karen Ann Quinlan and examines the responses from the public and the courts as the idea germinated that an individual might determine the time and manner of his or her death. *Quinlan* brought general recognition by the American legal system of the right-to-die and as such, marked the beginning of the movement. It forced people to consider, perhaps for the first time, that because of medical technology and unwanted medical treatment, life could be more feared than death. Over time, state and federal courts removed medical decision-making authority from the proprietary hands of the medical profession and gave it to the patient. The Hemlock Society provided like-minded people with a forum to press cohesively for the legalization of assisted suicide. Doctor Kevorkian raised public awareness as the nation watched other countries deal with this sizzling topic.

The issue of PAS for the mentally competent, terminally ill adult has become a bitter struggle between the American people and those institutions that provide a formidable check on the right-to-die movement. The Roman Catholic Church is terrified that its hypocrisy will be exposed, and recognizes that if it loses on this civil right, the foundation of its dogma of God's supreme authority over human behavior will have been destroyed. The medical profession, historically opposed to regulation and oversight of any kind, is angry about its dwindling power, and is motivated by self-interest and greed. The government, for its part, is too cowardly to leave the sanctuary of safe political cover.

The opposing forces of activism and restraint have produced political and legal reforms, the results of cultural changes, declining institutions, demographic shifts—in simplest terms, of people and events. Physician-assisted suicide has arrived, and Oregon has legalized it. The Supreme Court has left the issue to the states. Overriding all other considerations, the cost of health care in an aging society demands exploration of a shortening of the dying process to eliminate wasteful procedures and unwanted care.

In the next century, when historians focus on the key social issues that engaged Americans in the last three decades of the twentieth century, they will undoubtedly be struck by the protracted struggles for two rights involving people's control over their bodies: medical abortion and physician-assisted suicide. Both options, according to opinion polls, were wanted by a majority of the people. Yet many politicians, judges, and church leaders fought to deny the right of an adult to make decisions about these most basic of human events—birth and death.

Thus was a nation divided, between one side comprising millions of people who wanted straightforward choices about their lives, and the other, smaller numerically but supremely powerful in its manipulation of the controlling mechanisms of society. In this power struggle the popular vote has tried to overcome the strength of those in command of legislation, despite the latter's access to substantial organizational political clout and financial influence.

The fight for a woman's right to choose lawful, medical abortion has lasted more than twenty-five years. Legalized in 1973 by the U.S. Supreme Court in *Roe* v. *Wade*, the law has had to be constantly defended against neutralization by the forces of the Christian right in Congress, the courts, and state legislatures. A foreigner arriving in the United States today could be forgiven for thinking that abortion was still a crime, so vociferous and persistent are the attempts to stop it. A woman's right to control decisions about her body has barely survived the onslaught, a few extremists having resorted to the shooting of doctors and the bombing of clinics.

Another, similarly protracted struggle is developing as battle lines are drawn for the second war over "choice." The most common illusion entertained by people who either come fresh to the subject of assisted suicide or are anxious to scoff at it is that euthanasia has to do with cutting off other people's lives before they are ready to die. We have the Nazi propaganda machine to thank for that myth, and also their misuse of the word "euthanasia," which means "good death" and has come down to us from the Greek *eu* (good) and *thanatos* (death). As well as slaughtering some ten million Jews, Gypsies, homosexuals, Russian prisoners of war, political dissidents, and common criminals, the Nazis in their madness also set about exterminating their own mentally or physically handicapped people.

Historical records point to at least one hundred thousand such murders, with a great many more—mainly deformed babies—unrecorded. Covering their tracks so as not to cause alarm among their own people, the Nazis pretended that these were mercy killings, shrewdly mislabeling them part of the "Euthanasia Program." The purpose of the slaughter was in fact twofold: the creation of a master race and the elimination of those whom they considered to be living a "life unworthy of life."

Hitler and his cronies gave humanity a terrible example of mass murder, which must never be forgotten. By no stretch of the imagination were these "good deaths." Choice in the matter did not exist. Yet to tell a person today in, say, Peoria, Illinois, who is suffering abominably from terminal cancer that he or she cannot have lethal drugs because of Nazi Germany's record is not only the height of absurdity but cruel and irrelevant. Two decades of debate on the right to die have cleared away most of the general public's concern that legalizing an assisted death resembles Nazi crimes.

Thus, in this book we are not afraid to use the word "euthanasia" where appropriate, accepting that its modern definition has gradually been modified to mean "help with a good death." Nor will we back away from the word "suicide," as many do. But we will preface both words with qualifying terms: *voluntary* euthanasia, and *physician-assisted* suicide. True, many people are more comfortable with such euphemisms as "aid in dying" and "self-deliverance," but if the right-to-die debate is to get anywhere it must be honest in its use of terms.

To avoid the confusion resulting from the use of "I" by two authors, we have decided to refer to ourselves in the third person.

Throughout this book "euthanasia" means general help with a good death by whatever methods; "voluntary euthanasia" means a dying patient asking a doctor for a lethal injection; and "physician-assisted suicide" means a dying patient asking a doctor for a prescription for lethal drugs to be self-administered. As this book is almost entirely about physician-assisted suicide, we shall use the initials PAS. The so-called right-to-die movement in the United States and the rest of the world is concerned solely with securing death with choice and dignity for competent adults who are close to the end and asking for a speedier release from unbearable suffering. This movement, which has its roots in classical Greece, resurfaced quietly in the 1930s and then took off popularly in the 1980s. It seeks neither societal acceptance nor laws for ending the lives of the mentally ill and incompetent, the disabled, minors, and malformed babies. The most vulnerable among us are entitled to society's compassion and appropriate care. To lump all these quality-of-life and dignity-in-death problems together, as some do, serves only to confuse the issue and delay the help many sectors of society cry out for. This book is solely concerned with terminal illness, whose significance is illustrated by the statistic that some 2 million people face this fatal condition in the United States every year.

This book also examines why in an America world-famous as "the land of the free," a nation founded mostly by people fleeing religious and political persecutions on other continents, the Roman Catholic Church is passionately opposing the right of people not of its faith to have a lawful assisted death. It is as though Jehovah's Witnesses were forbidding the rest of the population blood transfusions, or Christian Scientists barring others from medical care. While the Roman Catholic Church is the most vocal and active opponent of PAS, many other sectors of the Christian and Jewish faiths also oppose it. Do we live in a society whose laws must still be governed by the dogmas of the Judeo-Christian religions, or should secular, commonsense, and humanitarian politics help us to frame our laws? Though euthanasia in any form remains a crime in most of the United States, the American Catholic bishops can be expected both to continue to try to undo the Oregon law and to stop its spread to other states. At what point in this contest, constitutional law scholars may well ask, will their efforts become an infringement of the traditional separation of church and state in the United States?

Historically famous for keeping its head in the sand until the forces of reform have swept past, the American Medical Association (AMA) leadership also trenchantly opposes any form of assisted death as ethically unacceptable. But the AMA's membership is declining (down to 42 percent of all doctors), with many of its own members in revolt over its conservative policies. Thousands of doctors—so independent studies show—already covertly help some patients to a quicker death. Oddly the AMA does not condemn this "back-alley" euthanasia but concentrates on opposing the regulation of open, thoughtful, legal procedures. Unfortunately the AMA's political clout makes it nearly impossible to conduct a high-quality study of the euthanasia issue. Thus in the United States—in contrast to the Netherlands, which for twenty-five years has had an open-door investigative policy—we are blundering forward into an area of human behavior that is emotionally, ethically, and medically extremely sensitive. False moves could cause more suffering.

Many politicians—none more so than President Clinton—are playing games with the euthanasia issue. Afraid of calls for voter boycotts by the churches, and still in awe of the power and the purse of the medical profession, elected representatives look over their shoulders and hastily damn any fact-gathering or law reform. One example: Who can explain why 60 to 75 percent of Americans want PAS yet 100 percent of U.S. senators vote against it? They are either very out of touch with the average elector's views or being leaned on by special-interest lobbyists. President Clinton has sternly defended a woman's right to choice over abortion. But his humanity does not extend to help for the dying. His knee-jerk reaction in 1997, lacking any examination of the pros and cons, was quickly to sign into law a bill forbidding federal funds to be spent on PAS.

The extreme timidity the establishment has demonstrated over the PAS issue sends a clear message to the public: If you want this ultimate in civil liberties you must use the ballot box to achieve it, as voters in Oregon did. This being an issue in which everybody—from blue-collar worker to university intellectual—has strong and often fixed views, the next decade in the United States promises to be a contentious one.

PART ONE

The
Impetus
for
Change

Medical Technology's Onslaught

Public interest is the lever that activates the government and other institutions to formulate public policy. Members of the community, from block associations to the U.S. electorate, raise issues and express preferences by the election of officials, by initiatives and referendums, and by the determination of special-interest-group activity. The government, in response to its constituents, provides public policy. Other institutions modify or change their official policy as public pressure dictates.

The right-to-die has become a matter of immense public interest and concern. What began as minimal interest in the 1930s, escalated in the 1970s with the plight of Karen Ann Quinlan, and continued with the California and Washington referendums—followed by the Oregon initiative—has culminated at the end of the twentieth century in the U.S. Supreme Court's deciding the constitutionality of a mentally competent terminally ill adult's right to determine, with the aid of a physician, the time and manner of his or her death.

The Supreme Court addresses a divisive social issue only when that issue has generated enough interest, intensity, and conflict over an adequate period of time to demand some kind of legal resolution. The Court seldom seeks the authoritative role on a red-hot social issue such as PAS. Quite the contrary, it generally tries to avoid it. Public interest, however, pressured the Court to consider this controversial social issue. As it turned out, the Court left the matter to the states, but its very consideration of the issue signals that PAS has become part of a mainstream debate. However, far from establishing what might be called "A Policy for the Right-to-Die Movement," the Oregon initiative and the Supreme Court ruling add more pieces to the jigsaw puzzle of the ongoing struggle. The individual states will decide whether PAS will be allowed, and they will formulate public policy based on public demand.

Public interest and policy do not appear and grow in a vacuum. Right-to-die policy is developing as the result of the " 'policy forces' of restraint, activism, and mediation: pressures and stresses that push, pull, and shape policy into one form or another."[1] This approach allows us to understand right-to-die policy, in the United States at the end of the twentieth century, as the result of the forces of activism overwhelming the forces of restraint, forcing the government to act.

These forces of activism have compelled the culture of medicine, the economics of health care, state and federal courts, and legislatures in all fifty states to deal with the right-to-die. Forces of restraint are also at work, and have until recently kept PAS submerged as an issue of extensive public discussion. Though the forces of activism overcame the forces of restraint on the issue of forgoing life-sustaining treatment, the struggle against PAS continues. Institutions with a vested interest in maintaining the status quo attempt to hold the line against change. Political scientist James Hoefler says these same "forces of restraint are strong enough to limit the scope of right-to-die policy and slow its development," even as they lose to popular opinion.[2]

What are these forces of activism that drive public support of assisted death, that are responsible for raising public awareness of the suffering patient who lacks all hope of ever regaining a meaningful quality of life? Why does one Gallup poll show that 75 percent of Americans believe doctors should be allowed to end the lives of terminally ill patients by painless means if the patients request it?[3] Why do an even higher 78 percent of adults believe that PAS should be legalized by the federal government?[4] Why are newspapers across the country now endorsing the practice in their editorial pages? Why did Oregonians ignore intense pressure from establishment forces and vote in favor of assisted death? What has happened in our culture that the two largest and most influential courts of appeals have ruled, in effect, that laws dating back to the nineteenth century, prohibiting assisted suicide, need no longer pertain to late-twentieth-century Americans? What do Americans know now that they did not know before? Again, Why Now?

A number of factors have brought society to the point where a majority favors the voluntary termination of life to avoid unrelenting pain and suffering. Dramatic advances in technology since World War II, the rise of AIDS as a national plague, the decline of the doctor-patient relationship, the economics of health care, and the medical profession's lax attitude toward pain control and comfort care, combined with the expectations of entitlement and autonomy generated by the "rights culture" of the 1960s, all give rise to the expectation of a quality death with personal input. The right-to-die movement is consistent, furthermore, with the baby boomers' increasingly influential creed: "I want what I want when I want it, especially if it will make me feel better."

It is incontrovertible that fear of dying in the cold, impersonal clutches of modern medical technology has given a major boost to public acceptance of a hastened death. Technology has pushed the assisted-death issue to the forefront. Americans are uneasy about the cost and the impersonal technological arrogance of modern medical care, and they fear a prolonged death that diminishes their dignity and burdens their loved ones. Technology creates scenarios that raise questions about the dying process.

Henry R. Glick, professor of political science and research associate at the Institute on Aging at Florida State University, sees no end to medical innovation and the power of doctors and new machines to prolong life—and the resulting liabilities for the elderly and the seriously ill. "Changes in the technology and the practice of medicine, coupled with traditional medical training and ethics that champion conquering disease and preserving life, and doctors' fears of liability for discontinuing treatment have all created a specter of a lingering death for many terminally ill or comatose patients and the growing elderly population," says Glick. "Modern medical tools are valued lifesavers for accident victims and those suffering from reversible serious illness or undergoing surgery, but the new technology can also be a threat to the elderly and the hopelessly ill who inevitably will die, but not quickly or easily because the same machines that preserve life can exacerbate inevitable death."[5]

How did technology, once regarded so positively, become so objectionable as to start a new social movement worldwide? Before the 1950s, when doctors and nurses practiced without benefit of modern medicine, the right-to-die was of little concern, since medical science was unable to extend appreciably the lives of terminally ill patients. People understood that death was inevitable and unavoidable. Daniel Callahan, founder and former president of the Hastings Center, which studies ethical issues in medicine, says that death

> was seen across the entire life cycle, from children to elderly people. Medicine could do very little in the way of cure or in the extension of life. That came from better sanitation, nutrition and housing, not through medical intervention. Medicine provided comfort care and palliation. Most importantly, the cultures of the prescientific era developed various religious and cultural rituals to help people cope with death and grief. Even though death was feared, it was accepted and placed in the context of people's lives.[6]

Most people died at home without medical treatment or technology. In 1949, 50 percent of the U.S. population died in institutions—hospitals, medical centers, or nursing homes. In 1958 the figure was 61 percent. Two decades later the number had risen to 71 percent. Now, over 80 percent die in medical institutions. In the past death came naturally, and when aid in dying was appropriate, the privacy of the domestic bedroom shielded a doctor who deliberately overmedicated. Little was written about the care of the dying. Death occurred through the natural progression of life. The absence of sophisticated medical procedures made illness more likely to be deadly than it is today. Certainly death then was swifter. The permanently unconscious patient died quickly from additional complications or starvation, whichever occurred first. Pneumonia, influenza, tuberculosis, and common infections produced rapid death before the invention of penicillin during World War II. Technology has dramatically changed the trajectory of illness. We now have long periods of functional decline.

Technological advances during World War II dramatically changed the prognosis of the dying patient as well as the mind-set of the nation. Penicillin, first used in military hospitals, and, later on, other antibiotics, enjoyed widespread use and were responsible for the control of acute and communicable diseases. By the 1950s technological wizardry had come to the forefront with stunning results. The decade was alive with possibilities. According to Glick, the public was justifiably awed as

> surgical techniques improved, and cancer patients, for example, could undergo surgery that might not cure but could postpone the ravages of illness. Developments during this period included intravenous feeding, new drugs to fight infection, and cardiopulmonary bypass machines and coronary angiography for open heart surgery and for studying coronary circulation. In the 1960s, ventilators, cardiac resuscitation, kidney dialysis, organ transplants, artificial heart valves, and more antibiotics were added to the medical arsenal. Computer axial tomography (CAT scanners) and nuclear magnetic resonance imaging (MRIs), which were superior to x-rays, appeared in the 1970s and 1980s. New drugs for fighting the progression of AIDS and other diseases are on the way, and organ transplant and artificial skin technology is improving.[7]

Following the war, the United States underwent a massive transformation, driven primarily by prosperity and technological advance. Both world wars and the Great Depression were things of the past, and the country was ready to tackle all its problems. The mood was optimistic, and the air was alive with apparently limitless possibilities. The impressive advances in well-being, including consumer products and services, were introduced primarily in the twenty-five years following World War II.

Much of what we take for granted every day stems from that postwar era: In 1945 almost no one had a television, yet by 1994, 97 percent of Americans had color TVs; in 1940, U.S. commercial aircraft carried 3.5 million passengers, yet by the mid-1990s, the total exceeded 400 million; and, introduced in the 1960s, oral contraception—the Pill—revolutionized birth control, making it easier for women to work, families to limit their children, and couples to engage in sex without fear of pregnancy. Highways, automobiles, communications, home appliances, computers, and farm machinery expanded the constantly growing list of consumer-oriented innovations.

The public, surfacing from thirty years of hard times, saw technology as a means of winning the war against death, says journalist Robert J. Samuelson:

> Once a problem had been identified, it became the enemy and could— as the Second World War had shown—be defeated with the right tactics and weapons. Sometimes the metaphor was applied explicitly, as with the 1960s War on Poverty or the 1980s "war on drugs." More often it was simply a frame of mind that Americans adopted when confronted with society's imperfections. . . . Both the war and the Depression seemed to discredit the notion that "just leaving things alone" was the best way to proceed. The postwar style of politics would blend the two experiences into the "politics of problem solving." The phrase conveyed a faith that, as a nation, we might solve whatever problems presented themselves.[8]

President John F. Kennedy told Americans in 1961 that the United States would put a man on the moon by the end of the decade. Work began, and the goal was achieved. With this dramatic accomplishment the conquering of any technological frontier seemed not only worth conquering but capable of being conquered. Hoefler comments: "Questions about whether going to the moon was really the right thing to do with the billions of dollars spent on that pursuit got very little attention at the time. Instead, it seemed as if the collective American reaction to the idea was 'if we *can* (and of course we can), then we *should*.' "[9]

The twenty years following the close of World War II have been called "the Gilded Age of research, the triumph of laissez-faire in the laboratory," writes David J. Rothman, professor of social medicine and history at Columbia University and director of the Center for the Study of Society and Medicine at the Columbia College of Physicians and Surgeons.[10] The thrust of public policy was to finance organizations and individuals able to continue the spectacular achievements in medical research that had begun during World War II. The victories over smallpox, typhoid, tetanus, yellow fever, and other infectious diseases were recounted. Americans reveled in the exhilarating certainty that humanity was approaching a time when some of the most dreaded diseases could and would be wiped out, and this certainty was fostered by the research community and the press. No science fiction achievements, however grandiose, seemed unrealistic. The discovery of the "miracle drug," penicillin, served as proof of the unlimited possibilities that existed to reduce human suffering.

Society began its infatuation with technology as a result of this infectious excitement. The medical community was no exception. It began functioning under what is known as the "technological imperative": the belief that it is obligated to use whatever medical treatment and technology is available, for as long as possible, however small the potential benefit, however high the emotional, mental, physical or financial cost to the patient and his or her family.

Political figures joined the all-out battle against diseases and the National Institutes of Health embodied the national mandate. Congress appropriated approximately $700,000 for the NIH in 1945. Rothman points out: "By 1955, the figure had climbed to $36 million; and by 1970, $1.5 billion, a sum that allowed it to award some 11,000 grants. . . . Indeed, the scope and significance of NIH operations were such that through the 1980s, practically every chairman of a basic science department in major American medical schools was at some point in his career an NIH fellow or NIH grant recipient."[11]

The technological explosion perpetuated the myth that medical technology could cure all the diseases that plague us, and perhaps even eliminate death itself. As a result the government has continued to invest more money in finding new and better cures. In 1983, for example, $6 billion was spent on health research alone. The expectation for each year in the 1990s well surpassed $10 billion.

An early contribution to this technological explosion, introduced in 1952, originated in Denmark during the worldwide polio epidemic. Seeing a large group of children in his clinic and knowing they would die, an anesthesiologist in Copenhagen introduced the technique of using airbags to pump oxygen into the lungs of these failing patients. The technique worked, but it required continuous pumping to be effective. All the medical students of the Copenhagen Medical School and all of the nurses in the hospital spent a week pumping oxygen into the children's lungs, saving many of them from certain death.

It was apparent that this innovation was useful but impractical in its current form. And so, by attaching a mechanical pump to the airbag instead of a student or a nurse, medicine created the first artificial respirator. This piece of technology became popular in both the United States and Europe, so that virtually every hospital had at least one respirator by the mid-1950s. Bioethicist Stanley J. Reiser speaks of its wonders: "It was a miraculous machine in that patients coming into hospitals with acute respiratory failure, stroke from drug overdose, or in diabetic coma could be treated in the hope that the natural breathing mechanism would be restored and the technology could be removed."[12]

This emphasis on technology has brought mixed blessings. The increasing medical possibilities have had, in general, very positive effects. More patients survive, fewer patients have severe handicaps, and certain suffering is reduced. On the other hand, medical advances in diagnosis and treatment have also made it difficult to get off the inexorable medical treadmill. There is always a promising new treatment to be tried, and doctors play down the low success rate, placing an often unrealistic emphasis on "hope." For the first time in history, physicians have the ability, knowledge, and sophisticated technology to sustain the physical life of patients with no regard to the quality of life they are willing to endure. The dying process is often merely prolonged, with no known way of bringing the patient back to more than a subhuman existence.

These mixed results are reflected in Reiser's account of a Viennese anesthesiologist, Dr. Bruno Haid, who enthusiastically used this miraculous respirator, only to see, like others, the dark side of the technology and the wasteland it often leaves behind:

> For they saw that while many of the patients they treated indeed survived because of this machine, not all of them survived to become functional in the way they had been before being overtaken by illness. A number of them were not dead, but in some ways they did not seem to be alive. They lingered, lingered in this never-never land between functioning life and death. And as some of his patients remained in this state, Haid came to face dilemmas to which he had no solution.[13]

When death finally does take place, says Sherwin Nuland, physician and author of the best-seller, *How We Die*, it is usually not the classic bedroom scene, quiet and subdued with respectful friends paying last respects and family gathered around the bed to say farewell. Nuland describes the more common scene as one of

> beeping and squealing monitors, the hissing of respirators and pistoned mattresses, the flashing multicolored electronic signals—the whole technological panoply is background for the tactics by which we are deprived of the tranquillity we have every right to hope for, and separated from those few who would not let us die alone. By such means, biotechnology created to provide hope serves actually to take it away, and to leave our survivors bereft of the unshattered final memories that rightly belong to those who sit nearby as our days draw to a close.[14]

Technology has created problems, particularly for the terminally ill patient, when the "technological imperative" has taken precedence over the individual's beliefs, values, and preferences. By the 1950s, techniques that had been developed to serve human interests, and that often did so brilliantly, began to override and even displace human priorities. Since then many treatments have been used overzealously. It is ironic that modern medical tools, so beneficial to the accident victim and to those sustaining a reversible illness, can be so detrimental to the elderly and hopelessly ill who suffer further at the hands of "progress."

Cardiopulmonary resuscitation (CPR) is a good example of treatment yielding unintended consequences when used indiscriminately, as is frequently the case. CPR refers to the medical techniques used to restart a patient's heart and breathing when the patient suffers heart and pulmonary failure. CPR may involve such simple efforts as mouth-to-mouth resuscitation and external chest compression. Advanced CPR may involve electric shock, insertion of a tube to open the patient's airway, injection of medication into the heart, and, in an extreme case, open-chest heart massage. CPR can be a true lifesaver when used on the healthy and strong patient, typically an accident victim, for whom it was initially intended.

Research has shown, however, that ill or frail patients with cardiac or pulmonary arrest are unlikely to benefit from CPR, even though it is almost routinely given them. For the elderly and those in the final stages of terminal conditions, cardiopulmonary arrest lets death occur peacefully and painlessly. If such patients are resuscitated, however, there is a high probability that the brain and other vital organs will be damaged from lack of oxygen, leaving the individual in an even worse physical condition. Also, if revived, these patients are typically transferred to costly intensive-care wards, where dying is forestalled only temporarily but the dying process is prolonged, at great emotional and financial expense to the family.

Technological innovations provide mechanical breathing, food, and water to patients who would otherwise have died long ago. There are approximately fourteen thousand patients in a persistent vegetative state at any given time, like Karen Ann Quinlan, for example, with complete loss of mental functions, unconscious, unaware of herself or the surrounding environment. These patients are experiencing neither pain nor emotion, yet are able to survive for ten, twenty, and thirty years on a respirator, with a type of artificial nutrition and hydration only available for the last twenty-five years.

One of Quinlan's physicians, Dr. Joseph Fennelly, has harsh words for the effects of our idolization of technology:

> World War II we believed was won by technology—The Nordan Bombsight, radar, and for a really big finish, The Atom Bomb. Now we were ready for the Last Battle. The Battle Against Death Itself! And this battle would be won, as the war was, by high technology. . . . Cardiac resuscitation, moves from bench science to its use on virtually every patient. The failures from this technique, the comatose patients, are closeted in the nursing homes or at home. The families suffer spiritual and economic bankruptcy. The "failures" of our successes were denied in the blaze of unexamined "progress." Death became regarded as a failure and the terminally ill as embodiments of that failure.[15]

This obsession with the eradication of death, added to our near deification of technology, has prevented many health care providers from knowing when to stop, when to say, "Enough." Daniel Callahan calls this approach "technological brinkmanship." As a nation, he warns, "We believe that we should run the machinery of medicine at top speed right to the edge of the cliff called 'futility' and then stop it, just before it begins to do real harm to the patient. The trouble with this practice of brinkmanship is that it does not work well. Not at all. We cannot control our technologies with the precision necessary to stop at just the right moment, going as far as we can but not a bit further."[16]

Financier and philanthropist George Soros correctly observes that this emphasis on treating and curing diseases has altered the practice of medicine, bringing severe shortcomings with our successes. Soros argues: "We have created a medical culture that is so intent on curing disease and prolonging life that it fails to provide support in that inevitable phase of life-death. Advances in high technology interventions have contributed to this weakness in our medical system, deluding doctors and patients alike into believing that the inevitable can be delayed almost indefinitely."[17]

Why this overuse of technology and the unbearable consequences that often follow? Why can't health care professionals control technology instead of letting technology control them? The tendency toward excessive or inappropriate use is prompted by physician training, fear of malpractice, greed, methods of reimbursement, consumer demands, cultural priorities, and denial of death. First, doctors are trained to heal and cure, not to comfort and console. They are also trained to use all the state-of-the-art medical technology at their disposal to defeat the avowed enemy, death. The death of a patient is often perceived by the medical community as a failure of the doctor. Perhaps as a result of their training, physicians tend to overtreat uselessly in an attempt to protect their fragile egos. When patients fail to respond to treatment, says Hoefler, doctors perceive a blow to their self-esteem, which they promptly counteract with even more aggressive treatment.

Moreover, death is a taboo subject in our culture. And, like most taboo subjects, we both deny and fear it. Whereas death was openly discussed and sex was taboo in the Victorian era, quite the opposite is true today. Sex appears in most aspects of everyday life in the nineties, yet we keep death shrouded in euphemisms, sanitized, and hidden from view whenever possible. "Death was difficult to deny before the modern age," writes Hoefler in *Deathright*, "since there was simply too much of it around. But geographic mobility increased the emotional and social distance between family members, and industrialization helped put senior citizens—those most likely to die—out to pasture. And urbanization facilitated the scattering of the extended family and precipitated the abdication of responsibility of caring for both the dying (to the hospitals) and the dead (to funeral directors)."[18] These historical processes have robbed us of the understanding that death is the natural culmination of life, part of the natural order of things. We are so distanced from it that we can almost deny its existence.

In addition, when a physician contemplates withholding treatment or using less aggressive treatment, the fear of a medical malpractice lawsuit quickly pushes more conservative treatment from his or her mind. In fact, medical liability *is* a valid concern in medical practice. Three-quarters of all obstetricians and gynecologists, one-half of all surgeons, and one-third of all physicians will be sued at least once during their medical career.[19] Some doctors think it is malpractice not to use all available technology and fear that their patients will think similarly. However, the fear that cooperative physicians will be slapped with a criminal or civil multimillion-dollar lawsuit for the untimely death of a patient whom they have not treated aggressively, at the request of the patient or the patient's surrogate, is not grounded in reality. Such suits are rare to the point of nonexistence.

Doctors and hospital administrators have repeatedly taken the cases of comatose, dying patients to court, begging for guidance and protection from civil and criminal liability. They have repeatedly received both. The courts have done their job admirably, reiterating that treatment decisions are to be made by the patient or by the patient's proxy or surrogate through Living Wills and Health Care Proxies. These documents contain instructions regarding future medical care, including life-sustaining measures, in the event of decision-making incapacity. It is not the role of either the physician or the health care institution to make decisions about forgoing treatment. Courts have clearly stated, in the cases of Karen Ann Quinlan and Nancy Ellen Jobes in particular, that the medical profession's role is not one of medical decision-maker—that role is the prerogative of the patient or surrogate. In *In re Jobes*, where a nursing home rejected a family's request to discontinue the tubal feeding of their thirty-two-year-old daughter who had been in an unconscious state for seven years, the court ordered that the artificial feeding be stopped and said: "Courts are not the proper place to resolve the agonizing personal problems that underlie these cases. Our legal system cannot replace the more intimate struggle that must be borne by the patient, those caring for the patient, and those who care about the patient."[20] Yet health care professionals return to the courtroom time and time again for legal protection before discontinuing treatment.

There is a new legal trend, however, whereby doctors are beginning to incur liability for *continuing* treatment *against* a surrogate's wishes on behalf of an incompetent patient. Patients are filing lawsuits to hold medical professionals responsible for disregarding end-of-life directives. While juries have rarely faulted doctors in the past for keeping a patient alive, this is changing.

For example, a young woman in Michigan, Brenda Young, had a history of progressively worsening seizures, which her doctor had warned her would eventually leave her severely disabled. Hoping to avoid precisely the situation she later faced, she signed a Living Will and a Health Care Proxy authorizing her mother to stop all life-support treatment if she became incapacitated. When she suffered a particularly severe seizure, she was put on a respirator, despite her mother's insistence that she did not want this life-sustaining treatment. Young emerged profoundly disabled, thrashing and screaming for hours at a time, requiring total care. The family sued the hospital for continuing unwanted medical treatment and ultimately, in 1996, won a $16.5 million judgment.

Money, fueled by consumer demand, is another reason for the excessive use of high-tech medical care. Some suggest that certain physicians overtreat their patients out of simple greed. There is certainly money to be made from keeping the hospital beds full. Sustaining lives is, to be sure, more profitable for all parties in the business of billing and receiving money for services. Dead patients generate no income for either the physician or the hospital. Moreover, expensive machinery, once purchased, must be utilized in order to support the original cost plus maintenance.

Unbelievable as it is, there is no classification under which a doctor can bill for end-of-life comfort care. It was only as recently as 1996 that the medical profession officially acknowledged that some of the care delivered in hospitals is palliative (comfort care). Consequently using medical machinery is more profitable, for the doctor and hospital alike, than is tending to the emotional and spiritual well-being of the patient and his or her family, for which there is absolutely no reimbursement. Unable to bill for such care, small wonder that doctors rarely provide it. A new diagnostic code, however, is a positive step toward reimbursing professionals for services that—it is to be hoped—they will render more often, since comfort care is crucial to the improvement of deficient end-of-life care.

It is not only doctors who promote the overuse of technology in medicine. Consumer demand also plays a powerful part. Technology offers the possibility of a cure to patient and family alike, promising eternal hope. Often that hope performs miracles. More often, however, it falls short, with the patient tethered to tubes protruding from every orifice of the body—sometimes conscious and sometimes not, yet never functioning with the anticipated quality of life. Nevertheless the yearning for highly specialized techniques and procedures turns into expectations that, however unreal, are then turned into public demands. The public has bought the myth that death is avoidable, that the cure is out there. It may be too late for any specific patient, but these expectations pressure the hospital and the doctors, who often acquiesce, acquiring excess equipment and gadgetry to satisfy future consumer demand.

Although powerful modern medical technology has become venerated and pervasive, heightened social and political concerns have nonetheless emerged over the right of the individual to restrain the use of technology and to control the time and manner of his or her own death. A backlash has developed against the mechanical and the impersonal. Americans are uncomfortable with the cold technological arrogance of modern medicine, and they fear being kept alive in ways that constitute an affront to their dignity and a burden to their loved ones—when no reasonable expectation of recovery exists.

A revolution against such care is taking place. Increasingly patients, family members, and members of the medical profession are making the decision to forgo life-sustaining treatment and the agony of a prolonged death. People are attempting to regain or maintain the control they have either lost or fear losing. "Managed death," as it is called, has become routine. Indeed, of the 1.25 million deaths in medical institutions every year, 70 percent are "managed" or right-to-die cases. According to the American Hospital Association (AHA), a great many of the "6,000 deaths that occur in this country every day are somehow timed or negotiated by patients, families and doctors who . . . armed with an amazing array of death-delaying technology . . . reach a very painful and a very private consensus not to do all that they can do and let a dying patient die."[21]

Individuals have had, for many decades, the legal right to refuse unwanted medical treatment, including life-sustaining treatment, and the use of advance directives can be employed if the patient is unable to make these decisions. Advance directive is a term that encompasses Living Wills, Health Care Proxies and Do-Not-Resuscitate orders that authorize another individual to make medical decisions for an unconscious or mentally incompetent person whom technology, in one form or another, has kept alive up to that point.

However, not all seriously ill patients are being kept alive by powerful and modern medical technology as death approaches. There is, therefore, elevated public disquietude about those individuals *not* currently connected to life support who want to determine the course of their impending deaths with the aid of a physician. It is with these patients in mind that Oregon legalized PAS and that challenges were filed against laws prohibiting the practice in Washington and New York. The focus has thus turned to mentally competent, terminally ill—adults not on life-sustaining treatment—who wish to hasten their inevitable death with a doctor's prescription for lethal drugs.

The right-to-die is an evolving concept, one that connotes that death, in an intolerable situation, is preferable to life. It designates the authority of the individual over the paternalism of the medical profession, religion, and the law. Above all its basis is choice—the choice of the terminally or incurably ill to speed up the dying process when little or no quality of life remains, on or off life-sustaining technology.

Indeed, the Second Circuit Court of Appeals found no important difference between the choice of forgoing life-support and having a physician's help in hastening death. Neither one results in a natural death, ruled the court:

Indeed, there is nothing "natural" about causing death by means other than the original illness or its complications. The withdrawal of nutrition brings on death by starvation, the withdrawal of hydration brings on death by dehydration, and the withdrawal of ventilation brings about respiratory failure. By ordering the discontinuance of these artificial life-sustaining processes or refusing to accept them in the first place, a patient hastens his death by means that are not natural in any sense. It certainly cannot be said that the death that immediately ensues is the natural result of the progression of the disease or condition from which the patient suffers.

Moreover, the writing of a prescription to hasten death, after consultation with a patient, involves a far less active role for the physician than is required in bringing about death through asphyxiation, starvation and/or dehydration. Withdrawal of life support requires physicians or those acting at their direction physically to remove equipment and, often, to administer palliative drugs which may themselves contribute to death. The ending of life by these means is nothing more nor less than assisted suicide. It simply cannot be said that those mentally competent, terminally-ill persons who seek to hasten death but whose treatment does not include life support are treated equally.[22]

Callahan does not mince words in his direct advice on how individuals can personally avoid the powerful clutches of technology, keeping in mind that fewer than 20 percent of the population die *outside* hospitals or nursing homes. "It is going to be increasingly important to keep critically ill people out of hospitals in the first place. If you don't want to die a high-technology death, stay away from the places where they provide high-technology medicine," he warns. "Stay at home if at all possible, any other place than the hospital. Go out in the woods; don't go near those places. If you don't want to be over-treated, stay away. We have to help people to die at home or in hospices."[23]

The current presumption of "when in doubt, *treat*," has often resulted in technology being used because it is *there*, not because its use is justified by patient need. To rely so heavily on technology and biological functions to define the states of life and death is to deny the very social, emotional, and spiritual aspects of life that give it meaning. In their zeal to fashion new and improved technologies, many doctors have promoted measures that are inappropriate and whose applications often have horrendous consequences. Their efforts have provoked a backlash of disapproval from the public and have provided an impetus for the right-to-die movement and changing public policy. As such, medical technology's onslaught is one of the most powerful forces of activism, as well as an essential answer to the question Why Now?

C h a p t e r   2

The Rights Culture's Impact

Every so often "a pure flame of political rebellion shoots up somewhere and with amazing speed spreads in all directions, until half the countries on earth have been scorched," writes journalist Paul Berman.[1] Such a conflagration occurred during the American Revolution in 1776. A similar phenomenon took place in 1848, when an insurrection broke out in Paris, from which the ideas of nationalism and socialism ultimately spread across much of Europe. The Bolshevik uprisings in Russia in 1917 showed much the same pattern, based on the idea of constructing "a new socialist society on the basis of locally organized workers' councils."[2]

The student rebellions in the years around 1968 were an even larger phenomenon of a flame that touched and ignited the four corners of the world. The legacy of that era continues to impact every aspect of our nation's cultural, social, and political makeup as we approach the twenty-first century. It also affects the desire to control one's death. Without the legacy of the 1960s, what is now legal in Oregon would probably still be second-degree manslaughter today.

Radical students' conceptions of a utopian society at that time generally contained such features as a commitment to freedom of thought and action, which wanted to replace the confining bureaucratic modern state, the capitalist corporations, and the administrative unions. There was talk of autonomy, of operating free of all outside controls, in this utopian future world. There were calls for being true to oneself, with furious condemnations of government, religion, education, medicine, and all other implacable "enemies" of the new world order. Single-issue campaigns for enfranchisement became commonplace. Outdated ideas about gender, color, class, and sexual orientation were tossed to the winds, as campaigns arose to lead one sector of society after another "upward from the gloom of bottom-place standing in the social hierarchy into the glorious mediocrity of the American middle."[3]

Walt Whitman's and John Dewey's writings on democratic thought were often incorporated into these visions of the ideal society. While Whitman never dismissed the traditional structures of a constitutional government, democracy for him always meant something more. It meant a society in which people actively participated and fulfilled themselves. Personal input was paramount. Democracy was utopia, not a compromise. " 'Resist much, obey little,' was Whitman's maxim (italics and all), tendered as an incendiary guiding principle for civic affairs."[4]

In an essay written in the 1930s, Dewey, the Vermont sage, whose intellectual roots lay partly with Whitman, had discussed the "keynote of democracy," which he defined as "the participation of every mature human being in the formation of the values that regulate the living of men together. *All those who are affected by social institutions must have a share in producing and managing them.*" [emphasis added]

These were some of the core ideas that underlay the student rebellions of the 1960s. Of all the left-wing organizations, the Students for a Democratic Society (SDS) was the most powerful. Tom Hayden, one of the leading social activists of the decade, in his first draft of the SDS's manifesto, more commonly referred to as "the Statement," spoke of "participatory democracy," a catchy phrase, although it meant different things to different people. The most famous passage claimed: "We seek the establishment of a democracy of individual participation, governed by two central aims: that the individual share in those social decisions determining the quality and direction of his life; that society be organized to encourage independence in men and provide the media for their common participation." Regardless of its exact interpretation, its central message was clear: Participate in decisions that affect your well-being, take control of your life, and reject the oppression of authority.

This call for moral activism drew students to the SDS and showed them that they could choose to be democratic participants. The Vietnam War was the antithesis of participatory democracy. Its very inception was the decision of an elite, with no popular debate or democratic consensus. The war, environmental concerns, the high cost of the Cold War, the use of nuclear power—all of these and other concerns converged in the sixties and the seventies. People waged war on the authoritarian state and viewed almost every aspect of society—including government, medicine, and religion—with suspicion, distrust, and criticism, and deplored their paternalistic ways. The strident language of the radical left denounced the police as "pigs" and its ideological opponents as "fascists." Students aired emotions that had never been aired before, and brought crashing to the ground taboos, limitations, and restrictions formerly regarded as basic to civilization.

The student uprisings did not focus on political insurrection alone, but on cultural and moral insurrection as well. Whole groups in society—blacks, Latinos, women, homosexuals, and, by extension, anyone else who had suffered as a result of prejudices—expressed grievances and demanded the right of equal treatment. They borrowed from the new political left the language of "oppression," "occupation," "revolution," and "resistance." These outbreaks marked the beginning of the era of civil rights, gay rights, feminism, consumerism, the right to die a dignified death, and a host of other movements that would define future decades. A society of individual rights emerged. The idea of participatory democracy was the foundation of the new social order, in which individuals began sharing in the social decisions determining the quality of their lives and of their deaths.

The symbolic high point of the global rebellions of the late 1960s was reached in Paris on May 10, 1968. During "the Night of the Barricades," more than twenty thousand students marched through the Latin Quarter, "threatening vague unimaginable revolutions against the prejudices, power, practices, and hierarchies of every conceivable thing that could be labeled a yoke on the neck of mankind."[5] Shouting slogans to his followers, a student from the University of Nanterre, standing on a bench with a bullhorn in his hand, might well have been a protester endorsing physician-assisted death outside the U.S. Supreme Court building one cold January day in 1997: "There are no marshals and no leaders today! Nobody is responsible for you! You are responsible for yourselves, each row of you responsible for itself! *You* are the marshals!"

Americans have always cherished their individual rights. We are predisposed, says Hoefler,

> to celebrate individual liberty, broadly construed, at the expense of almost everything else. The right to free speech (even when libeling public figures in the press), the right to bear arms (without restriction), the right to freely associate, protest, and petition the government (regardless of how unpopular the group or the cause), and the right to privacy (including the exclusion of illegally obtained evidence in criminal proceedings) are just a few manifestations of the rights-oriented culture in which we live. Liberty—the freedom to do what we will in pursuit of our own desires—is an essential element of our political heritage.[6]

The 1960s, however, elevated individual rights to a new plateau and generated a new group of civil rights, with promises, reports Hoefler, "that individuals would be treated fairly in their interactions with 'the establishment,' if establishment is broadly defined to include all sorts of authority figures and power brokers in both the public and private sectors. The increasing predisposition of individuals to claim these rights is a phenomenon we refer to as the emergence of a rights culture."[7]

The rights culture of the 1960s strengthened the values of individualism, participation, self-determination, and autonomy. The raison d'être of the right-to-die movement, these values are thus the natural extension of other individual expressions that the nation has incorporated since the late 1960s: The movement and our culture go hand in hand.

The right to self-determination has been described as "the freedom each individual has to choose a lifestyle and course of action."[8] For more than four decades the student-rebels-turned-baby-boomers have directed public policy and mass culture in their quest for individual expression and self-determination. A major argument in favor of PAS is the individual's right to self-determination—to control the time, place, and manner of death, outside the purviews of government, religion, and medical authority. Supporters of that right believe that free choice justifies PAS.

More than one hundred years ago the Supreme Court declared the importance of every individual's right "to possession and control of his own person,"[9] but it was not until the 1960s that the Court seriously invoked the right of self-determination. It was then that the justices expanded the perimeters of the right to privacy. Those years saw it strike down laws prohibiting the distribution of contraceptives and a law forbidding interracial marriages. Consistent with the prevailing ideas of self-determination and autonomy, the Court found that the constitutionally protected right to decide whether or not to have an abortion is encompassed within the right to privacy, an absolute right during the first trimester of pregnancy. These and other new civil rights, better known to the legal trade as "penumbral rights," became part of the nation's lexicon as well as its normal expectation.

The laws of the last four decades reflect society's belief that there is a realm of personal liberty which the government may not enter—that "every human being of adult years and sound mind has a right to determine what shall be done with his own body."[10] In 1992 the Court summed up these earlier decisions when it reiterated that "our law affords constitutional protection to personal decisions relating to marriage, procreation, contraception, family relationships, child rearing, and education."[11]

Until the 1960s the practice of medicine was a paternalistic affair. Doctors were seen as wise fathers exercising total control over patient care. The sixties revolt led to more patient autonomy—putting the patient in charge as a paying customer. Then came a devastating event that deeply affected doctors, patients, their relationship, and public perception of the medical profession. An article described experiments done on humans without their consent.[12] These experiments quickly became linked to the rights movements that were gaining strength in the sixties, largely because of the victim status of the subjects, who were drawn disproportionately from among the poor, the blacks, the physically or mentally handicapped, the elderly, chronic alcoholics, newborns, and the incarcerated. As groups they lacked the opportunity or the ability to exercise choice. In one sense or another they were all devalued or marginalized by society.

The new skepticism toward the exercise of paternalism thus focused on medical researchers. News of what happened fostered a distrust of medical researchers and, by extension, of family doctors and the entire medical profession. Trust eroded as patients felt forced to protect themselves from their own physicians, reinforcing the emphasis on personal rights over the communal good, of us-versus-them hostilities.

Whereas during the 1940s and 1950s Americans had great reverence for researchers and the many miracles that emerged from their laboratories, in the 1960s the public identified not with the researchers but instead with the subjects of the experiments and the harm they were likely to suffer in the labs. This change in perspective mirrored the much larger change in social thought that fostered a national identification with the underdog.

A similar shift of sympathies centered on the ill and the dying, and the harm they were likely to suffer at the hands of the medical profession. This widespread awakening of individualism demanded a wresting of control from the oppressive establishment. In the arena of the right to die, patients empowered themselves to take authority from the doctor-knows-best physician, the antiquated law, and the unwieldy control of the hospital.

Patients' rights and the right-to-die movement began to emerge as a viable political issue around the same time that Congress and the courts were heavily engaged in making new policy in constitutional rights and liberties. "The growing emphasis on the withdrawal of treatment would not have become an issue if medical technology had not advanced to a point where life could be extended significantly through artificial means, but the move to individual rights may have prompted greater awareness and sensitivity to the right to be free from unwanted medical care," says political scientist Glick.[13]

By the end of the 1960s technology had reached behemoth proportions, and patients needed protection. They wanted personal input into their deaths as well as their lives. A formal proposal for a patient-instigated directive came in the summer of 1969, with the appearance of Louis Kutner's groundbreaking article, "Due Process of Euthanasia: The Living Will, A Proposal." Reviewing the legal flaws in mercy-killing cases, Kutner determined that neither the defendant nor the victim—whose death may have been unwarranted—had sufficient protection. Moreover, when a terminal patient *had* requested help in accelerating death, "the current state of the law does not recognize the right of the victim to die if he so desires. He may be in a terminal state suffering from an incurable illness and literally forced to continue a life of pain and despair. Such a denial may well infringe upon an individual's right of privacy."[14]

Arguing that it was, by law, a patient's right to consent to or refuse treatment, and that the law recognized the inviolability of the human body, Kutner proposed a Living Will, "analogous to a revocable or conditional trust with the patient's body as the *res*, the patient as the beneficiary and grantor, and the doctor and the hospital as the trustees."[15] In short, while still healthy and mentally competent, the individual would indicate in the Living Will the extent of treatment to which he or she would consent in the future. In addition, if a doctor acted contrary to the patient's wishes, he or she would be subject to liability.

It was almost a full decade before Kutner's Living Will became a legal reality, and there is still no liability for the doctor who acts contrary to the patient's wishes. Nevertheless this bold idea was born of the individualistic thinking of the 1960s and was reinforced by the courts and Congress, elected in those years to empower the powerless.

The first and perhaps most important document to illustrate new societal attitudes and practices between doctor and patient was the twelve-point Patient Bill of Rights, formally adopted by the American Hospital Association (AHA) in 1973. A polite and toothless attempt, it nonetheless reflected the growing ideology of the concept of rights.

The thrust of the AHA Bill of Rights was to encourage etiquette and courtesy. "Rights" ranging from "considerate and respectful care" to "every consideration of privacy" were essentially matters of staff courtesy. The Bill also addressed the rights of all patients to equal access to treatment, to be told the truth about medical treatment, to confidentiality, "to refuse treatment to the extent permitted by law," as well as other basic legal rights derived from the doctrine of informed consent.

An offshoot of the Bill, and more practical than the Bill itself, was the emergence of the patient rights advocate, whom George J. Annas, professor of health law and medical ethics at Boston University, defines as

> a person whose job is to help the patient exercise the rights outlined in the state's or institution's Patient Bill of Rights. The advocate may be employed by the health care facility, prepaid health plan, an insurance company, a government agency, a consumer group, or the patient. The critical characteristic is loyalty: *the patient rights advocate must represent the patient*. This is essential because the goal is to enhance the patient's position in making decisions, not to encourage the patient to follow facility routine or to "behave."[16]

The Bill of Rights was followed closely by New Jersey's *Quinlan* decision in 1976 which spotlighted a family's struggle to disconnect a respirator from a daughter trapped in a persistant vegetative state. Shortly thereafter other state cases on the withholding and withdrawing of medical treatments based their verdicts on the right to privacy enunciated by the rights-conscious Warren Court of the sixties. *Quinlan* inspired a respect for integrity and autonomy at the end of life and reinforced the ideology of patients' rights. The decision led to the empowerment of the individual (through the legal documents of a Living Will and Health Care Proxy) against the physician and the hospital. These documents took their place "alongside the AHA Patient Bill of Rights in asserting the new stand against doctors."[17]

The perfect timing of this commitment to patients' rights in the 1960s and 1970s gave a splendid boost to the emerging right-to-die movement. Medical paternalism began to lose its authority, as many bioethicists allied themselves with the Quinlans, elevating individual rights over medical authority. As one after another spoke out for patient autonomy and championed patients' rights in general, bioethicists increased in stature and influence.

"Just when courts were defining an expanded right to privacy," says Rothman,

> the bioethicists were emphasizing the principle of autonomy, and the two meshed neatly; judges supplied a legal basis and bioethicists, a philosophical basis for empowering the patient. Indeed, just when movements on behalf of a variety of minorities were advancing their claims, the bioethicists were siding with the individual against the constituted authority; in their powerlessness, patients seemed at one with women, inmates, homosexuals, tenants in public housing, welfare recipients, and students, who were all attempting to limit the discretionary authority of professionals . . . All these movements looked at the world from the vantage point of the objects of authority, not the wielders of authority.[18]

Our concept of personal autonomy has broadened since the 1960s: Society now reflects the belief that our lives belong to us alone. With a large segment of the population—many of whom have witnessed the bad death of a parent—facing imminent death, the voice for a better death grows louder and more persistent. Assisted death for the mentally competent terminally ill adult who voluntarily requests it is the ultimate civil right, not unlike other minority rights fought for during that tumultuous and chaotic decade. As one California court put it, echoing the beliefs of the national majority: "The right to die is an integral part of our right to control our own destinies so long as the rights of others are not affected."[19]

Over the years the public has wanted more than the mere passivity of nontreatment—the withholding or withdrawing of life-sustaining medical technology. It has come to insist on more active participation from the medical profession, in the form of PAS and perhaps, one day, voluntary euthanasia. The different methods of assisted dying are steps on a continuum that will follow societal changes and demands.

John Finn, chief physician for Hospice of Michigan, sees baby boomers' fears and anxieties, including their desire to control their own death, reflected in the three jury acquittals of Dr. Jack Kevorkian in his home state. Finn believes that the jurors' decisions do not represent support for Kevorkian's particular brand of assisted suicide, regarding them instead as "a major indictment of modern medicine. . . . They're not happy with the state of affairs. They're looking at their own deaths and they want to have options available for them."[20]

It appears, in fact, that southeastern Michigan has granted Kevorkian the implicit authority to assist in suicides under the current law, so difficult is he to convict. Quite astonishingly prosecutors have openly admitted they will not press charges. Since juries will not convict, he operates in a "free suicide zone these days."[21]

In his third trial Kevorkian was indicted under a unique Michigan Supreme Court ruling that held that assisting a suicide could be prosecuted under unwritten legal traditions dating back to English common law. Characteristically, he denounced both the prosecution and the state of society. Impatient with the prosecutor, Larry Bunting, Kevorkian shouted: "This is not a trial! This is a lynching! There is no law! No law!"[22]

Between such outbursts Kevorkian argued that even under common law he had not committed a crime. "I gave them the means to end their suffering—which definitely meant their lives would end, yes. . . . But that was the only means available to end their suffering. This is what they wanted, it was medically justified, and for me, honoring the patient's wish—when medically justified—is the highest duty of a physician." The exchange that ensued typified the acrimony displayed throughout the day. " 'Patient autonomy is supreme?' Mr. Bunting asked. 'It is for me,' Dr. Kevorkian shot back. 'Does a human have an owner?' Mr. Bunting asked. 'Yes, himself,' Dr. Kevorkian said."[23]

If participatory democracy was the foundation of the new order of the sixties, so too, it is the banner under which Kevorkian and the rest of the right-to-die community congregate. In a society abundant with individual liberties, a free person may claim: "I am entitled to control my final destiny. It is my death. It is my decision." The student rebels of the sixties would applaud the landmark Oregon vote—as proponents of an assisted death should acknowledge the students for the seeds they planted. The legacy of the 1960s continues.

Chapter 3

The Decline of the Doctor-Patient Relationship

Societal changes and discretionary abuses within the medical community have led to a distrust of the medical profession and a decline in the doctor-patient relationship. This deterioration of confidence is yet another force of activism that has propelled PAS to its current mainstream status. The elements of trust that existed before World War II were strong enough to legitimize a paternalistic attitude on the part of the doctor. But when trust diminished, so did the public's willingness to accept the doctor's authority. Patient autonomy, spurred on by the rights culture of the 1960s, increased, and with it came further acceptance of the right-to-die movement.

The doctor-patient relationship lies at the very core of medical practice. As such it is fragile, because it is based on sincere trust that the doctor will do everything that lies reasonably within his or her power to provide the best health care possible under the circumstances, enabling the patient to feel as good and to function as well as possible under the circumstances.

Opinion surveys have, over the years, inquired into the degree of confidence that Americans have in various institutions including Congress, the press, universities, and the medical profession. The declines have been dramatic and nowhere more pronounced than in medicine. Looking at confidence in medicine from 1966–1994, the numbers speak for themselves: seventy-three percent (1966), forty-three percent (1975), thirty-five percent (1985), and twenty-three percent (1994).[1]

Widespread alienation from the U.S. health care system was the central finding of a survey released by the AHA, according to a poll of twenty-three thousand patients conducted for the nonpartisan National Coalition on Health Care (NCHC). The overwhelming majority of individuals lacked confidence in the "quality, cost and accessibility of medical care and the health-care system overall," according to American Health Line.[2] The study showed

that 80 percent of Americans believe something is "seriously wrong" with
the system, 87 percent say the quality of care needs improvement, and 80
percent blame the profit motive for compromising quality.

That Americans view insurance companies as profiteers comes as no
great surprise, but the identification of doctors and hospitals with this greedy
industry gives professionals pause. Dr. Henry E. Simians, president of the
NCHC, expresses concern over the level of current dissatisfaction: "Most
disturbing to us was the serious concern voiced about the quality of medical
care and the lack of trust in our system."[3]

Society has revered physicians and paid them well, since we believe that
our very lives rest in their hands. Doctors' incomes are even on the rise
despite fears that managed care will cost them dearly, reaching nearly
$200,000 a year on average in 1996. That is about fifty percent higher than
in 1987 according to an American Medical Association survey.[4] We are in
awe of their powers. We want what they have: the secrets to longevity. We
have put them on pedestals resembling those reserved for religious figures,
and have accepted their decisions as the gospel. But this adulation is a thing
of the past. What has so diminished the public's respect for and confidence
in the medical profession in general and the doctor-patient relationship specifically?

First society changed dramatically after World War II. Second, the medical establishment abused the trust that the nation had so confidently placed
in it. Time and again it positioned the individual physician, the medical
profession, and the national good over the best interests of the patient. More
recently it has disregarded patients' end-of-life wishes. Trust, inherently so
fragile, has gradually disappeared—and with it, any semblance of a
physician-patient relationship.

Much of today's public was raised with the nostalgic image of the country doctor trudging through the snowy night with lantern and black bag in
hand, tending to his patients in exchange for a homemade apple pie. These
men may have been as businesslike as the robber barons, yet the myth was
at least partially true. To be successful doctors *had* to be compassionate,
trustworthy, and caring, for these were the only commodities they had to
offer.

Homogeneity and intimacy cemented the relationships. Before World
War II, personal compatibility was an important criteria in choosing a physician. The common protocol was: "Choose a physician as you would choose
a friend." The medical caretakers were considered part of the family, often
helping the same individual in and out of this world. Doctors had long-
standing relationships with their patients, whose values they understood and,
for the most part, agreed with. And they made house calls, entering into the
homes and hearts of their patients.

All of that has changed, of course. Practically every development in
medicine after World War II distanced the physician and the hospital from

the patient and the community. The first of the structural changes was the disappearance of the house call, rapidly followed by the advent of technology, medical specialization, and subspecialization, as well as the sprawling medical center and hospital. Hospital stays shortened as the number of hospital beds grew larger. For any condition out of the ordinary, family-practice physicians send patients to specialists—not even necessarily in the patient's hometown—whom they have never met before, and who know nothing of their values or preferences. Increased worldwide mobility and specialization means that doctor and patient first meet at a time of medical crisis, with no previous relationship between them. While these developments have improved certain kinds of medical care, the relationship between physician and patient has suffered.

Advances such as X rays and MRIs, together with complex surgery, also put an end to the routine house call, together with the intimacy that went with it. The busy doctor in the impersonal setting focuses solely on the patient's physical ailment, leaving aside the traditional approach of considering the patient's total well-being. Doctors now learn more about the patient from the available technology than from conversations with the patient or the family.

The bonds of trust—born of similar religion, ethnicity, education, and locale—dissolved with the changing times. Rothman explains how the old-boy network gave way to meritocracy, fostering more anonymity, as the doctors who gained their "positions through merit might or might not share their patient's religious persuasion, ethnic identity, or social values. . . . After the 1950s, even sectarian hospitals no longer relied on such criteria as religion or ethnicity to select most of the house staff and senior physicians. . . . It became increasingly difficult to define what was Presbyterian about Presbyterian Hospital or Jewish about Mt. Sinai."[5]

Entering a hospital is beginning to have much in common with entering a hostile and alienating environment, a far cry from the familiarity of one's home complete with family physician. A physician at the University of Toronto emphasizes the importance—perhaps the necessity—of having a friend or relative at the bedside *at all times* to act as advocate for the patient and to monitor the quality of the treatment. "In the Third World they've always done this," says Dr. Carolyn Bennett. "The families come by with a little tent and camp by the hospital. We're not quite there yet, but we can't count on the hospital doing everything anymore," she says.[6]

Something else, however, was happening within the medical community in the decades following the war that lowered public confidence in the profession and contributed to the decline of the doctor-patient relationship even more. Physicians abused the power vested in them, running roughshod over patient trust. For this the medical establishment is responsible, unlike the societal changes that occurred through no fault of their own.

The decades following 1945 were filled with examples of human experimentation without patient consent. The exposés that followed revealed in compelling fashion how medical researchers in postwar America abused their discretion time and again. That they behaved as arrogantly and irresponsibly as they did was attributable in large part to the remarkable laboratory achievements which took place during World War II. Rothman remarks:

Clinical research had come of age when medical progress, measured by antidotes against malaria, dysentery, and influenza, was the prime consideration, and traditional ethical notions about consent and voluntary participation in experimentation seemed far less relevant. A generation of researchers were trained to perform, accomplish, and deliver cures—to be heroes in the laboratory, like soldiers on the battlefield. If researchers created effective vaccines, diagnostic tests, or miracle drugs like penicillin, no one would question their methods or techniques.[7]

There was widespread conviction among the medical profession that ethical considerations in this important research were best left to those doing the research—to calculate the risks and benefits to the subjects and to share information when and where they thought appropriate. The matter of consent was disregarded for lack of importance. The general good of the population had priority over the well-being of individuals, who had become dispensable in light of the common good. The industrial-military-governmental establishment was content to let the medical researchers do their work without interference, scrutiny, or regulation.

Subsequent events, however, showed that these researchers could not be trusted with a human life. With the dissemination of this knowledge, the doctor-patient relationship fell into disrepair, since it was now impossible to offset this lack of trust with the intimate relationship that the physician and the patient had enjoyed prior to the war.

The first indictment of research ethics, which inspired outsiders to emasculate the medical community, was also the one that began the public's disillusionment with the medical profession. Henry Beecher, an anesthesiologist on the faculty of the Harvard Medical School and on the staff of Massachusetts General Hospital, was a whistle-blower and muckraker in the tradition of Harriet Beecher Stowe and Upton Sinclair. He analyzed various human experiments that had recently taken place and went public with his findings in 1966, revealing in a compelling fashion how researchers in the post–World War II era had abused their powers. His six-page article documented twenty-two examples of human experiments, all of which endangered the health and well-being of their subjects, without their knowledge or consent. This information created a furor and outrage inside and outside the medical profession.

In some studies researchers had attempted to learn more about a disease. In others they tested new drugs or withheld a drug known for its healing power in order to test an unknown alternative drug. Examples 16, 17 and 19, in Beecher's article, provide a sample of what had gone unsanctioned and unregulated for so long:

> Example 16. This study was directed toward determining the period of infectivity of infectious hepatitis. Artificial induction of hepatitis was carried out in an institution for mentally defective children in which a mild form of hepatitis was endemic. . . . A resolution adopted by the World Medical Association states explicitly: "Under no circumstances is a doctor permitted to do anything which would weaken the physical or mental resistance of a human being except from strictly therapeutic or prophylactic indications imposed in the interest of the patient." There is no right to risk an injury to one person for the benefit of others.
>
> Example 17. Live cancer cells were injected into 22 human subjects as part of a study of immunity to cancer. According to a recent review, the subjects (hospitalized patients) were "merely told they would be receiving 'some cells'—the word cancer was entirely omitted."
>
> Example 19. During bronchoscopy a special needle was inserted through a bronchus into the left atrium of the heart. This was done in an unspecified number of subjects, both with cardiac disease and with normal hearts. The technique was a new approach whose hazards were at the beginning quite unknown. The subjects with normal hearts were used, not for their possible benefit but for that of patients in general.[8]

It was not possible to make the excuse that this research was carried out in makeshift laboratories by eccentric physicians. Thirteen of the twenty-two experiments were conducted in highly respected university medical schools, clinics, and laboratories: Harvard, Georgetown, George Washington, Emory, and Duke, to name just a few. The funders of the research were no less well known. They included the U.S. military (the Surgeon General's Office or the Armed Forces Epidimiology Board), the National Institutes of Health, drug companies (including Merck Sharp and Dohme, and Parke-Davis & Company), private foundations, and other federal offices (including the U.S. Public Health Service and the Atomic Energy Commission).

These experiments on humans without their consent were not isolated events. Indeed, the United States had already witnessed the tragedy of the unapproved drug thalidomide in 1962. The well-known result of this disaster was the birth of many children with birth defects—typically, warped or missing limbs. "Many of the subjects who had taken thalidomide had had no idea that they were part of a drug trial and had not given their consent," says Rothman.[9]

Beecher's whistle-blowing on the medical profession did not succeed in stopping physicians from experimenting without their patients' consent. The practice continued, with each exposé pushing the outraged public to demand regulation of medical researchers who were unable or unwilling to regulate themselves. More scandals occurred between 1968 and 1974, each one further eroding the trust between the medical professionals and the public. One well-known program, federally sponsored by the U.S. Public Health Service, took place in Tuskegee, Alabama, where more than four hundred black men infected with syphilis went untreated for decades.

There were also the experiments conducted at the University of Cincinnati General Hospital, funded by the Department of Defense. Physicians administered radiation to patients with terminal cancer without their consent. The subjects of both the Tuskegee and Cincinnati studies closely resembled one another: They were indigent and black, with no more than a grade-school education.

The Dalkon Shield, Depo-Provera (medroxyprogesterone), and DES (diethylstilbestrol) were all prescribed for patients, with no mention of known side effects and without consent, as physicians engaged in premature use of unproven and untested drugs and procedures. The early 1970s brought neonatal intensive-care scandals. To read articles on nursery care is to learn that the mind-set of the neonatologist was not significantly different from the mind-set of the researcher, for both would sacrifice the well-being of the particular patient in order to further the progress of medicine.

As the incidences of abuse accumulated in number, it became clear that the medical profession and its researchers needed outside regulation. Willard Gaylin, president of the Hastings Center, did not believe that professional medical associations, such as the AMA, would develop or enforce necessary safeguards. "These institutions," Gaylin contended in 1973, "were originally designed as protective guilds, and they still function primarily in that sense. . . . I suspect that they will always be more concerned with the protection of the rights of their constituents than with the public per se." He, like many others at that time, wanted to empower the patient. "Patient-consumers must no longer trust exclusively the benevolence of the professional. Basic decisions must be returned to the hands of the patient population whose health and future will be affected," Gaylin said.[10]

Open criticism of the medical profession increased as any remaining faith in its ability to self-regulate declined. Physicians even became critical of one another. Arnold Relman, editor of the *New England Journal of Medicine*, declared war on physician authority. Relman declared that medicine's recent decisions on termination of treatment and experimentation left "no possible doubt of its total distrust of physicians' judgment. . . . Physicians must not be allowed to use their own professional judgment, but should be guided instead by government regulations."[11]

Exposure of these scandals deeply affected public trust. A loss of faith in researchers developed into a reluctance to trust *any* doctors. Cynicism about authority was already high in the 1960s and 1970s as participatory individualism gained strength, and the medical deceptions fueled public antagonism. The scandals permanently changed the dynamic between doctor and patient. Suspicion and distrust clouded the relationship. Physician paternalism gave way to patient autonomy, raising the possibility that end-of-life decisions should be left in the hands of the dying patient, not the attending physician.

The pervasive disregard for the individual vis-à-vis the general good was particularly surprising, following as it did on the heels of the Nuremberg War Crimes Trials in 1945 and 1946. The American research community ignored the Nuremberg Code—the set of standards for ethical research that emerged from the trials—viewing it as irrelevant to its own work in human research. The opening provision of the Code states: "The voluntary consent of the human subject is absolutely essential. This means that the person involved should have legal capacity to give consent." The Code mandates that the research subject "should be so situated as to be able to exercise free power of choice." The Code also states that human subjects "should have sufficient knowledge and comprehension of the elements of the subject matter involved as to make and understand an enlightened decision." According to these principles, the mentally ill, children, and prisoners are not suitable subjects for research.

The Nazi human-experiment atrocities might have made the American medical profession exceptionally mindful of the need for vigilant regulation of research. The Nuremberg Code might have served as a model for American research guidelines. Instead research continued, with the attitude that the end justifies the means. The main criterion became "the greatest good for the greatest number," superseding the priority of the individual patient. The lessons of the war did not apply; the growing sentiment favoring individual rights was ignored; the fundamental principle of medical ethics—that the doctor's first priority is the well-being of the patient—did not hold sway in the laboratory. Human experimentation "pitted the interest of society against the interests of the individual. In essence, the utilitarian calculus put every human subject at risk. . . . Human subjects had to become their own protectors."[12]

Lawsuits, disciplinary hearings, and extensive media coverage followed the exposure of the scandals. Thus, for the first time, and in direct response to the abuses of discretion, major changes ushered an unprecedented degree of oversight and regulation into the laboratory. Federal regulations and peer oversight replaced decision making that had traditionally been left to the doctor's individual conscience.

It was during this time that twenty-one-year-old Karen Ann Quinlan lay in a persistent vegetative state while her parents attempted to have her respirator removed. They were opposed by the doctor and hospital who supervised Karen's care. The case evolved into a contest between physicians on the one hand and patients and their legal advocates on the other, over the contentious issue of who controlled medical decision making. Who ruled at the bedside? Doctors had presumed to represent the patient interest. With the *Quinlan* decision in 1976, however, and to the chagrin of the medical profession, that role went to the patient, with the support of lawyers and judges. The American people no longer accepted the notion of the beneficence of the doctor, and as the indiscriminate use of technology increased, they no longer trusted that the doctor would ease them out of this life to their satisfaction.

After *Quinlan* there was no disputing the obvious fact that medical decision making was "in the public domain and that a profession that had once ruled was now being ruled," says Rothman. After *Quinlan* medical decision making became the "province of a collection of strangers," with judges, lawyers, ethicists, religion and philosophy professors, and other outsiders joining doctors at their patients' bedsides.[13] Even Congress joined the growing ranks of those interested in medical ethics and decision making. Although some physicians helped guide their profession through these changing times, the majority, expressing themselves in the editorial columns of medical publications and from "witness chairs in congressional hearings, displayed a barely disguised disdain and hostility. They inveighed against the new regulatory schemes and the empowerment of lay bodies and boards, and when they suffered defeat, took the losses badly."[14] The nation looked and listened and was not impressed.

Despite the opposition and delaying tactics of physicians, Congress created the National Commission for the Protection of Human Subjects, charged with recommending policies for human experimentation. What the commission discovered was this: The medical profession was incapable of regulating itself and, left unsupervised, abused its discretion and America's trust. The commission concluded that the job of setting ethical standards must fall to the laypeople on the commission, displacing the usual physician control. The once-respected medical profession was stripped of many of its decision-making prerogatives, and paternalism began to wane.

It would be reassuring to end the human-experiment story with the new federal regulations of the 1960s and 1970s—to say that medical researchers and the groups that financed them saw the error of their ways, and that the health and well-being of the patient have reigned supreme ever since. Unfortunately, such has not been the case.

Indeed, information about experiments on people without their consent has continued to surface on a regular basis, the most recent controversial news surfacing as recently as the end of 1996. A new Food and Drug Administration rule allows emergency room physicians to use certain experimental drugs or devices *without* the informed consent of the patient if the medical condition warrants it. According to a Reuters report:

The new rule came about after HHS (Health and Human Services) and FDA realized that proposals to conduct certain types of research, including projects funded by the National Institutes of Health, could not proceed under guidelines regulating the protection of human subjects. HHS decided to waive informed consent restrictions in emergency circumstances if the institutions complied with federal guidelines. . . . Patients also had to be in life-threatening situations in which available treatments were unproven or unsatisfactory and the collection of valid data through randomized investigations was necessary to determine the safety or efficacy of particular treatment.[15]

The first protocol approved by the FDA in early 1997 was designed to test the use of artificial blood in trauma cases in which the patient's blood type is unknown. The requirement of informed consent, they said, was hampering research. Previous restrictions made it impossible to conduct certain types of research. Supporters of the new protocol claim patients will benefit.

Opponents are not so sure. They are deeply troubled by this openly acknowledged easing of the U.S. ban on medical experiments without consent, and predict dire consequences. " '1996 is the 50th anniversary of Nuremberg,' where trials of Nazi doctors concluded humans should never again undergo such horrific, involuntary experimentation, noted Georgetown University bioethicist Robert Veatch. 'In the United States, we are commemorating that event by adopting regulations that flat-out are in violation of the Nuremberg Code.' "[16]

The stakes in the ethics of human experimentation are high. Are doctors and researchers being given so much latitude as to discredit themselves once again by abusing their authority? As Rothman warns:

The awesome power of research, the fragility of a concept such as voluntary consent, the international nature of both medicine and disease, and the strength of the profit motive in health care—all mean that the basic premises that should govern clinical research are unsettled. Some of us, particularly attuned to history, worry about a cyclical trend: abuse generates oversight, which in turn seems too restrictive and is relaxed, and then new abuses emerge.[17]

News of the FDA change also brought criticism from Dr. Jack Kevorkian in the form of an article he wrote for the *Los Angeles Times*, "At Least My Patients Gave Consent." Referring to the experimental treatment of patients in hospital emergency situations without patient consent, Dr. Kevorkian writes:

Talk about hypocrisy! Never mind that such experiments are, the bureaucrats say, limited to "emergency and life-threatening" situations.

What we have just taken is a fast ride down the slippery slope, right to the absolute depths. Half a century ago, the "civilized" world self-righteously hanged seven German physicians for "crimes against humanity" in the form of medical experiments on helpless human beings. That done, we piously concocted the Nuremberg Code to ensure that such atrocities would never be repeated. So what do we have now? The FDA cheerfully sanctioning such experimentation through new guidelines that without any doubt would shamelessly violate the Nuremberg Code.

The federal government justifies its actions as being the only way to get certain medical data on humans, by saying it is for the benefit of humanity. Kevorkian points to the similarity with Nazi Germany: "Doubtless the seven German physicians who were hanged after the war had felt the same way."[18]

Annas indicts the deprofessionalization of medicine, which encourages the replacement of medical ethics with market values:

Medical ethics is likely to be followed by physicians only if society grants physicians legal immunity for following their medical ethics. Since *Quinlan*, physicians' groups have increasingly sought immunity before they would do anything, even judge the quality of practice of their peers, or develop an enforceable standard of medical practice. And as a result, American society now sees physicians more and more not as professionals governed by a strong ethical code, but as merchants who sell their goods and services to customers.[19]

The AMA substantiated Annas's contention when it agreed to an exclusive endorsement of nine Sunbeam products, including scales, air cleaners, massagers, thermometers, vaporizers, and humidifiers, in its first-ever arrangement with a commercial enterprise. In exchange for the use of the AMA name and logo on these Sunbeam products and in advertisements, the medical organization would receive a royalty for each item sold. The controversial deal produced a rash of protest, and the AMA, under pressure, eventually renounced its deal with Sunbeam.

Damage had been done, however, as editorials and articles pointed to the greed and commercialism of physicians. "An appalling decision," stated a *New York Times* editorial. "The AMA is cashing in its debilitated reputation as a guardian of American health and becoming a straightforward feather merchant," snapped Dr. Quintin Young, head of an advocacy organization called the Health and Medicine Policy Research Group.[20] Here was a concrete, well-publicized example of physician avarice that attracted the public's attention.

Jerome P. Kassirer and Marcia Angell, editors of the *New England Jour-*

nal of Medicine, wrote a joint editorial condemning the preposterous commercial venture. They also called the AMA's recent announcements of its goals of protecting patients and doctor-patient relationships nothing more than disingenuous attempts to preserve the income of its members. The editorial continued:

> What's wrong with the arrangement? Plenty. It is one thing to recommend health-related products on the basis of careful scientific scrutiny; it is another to enter into an exclusive marketing arrangement with a single company in which royalties are linked to sales. An exclusive moneymaking deal of this kind seriously undermines the credibility of the AMA at a time when the public's trust in the profession has already slipped to dangerously low levels. Financial incentives are dangerous. We have learned painfully that physicians respond to them. In a fee-for-service system, they may order too many tests and procedures; in a capitated system, they may order too few. When physicians have a stake in a laboratory, they send their patients there for studies, and when they have a financial interest in a hospital, they admit their patients there.[21]

Deeply damaging to any remaining trust between doctor and patient are the results of the most comprehensive investigation of death in American hospitals. The Study to Understand Prognosis and Preferences for Outcomes and Risks in Treatment (SUPPORT) reported surprisingly discouraging findings in 1995. The project's first two-year phase (Phase I) aimed to discover the character of dying in American hospitals. The investigators concluded that the hospital experience was unsatisfactory for too many seriously ill patients. For example, while 79 percent of Phase I patients who died while hospitalized had a DNR order, a full 46 percent of these were written within two days of death. Thirty-one percent of Phase I patients expressed a preference not to be resuscitated, but less than 50 percent of their doctors accurately understood this preference. Of the Phase I patients who died while hospitalized, 38 percent spent ten or more days in an intensive care unit, against their stated wishes. More than 50 percent had moderate to severe pain at least half the time throughout their last three days of life. On the basis of the findings, investigators isolated several disturbing features of hospitalized dying and put together an intervention expressly designed to resolve them.

Phase II tested whether a combination of interventions would improve the quality of terminal care. To this end, interventions were put in place. Attending physicians received computer-generated prognostic estimates and information about the patient's preferences for life-prolonging interventions. In addition, specifically trained research nurses facilitated discussions among physicians, patients, and family members. These interventions increased opportunities for discussions about life-sustaining treatments in the hope that informed patient decision making would be enhanced, resulting in fewer high-technology interventions and more humane dying for patients.

The results of Phase II were startling. The interventions expressly designed to resolve the deficiencies of Phase I did nothing to improve the specified problems. Increasing communication between doctors and patients did not help. There were no significant changes in the timing of DNR orders, in physician-patient agreement about DNR orders, in the number of uncomfortable days, in the prevalence of pain, or in the technology used. Physicians were portrayed as uncaring and arrogant. Patients' requests were ignored, and not routinely respected even if known. A full 41 percent of patients who had not discussed resuscitation or prognosis with their physicians had indicated a desire to do so. The level of dissatisfaction with the medical care also remained the same.

Bernard Lo, professor in the Division of General Internal Medicine at the University of California at San Francisco, sums up the grim results of the SUPPORT study in the *Hastings Center Report*:

> The findings do not depict gentle, peaceful deaths, but high technology run amok with poor communication, inadequate relief of symptoms, and little respect for patient preferences.[22]

The SUPPORT study showed what the public has long suspected—that doctors cannot be trusted to make the dying process as comfortable as possible. They also cannot be trusted to respect patient wishes to forgo life-sustaining treatment, or to provide adequate pain relief. Large numbers of people still die alone, in pain, and tethered to mechanical ventilators in intensive care units.

The AMA repudiates the practice of PAS on the basis that it violates the profession's mission of healing and would be likely to destroy the doctor-patient relationship. It professes a belief that legalization of the practice would undermine public trust in medicine's dedication to preserving the life and health of patients. Angell, in an editorial for the *New England Journal of Medicine*, believes the opposite: "Contrary to the frequent assertion that permitting physician-assisted suicide would lead patients to distrust their doctors, I believe distrust is more likely to arise from uncertainty about whether a doctor will honor a patient's wishes."[23]

Stephen Jamison, social psychologist, educator, and author, agrees with Angell:

> I would argue that one of the reasons behind the public demand for legal change in assisted dying is both patients' desire for more control and the *existing* lack of trust in the ability of physicians to relieve their suffering. If assisted dying were legally available as an extraordinary op-

tion under strict rules, and patients knew that if they were suffering, their issues of pain and dignity would be addressed, then public fear of the dying process might lessen and trust in physicians might consequently increase.[24]

PAS becomes a comforting option as death approaches. The overall decline in trust has led to a decline in confidence and to a revolution in the public perception of medical individuals and institutions. Knowing that their needs will not be met in a hospital setting, they endorse the assisted suicide movement. As Hoefler points out: "When trust declines, patients become more willing to question their doctors as sources of authority, and questioning leads to demands from patients and their families that they be included as partners when it comes to making health care treatment decisions, even when—or especially when—death is a real possibility."[25]

The personal connection between doctor and patient did not decline overnight. Instead, there has been a gradual erosion since the end of World War II, some caused by immense societal changes that separated the patient physically and emotionally from the general intern. The relationship, once based on the confidence that doctors would do what is best for their patients, has frequently turned into a belief that doctors will do only what benefits their profession or themselves. Though some of the blame lies with the medical community and some does not, the majority of the public has lost faith in traditional medicine and is ready to seek out the best possible death on its own.

A changing society combined with physician abuse have led to a decline in the doctor-patient relationship. To be sure, not all physicians have abandoned the moral high ground. Some continue as dedicated healers, not as hawkers of consumer products who arrogantly ignore or disregard their patients' end-of-life requests. Too often patients' needs are not met. A loss of public confidence and an erosion of trust contribute to the public's revised outlook on available, acceptable, and alternative ways of dying.

C h a p t e r   4

Poor End-of-Life Care

In the debate over physician aid in dying, both sides agree on two points. First, the medical profession has done an exceedingly poor job to date with end-of-life care, including the management of pain. The certainty that death is inevitable regardless of our attempts to defeat it has failed to increase high-quality palliative care or to make physicians recognize that the clinical care of the dying patient is a central and crucial component of modern medicine. Too many patients are treated not with comfort-providing medications and human contact, but with unwanted and unwarranted technological intrusions.

A report from the Institute of Medicine details the crisis surrounding the care of the dying in the United States. "Doctors neglect, even avoid, the patients they cannot cure. Doctors often ignore their dying patients' preferences for care. Doctors often fail to address their dying patients' physical suffering. Instead, continued, unnecessary medical treatment often contributes to the dying person's pain," says Dr. Ira Byock, president of the American Academy of Hospice and Palliative Medicine.[1]

Dr. Christine K. Cassel, an expert on end-of-life issues, is chief of the Division of General Internal Medicine at the University of Chicago Medical Center. "It is necessary for the health care professions and the institutions where most people die to come to terms with their responsibilities to provide better clinical care for those who die in their charge," says Cassel:

> This is no small challenge since it confronts deep-seated attitudes, fears and anxieties of society at large and of the modern institutions of medicine, dominated by the miracles of science and technology and the culture they have spawned in which death is viewed as a failure—something shameful and peripheral to the prevailing standards of excellence inherent within the medical profession.[2]

Even the AMA confesses its neglect of the dying patient. "It's a professional obligation which we've forgotten over the last couple of decades in our zeal to save lives. We need to provide the kind of comfort, the kind of dignity, the kind of control that people are looking for," says Dr. Linda Emanuel, the organization's vice-president for ethics standards.[3] Dr. Thomas Reardon, the board chairman, agrees. "The issue," concedes Reardon, "is [that] the profession needs to do a better job."[4]

Second, there is agreement that—in addition to poor end-of-life care—the medical profession's failure to care adequately for patients in their final days has increased enthusiasm for the right-to-die movement. Members of the public are increasingly aware of atrocious end-of-life scenarios and see a hastened death as the only way to retain dignity and control. Advocates of legalization often point to the plague of "prolonged dying" as justification for ending the deplorable conditions.

In 1977, 38 percent of Americans agreed that "a person has a right to end his or her life if this person has an incurable disease." By 1996 the figure had increased to 61 percent. Surveys of the general public show current support for assisted suicide in the 60 to 78 percent range.

Fear of a painful death, says Dr. Mitchell Max, is one reason that ill patients ask for their doctor's help in dying. "Pain is the reason Jack Kevorkian has been so successful," says Max.[5] Pain, however, is only part of the sorry picture of death in the United States. Loss of control, fear of being a burden, abandonment, loss of dignity, and the cost of medical care are all reasons for the consistently overwhelming support for an assisted death when a person is terminally ill and in extreme suffering during the final stages preceding death.

"The increase in the popularity of legalized euthanasia is . . . a vote of no confidence in the medical profession," writes antieuthanasia activist Wesley J. Smith in his book, *Forced Exit: The Slippery Slope from Assisted Suicide to Legalized Murder*. "Many supporters (of euthanasia) are afraid—nay, terrified—at the prospect of being victimized at the hands of an out-of-control doctor who, they fear, will hook them up to a machine and force them to suffer as cash cows lingering in an agonizing limbo until they die or their health insurance runs out—whichever comes first. Thus, euthanasia is sold as a guarantee of sorts against both suffering and financial difficulty."[6]

That end-of-life care is not all it should be is not a novel complaint. Beginning with Dr. Elisabeth Kübler-Ross in the 1960s, critics saw serious deficiencies in an institutional denial of death, an obsession with technology, and physician inability, emotionally and/or clinically, to deal comfortably and competently with human mortality. Indeed, "inadequate education in the management of the terminally ill . . . is probably one of the greatest failures in today's professional education," opined medical observers in 1972.[7]

In a 1977 editorial in the *New England Journal of Medicine*, Dr.

Kathleen M. Foley, director of pain management at Memorial Sloan-Kettering Cancer Center (New York), wrote: "The lack of training in the care of the dying is evident in practice. Several studies have concluded that poor communication between physicians and patients; physicians' lack of knowledge about national guidelines for such care, and their lack of knowledge about the control of symptoms are barriers to the provision of good care at the end of life."[8]

Nothing has improved in the intervening twenty-five years, even though the profession repeatedly said, "We'll fix everything. Leave it to us." The public has run out of patience, and the popularity of an assisted death has soared.

What is the alternative to the current system, under which the preservation of life is the overriding concern and death is viewed as a personal and professional failure? Why does palliative care (also known as "comfort care" and "supportive care")—the study and management of patients with active and progressive diseases for whom the prognosis is poor—run so counter to the goals of most American medical practitioners? The focus of palliative care is broader than just keeping patients free of pain—or "comfortable," as the euphemistic usage goes.

The World Health Organization (WHO) Expert Committee on Cancer Pain Relief and Palliative Care provides a thorough definition of palliative care:

> Palliative care is the active total care of patients whose disease is not responsive to curative treatment. Control of pain, of other symptoms, and of psychological, social, and spiritual problems is paramount. The goal of palliative care is the achievement of the best possible quality of life for patients and their families. Many aspects of palliative care are also applicable earlier in the course of the illness, in conjunction with anticancer treatment.
>
> Palliative care: affirms life and regards dying as a normal process; neither hastens nor postpones death; provides relief from pain and other distressing symptoms; integrates the psychological and spiritual aspects of patient care; offers a support system to help patients live as actively as possible until death; offers a support system to help the family cope during the patient's illness and in their own bereavement. Radiotherapy, chemotherapy, and surgery have a place in palliative care, provided that the symptomatic benefits of treatment clearly outweigh the disadvantages.[9]

Comprehensive care is not limited, of course, to cancer patients. It is for all patients. Palliative care is at the heart of hospice, which provides aggressive comfort care in a patient-oriented setting. Hospice is the one success story in the care of the dying.

Dame Cecily Saunders founded the first hospice, St. Christopher's, in London in 1968, for the sole purpose of easing the suffering of the terminally ill. Hospice has provided an alternate, though still underused, way of dying ever since then. In essence, the goal of hospice is not to preserve life but to make whatever life remains meaningful, the end result being a peaceful death.

While acknowledging the many benefits of modern medicine, a group of clergy, health care workers, and other thoughtful people began wondering in the 1970s whether institutionalized deaths, depriving the natural process of dying of its family ties, had not robbed dying of its dignity. Out of their concerns, and in reaction to the prevalence of a technological and impersonal death, hospice care was born in the United States. The natural process of dying was returned to the home.

The first American hospice was started in New Haven, Connecticut, in 1974. In 1977 the National Hospice Organization (NHO) was born, and by 1983 its *Guide to the Nation's Hospices* listed 1,700 organizations servicing 100,000 patients nationwide. The movement has experienced extraordinary growth since then, with more than 2,600 hospice programs now in all fifty states, the District of Columbia, and Puerto Rico. Hospice helped approximately 400,000 Americans die in 1996—almost one out of every six deaths.

As much as being a facility, hospice is a philosophy of caregiving. The National Hospice Organization describes the hospice philosophy and how it works:

> Hospice is a special kind of care designed to provide sensitivity and support for people in the final phase of a terminal illness. Hospice care seeks to enable patients to carry on an alert, pain-free life and to manage other symptoms so that their last days may be spent with dignity and quality at home or in a home-like setting. . . . Hospice services are available to persons who can no longer benefit from curative treatment; the typical hospice patient has a life expectancy of six months or less. Most receive care at home. Services are provided by a team of trained professionals—physicians, nurses, counselors, therapists, social workers, aides, and volunteers—who provide medical care and support services not only to the patient, but to the patient's family and loved ones. The primary physician usually refers the patient to hospice. Referrals can also be made by family members, friends, clergy, or health professionals.[10]

The emphasis is on comfort care rather than curative treatment, using sophisticated methods of pain control that enable the patient to live as fully and comfortably as possible. In addition to the physical needs, hospice focuses on the social, emotional, psychological, and spiritual needs of the patient and his or her family. Hospice helps the patient and family address their fears of pain, suffering, loss of control, and dying. It also provides support for survivors in the form of bereavement care for up to thirteen months following the death.

Although hospice patients spend 90 percent of their time in a personal residence, some patients do live in nursing homes or hospice centers. Hospice offers help and support to the patient and family on a twenty-four-hours-a-day, seven-days-a-week basis. To assist the family with a home-based patient, professional teams visit the home. To give family members a break, trained volunteers provide "respite care."

Hospice does nothing to either speed up or slow down the dying process. The official position of the NHO condemns an assisted death, although individual hospices are divided on the subject. Common arguments against the practice assert that hospice, and palliative care in general, obliterates the need for physician aid in dying. Hospice leaders contend that interest in assisted suicide will recede as palliative care and effective pain management become more available.

Assisted-suicide supporters, on the other hand, argue that both options are necessary for the terminally ill for two reasons. One is that, no matter how skillfully it is treated, pain is untreatable in roughly 5 to 10 percent of all cases. The second is that pain is by no means the sole consideration of a person considering suicide. In terminal patients suffering is distinguishable from pain. Whereas pain can be treated in a vast majority of all cases, suffering cannot. Feelings of abandonment, loss of dignity and integrity, and fear of being an emotional and financial burden cannot be treated by increased medication or technological innovations. Sedated, incontinent, unable to feed oneself, and unable to communicate—this is suffering, which no amount of pain medication, antidepressants, or counseling can do anything to ease.

The greater the number of people whose suffering can be relieved by a physician, "the more we are pleased," says the Hemlock Society. "We are not into trying to get large numbers of people to end their lives. But we want that option of aid in dying to be available for the few people who may need it."[11]

Whereas conventional wisdom says that dying people seek a doctor's help because of intense pain, five recent studies have unexpectedly found that most patients are "motivated by psychological factors—often depression—not by unbearable physical suffering." The other factors, along with depression, include hopelessness, anxiety, a sense of loss of control, dependence on others and loss of dignity, says Dr. Ezekiel Emanuel of the Harvard Medical School.[12]

The Netherlands' 1991 *Remmelink Report*, the world's most comprehensive study of assisted suicide and euthanasia, found that pain was a motivating factor in less than 50 percent of the patients who requested a physician-assisted death. "The patients made the request for reasons of loss of dignity (mentioned in 57 percent of cases), pain (46 percent), unworthy dying (46 percent), being dependent on others (33 percent), or tiredness of life," it concluded.[13] Surprisingly, pain was the *sole* motivating factor in only 5 percent of the assisted-dying cases.

According to Marcia Angell, editor of the *New England Journal of Medicine*:

> I have no doubt that if expert palliative care were available to everyone who needed it, there would be fewer requests for assisted suicide. Even under the best of circumstances, however, there will always be a few patients whose suffering simply cannot be adequately alleviated. And there will be some that would prefer suicide to any other measures available, including the withdrawal of life-sustaining treatment or the use of heavy sedation. Surely, every effort should be made to improve palliative care, as I argued 15 years ago, but when those efforts are unavailing and suffering patients desperately long to end their lives, physician-assisted suicide should be allowed. *The argument that permitting it would divert us from redoubling our commitment to comfort care asks these patients to pay the penalty for our failings. It is also illogical. Good comfort care and the availability of physician-assisted suicide are no more mutually exclusive than good cardiologic care and the availability of heart transplantation* [italics added].[14]

Like most advocates of physician aid in dying, Doctor Angell is equally supportive of hospice and grateful that it is becoming more of a mainstream choice for patients given access to it. Unfortunately, it is the answer for only a small proportion of dying patients. Although as many as 85 percent of American adults would prefer to die at home with their loved ones, their pain under control, only 17 percent of dying patients are part of a hospice program. There are several reasons why the numbers are not larger.

First, hospice is available *only* to the patient who is predicted to die within six months. Therefore, it is overwhelmingly used by patients dying of cancer (about 80 percent) and more recently of AIDS, since the timing of these deaths can be predicted fairly accurately. The same qualification applies to PAS. While most of the population dies from heart disease, strokes, and respiratory and other chronic diseases, these people are usually not eligible for hospice programs or assisted suicide because the timing of their deaths is too uncertain.

Second, doctors must talk to their patients far enough ahead of time to implement hospice care. Many doctors, however, are uncomfortable discussing death and/or dealing with the family's grief. Annas comments on what the SUPPORT study tells us about physician-patient communication:

It is worth underscoring that American physicians are not just uninterested in communicating with their patients in general, they are particularly uninterested in communicating prognosis information. . . . Tolstoy tells us, however, that such refusals to confront the death of a patient with the patient are not unique to our country or our century: "What tormented Ivan Ilych most was the deception, the lie, which for some reason they all accepted, that he was not dying but was simply ill, and that he only need keep quiet and undergo the treatment and then something very good would result."

Medical students and residents are taught that talking is a waste of time, distracting from the time available to do real medicine. And when even doing real medicine cannot help the dying patient, students and residents quickly learn that the attending physicians are uninterested in having discussions with patients or families about death or pain.[15]

A 1998 study published in the *Journal of the American Medical Association* confirms the belief that doctors are frequently not honest about a patient's prognosis. Most terminally ill patients believe their odds for survival are far greater than they really are, research shows. Physicians contend they have trouble being realistic with their patients for fear that they will lose hope. Whatever the real reasons are for not setting their patients straight, these false hopes increase suffering. A study of terminally ill cancer patients shows that false hope leads overly optimistic patients to choose futile, aggressive treatment, which only adds to their pain and precludes enrollment in a hospice program.

Third, hospice care usually involves home care, which for many people is not a viable option. They either live alone or are not blessed with a family member who can be home twenty-four hours a day to provide support and assistance.

Finally, most medical students receive no training in the advantages of hospice. This is partly because hospice care takes place outside a formal medical center and partly because palliative care is a low-status topic in the medical hierarchy. Indeed, Cassel points to the unfortunate fact that "in those teaching hospitals with hospice units, residents often do not follow patients who are transferred to hospice because 'it is not a learning experience.' "[16] Apparently "real" doctors do not do hospice. Moreover, with most Americans dying in either hospitals (61 percent) or nursing homes (17 percent), medical residents are left without experience of or rapport with this alternative to an institutionalized death.

What, according to Foley, is the suffering that hospice and other institutions seek to eradicate, that can force a terminally or chronically ill patient to take his or her life? There are three major components: pain and other physiological symptoms; psychological distress; and existential suffering, described as life without meaning or hope. These components are inextricably connected, and the perception of distress in one of the three intensifies the distress in the other two.

Pain is the most common symptom in dying patients. It is also the one that dying patients fear the most. Cancer pain *can* be well treated in up to 80 percent of patients by using adequate amounts of available oral medications. More aggressive treatments are able to control the pain in an additional 10 percent of patients, leaving only the final 10 percent unable to be helped, even with optimum attempts. The fact that cancer patients and those suffering from other diseases *can* be treated, however, does not mean that they *are* being treated.

A 1994 study conducted in fifty-four cancer clinics, published in the *New England Journal of Medicine*, found that physicians undertreat pain to the extent that 42 percent of patients with moderate-to-severe cancer pain do not receive enough medication to deal with it.

According to data from other U.S. studies, pain management was seriously inadequate in 56 percent of outpatients with cancer,[17] 82 percent of outpatients with AIDS,[18] 50 percent of hospitalized patients with various diagnoses,[19] and 36 percent of nursing home residents.[20] A 1995 study published by the *Journal of the American Medical Association* found that more than one-half of nine thousand terminally ill patients spend their dying days in moderate-to-severe pain. Other studies put that figure at closer to 70 percent.[21] In a yearlong review, a twelve-member committee of the Institute of Medicine found that in 1997, 40 to 80 percent of patients with cancer, AIDS, and other diseases reported inadequately treated pain.[22] These numbers are unconscionably high.

Pain management does not pertain solely to the terminally ill. A recent AMA briefing revealed that seventy million Americans are affected by undertreated chronic pain not associated with a terminal illness. It is pain from arthritis, lower-back troubles, and respiratory problems, among many other illnesses and conditions, that makes life so difficult to navigate.

Pain is often evaluated from the perspective of the beholder rather than that of the sufferer. Doctors prescribe less pain medication to members of minority groups, including women and the elderly, than to younger or middle-age white males. Of these underserved patients, those who were perceived by their physicians as "less ill" were more likely to receive less pain relief.

Not only patients and their surrogates claim inadequate pain management; doctors agree. A 1993 study in the *Annals of Internal Medicine* reports that 86 percent of oncologists admit that their patients lack sufficient medication. Whatever the actual percentage and regardless of who quotes the figures, a clear picture emerges: People who are terminally or chronically ill receive seriously inadequate pain medication—and some groups receive even less than others.

Uncontrolled severe pain lowers the quality of life, interrupting such everyday practices as sleeping, eating, and socializing with others, to say nothing of its psychological and existential effects. Meanwhile other physical symptoms further erode the remaining quality of life. The most common forms of distress in the days and weeks that precede death include shortness of breath, nausea and vomiting, fatigue, delirium, confusion, restlessness, disturbed bladder and bowel function, and general physical wasting and malnutrition. Few physicians are well prepared to deal effectively with these problems, let alone intensive, invasive pain.

Physical symptoms are not the only ones that affect the terminally ill, who suffer psychologically as well. Dying patients tolerate high degrees of depression and anxiety, with thoughts of suicide. This type of existential suffering manifests itself in feelings of meaninglessness, hopelessness, and futility, leading to intense psychic pain, which can be equal in discomfort to physical pain. Emotional and social needs go as undetected and unaddressed as physical symptoms.

Research tells us that 50 to 80 percent of dying patients experience death anxiety. More than 60 percent of patients with advanced cancer have psychiatric problems, depression, anxiety adjustment disorders and delirium being the most prevalent. Moreover, major depressive disorders occur in 9 to 17 percent of terminal patients with an additional 4 to 9 percent experiencing minor depression.

Sometimes the physical or psychological pain is simply too much to bear. The choice to hasten a death may be an expression of a thoughtful weighing of the benefits and burdens of further treatment. This decision is also called "rational suicide" and usually reflects "long-standing and strongly held values or beliefs," conclude a study of psychiatrists sponsored by the American Psychiatric Association (APA).[23] A national survey of attitudes toward death finds that "concerns about being a burden and retaining some dignity during dying in accordance with one's ego ideal may now determine a decision to refuse further treatment," or actively to seek out the means to commit suicide.[24]

Medicine today has the means to relieve the agony of the overwhelming majority of dying patients. It could alleviate the discomfort of many other people saddled with chronic pain. Effective pain medication exists, what is lacking is the will to use it. A number of forces continue to thwart efforts to improve not only pain management but also overall care before death. In turn this lack of sufficient and compassionate treatment serves as a powerful argument for legalizing PAS.

———

Why, in a medically sophisticated country with almost limitless research tools available, with the most exacting technology the world has ever known; why, with the pills, pumps, and slow release drugs, with opiates, nerve blocks, epidurals, and endless amounts of safe drug dosages available to physicians; why do so many people still die in excruciating pain? And why is so little attention paid to the general care and well-being of the terminally and incurably ill? When medicine has done all it can, and it is only a question of time before death arrives, why do physicians abandon the patient? Why is American end-of-life care so abysmal?

Barriers to the prevention of physical and emotional suffering fall into three basic categories: lack of knowledge and skills among health care providers, valid and invalid concerns and attitudes of health care providers, and valid and invalid concerns and attitudes of patients.

The biggest obstacle to adequate treatment and care of pain is lack of knowledge and skill among health care providers. Doctors are ignorant about the techniques of pain relief, unaware of medications and other treatments that are available and effective. Pain specialist Foley says that physicians are "educationally incompetent" to care for dying patients. "They're not educated in death and dying. We don't teach it in medical schools, and they don't have experiences in hospices."[25]

Most providers are inadequately trained to detect and manage the physical symptoms and emotional distress that are routinely associated with the care of the ill and, especially, the dying patient. Many doctors simply do not know how to prescribe properly the extraordinarily high doses of narcotics that some dying people require. Medical schools are organized to prepare students "to treat disease, to cure, to stave off death."[26]

There is virtually no training in pain management or palliative care, and students are rarely given the opportunity to "develop the skills required to honestly describe the patient's condition to the patient and family, to listen for the patient's understanding of his or her illness, or to stay in a relationship with the patient and family despite the physician's own personal discomfort in the face of death and decline," says social scientist and educator Mildred Z. Solomon.[27]

Only a small fraction of medical residency programs offer a course in pain management. Even fewer teach palliative medicine, which involves caring for the pain, psychological distress, and fears of dying patients and their families. According to the AMA's report on medical education, only five of the 126 medical schools in the United States require a separate course in end-of-life care. Of the 7,048 accredited residency programs in place, only 26 percent offer a course on the medical and legal aspects of care at the end of life as a regular part of the curriculum.

If medical literature reflects the priority accorded end-of-life treatment, it is safe to assume that it ranks near the bottom. *The Cecil Textbook of*

Medicine, used by most medical students, devotes only 3 of its 2,300 pages to the care of the terminally ill. Another classic, *Harrison's Principles of Internal Medicine*, bluntly states, "The discovery and cure of potentially serious disease represents a far greater service to one's patients than ministrations in the course of an incurable condition."

Literature for physicians is no more enlightening than literature for students, and equally indicative of our avoidance of the topic of death. A federal pamphlet on HIV for physicians never mentions that AIDS is a fatal disease. It recommends making arrangements for child care when the parent gets sick, but says nothing about the long-term care of the child when the parent dies. George Soros describes medical literature's dearth of information about death at the end of the twentieth century: "It is easier to find descriptions of the way people die and what can be done to ease their death in the medical textbooks of the turn of the century than in today's voluminous literature on the treatment and cure of diseases."[28]

People suffer needlessly because the existence of their pain is undiagnosed, the source unknown. Pain management and palliative care are not generally a part of the medical education's lexicon. "Consequently, when most doctors begin practicing medicine, pain is not even in their awareness. A recent study found that half of hospital patients who were in substantial pain were never even asked by their doctors and nurses how much they hurt," write journalists Shannon Brownlee and Joannie M. Schrof in a cover story on pain for *U.S. News & World Report*.[29]

This gap in medical education is not unique to the United States. The focus on cure rather than care exists in almost all "developed" countries. In a 1994 survey of Canadian medical schools, for example, *not one* of them offered a full palliative care course.

The situation is no better in Israel. Despite the fact that there are more doctors in Israel per person than in any other nation in the world, "in at least one area, the treatment of pain, many Israeli doctors remain in the dark ages— not for lack of equipment or funds, but out of inexcusable ignorance." A survey by the Israeli Pain Society found that 33.3 to 50 percent of patients in the early stages of cancer experience pain, as do 70 percent to 90 percent in the advanced stages. Physicians believe that pain can be controlled in 75 percent of cancer patients, yet this pain is controlled in only 17 percent with any success. The reason given? Poor to nonexistent medical school training. Israeli physicians rated their own medical school training in pain as "poor to very poor. There are no formal courses on palliative medicine in any of Israel's four medical schools. Palliative care is not a required subject for doctors, even for oncologists," admits the *Jerusalem Post*.[30]

American doctors acknowledge the inadequacy of their skills and understanding of medications and other treatments that are available and effective. In a study of 1,177 physicians who had treated a total of more than seventy thousand cancer patients in the prior six months, *76 percent of the doctors cited lack of knowledge as a barrier to their ability to control pain, an inexcusable statistic in this day and age.* The fact that doctors acknowledge these deficiencies, and yet fail to correct them by taking continuing education courses or by other informational means, speaks volumes about the low priority the medical profession gives to relieving patient suffering and distress.

Among other obstacles to satisfactory end-of-life care are the valid and invalid concerns and attitudes of physicians. Health care providers actually erect their own barriers to good treatment and pain management. These impediments emanate from fear of death, to misconceptions about narcotics, to a hostile attitude toward the dying process itself. A well-justified fear of criminal prosecution is another problem. The art of medicine requires physicians to know the difference between saving someone for living and saving him or her as a test of technological skills. It also requires them to make peace with the enemy—death—and to help the patient come to terms with it. And this requires talking with the patient, something that physicians, by all accounts, find it difficult to do.

In his keynote address at a conference on end-of-life care held at New York City's Columbia Presbyterian Hospital, Richard S. Blacher, professor of psychiatry at Tufts University School of Medicine, talked about why death is so very difficult for health care providers to discuss, yet so necessary if one is to help a patient have a "good death":

> "Doctors and nurses may have less tolerance for dying than other people," he said. "This is one of the problems that confront us, for death, after all, is our enemy and also a blow to our pride in our ability to preserve life." Blacher recalled a time when the medical staff of a coronary care unit asked him to go into the room of a dying 85-year-old patient and "stop her." What she was doing was calmly giving her sons detailed instructions for her funeral arrangements and what they should do with her possessions. "I sat down and listened to the serene conversation, a conversation the medical staff found intolerable because she was saying that she expected to die, and dying was against both the expectations of the staff and perhaps even against the rules of the coronary unit."[31]

Dr. Balfour Mount, chair of palliative medicine at McGill University and founding director of the Palliative Care Service at Montreal's Royal Victoria Hospital, concedes that poor listening skills prevent providers from hearing the needs of the terminally ill. In addition, Mount believes physicians' "intrinsic anxiety about death" is one of the main reasons patients' needs are not met. Humans have a deeply rooted, existential fear of death that lurks suppressed in our unconscious most of the time. This anxiety results in physicians' avoidance of dying patients. Doctors and nurses visit less frequently and stay for shorter periods. This avoidance translates into abandonment in the eyes of the patient, one of the main criticisms of the medical profession. These unaddressed fears, says Mount, prevent the health care system from providing good and compassionate care for the dying.

Sherwin Nuland goes a step further, claiming that studies show that contact with death at an early age is one of the reasons why people go into medicine. Moreover, because the subject of death can trigger inner fears, doctors become uncomfortable, reluctant, and even incapable of attending to the comfort and well-being of the patient whose death is imminent: " 'Doctors have a greater fear of death than any other profession. One of the reasons we deal so badly with end of life issues is because it brings back all of these primitive fears.' The situation is complicated by the fact that doctors are trained to save lives and when they lose a patient it can be devastating. 'I don't think I ever lost a patient when I didn't feel I should have done something more to save them.' "[32]

Communication is a necessary part of preparing for a good death. Many physicians fear, however, that planning "palliative care for the end stages of dying will disturb the protective mechanism of denial and thereby distress the patient and family," write anesthesiologists and pain experts C. Richard Chapman and Jonathan Gavrin.[33] Whether this is a convenient rationalization depends on the reality of the situation. Justifiably or not, the family and doctor often conspire to keep the fatal prognosis from the patient, thereby limiting any constructive planning for future comfort care. The question remains of who in this scenario cannot face his or her mortality—the doctor or the patient?

The two most serious barriers to sufficient medication are fear of addiction and fear of prosecution. Fear of addiction is not a valid concern. Doctors are afraid of turning their patients into drug addicts, even though it has been proved that pain patients rarely become addicted. Quite validly doctors are also afraid of being branded drug pushers and losing their medical licenses or, worse,—charged with murder. "We have a system right now oriented toward drug-addiction control that sees narcotics as drugs of abuse," says Dr. Diane Meier, geriatrics and palliative care specialist at New York's Mount Sinai Medical Center, who believes a change in pain medication regulations is long overdue. "Physicians are fearful of being sanctioned for appropriately prescribing opiate analgesics," she says.[34]

A recent study found that more than 50 percent of doctors fear prescribing narcotics, even though they acknowledged that their patients would benefit from them. To avoid attracting the attention of drug enforcement agencies and state medical boards, doctors who will initially prescribe narcotics usually refuse to prescribe refills. Others give their patients doses that are too low to alleviate the pain. Reluctance to provide large doses of narcotics is justified, however. Last year more than 120 doctors who were prescribing—some would say overprescribing—narcotics for pain had their licenses revoked or suspended. Some were even charged with murder if the patient died. Such is the backlash from the recent success of the PAS movement, which has brought the practice out in the open and left it more vulnerable to opponents who are poised to jump on anyone when PAS is suspected.

The only painkiller strong enough to relieve most intense pain is morphine, a narcotic derived, like heroin, from opium. Scientists are convinced that most kinds of severe pain can be treated safely and effectively if doctors will make more liberal use of narcotic drugs, especially morphine. The public and the law view these drugs with suspicion, as substances characterized by abuse and restricted by state and federal law. *Time* reports on the fears but also the miraculous benefits of morphine, which not only relieves the suffering but also aids the patient in actually getting better faster:

> Narcotics. The word conjures up images of dope peddlers, undercover cops and mandatory prison terms. No matter that morphine is more effective than most prescription-strength painkillers. No matter that the vast majority of patients today can take the drug without becoming addicted. Quite a few doctors, a large number of their patients and much of the health-care establishment want no part of it. Even specialists in the treatment of pain who prescribe narcotics on a regular basis refer to the drugs as "opiate medications," as if calling them by a different name would counter their shady reputation.[35]

There is uninformed prejudice within the medical community, as well as within society as a whole, against using narcotics—even when indicated. This prejudice arises out of the incorrect belief that they will turn law-abiding citizens into drug-crazed morphine addicts. This is nonsense, and it indicates a failure to distinguish between the abuse of these drugs and their purposeful use to treat legitimately painful conditions.

Clearly there is a potential for abuse, but any argument against using strong medication to relieve pain for the terminally ill has no credibility for five specific reasons. First, addiction to prescribed opioids is rare, "occurring in from 1 in 1,000 to 1 in 10,000 cases. Still, states require physicians to complete multiple forms, limit the number of dosages prescribed at once, or forbid approval of refills over the telephone—barriers which make it difficult for patients cared for at home, in hospices, or nursing homes to get these medications," concludes a committee of physicians calling for narcotics reform.[36]

Second, medical literature describes how severe pain "eats up" the opioid medication in a way that prevents addiction. Moreover, unlike addicts who get high from the instant "rush" of the drug being injected into their systems, pain is relieved through consistent, steady doses over a course of time.

Third, if someone is going to die in a matter of days or even months and is in excruciating pain, it is ludicrous to let fear of addiction stand in the way of some quality of life. What possible difference would it make if a candidate *did* develop a physical or psychological dependence?

Fourth, there is confusion about what constitutes addiction and what is simply physical dependence. "Most people who take morphine for more than a few days become physically dependent, suffering temporary withdrawal symptoms—nausea, muscle cramps, chills—if they stop taking it abruptly, without tapering the dose. But few exhibit the classic signs of addiction: a compulsive craving for the drug's euphoric or calming effects, and continued abuse of the drug even when to do so is obviously self-destructive," write Brownlee and Schrof.[37] If physical dependence *does* occur, a gradual reduction of the medication, called withdrawal therapy, will take care of the symptoms.

Finally, when addicts take drugs they are lost to themselves, their families, and society. When a person with chronic or terminal pain takes drugs, he or she is able to return to a normal life of family and work. When addicts use drugs, they become less functional and more isolated, and they move away from the mainstream. On the other hand, when pain patients use drugs, they become more functional and much less isolated, and they move *toward* the mainstream.

William Hurwitz was *not* afraid to prescribe narcotics—not, that is, until his medical license was revoked. Hurwitz, an internist in Virginia, is a case in point of what can happen to a doctor who helps patients combat pain with prescriptions for appropriate but high doses of morphine. The Virginia Medical Board said he was excessively and indiscriminately prescribing narcotics. His patients, however, said otherwise. One patient committed suicide after Hurwitz could no longer write a prescription for medication. The patient, on video, blamed the Drug Enforcement Administration (DEA) and the Virginia Medical Board for the pain that caused his death. "The war on drugs has turned into a war on pain patients. These patients are told, 'Go home. Suffer. Don't bother us.' And the patients are extorted into killing themselves because they can't get what should be available to anybody who needs it," says Doctor Hurwitz.[38]

Stratton Hill of M. D. Anderson Cancer Center in Houston, Texas, is one of the country's foremost authorities on pain management. He and Doctor Hurwitz were both guests on CBS-TV's *60 Minutes*. Doctor Hill had testified for Hurwitz in court. Discussing the chilling effect on doctors across the country of this type of sanction, Hill said: "We have to do something about the problem of regulatory boards insisting upon standards of practice that are based upon prejudice, biases and misinformation. The board has almost unbridled power, and they do whatever they want to. That's what's so scary to doctors."[39]

Physicians must now confront a new problem with the law. In addition to fearing that prescriptions for powerful doses of narcotics might provoke action from state and federal agencies, they must fear action from the religious and political right as well. As courts and legislatures have grappled in recent years with the issue of PAS, new attention has fallen on pain management in the context of death and dying. Attention has focused on the doctor, who may or may not have intended the patient's death when the morphine was increased. As long as the "intent" is to relieve suffering, the resulting death is an acceptable by-product of the initial good intent. If their "intent," however, is to hasten the patient's death, the resulting death can be interpreted as murder. This "logic" is known in religious and medical communities as the "double effect" and is legal. Right-to-die advocates contend it is assisted dying in disguise and hypocritical to pretend otherwise. Many doctors shy away from large doses of morphine for terminally ill patients to relieve the pain, fearing their "intent" will be questioned.

It is tricky business to determine the motivation of another. Now that physician aid in dying is in the spotlight, cases are occurring in which a doctor is reported for *intending* to hasten a patient's death. The doctor contends that his or her intent was to relieve pain, and that the medication inadvertently caused the death. Right-to-life advocates press the issue, saying the doctor is a murderer. The medical license is suspended, the case goes to court, and doctor is put in the defensive position, at great financial and emotional cost.

What happened to Ernesto Pinzon is an example of what physicians fear. His elderly patient, Mr. Gurrieri, was riddled with lung cancer; he was sweating profusely and struggling for every breath. Testimony revealed he had been given less than two days to live. The doctor administered his doses of drugs after Gurrieri's family urged him to do something to ease his persistent suffering. Gurrieri died shortly thereafter. Pinzon testified that he was simply trying to relieve the man's pain. The prosecution claimed he had intentionally killed the man to end his suffering. Pinzon was charged with the murder of his patient. The Florida State Board of Medicine suspended his license to practice medicine.

It turned out that a nursing supervisor had filed the complaint against him. Pinzon was acquitted, but not before his lawyer commented, "This is going to put the whole medical profession in jeopardy because no one is going to want to treat pain symptoms for terminally ill patients."[40] The jury foreman said later, "Who should be on trial here? Dr. Pinzon or the American medical community?"[41] The jurors agreed that they would be comfortable having him treat them or a relative with a terminal disease. This kind of scrutiny has made doctors even more cautious about prescribing the quantity of drugs that will really alleviate the pain. Pinzon could have faced the death penalty.

When the Supreme Court ruled in 1997 that there was no constitutional right to physician-assisted suicide, it required all states to ensure that their laws do not obstruct the provision of adequate palliative care, especially the alleviation of pain and other physical symptoms of people facing death. Essentially the Court guaranteed the right to palliative care for terminally ill patients.

Or, as Robert A. Burt of the Yale Law School wrote in the *New England Journal of Medicine*:

> A Court majority has found that states must not impose barriers on the availability of palliative care for terminally ill patients. This ruling would have the same status as the right to an abortion established by *Roe v. Wade*—that is, an individual right that cannot be overridden by state actions prohibiting or "unreasonably burdening" access to a physician's assistance. . . . The Supreme Court majority has thus provided an unexpected but strong and very welcome directive requiring states to remove the barriers that their laws and policies impose on the availability of palliative care.[42]

The law has always permitted the "double effect." The High Court ruling will have a positive effect on restraining state and federal medical boards from removing a doctor's license if overprescription is suspected. However, it will not provide relief from criminal prosecution if the patient dies and the doctor's intent is questioned. As long as doctors fear strangers' second-guessing their intent, patients will not get the pain relief they so desperately need and want. Until those against an assisted death cease interfering with what goes on between doctors and patients—ferreting out doctors who may have had the "wrong intent" when administering medication—physicians will not be free to make the best interest of the patient their first priority.

Effective pain management is more than shots and pills. It is more than prescribing strong narcotics, even if this were possible without fear of censure or prosecution based on "intent." Education and expertise, so often lacking, are critical. Soothing alternatives to oral narcotics, including the controversial use of marijuana, can control chronic debilitating pain in the following ways:

> *Transdermal duragesic patches that, when applied to the skin, provide a slow, steady release of medication that can last three days. *Implantable devices that deliver a steady stream of drugs to keep pain in control and prevent surges and the often-resulting overmedication. *Epiduroscopy. Using a camera attached to a catheter, physicians can identify which nerves are causing the pain and treat those nerves specifically with drugs. This process often is used in conjunction with intrathecal morphine, in which the drug is delivered directly to the affected nerves

through a catheter. *Spinal cord stimulation. A catheter carrying electric current is placed in the spine near the nerves causing pain, which blocks the perception of pain from reaching the brain.[43]

Doctors in the United Kingdom recently voted overwhelmingly to allow for cannabis products to be made legally available for medical use, a controversial medical issue in the United States. Proponents argue that if an individual is suffering, it is inhuman and barbaric to outlaw a product that would help him or her. Medicinal use of marijuana, however, encounters the same opposition as do large doses of narcotics to alleviate suffering—the war-on-drugs mentality and the resistance of regulatory boards, based on prejudice, biases, and misinformation. Similar to the controversy over physician-assisted suicide, the legalization of marijuana pits the public against the establishment in a bitter struggle. A 1997 poll shows that 60 percent of Americans support the medicinal use of marijuana.

Advocates contend that marijuana is useful for relieving internal eye pressure in glaucoma, for controlling nausea in cancer patients on chemotherapy, and for combating severe weight loss associated with AIDS and the human immunodeficiency virus (HIV). Its benefit as a muscle relaxant has brought relief to people suffering from multiple sclerosis and Parkinson's disease.

The citizens of Arizona and California legalized marijuana in 1996 for certain purposes. California, by a 54 to 46 percent margin, approved a law allowing the possession, use, and cultivation of marijuana, as long as the drug was for medicinal purposes. Arizona, by an even larger margin (65 to 35 percent) approved a law allowing sick people to receive a variety of controlled drugs, including marijuana, LSD, and heroin, for pain relief and the treatment of certain illnesses.

The Arizona and California initiatives emanated from two quite different concerns: relief for suffering patients and relief from a failed drug policy. Recent attention to the legalization of marijuana for the relief of suffering has also fostered comments about the need to change America's corrupt drug policy in general. "U.S. drug prohibition is now collapsing fast. America is in the incipient stages of 'Colombianization,' with every level—from the lowest sheriff to top officials of the U.S. Justice Department. The drug war has become unbelievably dirty and corrupt. It's not just bribes any longer: the police themselves are the gangsters," says Joseph McNamara, former chief of police of Kansas City and now a fellow of the Hoover Institute.[44]

Amid the hue and cry, the Clinton administration responded decisively, with Gen. Barry McCaffrey, the White House drug policy chief, leading the opposition to legalize marijuana for medicinal purposes. Federal drug policy overrode the state initiatives, as McCaffrey ordered the total prohibition of its possession or use for any reason, including the elimination of pain and suffering. Doctors who counseled patients to use marijuana would be excluded from Medicaid and Medicare programs as well as from the federal registry that allows them to write prescriptions, and would face criminal charges.

The government worked hard to validate its position. It claimed that marijuana has no medicinal value, that marijuana accomplishes nothing that legal drugs cannot do, and that its liberalized use as medicine would lead toward more liberal drug laws and more drug abuse. No scientific research had proved the drug's medicinal properties or its medical value, said McCaffrey. "Smoke is not a medicine. Other treatments have been deemed safer and more effective than a psychoactive burning carcinogen self-induced through one's throat."[45]

Dr. Robert Temple, an official of the Food and Drug Administration (FDA), pointed out that any drug, including marijuana, need not be proved superior to current medications in order to be approved by the agency. It does not have to be better than, or even as good as, an existing drug. It must only have medicinal value.[46]

Not surprisingly, the AMA, consistent with its pattern of resisting change, sided with the government, enraging many physicians who claimed intrusion into the relationship of doctor and patient. Physicians cited the medical profession's historic right to decide what is best for the patient. But what eventually took the wind out of the government's sails was an editorial in the prestigious *New England Journal of Medicine*. It advocated the freedom of doctors to prescribe marijuana for medical purposes and condemned the threat of government sanctions as "misguided, heavy-handed and inhuman. . . . What really counts for a therapy with this kind of safety margin is whether a seriously ill patient feels relief as a result of the intervention, not whether a controlled trial 'proves' its efficacy," wrote Kassirer, executive editor.[47]

A *Boston Globe* editorial expressed the majority opinion: "The states are clearly out front on an issue that the Clinton administration has chosen to play for politics. This is a matter of compassion, not image-making. If morphine and other addictive drugs can be prescribed and used responsibly under a doctor's care, there's no reason marijuana can't be used in palliative care."[48]

One of McCaffrey's themes was that scientific research has not proved the drug's medicinal properties or values. While the federal government and the two states were going at one another, the American Civil Liberties Union's education director, Loren Siegal, observed "that the government 'has consistently impeded research into medical marijuana' while maintaining that its effectiveness should be subjected to scientific scrutiny."[49]

Lawsuits, political posturing, study groups, and the government's slow retreat from its dogmatic position eventually left the prescription of marijuana not prosecuted, if also not actually legal, in California. The winning ballot initiative was undone by the Arizona legislature, and the medical use of marijuana remains illegal there. Despite the setbacks a number of previously unknown facts surfaced from the publicity surrounding the initiatives.

The widening national debate revealed evidence of marijuana's ability to reduce suffering and of the government's unadmitted awareness of its positive effects. Without question the most startling and contradictory piece of information to emerge from the dispute was the discovery of a little-known government program at the University of Mississippi that supplies marijuana to eight people across the United States for medicinal purposes, while at the same time disavowing its therapeutic value. It is the only legal marijuana project in the country. The university, under contract with the National Institute on Drug Abuse since 1970, has grown marijuana for these specific people and for research. In 1976 the university began supplying the drug under a separate program to be overseen by the FDA. The goal has been to "provide compassionate care to relieve symptoms from diseases such as multiple sclerosis, epilepsy, cancer, glaucoma and rare genetic diseases."[50]

The program, which costs two hundred thousand dollars a year to operate, supplies as many as three hundred marijuana cigarettes a month, even though federal law classifies marijuana as an illegal narcotic with no recognized therapeutic value. Although five of the original thirteen patients have died, the program stopped taking new patients in 1992, when the Department of Health and Human Services (DHHS) began its official policy of disclaiming knowledge of marijuana as a form of treatment.

Despite its name the Compassionate Investigative New Drug program is not a clinical trial. In fact, according to the *Oregonian*, which reported the story:

"the reports submitted regularly by the participants' doctors are used only to evaluate whether to keep them in the program. The reports have no effect on a policy that discounts the medical value of smoking marijuana". . . . The compassionate-care program exists today because of the FDA's longstanding policy to keep an individual in an investigative drug program "as long as they and their doctors think they're benefiting." Advocates of medicinal marijuana wonder why the government has not used this copious information.

Doing away with sanctions against marijuana involves more than mere fear of addiction or the stubbornness of the DEA or the bias of state regulatory boards. The financial stakes are high in this governmental drug-war effort to maintain the status quo, even if the public has voted otherwise. Meanwhile marijuana is covertly and increasingly used to control and relieve the symptoms from certain diseases—driven largely by the absence of other available medications.

———

Physicians are not the only ones to blame for poor end-of-life care in the United States. Patients are also responsible for not getting the end-of-life compassion and pain relief they need and are entitled to. A large number of patients contribute to their own misery by suffering in silence rather than speaking up and complaining. Some find it empowering "to endure," finding suffering a sign of moral strength. These patients concur with the belief system that "living with pain in stoic silence still is seen as a sign of moral strength, while taking drugs to relieve it is often viewed as weak or evil. 'We are pharmacological Calvinists,' says Dr. Steven Hyman, director of the National Institute of Mental Health."[51] These people come from the same school of thought as those religious groups opposed to assisted suicide on the ground that suffering has redemptive powers, that hardship brings us closer to Christ.

Other terminally ill people, including many AIDS patients, also choose to suffer their pain in silence because they do not want to be a burden or a nuisance to the attending physician. These patients see the doctor's role as the traditional one of curing, not comforting, and find any reference to pain not only burdensome but distracting as well. Others are afraid to be labeled as bad or troublesome patients. Some refuse to reveal worsening pain, afraid that it means the disease is progressing. Acknowledging the pain would break down the denial system, an important coping mechanism for many dying people. A number of patients believe that pain from diseases like cancer and AIDS is inevitable and uncontrollable, about which nothing can be done.

Other patients are afraid to use narcotics, even when pain is severe, for fear of addiction. Some also worry that taking narcotics early in the course of their illness will leave them with later pain that is immune to the narcotic. This concern is not valid, since the dose can always be increased as the pain mounts.

Too often those who do inform their doctors find them unwilling to prescribe stronger pain relief, which can result in the patient never mentioning it again. Or, worse, the request can be met with disdain and suspicion. Physicians may treat patients like drug addicts or criminals, the pharmacist may question the prescription, or the nurse may refuse to administer the medication. To avoid these humiliating reactions, the patient learns to suffer in silence.

Education to remove these widespread misconceptions and fears is the answer for doctors and patients alike. Pain management is moving into medical education and is being discussed more openly by society. Patients are beginning to ask for more comfort care. State medical boards' disciplinary activity for excessive prescribing of controlled substances has come under intense scrutiny. State legislators are sponsoring Intractable Pain Relief Acts.

The laws, if passed, would provide protection for physicians, nurses, and pharmacists treating pain in good faith. There is every reason to hope that with time, the obstacles to a peaceful death will gradually disappear.

Ironically, poor end-of-life care has increased support for the PAS movement which, in turn, is improving the nation's poor end-of-life care. It has taken two Oregon initiatives, the Ninth and the Second Circuit Courts of Appeals decisions, and two cases before the Supreme Court to make headway in any fundamental shift in the way medicine looks at itself and the patients it treats. Medical professionals are finally realizing that, despite stunning technological breakthroughs, not everyone can be cured, and that if they cannot be cured, the public will not settle for suffering and abandonment. With this in mind, medicine has been forced to focus on the patient's comfort along with the doctor's cure.

"It was a wake-up call to everyone that we needed to do a better job," says the AMA's Reardon of public support for assisted death. "As is the case with so many things in our society, sometimes you need a crisis to get your attention, to recognize the problem and to deal with it efficiently," he explains.[52]

Dramatic moves to effect change actually go back to November 1994, when Measure 16 was passed in Oregon, legalizing PAS. Supporters and opponents of Measure 16 agree that key public perceptions about medicine's lapses aided the measure's narrow passage. The passage of Measure 16, said an editorial in the *Oregonian*, evidenced

> a widespread belief that the medical profession was inadequately skilled and compassionate in helping dying patients; a broad sense that the dying were needlessly suffering from pain and depression; and an impression, bordering on a conviction, that physicians, often backed by relentless technology, were robbing patients of too much personal control in their final days, consigning them to what they and their families felt were deaths without dignity.[53]

Although approved by a tiny margin, the victory came as a surprise to the medical profession. Until the Oregon vote, doctors were only minimally reacting to assisted suicide or to their own inadequate care of the dying. It appeared at that point that Oregon only had "a month before the law would take effect. 'Man, everybody was hustling,' says Dr. Susan Tolle, the director of the Center for Ethics and Health Care at Oregon Health Sciences University. 'They couldn't do more to improve care for the dying in these 30 days.' "[54] Leaving it really no choice but to rectify its neglect, the AMA began scrambling, promising changes, sponsoring seminars and lectures on pain control and setting up task forces on end-of-life care.

Robert J. Samuelson, national columnist for *Newsweek* and the *Washington Post*, believes that the recent spotlight on aid in dying has finally exposed medicine's familiar and traditional approach to death and dying. This exposure has embarrassed the profession and given it no alternative but to respond. After all, society has criticized doctors since the 1960s for their obsession with technology. "The great irony," says David Mayo, a philosopher with the University of Minnesota's Center for Bioethics, "is that they didn't give a damn about palliative care until the Oregon initiative passed."[55]

The 1994 Oregon vote fueled improvements in the quality of that state's end-of-life care. The state has shown increased attention to comfort care in two ways. First, the rate of admission to hospice increased 20 percent in 1995 and continues to improve. Of Oregonians who die each year, 29 percent are doing so with hospice support, compared to the national figure, which is a considerably lower 17 percent. Second, Oregon currently leads the nation in the medical use of morphine to relieve pain. From 1994 through 1996, Oregon increased its use by 70 percent, due largely to fewer impediments to its prescribing practices than other states.

Despite persistent claims by medicine that the situation would improve, the continuing poor care offered dying patients has remained. The public lost patience and confidence, however, and began searching for a better death. The more information available, the more the public has supported physician-assisted suicide. The SUPPORT study, for example, confirmed that doctors ignore patients and their end-of-life requests. Physician aid in dying provides an alternative, as the public attempts to take control and fill a void that medicine has created.

As poor end-of-life care has influenced public interest and inspired support for the right-to-die movement, so has the right-to-die movement forced the medical profession to admit its inadequacies and begin making the necessary modifications, enhancements, and changes. The furor over aid in dying has had the dramatic, unexpected consequence of forcing mainstream American medicine to turn its attention to the dying to an unprecedented degree. Even opponents of assisted death confess that, as long as legalization does not result, all the initiatives, court battles, and enthusiasm for changes in the law will have been worth it, if it continues to improve the care of the dying.

The Impact of AIDS

The painful physical and emotional suffering associated with AIDS produces some of the most compassionate and compelling arguments in favor of PAS. Some ethicists argue that AIDS, with its highly predictable and sustained agony, is *the* disease that makes the case for assisted death. Also, since AIDS is the number one cause of death among both men and women between twenty-five and forty-four years of age, the sheer number of deaths caused by the epidemic has generated interest in finding a way to shorten the dying process.

For people with AIDS (PWAs) the choice is not between life and death, but rather between dying now or dying later. To that end "it is not so much a choice of death as a choice to end irreversible emotional and physical suffering of grave dimensions," writes Jeremy A. Sitcoff in a law review article.[1] The AIDS epidemic has combined forces with other cultural and behavioral phenomena in the late twentieth century to create public demand for changes in how we die.

In his graduate thesis examining the incidents of euthanasia and PAS among PWAs, Russel Ogden found a high correlation between AIDS and an assisted death. Of the PWAs he interviewed, almost 84 percent were personally considering an assisted death for themselves, while almost 45 percent had already made specific plans to end prematurely their pain and suffering. A full 100 percent favored a change in the law, from legalization to a more cautious reduction in the severity of the penalties.[2] For many PWAs a hastened death was the only solution that allowed them to set the terms and conditions on how they would complete their lives.

PAS and euthanasia among PWAs have not been well studied, but in addition to Ogden's work, research from the Netherlands contributes to the emerging connection between PWAs and an assisted death. Two separate studies show that both suicide and assistance in suicide are significant considerations for persons with AIDS. The Remmelink Commission conducted a comprehensive study of medically assisted suicide in the Netherlands, interviewing 405 physicians and reviewing seven thousand deaths to evaluate end-of-life decisions in that country. Results showed that "between 10% and 20% of all deaths among terminal AIDS patients involve euthanasia or assisted suicide."[3] A year later a smaller study conducted by the Netherlands Institute of Mental Health reported similar incidences of assisted suicide in AIDS patients. These results indicated that "euthanasia was discussed by 60% of all patients mainly because of their fear of dementia and physical deterioration," while AIDS patients actually died from euthanasia in 23 percent of the cases investigated. From these findings the authors concluded that "euthanasia is a major theme for people with AIDS."[4]

More than 235,000 Americans have AIDS. As of late 1996 the Centers for Disease Control (CDC) reports the cumulative number of deaths from AIDS to be 501,310. The impact of AIDS on these lives has been devastating. Uncertainty regarding health, reduced ability to work, and the corresponding decline in quality of life compounds the debilitation of an already incapacitating disease. Most PWAs suffer the losses of numerous loved ones and friends, as AIDS rips through the gay community and the nation, bringing isolation, loneliness, dependence, humiliation, and eventually depression to overwhelming numbers of people. Given the characteristics of the disease and the degree of related suffering, it is reasonable that a sizable proportion of PWAs prefers to avoid a lingering death.

The decision to abbreviate the prolonged dying process is not casually made, but is, to the contrary, the product of considerable discussion and planning. Action on the decision is initiated out of the understanding that there is no hope for recovery. "AIDS has succeeded in uncloseting much about sexual behavior and sexuality, perhaps it will also succeed in being the disease to uncloset euthanasia," Ogden optimistically suggests.[5]

A multitude of physical manifestations surround the disease. The most common pain syndromes for PWAs are neuropathy, joint pains (arthritis, arthralgia, rheumatic), skin pains (Kaposi's sarcoma, infection), and headaches. Wasting syndrome, a familiar component of the disease, leaves the body drawn and weakened to a skeletal condition. Two symptoms are associated with wasting syndrome. The first is a loss of body weight, which is usually progressive and may be accompanied by severe diarrhea. The second symptom is night sweats, which can involve fevers with dangerously high temperatures of 106 or 107 degrees Fahrenheit.

Also common among PWAs are a form of candidiasis and PCP. Candidiasis is an infection of the esophagus that causes major difficulty and discomfort when swallowing. PCP is a rare form of pneumonia that is common among individuals with AIDS. Symptoms of PCP include rapid, labored breathing, a nonproductive cough, and extreme anxiety because of the inability of the lungs to draw enough oxygen from the air into the bloodstream.

As more people with AIDS survive longer with combinations of drugs, many are confronting yet another serious health problem: cancer. Malignant tumors, particularly Kaposi's sarcoma and certain cancers of the lymph system, have been present since the disease was first recognized in 1981. But now the array of cancers is broadening. Dr. Valerie Beral of the University of Oxford in England says that studies have definitively linked five cancers with HIV infection. These cancers affect the skin and internal organs, the lymph system, the eye, the cervix, and the anus. Three other cancers, affecting the lymph and blood system and the muscles, are most probably linked to the infection. Recent studies have also suggested an increase in lung, lip, and testicular cancers among people with AIDS, but the link is currently uncertain.

Medical treatment often produces adverse side effects, adding to the general discomfort. Zidovudine (AZT), used to reduce the progression of the disease, must be carefully monitored to prevent anemia, blood disorders, and liver dysfunction. Chemotherapy further weakens the system. Physicians treat PCP, which occurs in 85 percent of AIDS patients, with antibiotics to minimize the onset of respiratory difficulties, but the treatment itself can cause low-grade fever, nausea, and vomiting.

Pain in PWAs is similar to pain among the general public—unrecognized and undertreated. A study reported in the *British Medical Journal* sought to measure the prevalence, severity, and impact of pain on quality of life for HIV patients; to identify factors associated with undertreatment of pain. The results? "From 30% of outpatients to 62% of inpatients reported pain due to HIV disease. Pain severity significantly decreased patients' quality of life. Doctors underestimated pain severity in 52% of HIV patients reporting pain. Underestimation of pain severity was more likely for patients who reported moderate or severe pain and less likely for patients whose pain source was identified or who were perceived as more depressed. Of the patients reporting moderate or severe pain, 57% did not receive any analgesic treatment; only 22% received at least weak opioids. Likelihood of analgesic prescription increased when doctors estimated pain to be more severe and regarded patients as sicker." The conclusion? "Pain is a common and debilitating symptom of HIV disease which is greatly underestimated and undertreated."[6] It is worth noting that it was the doctor's subjective determination of how much the patient was suffering that determined how much medication was prescribed, not the severity of the pain as described by the patient.

The problem of poor palliative care in the United States is further compounded in PWAs. Research has found that the majority of AIDS patients are members of stigmatized and marginalized groups within our society, "(i.e., infected drug users, gay males, females, low socio-economic status, and minority groups) and as such, they are placed at risk for insufficient connections to medical care in general and poor palliative care in particular. This disenfranchisement can lead to requests for assisted suicide that emanate from the despair and unnecessary suffering that stems from poor palliative care."[7]

AIDS dementia adds to the misery. It is the most common neurological complication (organic mental disorder) of AIDS, caused by the HIV virus invading the central nervous system early in the infection. The syndrome of AIDS dementia complex is characterized by disturbances in motor performance, cognition, and behavior. An estimated two-thirds of all PWAs will develop clinical dementia during the course of their illness.

A 1986 review of psychiatric disorders in AIDS patients at the Memorial Sloan-Kettering Cancer Center in New York City revealed that Kaposi's sarcoma was the single most common medical diagnosis among suicidal patients. Patients with AIDS and Kaposi's sarcoma who were suicidal frequently had prominent signs of delirium, often superimposed on AIDS dementia.

Such physical and mental symptoms are not the only hardships associated with AIDS; social factors intensify the emotional distress. These pressures lead to constant personal health assessments. PWAs are acutely aware of what to expect once diagnosed. They are likely to have witnessed poorly controlled pain, suffering, and loss of physical and mental integrity. Many have been the primary caretaker to a person enduring at least one of these losses. Waiting and watching for symptoms to appear, one young man with the HIV virus was ever vigilant. "I'd pose in front of the mirror and say to myself, 'You look great, but you're rotting inside,'" he confessed.[8]

One-third of Russel Ogden's sample group reported the loss of a partner to an AIDS-related death. The numbers of AIDS-related deaths known to each participant ranged from 0 to 180, with a mean number of 29. "To put such loss into perspective," writes Ogden, "many of the respondents indicated fatigue with attending funerals. Some commented that they had seen more death within their peer group, to one disease, than had their parents in a lifetime. Living with AIDS brings with it a heightened sense of mortality, and watching AIDS kill one's peer group is a constant reminder of the inevitability of death from AIDS."[9]

Stigmatization from inside and outside the gay community causes isolation and depression, two predictors of suicide, says Ogden. He discovered that 61 percent of responding PWAs gave accounts of subtle exclusion by other gay men not infected. Men without HIV/AIDS often choose not to associate with men carrying the disease. Respondents reported feeling alienated from society as well as from their peer support group.

Loss of control and a death without dignity—in pain and possibly violent—comprise the reasonable fears expressed by people with AIDS. "Death for me is easy, it's getting there with this illness, that is horrifying," admits one ailing patient. Sampling shows 78 percent are fearful of losing control as health declines. The decision to abbreviate the dying process is based on a desire to maintain dominion over the remnants of a deteriorating mind and body. A staggering 83 percent have witnessed AIDS-related deaths that were "violent," "excruciating," or "horrific." "Euthanasia is not a way of giving up, it is a way of stating one's final decision. For me, it is an issue of not wanting to lose control of how I relate to the world. It is a response to a desperate situation," said one patient. "In my experience, many who die of HIV die very violent, brutal, and painful deaths, because that is the nature of HIV," stated another man.[10]

Even though a great deal of progress is being made in the treatment of AIDS, and hope exists where it was absent previously, incidences of suicide for PWAs are astonishingly high in comparison to the suicide rate for the general population, or even among people with other terminal illnesses. In 1985 Dr. Peter Marzuk and a team of researchers from Cornell University Medical College conducted the first study examining the relationship between AIDS and suicide.[11] Marzuk's study found that among New York City residents with AIDS, the suicide rate in men between the ages of twenty and fifty-nine was thirty-six times higher than men in the same age group without the diagnosis, and sixty-six times higher than in the general population.

The idea that suicide may be an acceptable, rational option is rarely presented in professional literature. Traditionally, mental health professionals have denied and denounced the idea of "rational suicide." The literature on suicide, for the most part, is filled with statements proclaiming the irrationality of anyone who might even *consider* ending his or her life. It is argued that since anyone considering suicide is irrational, his or her outlook distorted by mental illness, the health care worker has the legal and ethical responsibility to intervene—that is, to persuade the patient to abandon such thoughts, to break confidentiality and notify others, and to hospitalize involuntarily as quickly as possible: anything to prevent clients from harming themselves.

James L. Werth, psychological counselor, clinician, and author, believes it is possible to make a rational decision to suicide. Because he does not consider suicide a crime that is "committed," he uses suicide as a verb without the modifier "to commit." He refutes the conventional wisdom that suicide can be equated with mental illness in all cases.[12] Werth is not alone in his beliefs; the mental health profession is slowly coming to recognize the existence of rational suicides. Indeed, Werth found that rational suicide is acceptable to 80 percent of psychologists questioned. Furthermore, 20 percent of the same respondents reported working with a client whom they considered to be rational in his or suicide thoughts. Not surprisingly, psychologists are forced to practice in a fashion not compatible with their belief system, due to justifiable fear about the legal and ethical repercussions of allowing a client, even one who is rational, to suicide. "I would take all steps necessary to keep a client from committing suicide even though I support rational suicide because his/her family could successfully put me out of practice and sue me, since by our state's law as well as the current ethics of our profession, we cannot exercise discretionary judgment about this. If the law were different, my actions might very well be different," confided a fellow psychologist.[13]

Werth's belief in a rational suicide operates on three premises: first, that rational suicide, including but not limited to assisted suicide for the terminally and hopelessly ill, is a legitimate option for some individuals; second, that traditional interpretations of mental health and ethical and legal standards of care do not allow for the possibility of rational suicide and therefore need to be changed; and last, that mental health professionals should consider the possibility that a person who wants to die is rational in this desire and consequently that the professional needs criteria by which the rationality of this decision can be assessed.

Based on responses from the psychologists he interviewed, Werth generated a set of conditions that would need to be met for a suicide to be considered rational:

> For a suicide to be deemed rational, the person must have a hopeless condition (e.g., a terminal illness, a painful condition, a disabling and/ or deteriorating condition, or chronic low quality of life), he or she must have arrived at the decision through his or her own free will, and he or she must have engaged in a sound decision-making process (i.e., non-impulsively consider all alternatives, consider his or her personal beliefs, consider the impact on others, and consult with significant others and with professionals—especially a mental health professional who can assess psychological competence that, for this sample, would include the absence of treatable major depression).[14]

To many PWAs suicide is a dignified option that is exclusively theirs to take—a sane, purposeful, and rational decision. According to one physician who treats PWAs, "people with AIDS and their advocates say that virtually everyone with the disease at least thinks about suicide when the end is near and wonders how it might be done."[15]

Many knowledgeable mental health experts believe that suicidal thoughts in AIDS patients constitute a coping mechanism instead of a manifestation of psychological imbalance. Thinking about suicide may help the individual to function with a greater sense of control in the face of a severe future threat. Researchers illustrate one patient's suicidal thoughts as representative of many others who reach for suicide, if only in their thoughts, as an option: "A close friend of 32 years (he is now 35) is dying of KS [Kaposi's sarcoma]. I try to imagine what I would do in his circumstances. This leads me to suicidal thoughts. . . . I guess I would do it if there was no other option and I was in a lot of pain. . . . *I think that thinking about suicide alternatives is a way for me to cope, or deal with the question of what I would do, if I were to develop AIDS* [emphasis added]."[16]

Not all PWAs are fortunate enough to have the support of a physician. Less savvy AIDS patients, much like the general public, request sleeping medication from several doctors in an attempt to accumulate enough lethal drugs to shorten their lives. Unlike what happens in the general public, however, friends often collect the leftover pills after a suicide and recycle them to another AIDS victim in need of a lethal dose, thereby continuing the underground access to sedatives, barbiturates, and narcotics. The problem, however, is that, when drugs come from various sources and with unknown shelf lives, it is almost impossible to judge their strength—resulting in botched suicides because of undermedication.

When such suicide attempts are unsuccessful, the dying individual is forced to resort to whatever means are available to complete the job—hanging, shooting, jumping, or suffocating. What began as death with dignity often turns into a sordid, messy end. In their efforts to avoid this horror, PWAs have indirectly become a driving force behind the legalization of PAS.

The AIDS epidemic has taken many lives, and the AIDS population has much to gain by a legal change permitting PAS. Surprisingly, however, AIDS activists have contributed minimally toward furthering the right-to-die agenda. Author Nina Clark speculates about the apparent lack of interest: "Some speculate that the AIDS community and the right-to-die faction keep each other at arm's length in an effort to avoid the stigma of the other group. In addition, AIDS activists feel they have enough to do in getting the public to understand about AIDS. Another reason that individuals afflicted with AIDS avoid becoming active in the right-to-die movement is that the AIDS community places much emphasis on living with disease, rather than preparing for death. Nevertheless, people afflicted with the AIDS virus tend to be younger patients, more insistent on their civil rights than elderly patients with Alzheimer's disease or cancer and as such, they are generally supportive, but have refrained from intense activism or verbal expression in favor of assisted suicide."[17]

The arrival of AIDS contributes one more motivation for obtaining control over the way we die. The slow deterioration of mind and body fulfills the requirements for PAS. The patient with AIDS is mentally competent—at least for a long while—and terminally ill, which means that in all medical probability, he or she can accurately be diagnosed to be dead within six months. Such accurate prediction of time left is usually possible with AIDS victims. The other requirement is that the patient must be an adult. The vast number of AIDS deaths occur among those between twenty-five and forty-four years of age. PWAs, therefore, are good candidates for an assisted death.

Few people would disagree that modern medicine has accomplished an extraordinary amount as a result of its shift into specialization and technological wizardry. Meanwhile, however, there have been significant side effects. Most important, human interaction has been replaced by a dispassionate approach, wherein the body is viewed as a machine to be fixed—lacking emotion, fear, and soul. The physician has become detached from the patient, while the dying patient feels increasingly frustrated and abandoned. So terrifying have the stories become about those who placed all faith in the health care community that the atmosphere is now conducive to taking personal control of the dying experience.

Changing societal dynamics—the onslaught of technology, the rights culture, the decline of the doctor-patient relationship, poor end-of-life care, and the AIDS epidemic—have caused us to focus on scenarios of the outdated ways we spend our final days. Paradigms that once worked are no longer emotionally satisfying or physically effective. As discontent with the dying process grows, public interest is pressuring the establishment to meet the demands of a changing culture and its emerging needs. This pressure is meeting stiff opposition, but cracks in the wall of resistance are beginning to show. Later we will examine the forces of restraint that are trying but failing desperately to maintain the status quo.

The stage is now set for the birth of a movement to meet the needs of a changing culture. The right-to-die movement begins its fledgling steps to improve the deplorable suffering of the dying patient. Groups organize, people become personalities, resistance raises its complacent head, state and federal legislatures respond to vocal constituents, the courts emerge as the patient's advocate, and the world joins in the struggle to change outdated public policy.

PART TWO

The
Birth
of a
Movement

C h a p t e r   6

At Last, New Rights for Patients

The right to die" is a shorthand phrase used by the courts. It is also the banner under which patients' rights advocates assemble. While there is no complete agreement on the meaning of the right to die, terms such as "right to die with dignity" and "death with dignity" are used to convey the concept of a desirable environment in which to spend one's final days. The legal basis of the right to die is the full wheel of death-and-dying law, made up of various cogs—a product of constitutional and common law and legislative and judicial decisions. It affects those who are competent and those who are not. It runs on a continuum from the right to know the truth about your medical condition all the way to the involuntary mercy-killing of the incompetent incurably ill. Most contemporary policy discussions and legal debates center around the withholding or withdrawing of medical treatment, including life-sustaining treatment, and PAS for the mentally competent terminally ill adult. There is, however, no national right-to-die law.[1]

The central feature of the right-to-die movement is the body of legal cases expanding the patient's right to refuse unwanted life-sustaining treatment, forcing doctors to withdraw such treatment if administered, and, eventually allowing medical professionals to assist terminally ill patients who want to end their intolerable lives. Regardless of which cog is focused on, the driving force is the right of the individual to have control over his or her physical person. People are entitled to the autonomy of decision making based on all the available facts and the personal integrity to be free of bodily and governmental intrusion, despite the advances of technology and the power of those who would disagree.

There are six predominant elements of the right to die, some cultural, some legal and political. Three of them arise from the doctor-patient relationship, concepts that have accumulated over recent centuries: the right based on the doctrine of informed consent, the right to know the truth about one's condition, and the right of the patient to hire and fire doctors. The remaining three elements arise from relatively recent law: rights conferred by U.S. constitutional and common law, including tort and criminal law, rights conferred by statutes that enable the individual to execute advance directives that express his or her wishes regarding medical care, and the right to enlist the help of a willing physician to hasten an inevitable death. PAS and voluntary euthanasia, as well as the right to forgo life-sustaining treatment, are all based on these overlapping elements.

Certain defining events in our culture change our expectations of others and our realities about ourselves—events of such proportion as to impact our most venerated and seemingly impenetrable institutions. Such an event took place in the mid-seventies. The results of the revolution, as many have called it, were achieved at the expense of one young life and through the pain, determination, and courage of one small-town New Jersey family.

The *Karen Ann Quinlan* case,[2] decided in 1976, was the first major right-to-die case in the United States. It was the first state high court decision ever handed down that extended a constitutional right of privacy to a refusal of life-sustaining treatment. The court's decision was the first step in the formulation of right-to-die public policy. It made famous the predicament of a patient in a persistent vegetative state who no longer had the mental capacity to exercise any decision-making options.

Quinlan forced Americans to consider, perhaps for the first time, issues involving end-of-life care. Karen Quinlan came to symbolize the struggle Americans faced over a death with dignity and the dehumanizing, advancing role of modern medicine. She gave the world a name and a face on which to focus its anxieties concerning the futile use of technology. She became famous as the one nobody wanted to be like. Hers was the prolonged death everyone wished to avoid. She changed the face and practice of medicine forever.

Concerns over the ravages of futile treatment had surfaced decades before the *Quinlan* litigation, but it was this case that grabbed the world's attention—that focused the public and forced the changes. From at least the 1950s, members of the public and the medical profession expressed concern over the need to curtail modern medicine. In 1958, at a banquet address to a chapter of the American College of Surgeons, Dr. John Farrell, chair of surgery at the University of Miami, "decided to forgo a 'light and amusing' theme befitting the occasion. Instead . . . he spoke of the patient's unnecessary suffering as doctors relentlessly and futilely fought death: 'In our pursuit of the scientific aspects of science, the art of medicine has sometimes unwittingly and unjustifiably suffered. . . . The deathbed scenes I witness are not particularly dignified. The family is shoved out into the corridor by the physical presence of intravenous stands, suction machines, oxygen tanks and tubes emanating from every natural and several surgically induced orifices. The last words . . . are lost behind an oxygen mask.' "[3]

Several years after *Quinlan*, in 1990, Nancy Beth Cruzan's case[4] catapulted the debate from a state to a national level. The evolution by no means ended with *Cruzan*, but in that period, bracketed between *Quinlan* and *Cruzan*, transpired massive legislation and scores of judicial decisions, the medical profession was revolutionized, patients took responsibility for their death, and death and dying rose to the top of America's social agenda. It was during these years that Derek Humphry founded the Hemlock Society, whose membership rose to 50,000. Dr. Jack Kevorkian began helping people die but no jury would convict him of murder, and the Netherlands permitted assisted death, even though it remained technically illegal. The right-to-die movement began to get off the ground in earnest. These years fairly boiled and bubbled with activity, as state courts and legislatures laid the policy foundations of the new movement.

The two cases dramatized the success and benefit of medical technology juxtaposed against its danger and destruction. They brought into clear focus certain institutional and cultural dysfunctions that had needed realignment for some time. They were highly significant for different reasons.

Similar in both scenarios were the courage and fidelity of two extraordinary families. Both young women lay in persistent vegetative states, with no hope of improvement, much less recovery. Since neither of them had left any written indication of her wishes about futile life support, both families were left with the uncertain consequences of battling the establishment for what they believed was right. One aspect that emerged from the private and public hardship of Joseph and Julia Quinlan and Joseph and Joyce Cruzan is the appreciation that a very few people can make a very big difference. Through perseverance, determination, and courage, the two families broke new ground in their struggles to free their daughters. In the process all of us benefited. The right of the competent patient and the right of the incompetent patient's surrogate to refuse treatment, even if it results in death, is now well established by state and federal authority.

How is it that this first young woman, Karen Ann Quinlan, started, from her deathbed coma, a chain reaction leading to medical, legal, ethical, and social changes in our culture so vast as to be one of the clear and bright lines of the twentieth century? What decision did her loving and courageous parents make that causes us now to reflect not so much on "How I want to die" but rather on "How I want to live until I die"?

Karen Ann Quinlan was a bright, generous, and energetic young woman of twenty-one when the tragedy occurred. What follows, unless otherwise noted, is an account of Karen's story written by her loving parents.[5] Sensitive and loyal to those around her, Karen delighted in typical activities of her age—having fun and hanging around with her friends. A former boyfriend remembers her as lighthearted: "Everything was laughs." Yet, with unusual prescience, she announced on several occasions, to startled listeners, that she would die young and go down in history. Karen's predictions came true—on both counts.

It was never entirely clear what happened to Karen Ann Quinlan during that evening of April 15, 1975. Out partying with her friends, she fell into a coma and was admitted several hours later to a nearby hospital in New Jersey. She had, according to her friends, consumed three gin and tonics. The doctor found Valium in her handbag. As far as anyone ever ascertained, the alcohol on an empty stomach—she had been on a starvation diet—caused her to stop breathing for two separate periods of approximately fifteen minutes each. Similar to Nancy Cruzan, the subsequent lack of oxygen to the brain caused her to fall into a coma. Brain function cannot survive after six minutes without oxygen. Although Quinlan was rumored to have taken a whole list of drugs, doctors found only aspirin and a small amount of Valium in her system.

Her condition further deteriorated. Within a short time, all the examining physicians agreed that she had suffered irreversible brain damage with no hope of recovery, or even of improvement, and that she was now in a permanent vegetative state. Julia Quinlan recalls how her daughter's body became distorted within days of the tragedy. Left alone, her body persisted in curling inward. Her knees were bent and pushed toward her chest, and her elbows pushed in toward her sides, while her wrists, bent yet rigid, were curled under her chin. Her hyperextended neck gave the impression of having been broken. Curled in a fetal position, head back, neck hyperextended, mouth wide open, she moved her head from side to side, her face grimacing. In order to prevent her body's involuntary curling and twisting, Karen's arms and legs were bound to wooden boards, like splints, in an attempt to straighten them out.

At the conclusion of each eight-hour shift, the attending nurse wrote brief reports on her condition, on sheets headed VITAL SIGNS—KAREN ANN QUINLAN. Some of the notations read as follows: "Seems as if she's in pain by facial expressions"; "Making crying sounds"; "Opens mouth and winces as though in pain"; "Moaning loudly at intervals this night"; and "Pt. [patient] crying with tears when mother is speaking to her." How absolutely heart wrenching for a parent to witness. "I don't care how logical and technical and medical you try to be, it is horrible to see your daughter suffering this way day after day, and stand by helpless," Julia Quinlan said.

Mrs. Quinlan recalls the standard procedures taken to keep Karen "alive":

> They monitored the respirator, recording the times when the patient was able to assist the MA-1 by breathing spontaneously. They regularly suctioned the cavity in her throat of mucus, to prevent a recurrence of infection. They tube-fed Karen and emptied her body wastes from the

Foley catheter inserted in her bladder. They dispensed medicines as ordered, bathed her, and every four hours recorded her temperature, pulse, respiration, blood pressure. Every two hours they turned her to a new position in a vain attempt to eliminate bedsores.

Late in the second week of May, approximately one month after Karen had lapsed into the coma, Julia invited her mother to their traditional Mother's Day dinner. On their way to the restaurant they stopped at the hospital to see the patient. They were not prepared for what they saw. Karen was, uncharacteristically, without the bedclothes that usually covered her deformed body. They looked down at Karen's body, shrunken and twisted into a position that seemed inhuman. There was a blanket stuck between her legs so the bones of one leg wouldn't cut into the other, and gauze pads between her toes to keep them from bruising one another. But the really unsettling part was the bedsores, so deep that the two women could actually see right to Karen's exposed hipbone. "And my mother was just standing there, with her mouth open but not saying a word," Mrs. Quinlan said.

What was the diagnosis and prognosis that this unassuming yet strong and courageous, deeply religious family found themselves confronting two to three times a day? Their daughter was in a persistent vegetative state. Persistent vegetative state (PVS) patients are permanently unconscious, with a complete loss of mental functions, unaware of themselves or the surrounding environment. Voluntary reactions or behavioral responses reflecting consciousness, volition, or emotion are absent. It is not uncommon, however, for patients to survive in this condition for five, ten, or twenty years, without ever regaining consciousness. The longest reported survival, without recovery, was thirty-seven years and 111 days.[6] Were Karen to survive that long, she would "live" until close to her sixtieth birthday.

Making the situation that much more painful for family and loved ones, following the initial coma, in which the eyes are closed, the PVS patient evolves into a condition of eyes-open unconsciousness—that is, the vegetative state. At any given time there are approximately fourteen thousand people in this limbo condition in the United States. "Patients in a fully developed persistent vegetative state do manifest a variety of normal brain stem functions. The patient's eyes are open at times, and periods of wakefulness and sleep are present. The eyes wander, but without sustained visual pursuit (that is, following people or objects in the room in a consistent, meaningful, purposeful fashion). The pupils respond normally to light. . . . The protective gag and cough reflexes are usually normal, which partially accounts for the long-term survival of these patients. . . . PVS patients, then, are awake but unaware," writes Ronald W. Cranford, a neurologist and medical ethicist on Nancy Cruzan's case.[7]

Of utmost concern to any parent is whether patients such as Quinlan or Cruzan experience any pain and suffering. While the possibility has been debated, Cranford, as well as the American Academy of Neurology, is convinced that patients in a persistent vegetative state do not. Family members, however, may find it difficult to take quite the medical profession's unequivocal position. Cranford explains:

> There may be, and often are, facial movements and other signs indicating an apparent manifestation of conscious human suffering. . . . In other words, PVS patients may "react" to painful and other noxious stimuli, but they do not "feel" (experience) pain in the sense of conscious discomfort of the kind that physicians would be obligated to treat and of the type that would seriously disturb the family. Families are often quite distressed by these subcortical and brainstem reflex responses, which they mistakenly interpret as a conscious interaction with the environment and an indication that the patient is experiencing distress. The family needs constant reassurance on this matter and, of course, the physician must be extremely confident of the diagnosis.[8]

Julia Quinlan was the first member of the family to face the reality of Karen's condition, to realize that Karen could linger on for weeks, months, or even years, and that ultimately she would die without ever regaining consciousness. By the end of May, a mere six weeks into this catastrophe, Karen's "weight had dropped from 115 pounds, when she was brought in, to 90 pounds. They kept feeding her high-vitamin mixtures, and still her weight kept going down. And she was so rigid that there was no way of circulating the intravenous, so they had to put a feeding tube through her nostrils, into her stomach," Julia explained. She knew, as much as she willed it otherwise, that there was no hope of improvement.

Gradually each family member, dealing with the pain and loss in his or her own fashion, painfully began to accept the prognosis. Karen would never recover. Not only would she not recover, she would also never even *improve*. A nurse gently helped them face the truth. "The thinking part of the brain is dead," she told them. The neurologist wrote in her chart, "Respiratory status is stable. However, neurologically, situation is hopeless." Further distressing the family was their knowledge that Karen would be the first to say, "Don't do this to me. Just leave me alone." She had, in fact, said just that.

Karen's family consisted of her parents and a younger brother and sister. They were a close-knit group, and they agreed at the outset that any and all decisions concerning Karen would be unanimous. If one member said, " 'No, I can't accept that. I can't live with that,' Fine. Then that's it. As long as something wasn't a family decision, we just would not bring it up again." And so it was that the united family looked to their religion for help. After three months, many prayers and much discussion, Karen's parents, both devout Roman Catholics, consulted their friend and priest, Father Tom Traposso, about the possibility of disconnecting the respirator.

They were advised by Father Traposso that they were not obliged as Catholics to use "extraordinary means" to prolong life. The use of a respirator in a case like this was, they were told, an "extraordinary means." Catholic moral teaching maintains that life is a basic but not an absolute good and that, therefore, not all means must be used to preserve it. As Pope Pius XII noted in 1957: "Normally one is held to use only ordinary means—according to the circumstances of persons, places, times and culture—that is to say, means that do not involve any grave burden for oneself or another. A more strict obligation would be too burdensome for most and would render the attainment of the higher, more important good too difficult. Life, health, all temporal activities are in fact subordinated to spiritual ends."[9]

The Quinlans would be well within the Catholic doctrine, said Father Traposso, in asking the doctors to remove the respirator. Therefore, after another unanimous family vote, Joe and Julia did just that. They went to Dr. Robert Morse, the attending physician, and requested that the respirator be disconnected so that Karen could die a natural death.

The health care professionals at the Catholic hospital agreed to remove the respirator at the family's request. Julia and Joe Quinlan signed a release form provided by the hospital. They had every reason to believe that this mutual agreement signified the beginning of the end. Unfortunately they were wrong, and the situation soon turned ugly. Three days after all parties had agreed to remove the respirator, Doctor Morse called Joe Quinlan at his office with a total change of heart. The doctor abruptly told Joe that he had a "moral problem" with disconnecting the respirator as planned and therefore would not go through with it. The hospital subsequently backed the doctor. The agreement was off; neither doctor nor hospital would disconnect Karen's respirator.

The hospital's attorney, it turned out, had recommended that Doctor Morse and St. Clare's Hospital not honor the agreement that they and the Quinlans had signed. When the Quinlans questioned why the health care professionals would not proceed as planned, the attorney replied, "You, Mr. Quinlan, are not Karen's legal guardian and not even responsible for her, since she is of age: twenty-one. Therefore, you have no right to recommend this action, the removal of the respirator. You will have to go to court and have a judge appoint you as your daughter's legal guardian, and then come back and make your request again." When Joe asked if the hospital would honor their request when guardianship was granted, the attorney coldly answered, "I don't know."

Julia and Joe Quinlan, like many of their successors in right-to-die cases, were soft-spoken people who had never been involved in any radical movement; they had never sought media attention. Deeply religious, their main interests were church and family. They were neither crusaders nor fighters, and no one would expect them to command world attention. However, they were willing to do anything within their moral code, methodically and with enormous courage, to help the daughter they loved. Therefore, with their backs to the wall and nowhere else to turn, the Quinlans hired a young, inexperienced Legal Aid attorney, Paul W. Armstrong, and went to court. Armstrong asked the court to appoint Joe guardian, for the purpose of authorizing removal of his daughter's respirator.

All they were asking of the health care providers, Joe Quinlan would repeatedly emphasize to the court and to the media, was for "permission to do physically what I had done mentally. And that was to put Karen in God's hands and let Him decide when she was going to die. Not the doctors. Not the machines or anything else. But just leave her in a natural state and let the Lord decide when He was going to take Karen."

It was apparent early in the trial that at least part of Doctor Morse's reluctance to disconnect the respirator stemmed from moral and legal insecurity. He testified that, like the Quinlans, he was a Roman Catholic. Unlike them, however, he had not heard about the concept of ordinary means versus extraordinary means of life-sustaining treatment. While debating his role in this scenario, he had looked to the church for moral approval to support his medical concerns. He found none. Finding no religious support or medical "precedent to support the Church's 'extraordinary means' concept," he telephoned the Quinlans, "and I said that I personally empathized with them. I know what they are going through. But I said I cannot break with medical tradition."

Moreover, similar to many physicians today who fear legal repercussions if they assist in a suicide, Doctor Morse feared legal liability for lack of legal precedent. Similar situations were customarily settled in the patient's hospital room or in the hospital corridors or waiting room, with the physician, not the family, acting as the decision maker. When questioned about his unwillingness to follow the parents' directive and unplug the respirator, the acquiescing Morse adhered to the cautious instructions of the hospital attorney: "There is no case that I can refer to. Nobody seems to be able to tell me of any case," he admitted. And, there being no precedent, the Doctor would take no chances.

On a rainy Monday morning, November 10, 1975, Judge Robert Muir ruled against the Quinlans in New Jersey's trial court. Joe would not be named guardian, and Karen would remain on the respirator: "There is no constitutional right to die that can be asserted by a parent for his incompetent adult child. The life-and-death decisions must be made by physicians—not by Courts of Law. The morality and conscience of our society placed this responsibility in the hands of the physician," said Judge Muir. For the most part the medical profession agreed with the judge, choosing to maintain the status quo by having all decision-making authority remain in their own hands.

Some physicians, like Dr. Christiaan Barnard, the South African heart transplant pioneer, disagreed with the verdict. He already believed what much of the population was rapidly recognizing: "The hopelessly ill should be allowed to die. Often doctors concentrate too much on keeping a patient alive. It's often a selfish attitude—a matter of feeding the ego of the doctor."

One week after losing in civil court, the Quinlans filed an appeal with the Appellate Division of the Supreme Court of New Jersey. Due to the "important issues presented by the tragic plight of Karen and her family," the New Jersey Supreme Court promptly announced that it would hear the case, thereby bypassing the Appellate Division. The New Jersey chief justice was a man named Richard Hughes. He and his wife had been scheduled to go on vacation when the case came before his court. At his wife's insistence they canceled their trip to Europe, so determined was she that her husband immediately address the Quinlans' compelling plight.

By now the family was emotionally stretched to the point where others might have given up the struggle against what seemed to be indomitable and immovable forces. The situation was becoming increasingly distressing: Their daughter, whom they continued to visit every day, was approaching nine months in a persistent vegetative state; the media were camped out on their front lawn, coming into the house frequently to ask questions, to warm up during rainy weather, and to use the bathroom; the Quinlans were receiving enough hate mail and open threats to have a state security guard posted outside Karen's hospital room at all times; there were endless meetings (and many confrontations) with doctors and attorneys; money was getting low; and there were Karen's two younger siblings to consider, Mary Ellen and John, who were going through rough times of their own.

Those who support any part of the right-to-die movement, even those who believe only in the availability of living wills, owe much to this loving and courageous family. They, like those who came after them, endured the legal struggles so that medicine was forced to respect the patient's wishes. The Quinlans had the determination and the perseverance to remain steadfast in their quest to do the very best for Karen. They possessed the inner strength to continue fighting the defenders of the establishment, those whose money, power, and prestige were threatened by change. Joe and Julia were superb communicators, commandeering the early support of the media. They never waivered in their wish to have Karen returned to her "natural state," after which they felt confident in letting God decide what would happen to their beloved daughter.

Mary Clement spent two days at a conference with Joe and Julia Quinlan in Princeton, New Jersey, in the spring of 1996. The conference, entitled Quinlan: A Twenty Year Retrospective, aimed "to provide the participants with an understanding of the impact of the *Quinlan* decision over the past twenty years, including legislation and judicial opinions in virtually every state, in Congress, and in the U.S. Supreme Court on advance directives and the 'right to die.' " Besides honoring the Quinlans, the conference paid tribute to the Cruzans, who were also present.

Clement was struck by the enormous support and consideration Julia and Joe demonstrated for each other. It was subtle but constant: the offer of a hand to steady a faltering step; the adjustment of a microphone when the spouse began to speak; the glass of water when hoarseness set in; and the eye contact when a particularly emotional time was discussed—always without speaking a word. They were extraordinarily attuned to one another. She remembers thinking at the time, Ah, so this is how they did it. Their devotion to each other undoubtedly sustained them throughout their ordeal.

On appeal, Armstrong asked the court to appoint Mr. Quinlan as Karen's guardian. The attorney offered prior statements showing that Karen would have wanted the respirator disconnected. He explained the family's constitutional right to ask for removal of the respirator and the lack of obligation on the patient's part to receive futile medical treatment. The right to refuse medical treatment is rooted in the First Amendment's freedom of religion clause. It was within the tenets of the Catholic faith to withdraw "extraordinary" treatment, and the Quinlans were merely exercising their religious beliefs. Moreover, there was a fundamental constitutional right to privacy, recognized by the Supreme Court only three years before in *Roe* v. *Wade*. In light of all these facts, Armstrong argued, there would be no criminal liability for the doctors or the hospital, since the homicide statute would not apply. Throughout the appeal, Armstrong stressed the importance of the decision being made by those closest to Karen.

Opposing the Quinlans, medical experts testified that removal of the respirator did not conform to medical practices, standards, and traditions. Removal of life support, they argued, could not take place at the request of the patient or family; this was a matter for the doctors to decide.

Chief Justice Hughes's court was willing to trust in the goodwill and good sense of patients and their families. It was open minded to a changing society in which medical technology often exceeded reason, and in which the medical profession was arrogant and greedy. The justices understood what people were beginning to fear—the prolongation of the dying process more than death itself. These justices did what they believed was correct, for Karen and for the nation. They were not afraid to deviate from the traditional standards, and they had the foresight to understand that the judiciary must rise to meet changing times and circumstances.

The New Jersey Supreme Court therefore overturned the trial court's ruling. Joe was appointed guardian. Chief Justice Hughes, writing for the unanimous court, ruled that there was no state interest strong enough to "compel Karen to endure the unendurable only to vegetate a few measurable months with no realistic possibilities of returning to any semblance of cognitive or sapient life." Whatever Joe Quinlan decided to do regarding his daughter "should be accepted by society, the overwhelming majority of whose members would, we think, in similar circumstances exercise such a choice in the same way for themselves or for those closest to them."

This 1976 decision represents the first judicial ruling to enunciate the constitutional right of privacy as the basis for withholding or withdrawing life support from an ill individual: "We think the State's interest contra weakens and the individual's right to privacy grows as the degree of bodily invasion increases and the prognosis dims. . . . It is for this reason that we determine that Karen's right of privacy may be asserted in her behalf, in this respect, by her guardian and family under the particular circumstances presented by this record."

In addition, the court eliminated all criminal liability for removing life-sustaining treatment: "We believe, first, that the ensuing death would not be homicide but rather expiration from existing natural causes. Secondly, even if it were to be regarded as homicide, it would not be unlawful."[10]

Author and law professor Norman L. Cantor praises the New Jersey court for its reconciliation of the sanctity-of-life and the death-with-dignity arguments:

It took courage and vision to rule as the *Quinlan* court did in 1976. The court could easily have found that letting an incompetent patient die was too delicate and problematic an issue to be resolved without legislative guidance. Contemporary voices of gloom and doom admonished that a sanctity of life ethic must prevail over a quality of life ethic (so that even a vegetative patient should be indefinitely sustained). According to those voices, consideration of quality of life in end-of-life decisionmaking would subject vulnerable patients to arbitrary judgments about unworthiness to live. A jurist argued less than a year after *Quinlan* that judicial authorization of withdrawal of life support from an incompetent being declares "that not every human life has sufficient value to be worthy of the State's protection, denies the dignity of all human life, and undermines the very principle [sanctity of life] on which American law is constructed."

To the eternal credit of the New Jersey Supreme Court, it rejected these vitalist pronouncements. Chief Justice Hughes instinctively understood that in an age of mechanical miracles, a sanctity of life imperative would sometimes entail prolonging undignified dying processes long beyond the pain that most people would wish. The New Jersey court understood that gravely deteriorated states can be reached that most people consider worse than death. The opinion enumerated two such states—permanent unconsciousness and a pain-wracked terminal existence.[11]

Armstrong, on the evening of the decision, joyfully exclaimed to his grateful clients that the opinion "was the kindest piece of judicial writing that's ever been presented." Their euphoria was short-lived, however, as the realization dawned that Doctor Morse had no intention of following the court's decision and removing the respirator.

Six weeks passed after Chief Justice Hughes's decision. Not only did the doctors make no attempt to remove the breathing apparatus, but Julia discovered that they had in fact placed Karen on yet *another* form of life-sustaining treatment. On one of her visits to see Karen, who was now running a fever, Julia was shocked at the sight of a "body temperature control machine"—*more*, rather than less, technology. When confronted, Doctor Morse acted as though there had been no court decision. He firmly stated that he intended to "follow *his* concept of what is standard medical practice." The doctor, blinded by his fear-based obsession with "following medical protocol," had decided to treat Karen, now in a coma for thirteen months, with the same aggressive treatment as the patient in the next bed, who had been hospitalized for only two days.

The Quinlans became increasingly distraught with the frustration of being ignored—especially after the court battles, the last of which they had won. "How long will you continue to do this?" asked Julia. The doctor's answer? "Forever." For Julia Quinlan this answer was the proverbial "straw." Even tempered and cordial up to this point, Mrs. Quinlan fled from the conference room weeping, soon to be followed by her equally anguished husband. The hospital supported Doctor Morse, reiterating its position that withdrawal from the machine would be "morally incorrect."

St. Clare's Hospital and Doctor Morse had once again backed Julia and Joe Quinlan into a position of having to fight—this time for implementation of the New Jersey court's decision. And fight they did, with the superb support of Paul Armstrong. Chief Justice Hughes had already ruled that the patient's father, as Karen's guardian, was authorized to find another doctor and hospital who would comply with their wishes. Left with no other option, Julia and Joe Quinlan set out to find more compatible surroundings.

After a vigorous and almost futile search, but with the help of the brave and compassionate Doctor Fennelly, Karen was moved on June 9, 1976, to Morris View Nursing Home. Dr. Robert Watson, the medical director, became directly responsible for her care. Although he had seen many patients in comas and in persistent vegetative states, Dr. Watson was unprepared for the sight of Karen. "She was so twisted that I couldn't even conceive the pain she would feel if she were to regain consciousness. One could only imagine the feeling if one would take a foot, twist it around a couple of times, and then tie it in that position, curled backward," he said.

Several days after her relocation, Karen Ann Quinlan was removed from the respirator. While this long-awaited event did not end the ordeal for the family, a traumatic phase of their lives was over. There would be no more tears from frustration, anger, or hope. There would be no more lawsuits, no more confrontations, and no more press conferences. Now, for the sake of their two remaining children, they would try to live a normal life again.

By this time, without her family's knowledge, Doctor Morse had weaned Karen off the respirator to the point that she no longer needed it, essentially making the court's decision ineffective. Therefore, still in an irreversible unconscious state, and off the respirator, yet receiving artificial nutrition and hydration, Karen lived for another nine years. Her loyal parents continued to visit her at least once a day, often twice. The Quinlans have been quoted over the years as saying that while they supported the withdrawal of such artificial "extraordinary means" as respirators, they opposed the withdrawal or withholding of such "ordinary means" as artificial nutrition and hydration. What they said was taken out of context, the Quinlans contend. They *do* believe that food and water, given artificially, can, in certain circumstances, be considered "extraordinary" treatment that may, according to church dogma, ethically be refused. The entire family discussed the possibility of removing Karen's food and water, but not everyone agreed. Consistent with the ground rules established so long ago, they did not pursue the option.

The demarcation between "extraordinary" and "ordinary" means of treatment has disappeared by 1998, and the Catholic Church does not distinguish between the two. In 1980, Pope John Paul II stated that patients may refuse even ordinary medical treatment when death is imminent and treatment is futile.[12] It is now consistent with church policy to withdraw or withhold medical treatment of any and all kinds.

"The one thing my wife was praying for continuously was that when Karen died, when the Lord did call Karen, she would be there . . . with her daughter," Joe Quinlan remembers. In July 1985 Karen died in her mother's arms, surrounded by other family members. As requested by the family, she was given only aspirin to fight the pneumonia that would claim her in the end. Antibiotics were withheld.

Karen's story personalized an issue that had previously seemed abstract. It captured the attention of the media and the public, who felt they actually knew this young woman who lay hooked up to a machine that kept her alive for no purpose. The nation knew Karen intimately—the court decision even referred to her by her first name—and its heart went out to her family. But the national sentiment that transcended all others was the enormous fear—the fear that *any one of us* could end up like her. Almost no one argued against the Quinlan family's request to disconnect the respirator. An overwhelming majority of the public approved the proposition in 1977 and 1981 Louis Harris polls, which found that Americans overwhelmingly believed that families "ought to be able to tell doctors to remove all life-support services and let the patient die."

It is impossible to overstate the importance of the *Quinlan* case. Public fear fueled the state legislatures and judiciaries to formulate public policy that would satisfy the questions being raised: What can individuals, competent or incompetent do to ensure that their last wishes will be honored? How can families avoid the Quinlans' predicament?

Motivated by Karen's case, and in an attempt to forestall litigation for patients in predicaments similar to Karen's, the California Natural Death Act, the nation's first right-to-die statute, was signed into law in September 1976. Seven more states passed laws the following year.

These laws legalized "advance directives," a general term that refers to any instruction or statement regarding future medical care. The two basic types of advance directives are the living will and the health care proxy, although others have evolved over time. A living will is a legal document that allows a competent adult to state the kind of care they want or do not want and under what circumstances, in the event of mental incapacity. It is a personal statement about what medical treatment is wanted or not wanted should the patient become incapacitated and unable to communicate. A living will's main purpose is to guide the doctor and agent in deciding how aggressively to use medical treatment to postpone death.

A health care proxy is a document that allows a competent adult to appoint someone he or she trusts to make decisions about medical treatment, including life-sustaining measures, in the event of decision-making incapacity. The designated individual is called the agent, proxy, or surrogate. The agent is given the power to speak at any time the patient is unable to speak for him or herself, not only at the end of life. It is essential that the agent knows whether the patient wants treatment continued for as long as it is effective, does not want it begun at all, or wants it stopped at a given time. In essence, the living will details the end-of-life treatments that the now incompetent patient does not want, while the health care proxy authorizes a designated surrogate to implement the instructions in the living will.

Advance directives become legally valid as soon as they are signed in front of the required witnesses. However, as long as one is able to make one's own decisions about medical care, these documents will not be used. They take effect *only* when patients lose the ability to make medical decisions for themselves. Advance directives can just as easily be used to request maximum treatment as to refuse treatment, although their focus is usually on the latter. All directives are grounded in the idea that only the patient has the right to control decisions about his or her health care.

It is especially critical in certain states to execute an advance directive. These states do not permit family members to refuse life-sustaining treatment without prior evidence that this is what the patient would have wanted. The courts in these states have held that life-sustaining treatment may not be withheld or withdrawn from incapacitated patients without "clear and convincing evidence" that the now incompetent patient had requested the refusal prior to decision-making incapacity. A living will provides that evidence.

Laws allowing either a living will or a health care proxy now exist in all fifty states. As of 1998, forty-five states and the District of Columbia have legislation that authorizes both living wills and the appointment of health care agents. Two states, Alabama and Alaska, authorize living wills but not health care proxies, while Massachusetts, Michigan, and New York have legislation that allows only the appointment of a health care agent but does not authorize surrogate decision making. Although public approval of these documents falls in the 90 percent range, only 10 to 15 percent of the population has actually executed one.

Over time, Americans are becoming aware of their right to make medical decisions. As statutes were passed and the media reported on them, people began to understand that they could preserve their right to make medical decisions through an agent. Most people remain, unfortunately, so uninformed about living will and health care proxy law that they feel helpless and intimidated when opposed by someone in the medical community and therefore succumb to pressure against taking advantage of their rights. The medical community is equally unsure of the law. Thus, inaction prevails and the patient remains hooked up to all that technology has to offer.

People need to know that they are on sound legal ground when trying to enforce living wills and health care proxies, which are governed by law. The individual, and subsequently the agent, may have to educate the physician. As patients, we have more rights than most of us are aware of. It is the competent patient's prerogative to accept or reject any treatment that is recommended by his or her doctor.

You have the right to receive information about your illness and the ways it can be treated. Your doctor will discuss the advantages and disadvantages of each treatment option, telling you the benefits, risks, nature, and purpose of each treatment. You may ask any questions you have about your illness and its treatments. You may want to talk to other physicians in order to get their opinions. You are entitled at any time to find another doctor or even to change hospitals. The final decision is yours alone.

You can accept your doctor's recommended treatment or you can refuse it altogether, although the final decision may be a joint one. Whether your doctor agrees with you or not makes absolutely no difference. Nor does it matter what your reasons are for rejecting life-sustaining treatment. The physician brings experience and expertise to medical decision making. You bring knowledge of your own personal values, goals, tolerances, and preferences. You can opt for a different treatment or decide you prefer no treatment at all. All these prerogatives transfer to the agent on the incompetence of the principal. The laws are in place: It is now up to the individuals to become knowledgeable and to execute the documents.

Twenty-nine state legislatures have addressed the issue of nonhospital do-not-resuscitate orders, documents that are also known as advance directives. Until very recently, a do-not-resuscitate order (DNR) was valid only *within* medical facilities, *not outside* them. Furthermore, an emergency telephone call to 911 brought emergency medical technicians who, when called to the scene, were compelled by law to apply every possible aggressive measure to a patient to keep him or her alive at all costs. They were legally required to undertake cardiopulmonary resuscitation (CPR) even when all parties agreed that it was futile. Elderly and dying patients frequently end up in the intensive care unit when CPR is inappropriately used on them. In such situations many people prefer to avoid this aggressive effort at resuscitation.

These twenty-nine states now provide another option. The previous DNR order, valid only *within* medical facilities, has been expanded also to govern DNR orders in a *nonhospital* setting. This means that at home or elsewhere outside the hospital setting (including in an emergency room), emergency medical services personnel will *not* perform CPR if the requisite document has been signed by a physician. The document must be prominently displayed to be useful. DNR bracelets are also available.

Neither the Roman Catholic Church nor the AMA immediately accepted the idea of advance directives. Even though certain Catholic scholars recommended that the church reverse its opposition to living wills, and the National Conference of Catholic Bishops endorsed advance directives in 1984, in states in which the Catholic population is large and the church especially powerful, such as Massachusetts, Michigan, and New York, living will laws have not yet been enacted. Glick explains the dynamics involved:

> These states generally rank high in policy innovation, but in this particular policy, it strongly appears that the Catholic church has successfully blocked legislation. However, the appellate courts of these states have served as important alternative sources of policy. While it might successfully oppose or limit legislation, the Catholic church and other groups cannot prevent individual citizens from putting an issue on the judicial agenda.[13]

The New York State courts have since validated the living will.

Beginning with *Quinlan* the courts have come forward to support terminal patients and their families in this quest for personal control. By standing up to the health care professionals, Joe and Julia Quinlan forced the judiciary to establish the individual's right to refuse treatment, even if the refusal causes death. It was the first right-to-die case where the court interjected itself into the sacred doctor-patient relationship as the arbiter of right and wrong. The involvement of the judiciary in formulating right-to-die policy, however, did not stop with the *Quinlan* decision. In conjunction with the legislatures, and often ahead of them, it has built on the New Jersey court's decision to encourage autonomy and self-determination.

Between 1976 and 1988, fifty-four right-to-die cases were decided by state courts. Except for the early adoption of living will laws in 1976 and 1977, state courts have actually outstripped state legislatures in adopting right-to-die policies. Judges are much less likely than elected state legislators to be influenced by special interest groups, which can affect court cases only indirectly by submitting amicus curiae (friend of the court) briefs. The more objective courts have generally "responded favorably to claims of privacy and patient or family control over medical treatment in the right to die."[14] Of great importance is the judiciary's case law, with its interpretation and reasoning, its application and its refinement of state statutes, which patients and health care professionals turn to each day for guidance in the termination of treatment.

Medical decision making should be resolved without the expenditure of time and money and without having to involve lawyers and judges in costly and protracted court battles. The patient is always the loser in court proceedings, since the dying process and the suffering are prolonged for the time it takes the issue to be decided. However, court provides the last resort. Nowhere was the impact of *Quinlan* more keenly felt than in the medical community. It brought new rules and new players to medicine. It served notice to the profession that its reign was over. The Quinlans challenged the monopoly of the medical profession over end-of-life issues, and they won. Patients and families have the starring roles now—all within the supportive purview of the law.

Before the New Jersey Supreme Court's decision in 1976, medical decision making was the province of the doctors, the arbiters of life and death. Rothman explains how the medical system operated:

> Well into the post–World War II period, decisions at the bedside were the almost exclusive concern of the individual physician, even when they raised fundamental ethical and social issues. It was mainly doctors who wrote and read about the morality of withholding a course of antibiotics and letting pneumonia serve as the old man's best friend, of considering a newborn with grave birth defects a "stillbirth" and sparing the parents the agony of choice and the burden of care, of experimenting on the institutionalized retarded to learn more about hepatitis, or of giving one patient and not another access to the iron lung when the machine was in short supply. Moreover, it was usually the individual physician who decided these matters at the bedside or in the privacy of the hospital

room, without formal discussions with patients, their families, or even with colleagues, and certainly without drawing the attention of journalists, judges, or professional philosophers. And they made their decisions on a case-by-case basis, responding to the particular circumstances as they saw fit, reluctant by both training and practice to formulate or adhere to guidelines.[15]

The ostensible enemy in *Quinlan* was technology, yes, but many people understood that the underlying issue was "who ruled at the bedside."[16] Professional outsiders now define the moral codes that guide physician behavior. After *Quinlan*, medical decision making became the province of a collection of strangers, with judges, journalists, clergy, philosophers, lawyers, ethicists, and legislators joining doctors at their patients' bedside. Though there was much disagreement among these diverse groups, they all agreed on one matter—the need to reduce physicians' discretion and enhance patients' autonomy. A new commitment developed, to collective as opposed to individual decision making. These outsiders who entered medicine joined together to create a new formality and impose it on medicine, insisting on guidelines and regulations. The changes that came to medicine generally came over the strenuous objections of doctors, giving the entire process an adversarial quality.

An example of collective decision making was the ethics committee, popularized in the *Quinlan* decision when the court, in a side comment, suggested that treatment decisions to discontinue life support be made by the patient, in consultation with a hospital ethics committee if problems arose. The ethics committee aspect of the decision has been the subject of much confusion and disagreement. Generally speaking, however, it is a nonjudicial multidiscipline body for dealing with significant medical and ethical problems confronting health care professionals. It includes not only physicians but lawyers, social workers, ethicists, clergy, and philosophers.

Doctors and hospitals were initially reluctant to accept these ethics review boards and their intrusion into the medical process. According to one survey, less than 5 percent of U.S. hospitals had them in place by 1983, seven years after *Quinlan*. However, with the encouragement of the President's Commission for the Study of Ethical Problems in Medicine and Biomedical and Behavioral Research in 1983, the percentage of hospitals reporting the existence of these committees jumped to 30 percent by 1985. Today, this commission expects *all* hospitals to have some sort of "deliberative and representative ethics body in place."[17]

The medical chart is an example of a formality that characterized this new decision making. Its introduction made extinct private communication between physicians as well as word-of-mouth orders. Medical charts became evidentiary of what had transpired, as written documentation replaced the less reliable verbal instructions.

In the recent words of Paul Armstrong, the Quinlans' attorney, the seminal case of Karen Ann Quinlan has served as a polestar in the evolving national debate on the care of dying patients. It is a landmark in medical and legal history. Today, almost a quarter of a century later, the 1976 decision of the late Chief Justice Richard J. Hughes, for a unanimous New Jersey Supreme Court

> still informs and authenticates the rights of us all to make fundamental treatment decisions at the end of life. The court's clear articulation of the common and constitutional law justification of the concepts of personal autonomy and bodily integrity continues to define the ongoing national debate. The constitutional notions of privacy and liberty, the central role of the family and the introduction of ethics committees at the bedside reaffirmed our basic belief in the integrity of the patient, family, physician and institution as proper cooperators in choices concerning life-sustaining measures.[18]

The legacy of *Quinlan* has seeped into the very fabric of our most venerated institutions. Society was ready and waiting for an incident that would generate enough noise to make public concerns heard about modern, high-tech treatment. Karen Ann Quinlan provided a focus for the public's feelings of powerlessness in the medical arena. Other forces, including a loss of confidence in the medical profession, were pushing disillusionment to the fore. The public was learning to exercise its authority over physicians as never before, a result of the "participatory democracy" ethic unleashed in the 1960s. A new paradigm began to emerge from one family's struggle. *Quinlan* lifted the shroud of secrecy that surrounded the taboo subject of dying and allowed society to scrutinize it under the light.

The questions of withdrawal and withholding of treatment opened up for public debate—at the kitchen table, on television, in the hospital waiting room, in the courtroom, and in the state legislature. The dying patient and the surviving family would never feel so powerless again.

The Birth of the Hemlock Society

The United States was introduced to the idea of medically assisted dying by Derek Humphry, who formed the Hemlock Society in 1980 and in the following twelve years built it from an unknown organization—initially regarded by many as distinctly oddball—operated from his garage on 32nd Street, Santa Monica, into a nationally recognized force for social change on the issue of the right to choose to die. His tools were his books on the subject and skills in public relations acquired during thirty-five years as a journalist. He knew how to talk to journalists, and could write quick press releases and advertising copy. Journalists respected him for having worked at all levels of journalism, from local weeklies to giant international journals. Humphry was also an experienced broadcaster on radio and television. A personal tragedy with his first wife, Jean, had introduced him to assisted suicide and eventually led to his forming Hemlock to work to change the law.

Humphry was born and raised in England, but due to a broken home (his parents were divorced when he was three) plus six years of family disruption during World War II, his education was skimpy, and financial circumstances dictated that he leave school at fifteen. Dreams of high school and university were shattered. Having the misfortune to be thrown into the workforce when postwar demobilization was in full swing, Humphry could not get journalistic employment in his hometown of Bristol. He borrowed money to take a train to London and, the next day, using the services of an employment agency took a job as a messenger boy in the London office of the *Yorkshire Post*, an influential regional newspaper. It was a start. Always anxious to move on, Humphry successively landed reporting jobs on the Bristol *Evening World* and the *Manchester Evening News*. By age twenty-five he was writing for a national newspaper, the *Daily Mail*. After a spell as editor in chief of a weekly newspaper, concluding that he was happier as a writer than an executive, he transferred to the London *Sunday Times*.

As he climbed up through the ranks of British journalism, he had enjoyed a good marriage of twenty-two years to Jean, who had borne him two sons, and they had adopted a third of mixed race. Their happiness was shattered when, in 1973, Jean contracted breast cancer that rapidly metastasized into bone cancer. Radical mastectomy, removal of the lymph nodes (already affected), chemotherapy, and radiation all failed to check the cancer. Within a year Derek knew she was dying and that the end was only a matter of time. The couple was not aware of any euthanasia movement—it was not then a subject of public discussion—and so had no preconceived views on the subject.

Jean faced her oncoming death with considerable courage, determined to make the best of what little life she had left. In mid-1974 her illness took a turn for the worse, and doctors told Derek she might not last more than a few days. But using her powerful will to live, plus superb medical care and nursing at Churchill Hospital in Oxford, Jean pulled out of the crisis. Yet she was a changed person.

Two things had changed Jean—her mother's death and watching other people die during long months spent in cancer wards. Five years earlier her mother had died of lung cancer in Jean's presence, and it was a "bad death" for two reasons. First, Beatrice Crane either did not fully realize she was dying or refused to accept it. Secondly, she was in unremitting pain at home during the final stages. Her mother's physical pain and emotional anguish had so deeply affected Jean that she privately resolved that such an unprepared death would never happen to her. During her own illness Jean spoke of witnessing the deaths of other patients in the hospital, with the family almost always arriving in the middle of the night, just too late.

When Derek returned to Churchill Hospital one day, he found Jean sitting up in bed, temporarily recovered from the near-death experience. His epiphany was at hand.

"Derek," she said, taking a deep breath,

> I simply don't want to go on living like this. It's been pretty bad this week and I want you to do something for me so that if I decide I want to die I can do it on my own terms and exactly when I choose. The one thing that worries me is that I won't be in any position to make the right decision, what with my being knocked senseless by all these drugs. I might be too daft to know whether I'm doing the right thing or not but I shall have a good idea when I've had enough of the pain. So I want you to promise me that when I ask you if this is the right time to kill myself, you will give me an honest answer one way or another and we must understand, both you and I, that I'll do it right at that very moment. You won't question my right and you will give me the means to do it.[1]

After a pause to absorb this surprising request, Derek told her that if their positions were reversed and he was the one dying of cancer, he would be asking Jean to help him die. It was an instinctive reply, because he had never previously considered the matter. Like many other couples in their early forties, thoughts of death, and of how dying might be handled, had not been considered. At the time he had no idea that this brief conversation would eventually completely alter the rest of his life. Almost immediately Derek sought out a physician in London who had been helpful to him some years previously when he was doing investigative reporting on administrative problems in the British National Health Service.

"Dr. Joe"—which is the only clue Derek has ever revealed to his identity—heard his plea for lethal drugs with which Jean could kill herself. He questioned him closely about her medical condition and concluded: "She has no quality of life left." Almost casually Dr. Joe telephoned the chief pharmacist at the hospital where he had privileges and asked which drugs would be most lethal in these circumstances. The conversation over, and reluctant to write out a prescription that could give him away to the authorities, he went to his drugs cabinet and gave Derek two substances, with instructions how to use them. "Never reveal that I did this," instructed Dr. Joe. The two men shook hands.

Both were about to commit the crime of assisted suicide under Section 2 of the Suicide Act of 1961, making them liable of conviction for up to fourteen years' imprisonment. The same act stipulated that Jean's suicide was no longer a felony; thus the two men were technically perpetrating a crime, but only to carry out something that was not a crime—a distinction that struck Derek as ludicrous. But immediately after Jean's request, he studied this particular law and noticed a caveat in it. A prosecution could not be directly brought by the police—as with most crimes—but only with the permission of the Director of Public Prosecutions. Having written about the administration of justice for the *Sunday Times* for many years, Derek knew that the current director was a man of humane and liberal tendencies. So he decided that the necessity of helping Jean to die was worth the small risk of prosecution.

To make Jean's last years more pleasant, the couple moved out of London to Langley Durrell, a village in Wiltshire, in the southern Cotswolds. The three-hundred-year-old stone house they purchased contained the grocery store for the village, which Jean took huge pleasure in running, although she had no retail sales experience. For about a year there was ample time for relaxation and reflection. Jean took a third course of chemotherapy, which gave her a welcome remission. Nine months elapsed between the making of the assisted suicide pact and Jean's death, but it was never discussed between the couple, although Jean would occasionally tell her women friends that she was "not planning to go to the end with this." Apparently these friends, who knew Jean's determined character, accepted these remarks and remembered them. These fairly offhand statements turned out to be fortuitous for Derek when the police went looking for evidence against him three years later. It showed that the suicide had been Jean's plan and not Derek's.

In March 1975 Jean's cancer returned with a vengeance, spreading from her bones to her vital organs. Back in the hospital, her doctors told her that there were no more treatments available for her condition. They promised to manage her pain and offered her the choice between dying in a hospital or at home. With her self-deliverance plan in mind, she opted for an ambulance to take her home. Accompanying her was a large bottle of what the British call "Brompton cocktail" and Americans call "hospice mix," which is a concoction of narcotic analgesics made up by trial and error to quell the pain of an individual patient. In overdose it is lethal, and could have been used in Jean's suicide instead of Dr. Joe's pills.

During the next three days Derek observed that Jean was saying goodbye to people and tidying up those parts of the bedroom she could still reach. He had noticed that once he had told Jean, months earlier, that he possessed the lethal drugs, she became calmer and even more ready to fight her cancer. In the week before her end she let a washbowl slip, bent forward instinctively to catch it before the water soaked the bedclothes, and snapped several ribs. Now she was bedbound, unable to reach the bathroom, and this seemed to be her signal to conclude her life. Those around her were amazed at her calmness. Derek alone knew of her plan up to this point, although a few days before her death he and Jean confided her intention to their sons. Generally stunned by the impending loss of their mother, they had nevertheless helped to care for her and sympathized with her in her suffering. The teenagers remained quiet and supportive.

When she awoke on March 29, Jean's pain was so intense that she was unable to move. Derek brought her painkillers, and once they had taken effect she was able to sit up cautiously in bed, propped up by numerous pillows.

"Is this the day?" Jean quietly asked Derek.

For a few moments he was paralyzed by the awesome nature of the question. She had decided to die. Although not unexpected, it was nevertheless traumatic to have to give permission to the person whom he loved most in the world to kill herself. Part of their original pact had been that Jean would not act without her husband's agreement; now he had to decide whether he concurred. He temporized for a moment by discussing Jean's present worsening condition, which might necessitate a quick return to the hospital, and then conceded that perhaps the time had come.

Sensing his acceptance, Jean immediately said: "I shall die at one o'clock. You must give me the overdose and then go into the garden and not return for an hour. We'll say our last goodbye here, but I don't want you actually to see me die."

As one o'clock approached, a calm and collected Jean asked Derek to get her the drugs, which he had decided would be best taken in a large mug of coffee with a lot of milk, plentifully laced with sugar to reduce the bitter taste of the barbiturates and codeine.

After the couple embraced for the last time, Jean's last words were "Goodbye my love." She immediately took the mug and gulped its contents swiftly. Derek ignored her request to leave the room, considering it better to ensure that nothing went wrong. Within seconds the drugs had knocked Jean out and she lay breathing heavily. At one point Jean vomited—the couple did not know of the importance of antiemetics to prevent sickness caused by swallowing so much medication—and Derek was terrified that she had not kept down enough of the deadly potion. He prepared himself to stifle her with a pillow if she showed signs of awakening because he had given his word that she would not awaken. Fortunately for both of them, within fifty minutes the drugs worked and respiration stopped completely. Jean lay peacefully at rest after all her suffering; Derek sat at her bedside dazed by the loss yet also filled with admiration for the courageous, determined, and dignified manner of her death.

Family and friends all knew of the way Jean had died, but nobody reported Derek's crime to the police. Most did not know it was a felony to assist a suicide. The treating doctor was called and signed a death certificate giving "carcinomatosis" as the cause of death, not realizing that she had accelerated her end. Subsequently Derek was asked many times if he ever regretted helping Jean kill herself. "No," he would answer. "I would feel guilty if I had refused her request and allowed her to continue suffering." Although only a small circle of close family and friends knew of his action, no one treated him differently than before.

After a period of mourning, Derek took Jean's deathbed advice to get on with his life as soon as possible. During her illness Derek had not considered writing about it, although some of his colleagues had suggested his doing so. But, as he gradually managed to distance himself from the sadness of her death, he thought about writing a long magazine article about the experience of helping a loved one to die.

Following his marriage to Ann Wickett, a year later, his new wife urged him to write a book about Jean's life and death, and she offered to help. An American who had studied psychology at Boston and Toronto Universities, and now a student at England's Shakespeare Institute, Ann was able to provide and express certain insights he could not. So, in his spare time, they sat down to put together a book that proved crucial in the drastic alteration of his life. Derek dictated the book as Ann probed into the background and motives of the story and suggested additions.

But when the book was finished in 1977, it proved difficult to find a publisher. Several London firms were quick to read it because Derek was an established, prizewinning author with what the English call a "good address" at the *Sunday Times*. But they were equally quick to return the manuscript. "Too harrowing, thus not saleable," was their shared opinion. The book was shown to several American publishers, who also rejected it. "Bring us your next book," they all said approvingly.

Derek knew this was an important story with a message, one worth publishing. He had observed that in the United States books about death sold steadily—*Death Be Not Proud*, by John Gunther, was a classic example. In desperation, he took the manuscript to London's newest and smallest publisher, Quartet Books, whose editor, William Miller, was more perceptive, liberal, and freethinking than most of his profession. Miller had published Derek's trailblazing book about racism in the British police, *Police Power and Black People*, in 1972. Within twenty-four hours Miller called Derek back and said: "Of course I'll publish it, but you must stand by the legal consequences and be prepared to defend your actions in the media and the courts if necessary." Accustomed to hostile publicity from his previous books on race, police, and civil liberties, Derek said he would do whatever was necessary when the book came out. Even given Miller's enthusiasm, the publisher offered only a five-hundred-pound advance and did not bother to keep the customary share of the film, paperback, and foreign rights.

When *Jean's Way* hit the bookstores in March 1978 it immediately sold out, earning a wave of publicity, nationally and internationally, considerably helped by a powerful television documentary shown on London Weekend Television. Suddenly Derek found himself defending assisted suicide in public, arguing on television with such notable opponents as Dame Cecily Saunders, the founder of Hospice, and Malcolm Muggeridge, the raconteur and popular philosopher. Intense and widespread criticism—notably from hospice leaders, such as Dame Cecily—of his action in helping Jean to die was offset by enormous support; people from all over the world wrote saying either that they, too, had helped a loved one die, or would want to be able to get that help if they ever needed it. People stopped him in the street to shake his hand.

After the media had no more angles for stories on Derek within a few days, they asked the director of public prosecutions what he was going to do about this clear confession to a crime in *Jean's Way*. He ordered a police inquiry so that he could—as the 1961 Suicide Act allowed—make a decision on whether to prosecute. Within days, the Wiltshire police traveled to London to meet Derek by arrangement in his lawyer's office. There Derek handed them a written confession to his crime, with the addendum that, if taken to court, he would plead guilty and ask for its mercy. The detectives officially warned Derek that he was under investigation for the crime of assisted suicide, and read him the British equivalent of his "Miranda rights." The police accepted his confession but followed up with a barrage of questions about the doctor who had supplied the lethal drugs. They seemed keener to get this person than Derek. Repeatedly Derek told them that he would never reveal the name of the doctor, so they were wasting their time. After an hour the detectives, who were not antagonistic but merely doing their duty, gave up and left.

In every other respect Derek cooperated with the police, giving permission to interview any members of the family, friends, and Jean's physicians, the latter being unaware of the suicide. The police found that this accelerated death was entirely Jean's plan, with Derek as a mere accessory. Six months later the public prosecutor ruled that he was exercising the discretion allowed him by law and would not prosecute. Of course he had only Derek's word that a crime had been committed, and a person may not be convicted of a felony on his or her own admission alone: There has to be corroborating evidence. By this time Derek was living in California, working for the *Los Angeles Times*, but he had left word with his lawyer and the prosecutor that if the decision was to take him to court, he would return voluntarily to Britain, avoiding messy extradition proceedings.

Events began to unfold that led Derek from being just a writer to becoming an activist as well. All his life he had been interested in causes, and had worked in campaigns in Britain to make the police accountable for misdeeds, for racial equality, and for civil liberties. When *Jean's Way* was a huge success in Australia, Derek was invited to that country for a joint book promotion and lecture tour. What impressed him most were the audiences, young and old, of varying levels of education, who packed the lecture halls. I must be saying something people want to hear, he mused. On his return to the United States he had more invitations, to speak to university groups, senior citizens' clubs, and Unitarian churches.

After the U.S. publication of *Jean's Way* in 1979, Derek was invited on all the major talk shows, television and radio, although the book sold modestly. But the visibility was enormous for what was now developing into a major cause for Derek. Easily able to contact him at the *Los Angeles Times*, requests poured in for help in dying, for advice, and urging him to do something about changing American law, which was just as punitive on the issue as that in Britain. The question most frequently put to him was: What are the most lethal drugs, and where do you get them? The Voluntary Euthanasia Society in London told Derek that it had some five hundred American members, and he was welcome to their names and addresses if he could use them.

Four years after *Quinlan* revealed the remarkable ability of modern medical technology to keep alive people who previously would have died of their conditions, Americans were becoming intensely interested in the wider issue of the right to die.

The idea was developing in Derek's mind that there ought to be an organization, similar to those in Britain and Australia, fighting for Americans' right to a chosen death. First he approached the two right-to-die groups in New York, Concern for Dying and the Society for the Right to Die (now merged as Choice in Dying) and asked them to branch out from advance directives into physician-assisted suicide. They declined, claiming that the United States was not ready for this. They were only interested in what is known as "passive euthanasia"—the disconnection of life-support systems in hopeless cases. Derek felt they were wrong not to extend their field because for him the evidence indicated a high degree of interest. He talked with Ann about his plan for a specialized group. She suggested it be called "Hemlock," and he agreed, adding "Society" as a clarification of what it was. Thus was born the Hemlock Society, America's first group to fight exclusively to change the law on assisted suicide for the terminally ill. In a taped interview with 60 Minutes, Derek told interviewer Mike Wallace of his intentions, thereby committing himself to rapid action. (At the time of this interview in 1979 Wallace did not betray any sympathy for the emerging assisted-suicide cause, but in recent years he has been openly supportive.)

At the height of the rumpus over Jean's Way in London in 1978, the Evening Standard had asked Derek for a feature-page article that appeared under the headline of THE RIGHT TO DIE WITH DIGNITY. In the article Derek, though a novice in this field, presented a four-point charter for legislation:

1. The patient must know the essentials of his situation, the available therapies, the alternative prognosis and possibilities. He must be fully aware that euthanasia is irreversible death.
2. The patient must have voluntarily requested euthanasia, preferably repeatedly, confirming that the present situation and all available alternatives are unbearable to him.
3. He must be incurable, with no possibility of alleviating his suffering in a manner acceptable to him. Death must, in his informed and considered opinion, be the only acceptable solution.
4. Euthanasia must be applied by the attending doctor.[2]

Making allowances for the then poorly defined meaning of words such as "euthanasia," this appears to have been the first published charter for assisted suicide in the English-speaking world. (The Dutch had been working on such propositions for the previous five years.) Developing his original ideas, Derek two years later drew up a draft charter for the aims and objects of Hemlock, circulating it to dozens of legal and health professionals in California whom he knew were interested in the subject. In essence it said that Hemlock would provide information so that people who were dying could end their own lives with dignity, and, in the long term, Hemlock would fight for a reform of the law. It would be a nonprofit California educational corporation with a board of directors and a small staff.

In California, where the national organization was to be based from the outset, suicide was not a crime, but under Penal Code 401 any form of assistance was felonious, punishable by up to five years' imprisonment. As much as Derek researched, he could not find a single instance of an assisted suicide conviction since the law had been passed in 1897. Although some warned him against starting what critics would label a crazy pro-suicide club, he relied on his public relations skills to get it across to the law enforcement authorities and the public that this was assistance only for the terminally ill and the irreversibly ill purely on a voluntary basis, with a long-term aim of democratic law reform to permit the procedure under regulated circumstances. Thirty-two other states had specific laws punishing assistance in suicide, while the remainder considered it murder or manslaughter. Law reform on this scale, with such a controversial issue, was obviously a mountainous task, but Derek told supporters from the start that it would probably take twenty years to achieve.

The original draft charter—or mission statement—of Hemlock read as follows:

CHARTER PRINCIPLES, 1980

1. Hemlock's objective is to promote a climate of public opinion which is tolerant of the right of people who are terminally ill to end their own lives in a planned manner.
2. Hemlock does not condone suicide for any primary emotional, traumatic or financial reasons in the absence of terminal illness. It approves of the work of all those involved in suicide prevention.
3. Hemlock will not encourage terminally ill people to end their lives, believing this action, and its timing, to be an extremely personal decision, wherever possible taken in concert with family and friends.
4. A book providing information about methods and strategies of planned death with dignity will be supplied to members upon request. (This book is in preparation and not immediately available.)
5. Hemlock speaks only to those people of like mind who approach it out of mutual sympathy with its goals. Views contrary to its own which are held by other religions and philosophies are respected.

Those who received the draft charter were invited to a meeting on July 16, 1980, at the Los Angeles home of Richard Scott, a physician and lawyer, who had told Derek of his interest. About twenty people turned up to discuss the issue of whether the United States needed an organization to fight for the right of a dying person to end his or her life. Derek had got to know them all while researching a series of articles for the *Los Angeles Times*, "The Quality of Dying in America," and he had a good idea where their sympathies lay. There was a lively discussion for two hours on the need, or lack thereof, for a group like Hemlock. Finally, when Derek, who was chairing the meeting, called for a vote on the necessity or otherwise of such a group, acceptance was unanimous. Then he asked those willing to join such a group to step forward. Only one person did. Astonished, Derek asked them how they could on the one hand approve of such an organization, while on the other they failed to support it? Some muttered that their legal, medical, nursing, or psychological practices could be affected. Some said their children attended Catholic schools and might meet resentment; others, that their homes might be bombed by the same fanatics who were attacking abortion clinics.

Only Gerald A. Larue, at that time professor of religious studies at the University of Southern California, offered to put his name down for the new organization. "If we believe in a cause then we must be prepared to back it," he said. Larue was well known in California academic circles for his iconoclastic views of many subjects, religious and otherwise. Many years earlier he had pioneered courses in "Death and Dying" in which he had not avoided addressing all forms of suicide. The next day Derek asked Larue to be president of Hemlock. He exclaimed: "Why me?" Derek replied: "You're the only person available!" Derek appointed himself executive director, and Ann served as treasurer of the tiny group.

On August 12, 1980, Derek booked the hall of the Los Angeles Press Club, where most press conferences are held, to announce the arrival of the Hemlock Society. Derek and Larue mounted the podium before the assembled reporters and cameramen, but Doctor Scott and Ann Wickett held back, still nervous as to how Hemlock would be received. Less than an hour before the press conference started, a woman who had heard about the new organization approached Derek with a request to join, so he signed up Shirley O'Connor, who remains a member in 1998.

Every person who had ever contacted Derek on this issue, along with the five hundred American names and addresses passed on by the London organization, was contacted by mail, and the membership topped one thousand within a few months. What the members most wanted, Derek now set out to provide: a book on how to end one's life through the use of drugs. Richard Scott, who joined Hemlock's board of directors once he had seen that its public reception had escaped problems, advised him to get true accounts of terminally ill people's own suicides and report them in great detail in a book. His advice was that, in the United States, a writer could not be sued or prosecuted for telling the truth. Within the stories should be given the exact quantities of drugs ingested and the consequences.

Hemlock appealed to all its members for personal stories of helping another to die. The response was huge, and soon Derek had all the material he needed to write *Let Me Die Before I Wake*, at which point, in 1981, he ran out of money. Up to then he had been financing Hemlock and himself with the royalties from *Jean's Way*, but these were now declining. A letter was sent to all Hemlock members, by now some three thousand strong, telling them that the book was in manuscript form but finances were lacking for its printing. Members were asked to order and pay in advance. About two thousand members trusted this offer, and soon Hemlock had enough cash to print the book and mail it out to the subscribers. *Let Me Die Before I Wake*, constantly updated and revised, continued to help terminally ill people end their lives, additionally supplying Hemlock a steady cash flow for the next ten years. When the book first appeared in 1981, Hemlock, out of caution, confined it to members only. However, protests came from some in the book trade that this was "not the American way," so at the start of 1982 the book was thrown open to libraries and sale in stores. It attracted very little media attention, which at that time did not take assisted dying with much seriousness. But right-to-die supporters for the next ten years bought it at the rate of approximately twenty-five thousand copies a year. The CBS-TV series *60 Minutes* developed a second segment on hastened deaths; while the first, broadcast in 1980, centered on Derek and Jean, five years later the approach to the subject was broader. The second segment featured people living in Arizona going across the border into Mexico to purchase lethal drugs, cheaply and legally, and taking them home for storage in shoeboxes and clothes closets. Derek's only involvement in this show came when the travelers, having language difficulties, were seen showing pages of his how-to book to pharmacists in Mexico and asking for the drugs listed there.

Not wanting to be stigmatized as an organization with only a "suicide manual" on offer, Hemlock was quick to publish other books on the subject, notably reprints of *Jean's Way* and Doris Portwood's *Commonsense Suicide*, which introduced the idea of "balance sheet suicide" for the elderly. Mrs. Portwood argued that there might be a stage in an aged person's life when the combinations of failing health and advanced years might enable the individual to justify to him- or herself deliberately drawing it to a close. Hemlock also commissioned Dr. Larue to write *Euthanasia and Religion* (1985), which sold widely to colleges and libraries. A paperback original, it was the first easy-to-read description of how the many religions in the world viewed suicide and assisted suicide.

Books on the right to die were regarded with disfavor as inevitable money losers by the mainstream publishing industry until TV reporter Betty Rollin's story of helping her mother to die, *Last Wish* (1985), became a *New York Times* bestseller. This sales breakthrough spurred Harper & Row, a major New York publisher (now HarperCollins), to commission Derek to write a full length history of euthanasia, *The Right to Die* (1986). Unable to complete it himself within the nine months specified by the publisher, Humphry brought in Ann Wickett and two more researchers. At that point general information on the right-to-die was limited. It needed to be dug out of university archives, libraries, and old newspaper files, in contrast to the mid-1990s, when a plethora of articles and books exists on the once-taboo subject.

A by-product of this book was that the royalties (some forty thousand dollars) enabled Hemlock permanently to expand its library and research services. *The Right to Die* was also published in Britain, and in translations in Spain and Germany, which, together with the international acceptance of *Jean's Way* (five translations), started to give Hemlock its international reputation. Nevertheless, membership was confined to the United States. When foreigners sought to join, Hemlock encouraged them to join their own national group, or to form one of their own.

Throughout the 1980s, when the right to die was a low-priority public policy issue, Hemlock organized national conferences that attracted considerable attention from the public and media. The first chapter was set up in Tucson, Arizona, in 1983, when Derek was asked to speak at the City Center YWCA. He arrived expecting an audience of 20 but found to his astonishment that it numbered 120. A vibrant chapter was immediately set up and flourishes to this day. It was followed by eighty more by 1990. Derek's technique in forming chapters was to go to a city after writing to all the local members that he would be speaking at a certain place—usually the Unitarian Church hall—at a specified time. (In the early years of Hemlock, Unitarians were by far the most openly supportive of the organization.) He would also inform the media that he was there, with the object of setting up a local Hemlock chapter, which invariably intrigued them. Derek would encourage those who turned up to the meeting—sometimes several hundred, more often a dozen or so—to begin their own chapter, handing out a leaflet with guidance on how to do so.

Gradually, Hemlock came to be widely known, even if not accepted, throughout the United States. Derek's main avenue for securing visibility for the cause was talk radio. He employed the long-established Hollywood radio publicist Irwin Zucker to get him bookings on shows. In a busy year Derek talked on as many as three hundred shows, at the end of each broadcast giving out Hemlock's address and telephone number. The partnership between him and Zucker was a fruitful one. Talk-show hosts discovered that the right-to-die topic attracted plenty of listeners, with abundant call-ins; everybody had a view on the matter, a question, or a horror story to tell of a loved one's death. Derek averaged about twenty-five television shows, local and national, in a year, using his books as the entrée.

Through the 1980s Hemlock was only Derek and three clerical assistants, with his wife, Ann, as a part-time employee working mainly as an editor of the organization's publications. Even as the organization prospered and could afford more qualified staff, many people were reluctant to have the embarrassment of telling others that they worked for such an unusual organization. But by the 1990s, as the right-to-die issue achieved national awareness and a measure of respectability, staff were more easily recruited.

In 1985, as public acceptance grew larger, the organization became bolder and started publishing drug charts in its newsletter, *Hemlock Quarterly*, and sending reprints for two dollars to all who wrote and asked. The membership, only a small percentage of whom were terminally ill, was always hungry for information on lethal drugs and how to get them. They had no intention of suiciding now, but knew that the time may come. The newsletter catered to this demand whenever possible. How many terminally ill people ended their lives with the information in *Let Me Die Before I Wake* and the newsletter will never be known, although Derek estimates that it was in the thousands over a period of ten years.

By 1987 Hemlock's membership totaled fifteen thousand. Within two years it had doubled. The reason for the spurt in growth was the attempt to qualify a ballot initiative in California in 1988, which, if it had passed, would have legalized voluntary euthanasia and physician-assisted suicide for terminally ill adults. The attempt failed miserably in terms of signatures gathered because Hemlock, and its political arm, Americans Against Human Suffering (renamed, in 1993, Americans for Death with Dignity), lacked the money to finance paid signature gathering, which is essential in such a huge state as California, where some four hundred thousand signatures are required to get on the ballot. But the publicity surrounding the attempt, particularly the scrutiny given to the wording of the first such law ever published, was so large that supporters who had been previously unaware of Hemlock enrolled in droves.

What sort of person was attracted to an organization devoted to the depressing subject of "dying"? A survey of Hemlock members in 1995 found that only 7 percent were terminally ill, turning on its head the myth that only dying people joined the group. The membership's feelings on religion are perhaps the most interesting. The survey found that 35.5 percent had no religion, 31.1 percent were Protestant, 12.6 percent were Jewish, 3.5 percent were Roman Catholics, while 17.2 percent said that they believed in a nonmainstream religion. The survey's overall conclusions were that "Hemlockers are older, married, Caucasian, predominantly female, with grown children . . . highly educated, financially stable homeowners, politically active and informed, and tend to be 'slightly left of center' . . . both mentally and physically healthy and concerned with investigating future health related life options . . . interested in fighting to preserve their right to individual self-determination in terms of right to die."[3]

By the time the 1990s loomed, Hemlock had grown into an influential organization and could no longer be run from a rented house. Larger and more suitable premises were required than the organization could afford in Los Angeles. A library was an essential requisite, now that the subject was increasingly popular with scholars and writers. Tiring of Southern California after ten years, Derek decided to move Hemlock to Eugene, Oregon, where costs would be lower and the quality of life better for himself and Ann. With the board's agreement, Hemlock moved to expanded headquarters, and its growth continued unabated.

Gerald Larue had consistently been reelected president of Hemlock, but when the organization moved to Oregon in 1988 he felt it was time for him to step down. The board of directors recognized his years of dedicated service by electing him president emeritus. Larue had left Derek pretty much alone to run Hemlock, turning up only to chair the monthly board meetings at which serious policy decisions were made. His academic prestige, powerful charismatic presence, brilliant public speaking ability, and gracious personal manner had been significant assets to Hemlock over the years.

Throughout 1990 Hemlock's membership soared by ten thousand to thirty-nine thousand, and if couples were counted the membership hovered around fifty thousand. At this point Derek took a sabbatical summer to write a how-to to replace the aging *Let Me Die Before I Wake*. When that book had been written ten years earlier, it had been extremely cautious in its approach to "self-deliverance" (a term Derek introduced and popularized for those who disliked the word "suicide"). Now there was a much more enlightened attitude toward the terminally ill accelerating their ends with lethal drugs. Supporters were now ready for a blunter, more honest approach. Moreover, ballot initiatives were in the planning stages in Washington State and California, which would need huge financial aid if they were to do better than the abortive California initiative in 1988. Derek poured into the new book everything he had learned over the previous fifteen years, this time writing in a much more direct and instructive way. When finished, he entitled it: *Final Exit: The Practicalities of Self-Deliverance and Assisted Suicide for the Dying*, little realizing how famous and successful it would become.

Final Exit was offered to numerous American publishers by Derek's literary agent in New York, Robert Ducas, but all rejected it. It was the same story in Australia and Great Britain. At the time this book was ready, Hemlock's other publications were being distributed by Carol Publishing, a medium-size publishing house in New York. Steven Schragis, the owner, offered to publish *Final Exit*, but, to his astonishment, his staff refused to cooperate. Schragis was reluctant to defy his staff but treated the matter as a personal crusade. He offered to lend Derek the financing to publish it himself, so confident was he that he could recoup the money from his share of the sales. Derek declined, saying that Hemlock could afford to publish the book. If it succeeded, the organization deserved and needed the profits.

When it appeared in February 1991, only Hemlock members realized its usefulness, snapping up a quarter of the forty thousand copies Derek had printed. Two hundred copies went out to reviewers, writers, and right-to-die experts, but after six months not a single paragraph had been printed about it. Recipients either did not understand the book, hated it, or regarded the subject matter as unimportant. Many bookstores had it on their shelves without realizing what a ticking time bomb they were stocking. Schragis never lost faith in the book and pushed the New York media to take notice. None did, until at a dinner party he met Norman Pearlstein, then editor of the *Wall Street Journal*, and told him about this unusual book. Pearlstein next day asked reporter Meg Cox to write an article for the "Marketplace" column about the book. Cox tracked Derek to his holiday spot in England, interviewed him about his reasons for writing such a strange book, and asked him who in the United States he thought would hate *Final Exit*. He mentioned the Hastings Center, the National Right to Life Committee, among others, and the spokesperson there dutifully condemned the book. Susan Wolf, a lawyer and researcher at Hastings, told the *Journal*: "The troubling possibility is that people may get hold of this and kill themselves when they're in the throes of a reversible depression or some other state for which they could get help." Burke Balch, an official of Right to Life, described the book as "a loaded gun."[4]

The newspaper article appeared on the second Friday in July. By Monday, *Final Exit* had sold out of bookstores. Schragis called Derek from New York and asked for more copies. "Okay, I'll print another ten thousand," he replied. "No, you don't understand," Schragis said, "I want another one hundred thousand." The book sold like wildfire. People were lining up in bookstores when they opened for business to snap up the daily allocation. A common joke at the time was that only in New York would you have to get in line to buy a book on how to commit suicide. Derek was invited onto all the major television talk shows, and *Time* and *Newsweek* devoted pages to the book. In downtown Manhattan a demonstration marched through the streets protesting its publication. Canadian newspapers howled that it should not be allowed to cross their border, but the bookstores there sold it by the tens of thousands. By August it was on the *New York Times* best-seller list, where it remained for eighteen weeks. During September, *Publishers Weekly* ranked it the best-selling nonfiction book in North America, and it finished as the fourth best-selling nonfiction book for the entire year.

If ever there was an instance where the public's taste and the establishment's standards were in direct conflict, this was a classic. The more the churches and the ethicists and the right-wing columnists roared against the book, the more the public went out to buy it. It was perhaps the most talked-about book in America in the fall of 1991: Just how could a book on how to kill yourself become a number one bestseller? What did this mean? Was the United States entering a period of nihilistic, suicidal behavior? Those commentators who took the trouble to read the book saw that it was addressed, in a careful, responsible manner, only to the dying. It was not, as thought by people who had not read it, a book advocating suicide in all and any circumstances. Moreover, advance directives such as Living Wills and Durable Powers of Attorney for Health Care were by now available in almost every state and confirmed by court decisions. Passive euthanasia was now accepted and lawful, so why not active euthanasia also, provided it was voluntary?

Hemlock grossed more than $2.2 million from book sales before they peaked at 550,000 copies. Over the next few years, hardcover and paperback editions and twelve foreign translations took sales of the book to well over one million. After printing costs, royalties, and commissions were deducted, Hemlock netted about a million dollars—money they were about to pour liberally into ballot initiatives to try to make assisted dying no longer a crime. Over the years Hemlock, the only "moneybags" in a movement made up mostly of elderly middle-class people on pensions, gave this backing to state initiative campaigns: California, 1988, $210,000; Washington, 1991, $300,000; California, 1992, $100,000; Oregon, 1994, $205,000; Oregon, 1997, $142,000; total: $957,000. Although the windfall of *Final Exit's* huge earnings provided much of its revenue, Hemlock also received thousands of small donations ($109,000 in 1992). Fees from its membership, now reaching an all-time-high total of 45,000, were regularly topping a half million dollars a year.

After twelve grueling years, Derek, staggered by his startling and unexpected fame, began to think that it was time to hand over the reins of Hemlock. Now sixty-two, he had no private pension because, until recently, Hemlock had been unable to afford such a plan. He quickly invested his royalties from the book, informing Hemlock that he was retiring in order to be a freelance writer and lecturer on death with dignity. "I believe in going when at the top, when the organization is in excellent administrative and financial condition," he told the board. "I need a rest and a change." A new executive director was appointed, but did not fit in well with a board that, in the aftermath of Derek's dominating style, was determined to micromanage Hemlock. He resigned after two years. By 1997 Hemlock's membership had been halved to around 22,000, leaving the third executive director, Faye Girsh, a sixty-something forensic psychologist who had been the founder and president of the nation's best Hemlock chapter, in San Diego, with the uphill task of rebuilding the organization. By 1998 a revitalized organization had branched more heavily into political work to change the law in several states, and was regaining much of the lost membership.

By this time other right-to-die groups were springing up across the United States to carry on the fight for law reform state by state. Only state law, not federal, is directly involved in the right to die. Hemlock had once had a virtual monopoly on the theme of PAS, but by 1998 there were ten related organizations, all vying for donations and memberships in a relatively small pool of active supporters:

1. Americans for Death with Dignity (California)
2. Compassion in Dying Federation
3. Death With Dignity National Center
4. Euthanasia Research and Guidance Organization (ERGO!)
5. Dying Well Network (Washington State)
6. Friends of Dying Patients (California)
7. Hemlock Society USA
8. Merian's Friends (Michigan)
9. Oregon Right to Die (Portland)
10. Oregon Death with Dignity Legal Defense and Education Center (Portland)

The majority of the workers in these organizations had been associated in one way or another—as officers, employees, or members—with Hemlock over the previous decade. What Derek had tentatively started in his Santa Monica garage in 1980 had become hydra-headed, spawning in the 1990s a powerful movement for social and legal reform on the right to choose to die. If Derek had not started the movement in the United States when he did, someone else would eventually have done so, so strong was the muffled public outcry for action. But in all likelihood it would not have begun for another five or ten years, probably when Doctor Kevorkian surfaced in 1990.

Step Forward, Step Backward

One might have predicted that an important case would emerge from all the legislation and litigation in lower state courts following *Quinlan*; the right-to-die movement was gaining momentum. *Cruzan v. Director, Missouri Department of Health*[1] turned out to be the one. It was the first time the Supreme Court had addressed the constitutional right of a person to refuse life-sustaining treatment, and media attention was rivaled only by *Quinlan* as the country focused once again on the right-to-die issue.

On January 11, 1983, an attractive and outgoing twenty-five-year-old from Missouri lost control of her 1963 Nash Rambler and was thrown out of the car as it crashed. That young woman, Nancy Beth Cruzan, lay face-down in a ditch for about fifteen minutes without breath or a heartbeat, after which time a state highway patrolman and paramedics discovered her and began resuscitation. Her lungs and heart began to work again, but her brain was already damaged. She remained in a coma, ultimately descending into a permanent vegetative state. As with Karen Ann Quinlan, her body continued to perform some functions, yet she would never regain consciousness. She was sustained by food and water, administered through a feeding tube surgically implanted in her stomach.

Her parents, Joyce and Joe Cruzan, waited four painful years. Reluctantly accepting that she could continue like this for many decades without improvement, they finally requested that the artificial nutrition and hydration be removed, allowing Nancy to die. Medical personnel, however, refused. Out of love for their daughter and respect for what they felt she would have wanted, they petitioned the courts to allow removal of the feeding tube. Early in 1988, Judge Charles E. Teel, presiding over the Probate Division courtroom in Jasper County, Missouri, granted their request. The Cruzans' elation, however, was short-lived, as the state immediately filed an appeal, claiming that removal of the feeding tube would constitute criminal homicide. The case eventually moved from the Jasper County Courthouse to the Missouri Supreme Court.

The Missouri Supreme Court refused the Cruzans' request to make decisions on Nancy's behalf. The New Jersey Supreme Court, in *Quinlan*, operating under the philosophy that incompetence should not compromise the rights of patients, had ruled that the only practical way to prevent destruction of the right of privacy was to permit the family to exercise it on behalf of the patient. In the years that followed, other state courts had agreed with the *Quinlan* constitutional balancing test—that under certain circumstances an individual's right to privacy outweighs the state's interest in the preservation and sanctity of life.

The Missouri court, however, rejected this balancing test, declaring that the state's interest in the preservation and sanctity of life should prevail, thus necessitating the preservation of even the most elemental level of life at any and all cost to patient and family. Moreover, Missouri had a high standard to meet in order to withdraw treatment from an incompetent patient. It required that the now incompetent patient must have left "clear and convincing evidence"—articulated while the patient was still competent—of his or her wish to have life-sustaining treatment withdrawn. In Nancy's case no one was able to say that while she was competent, Nancy had expressed the wish to be allowed to die under these circumstances. Since there was no "clear and convincing evidence" that she would have wanted to be disconnected from the feeding tube, the continuation of her existence, said the court, was the wisest course to follow.

Joyce and Joe Cruzan appealed to the U.S. Supreme Court for help. Prior to this case, the Court had refused to hear four cases in which the right to die was central. Much to everyone's surprise, the justices agreed to hear *Cruzan*, marking the first time the Court had addressed the rights of competent or incompetent patients to refuse life-sustaining treatment. Cruzan was, therefore, the first right-to-die case before the High Court, elevating the issue to the federal level.

In a 5–4 decision, the Court acknowledged that "for purposes of this case" the Court would assume that the U.S. Constitution would grant a competent person a constitutionally protected liberty interest in the right to refuse all forms of life-sustaining medical treatment, including artificial hydration and nutrition. The Court's statement that it could be inferred from prior decisions that competent patients have a constitutional right to refuse treatment, while not surprising, was welcome. The decision recognized, therefore, a constitutional right to die.

Nevertheless, the Court tempered its finding with the determination that nothing in the U.S. Constitution prevented Missouri from requiring "clear and convincing evidence of a person's expressed decision while competent" to have hydration and nutrition withdrawn in such a way as to cause death. Since Nancy had left no such evidence of wanting a feeding tube withdrawn when she was still competent, the Supreme Court sided with the state and remanded the case back to Missouri.

It is a somewhat confusing decision. On the one hand it established a constitutional right to forgo treatment even if death results. On the other it allowed Missouri to keep its very high standard, and since the Cruzans could not meet it, they lost the case. Nancy remained connected to the feeding tube planted in her stomach. A right to die was won, but the Cruzans lost the case.

With the case back in the probate division, several of Nancy's friends suddenly remembered conversations in which she *had* expressed her wish not to continue in a condition like the one she was now in. Her doctor therefore dropped his opposition to the removal of the feeding tube. The judge ruled that, indeed, there was now "clear and convincing evidence" that Nancy would not have wanted to be kept alive under these circumstances.

The tube providing nutrition and hydration was removed the next day, as Nancy's family began an eleven-and-a-half-day vigil. In the middle of the night on December 26, 1990, Joe Cruzan woke William Colby, the attorney who had represented the family in its journey from the trail court to the Supreme Court. Joe broke the news to Colby that Nancy had just died. The day after Christmas in 1990—almost twelve days after the feeding tube had been withdrawn, nearly seven years after her automobile accident, and almost three years after the first court hearing—Nancy Cruzan died.

The family was by the bedside as Nancy simply quit breathing and mercifully left. She showed no sign of distress or discomfort. Her tombstone reads:

> BORN JULY 20, 1957
> DEPARTED JAN. 11, 1983
> AT PEACE DEC. 26, 1990

Colby recalls that evening: "When Joe saw Nancy was no longer breathing, he reached up and gently closed her eyelids. His Uncle George, who had been outside the room, walked down to the nurses' station and said, 'It's over.' As we wound up the conversation early that morning I asked Joe, 'What are you going to do now?' He replied, 'Well, I guess we are going to go home.'" Colby goes on to say that, unfortunately, the years of public battle left the Cruzans too scarred ever to return emotionally to the place they once knew. The wounds ran too deep. At the 1996 commemorative conference in Princeton to honor the Quinlans and Cruzans, the Cruzans' attorney remarked that part of the two families' "solace today, no doubt like most families gathered at this conference, is in the belief that through their struggle, others may learn."[2]

Chris Cruzan White, Nancy's sister, spoke at that conference. In a moving talk on what she had learned from Nancy's experience, Chris stated emphatically that medical technology does not have all the answers. She warned the audience that family and friends *must* stand up for loved ones and petition on their behalf, since doctors, on their own, will not do anything about terminating life-support treatment. She emphasized that communication is the key to getting one's wishes honored and to avoiding an end-of-life experience like Nancy's. Colby agrees that as each individual communicates more openly and provides more information while healthy, the "greater the chance that we will empower those loved ones to ask the right questions and make and stand by the decisions we would choose at the end of life. . . . The legacy left us by Nancy Cruzan, Karen Ann Quinlan, and the rest of our unfortunate heroes is that we must all keep working to spread the message of communication."[3]

The toll on the family continued long after Nancy was finally "at peace." Almost six years later the *Detroit Free Press* reported: "Joe Cruzan, 62, a sheet-metal worker whose family crisis sparked a heated national right-to-die debate, committed suicide Saturday at his home in Carterville, Missouri. Friends said Mr. Cruzan never recovered from the emotional drain of his daughter, Nancy's, car crash and the ensuing court battle to remove her from life-support."[4]

To the many proponents of the belief that close family members ought to control life-and-death decisions over incompetent patients, the *Cruzan* ruling was a shock, a betrayal of the reason and compassion of the *Quinlan* court. Missouri's rule, in effect, resulted in the expulsion of families from the decision-making process, and the Supreme Court sanctioned it. *Cruzan* did not affect the cases of competent patients or cases in which the incompetent patient has left clear evidence of his or her wishes prior to incompetency. It did, however, profoundly affect situations in which the incompetent patient has left no advance directive—like Nancy and Karen. It severely limited the incompetent patient's surrogate to refuse unwanted treatment on his or her behalf and, in so doing, ignored the basis of *Quinlan*. How an incompetent patient is treated, therefore, depends on the laws of the state where he or she lives. It points to the importance of executing an advance directive, especially in those states that have Missouri's high standard, such as Michigan and New York.

Cruzan's judicial indifference to the *Quinlan* legacy provoked outrage. The Supreme Court had turned its back on the family. Armstrong, the Quinlans' attorney, minced no words in showing his displeasure over the antifamily ruling:

Simply put, a mere majority of the Supreme Court ignored Nancy Cruzan's wishes and those of her parents and sister, and out of an oft proclaimed obeisance to a sterile notion of federalism, acquiesced to Missouri's obdurate rejection of fundamental familial rights, duties and obligations. For five members of our nation's highest tribunal, it is more important to leave these questions to the "laboratory of the states," than

to allow Nancy Cruzan's parents to decide to free her from the laboratory of modern medicine and technology.

The United States Supreme Court, by recognizing a competent patient's constitutional right to make personal medical decisions and rel-
egating to the states the development of procedures for recognizing and
vindicating choices on behalf of incompetent patients, impels us to revisit the pronouncements of the New Jersey Supreme Court. In contrast,
New Jersey's highest court operates on the assumption that the surest
defense of people against abuse is the defense of the free exercise of
their rights. It declared that incompetence should not compromise the
rights of patients and ruled that the only practical way to prevent destruction of constitutional rights is to permit the family to exercise it on
behalf of the patient.[5]

Annas viewed the "bloodless" and "antifamily" decision as one more step
toward a government that sees "citizens merely as means to an end." In a
scathing article in the *Hastings Center Report*, Annas likens the Court's treatment of Nancy Cruzan to behavior that might be expected from China, not
the United States. He also provides a commentary on why this decision
occurred:

> Had the Cruzan family been in China when Nancy Cruzan suffered the
> accident that left her in a persistent vegetative state, and had China
> done to the Cruzans what Missouri had done to them, outrage would
> have rung throughout the United States. The commandeering of Nancy
> Cruzan's living body by the Chinese government would likely have been
> condemned by the White House, the State Department, and the Attor-
> ney General. Nancy's parents who know and love her better than anyone
> on earth, would have been seen as her natural protectors, the state as
> an unpredictable predator. Most Americans would likely have found it
> easy to see that both her and Nancy's family's rights were being uncon-
> scionably violated, and have thanked God that we live in a free country
> where arbitrary governmental actions are restrained by a Constitu-
> tion. . . .
>
> The U.S. Constitution is becoming irrelevant as a source of pro-
> tecting U.S. citizens from the growing power of the state and modern
> technology. With the decline of U.S. political, economic, and military
> influence in the world, our government seems ever intent on turning
> inward against its own people. In the 1960s this might have been seen
> as a call to action. But in the apathetic 1990s we will witness not
> meaningful political debate, but a battle of sound bites and slogans. . . .
> It is incredible that anyone would view this as a positive result.[6]

Nancy Cruzan's story did not cause the massive changes wrought by

Quinlan, although the nation undisputedly felt her impact. It alerted more people to the necessity of signing advance directives; the U.S. Congress entered the realm of the right to die; and it generated an increase in state lawmaking and judicial policy making. It raised fear in pro-life opponents that the pro-choice group was making progress; it provoked more conversation among ethicists; and it angered and discouraged others who felt the decision was a setback for the goodwill and authority of the family. If *Quinlan* made the public say, "I don't want to end up like Karen Quinlan," *Cruzan* provoked the public to say, "I had better sign an advance directive so I don't end up like Nancy Cruzan."

Not since the mid-1980s, when so many states enacted living will and health care proxy laws as a result of *Quinlan*, have so many state legislatures enacted new laws or amended old ones as in response to *Cruzan*. Following the *Cruzan* decision in June 1990, four more states enacted living will laws, and eighteen states amended their living will statues. Two of the new laws and ten of the new amendments include provisions for terminating treatment in cases of permanent unconsciousness. Five laws now include surrogate decision making as part of living wills, and all the new laws permit the refusal of artificial feeding.

Moreover, legislatures have begun to adopt other kinds of statutes to address other issues raised by end-of-life decision making. There are now statutes in thirty-four states listing those who are able to terminate treatment for patients who lack an advance directive. A growing number of states address the two issues of Do-Not-Resuscitate orders and incompetent pregnant women, who are sometimes prohibited from forgoing treatment.

Since 1991 a few states have enacted laws to increase the chances that advance directives will be filled out and will be effective. Maine requires that Living Will forms be provided to all applicants for driver's licenses and for hunting licenses. Illinois requires that possession of a Living Will be noted on the driver's license. Oregon requires all health care facilities to provide advance directives to all adult patients. It would be beneficial to their residents if more states addressed the issue with equal creativity.

With Nancy's prolonged dying process in mind, Congress enacted the Patient Self-Determination Act, which took effect on December 1, 1991. Its goal is to help ensure that all Americans have the opportunity to fill out advance directives, so that the wishes of incompetent patients with respect to termination of medical treatment will be clearly known by family and friends. Congress acted with the intent to educate Americans about their need to put their desires in writing to avoid increasingly unwanted life-sustaining technology.

The act requires that all United States hospitals, nursing facilities, health maintenance organizations, and other health care delivery systems receiving federal funds, most notably Medicare and Medicaid, develop written policies regarding advance directives. These organizations must also provide all admitted patients with written information explaining their right to accept or refuse medical treatment, and advance directives must be made available to them. This federal act imposes four more requirements on the provider organizations. They must provide: (1) education for the community and staff on advance directives; (2) documentation in the patient's chart as to the existence of advance directives; (3) written policies and procedures to implement the patient's refusal of treatment; and (4) written information to the patient on the policy and philosophy of the medical institution.

In theory, the congressional act sounded like a real gain for patients' rights groups and was, at the time, applauded as such. [The act became the latest vehicle for promoting autonomy about the way they lived and the way they died, requiring hospitals and other health care institutions to inform patients about their rights to control health care decisions.]

In practice, however, when patients are admitted to acute care hospitals or nursing homes, they are frequently too ill, too confused, too anxious, or in too much pain to make a rational, thoughtful decision about future care. The best time to execute an advance directive is *before* a crisis occurs, when decisions can be thoughtfully made and calmly communicated to friends and family alike. We know that most patients have not had any sort of meaningful discussion with their physicians about the type of treatment they want at the end of life. Patients are waiting for the doctor to initiate the discussion, but doctors remain convinced that to do so would upset the patient and undermine his or her trust.

Despite the 1991 federal law, Massachusetts health leaders revealed at a conference in April of 1998 that "everyday care is falling far short of the law's intent." The effort to honor patients' wishes is failing on multiple fronts, says David Clarke of Massachusetts Health Decisions: "Health care providers lose advance directives, they don't enforce them, families disagree about them, patients don't sign them. It's a mess."

Results of a new survey of 190 health-care institutions were presented at the conference: Only one-third reported they have trained their staffs on advance directives, as the federal law requires; three-quarters of health care institutions have done no community education on advance directives, another federal requirement; and slightly less than one-half of health care institutions and agencies said they had no committee, task force, or designated group to implement the requirements of the federal law.[7]

In the wake of *Cruzan* and the Patient Self-Determination Act, federal policy on the right to die now exists, but neither the Supreme Court nor Congress has developed standards and rules that come close to the scope of policies created by the states. The states are to be commended for what they have done in the last few decades. Nevertheless, both federal moves are incremental changes in the right-to-die movement and create a limited national policy. Small steps are common practice for the government, especially on controversial issues.

Every state now has advance directive legislation on the right to refuse treatment and most have developed a rich body of law, supporting the autonomy of the patient and the right of the surrogate to make decisions when the patient is unable to do so; New Jersey has continued as one of the most progressive. The right-to-die movement becomes more defined with the Patient Self-Determination Act, but far from resolved.

The unsung heroes of the right-to-die movement are the families who made the decisions to challenge the powerful groups that control our society. They persevered despite the hostilities of those who so vehemently disagreed with them. The Quinlans and the Cruzans are aware of their daughters' powerful influence on the patients' rights movement: "I think if it wasn't for our case, the public would not be as well-informed as they are. Before our case, I don't think that many people were aware that they had the right to make a decision on their treatment, or to make a decision that they can refuse treatment," says Julia Quinlan. She adds that before their experience with Karen, "I always felt that . . . when you go to the doctor you would just do and say whatever he tells you. You wouldn't ask him questions. It was like he was God. Now people realize we have the right to ask questions. We have the right to refuse treatment. People are aware of that now as a result of our case."[8]

Today Karen lives on in her parents' memories and through the hospice program, the Karen Ann Quinlan Center of Hope, established as a memorial to her, operating in New Jersey's Warren and Sussex Countries. It is available to all families, regardless of whether or not they can pay. Karen, as she herself predicted, went down in history. Nancy has joined her. By the time Nancy Cruzan died in June 1990, another person was in the process of joining the roster of names forever synonymous with the right-to-die movement. Dr. Jack Kevorkian had, the same month, assisted in his first suicide.

A Tale of Two Doctors

The sudden appearance in 1990 on the right-to-die scene of Dr. Jack Kevorkian transformed the issue from polite debate and courteous informational assistance (Hemlock's way) to in-your-face, controversial death-on-request operated by the retired Michigan pathologist. The media could not get enough of him—a doctor actually killing patients!—making him a household name within weeks. Here at last was a physician who was willing not only to help people die but to make every death a media event, holding press conferences, even issuing short videos of the patient's death request.

In less than a year a second American doctor—this time from mainstream medicine—came forward and confessed in the nation's most prestigious medical organ, the *New England Journal of Medicine*, that he had helped a dying woman patient to commit suicide. Dr. Timothy E. Quill delicately and persuasively wrote out his reasons for breaking the law, and the taboo, on PAS. Those in medicine who silently supported PAS but resented Doctor Kevorkian's unusual way of practicing, breathed a sigh of relief that one of their number was courageous enough to confess that he had committed "the unmentionable act" but with a more careful mode. Yet Kevorkian came first and was always better known to the masses.

Thousands of physicians in the United States and elsewhere accelerate the deaths of some patients whose end-stage suffering is terrible. Sometimes they leave a large amount of lethal drugs at the bedside, warning the patient that too many would be deadly. Doctors often increase the analgesics needed to stop pain to such an extent that they also bring life to an end (the "double effect"). Occasionally they perform direct injection of a lethal substance into a part of the body (usually the anal orifice) where the needle puncture is not visible. Rarely is this done in a hospital, where an opponent might report the "crime," but more often in the patient's home, followed by silence on the part of all concerned.

But here was Doctor Kevorkian brazenly helping people to die—with a home-built "suicide machine" no less—taking the corpse to the medical examiner's office, then describing to the press exactly how the death was brought about. The resulting public response was either outrage or acclamation, depending on their attitude toward euthanasia.

Kevorkian claimed the alleviation of suffering as his overriding motive, and he has never been shown to accept a penny from patients. He also aimed to change the way the leaders of medicine viewed assistance in dying. The target was the powerful AMA, to which 40 percent of physicians belong, and whose leaders trenchantly oppose the procedure under any conditions. Much criticized for promoting a media circus surrounding death, how else could Kevorkian's campaign succeed unless it was public knowledge?

From about the tenth assisted death onward, Kevorkian's notoriety enormous, American public opinion divided into two distinct camps: One side worshipped the ground he walked on, regarding him as a messiah leading the long-awaited breakthrough into compassionate medicine; the other side (including much of the medical profession) saw him as an eccentric, poorly qualified in medicine, and overly obsessed with the subject of death. The adjective most widely used by his critics, or those who did not, or chose not, to understand him, was "weird."

Leaders of the right-to-die movement were also divided on whether Kevorkian was a help or a hindrance to their cause. On the one hand he had raised the public awareness of the issue 100 percent, yet on the other, was it death with dignity to die in the back of a rusty Volkswagen camper or a motel room, far from home, and at the hands of a doctor the patient had known only for a day? What troubled the right-to-die groups was Kevorkian's insistence that euthanasia was purely a medical matter, and that the law had no business getting involved.

Humphry wrote in 1992:

> By helping three people who were not in the usual sense "terminally ill," Dr. Kevorkian has widened the debate over the ethics and legality of the right to choose to die. I believe this widening to be regrettable because the Hemlock movement and its sister organizations are close to the point of success in law reform. . . . Hemlock has spent ten years bringing the medical profession around to accepting its point of view. We believe 60 percent of doctors are on our side, as long as the law is changed. Now Dr. Kevorkian has muddied the waters.[1]

Some Hemlock members resigned in protest against the organization's criticism of Kevorkian, but generally speaking most members welcomed Kevorkian's campaign while quietly pushing forward themselves on law reform.

Kevorkian's view of the Hemlock Society sprang from his profession as a doctor. "It's a lay organization that unfortunately won't succeed well because the medical profession doesn't like taking orders from lay people," he said. "They are opposing what I'm doing openly and very forcefully, because they call me a loose cannon and a radical. They like step-by-step. They think this is a first step and then we'll change the law. There they go—a law, a law. Because they're not doctors, they've got to rely on a law to get what they want, and it's not the way to go."[2]

Hemlock's reply was to point out that the medical profession ranked among the most legally regulated professions in existence. Until the law making assisted suicide a felony in all the other states was abolished, very few doctors would follow Kevorkian's example, and he was obviously incapable of helping everybody who wanted hastened death in the United States. The right-to-die movement claimed it was focusing on the bigger picture and taking the long view of the situation.

Public opinion polling by the Harris organization in 1993 showed 50 percent of the public supported Kevorkian in March. By November, after he had been on a hunger strike to protest his being kept in jail for refusing to post a fifty-thousand-dollar bond on an assisted suicide charge, his support increased to 58 percent. In the second poll, 73 percent said that the law ought to change to permit PAS.[3] When Kevorkian stated that he would die of starvation rather than post bond, and began a hunger strike, many people who had been unsure now became convinced of the absolute sincerity of his motives. The hunger strike lasted seventeen days, at which point a judge reduced the bond to one hundred dollars. Television pictures of an emaciated Kevorkian being taken to a hospital in a wheelchair evoked a national wave of sympathy and admiration.

Kevorkian injected life and action into the smoldering right-to-die debate. It needed a maverick like him to do so. Whereas most doctors have families, well-paid, upwardly mobile careers, and many material possessions, Kevorkian had never married, was penniless, and owned no home, motor cars, or boats, so could not be sued for monetary damages. He was in his sixties; his career as an employable pathologist was over. Hospitals found his views and practices too startling to have him on staff. A man of very modest personal needs, he existed on small pensions. Necessarily he was a man of iron determination, not frightened of institutions or authority, and possessed strong opinions based on his life and extensive research. The prospect of a spell in prison never seemed to daunt him.

The only son of Armenian immigrants, Kevorkian was born in Pontiac, Michigan, in 1928. He attended the University of Michigan, as an undergraduate and as a medical student, interned at the Henry Ford Hospital in Detroit, and then spent more than a year as an army medical officer in the Korean War. Back in civilian life, he did residencies at Pontiac General

Hospital and Detroit Receiving, where his interest in the final moments of dying people developed.

Always more of an activist than a theorist, Kevorkian presented himself one day at Ohio State Penitentiary and asked the warden if he could interview men on death row about their attitudes to medical experimentation on themselves. The warden allowed him to talk to two condemned inmates, one of whom supported the idea if it would help mankind, while the other would not commit himself. Kevorkian began to develop a scientific paper outlining his ideas for experiments using criminals about to be executed: It had to be voluntary, painless, and done only by physicians with special training. Scientific and medical journals refused to publish his paper. In 1958 he was allowed to present it to a meeting of the American Association for the Advancement of Science, in Washington, D.C., drawing some criticism from the press. The chairman of the Pathology Department at the University of Michigan, embarrassed by the publicity, asked Kevorkian to stop talking about this or quit, which, characteristically, he did, immediately moving to Pontiac General Hospital as a pathologist. In his new job Kevorkian heard that Russian doctors were experimenting with transferring blood from corpses to injured people. If he could perfect the technique, Kevorkian reasoned, it could be used on the battlefield to save the lives of seriously injured soldiers. His physician colleagues thought the idea was unnecessary because there was ample blood available, but Kevorkian persisted. His research was eventually published in *Military Medicine* in 1964. Then, hoping for a grant for further work, he approached the U.S. Defense Department, which rejected his application. In 1970 Kevorkian became chief pathologist at Saratoga General Hospital, Detroit, a position he held for six years before moving to California, where he worked for several hospitals in the Los Angeles area.

In 1986 Kevorkian published a startling article in a German journal, *Medicine and Law*, in which he made a case for "the extraordinary opportunities for terminal experimentation on humans facing imminent and inevitable death."[4] He argued that just because the Nazis had done such experiments in a forcible and brutal way did not invalidate the case for doing medical research on condemned people in a voluntary and painless way. In the same article Kevorkian strayed into the right-to-die issue for the first time, spending several pages discussing the suicide of sick people, and suggested that this was also a fruitful area for research and experimentation. His constant mixing of ideas for experimentation and organ harvesting with arguments for euthanasia confused and worried many people who wished them to be seen as separate ethical issues.

In 1987 Kevorkian began inserting small classified advertisements in Michigan newspapers. A typical one read: "Is someone in your family terminally ill? Does he or she wish to die with dignity? Call Physician-Consultant," and gave a telephone number. So far as is known, no one responded to these advertisements. He also had business cards printed, which said: "Jack Kevorkian, M.D. Bioethics and Obitiatry. Special Death Counseling by Appointment only." Kevorkian attempted to introduce two new words into medical jargon—"obitiatry," the study of death; and "medicide," a doctor helping a person to die.

A Detroit journal, *Healthcare Weekly Review*, wrote him up in August 1987, accurately foretelling what Kevorkian would accomplish over the next ten years: "Kevorkian says he fully expects to be arrested after supervising the death of his first patient, but says he welcomes prosecution because it will force government, the public, and organized medicine to face the issue."[5]

The next year, when Kevorkian was back in California, he approached the Hemlock Society, then based in Los Angeles, with the idea that he open a suicide clinic. Hemlock would refer dying patients interested in euthanasia to him, and he would help them to die. When Humphry pointed out that the group was in the middle of its first attempt to modify the law prohibiting assisted suicide in California, Kevorkian responded that their cooperation would reap enormous publicity and thus help the campaign. But Humphry argued that it was not feasible simultaneously to break the law and democratically to reform it. Additionally, Humphry had always dismissed the idea of "suicide clinics" as vulnerable to abuse and unnecessary; he preferred a quiet, legal procedure negotiated between doctor and patient, carried out at home. Disgusted, Kevorkian never spoke to Humphry again, thereafter referring to him as "just another hypocrite."[6] Humphry respected Kevorkian's courage and determination, but realized that they were on separate paths to the same goal: Kevorkian's to alter the medical profession's attitude, and Hemlock's to change the law.

Kevorkian returned to his home state, which—as he and others had noticed—was unique in having no specific law forbidding assistance in suicide. There was no such law on Michigan's statute books and never had been, but neither was there one permitting assistance. Kevorkian developed the idea that people could be helped to die by physicians not by direct lethal injection by syringe but by themselves pushing the final button of equipment to which they were attached. His scheme—later repeated in Australia, when in 1996–97 the Northern Territory legalized euthanasia for ten brief months—was to have a doctor assess the suitability of the patient for accelerated death, then connect the patient to bottles of lethal drugs. But it would be the patient—via a button—who would actually make the ultimate decision and take the physical action to infuse the poison into his or her bloodstream. This kind of assistance, Kevorkian reasoned, had two advantages: He would not be killing the patient, but he or she would be committing suicide, and under legal precedent he could not be prosecuted in Michigan; ethically the patient had the responsibility for the final decision to die, thereby relieving the doctor of it, although of course the doctor played a significant part in providing the drugs and inserting a needle into the patient's vein.

Kevorkian never entertained the "Hemlock method" of accelerated death—taking overdoses by mouth—because he knew that infusion directly into the bloodstream was more effective and faster. Hemlock knew this as well, but their desire was to help people suffering unbearably who could not get a doctor to assist. Death by lethal injection was something for the future, after difficult law reform, Hemlock reasoned.

Whether he intended it or not, Kevorkian's public relations coup was stimulated by the novelty of his "suicide machine," the like of which had never before been heard of. It fascinated the media and the public. Built of scrap aluminum, it consisted of three inverted jars of drugs suspended from a frame with tube connections to needles, which were inserted in the patient's arms. A tiny motor from a toy car powered the intravenous lines. First, cardiograph electrodes were connected to the patient's arms and legs, which monitored the vital signs so that Kevorkian could know exactly when the patient was dead. Then the patient was connected intravenously to a harmless saline solution. When ready to die, the patient pushed a button that caused a valve to shut off the saline and to open the adjoining line to a bottle of pentothal, which induced sleep within about thirty seconds. A timing device connected to the line between the second and third containers triggered after one minute, causing an infusion of potassium chloride and succinylcholine (a powerful muscle relaxant). Death occurred within six minutes.

Brash as ever, Kevorkian appeared on television with his machine and was written up in *Newsweek*. There was no longer any need for him to spend his tiny income on small advertisements in local papers—he now had the national stage. His first patient was not long in coming. Janet Adkins, a Hemlock member in Portland, Oregon, was suffering from early Alzheimer's disease, and wanted help to die. Like many other people, she did not want to risk taking her own life in case she botched it; her own doctors would not help her, so she approached Kevorkian. After studying her medical records, Kevorkian agreed to help. Mrs. Adkins and her husband flew to Detroit in June 1990. On arrival she and her husband talked with Kevorkian; he questioned her closely about her views on her condition and stressed the unalterable significance of her decision, making sure this was preserved on video. Next day he helped her die with his suicide machine. The site of the death act became a matter of considerable controversy. It had to be in the back of Kevorkian's rusty old Volkswagen camper on a campsite because, although he searched extensively, no one would rent or lend him premises in which to carry out such an unusual action. Kevorkian installed curtains in the camper for privacy, and by his account Mrs. Adkins died quickly and peacefully. He then informed her husband and the local medical examiner's office. The *New York Times* heard about it almost immediately and devoted most of the next day's front page to a lengthy report, touching off a national and international controversy.

"Any such thing as a suicide machine is a moral abomination," said a spokesman for the Archdiocese of Detroit. "God alone is the author of life, from beginning to end."[7] "Most physicians are repulsed by the thought of it," said Dr. David Harold, a member of the board of the Medical Society in Oakland County, in which Janet Adkins had died. "We are in favor of promoting and prolonging and helping people with their lives. Here's a case where you've got the shopkeeper selling you the gun."[8]

As if it were not sufficiently contentious that an unknown pathologist had openly performed voluntary euthanasia on a woman not his patient, fuel was added to the debate by Mrs. Adkins's condition. That she had Alzheimer's was not in doubt, and was later confirmed by autopsy, but it was in its early stages. A week before her death she had been physically fit enough to play tennis. Critics deplored her decision to die so soon, and psychiatrists declared that it would not have happened if she had been in their care. But what these largely self-serving arguments ignored was Mrs. Adkins's wish to die—her "right to die," if she chose. As to the tennis game, she was not mentally capable of keeping the score. Her argument for death was that she would soon lose control of her faculties and her life, unable to make a competent decision about anything. Up to this point she had been able to discuss her accelerated death with her minister, her family, and her psychotherapist, who all agreed that it was her choice. A vital and purposeful woman, she could not bear the thought of life without a mind. As her husband argued subsequently in many public talks, if voluntary euthanasia had been legal, his wife could have made a pact with a local doctor and lived on for quite a while until her condition worsened.

The vague state of Michigan's law on assisted suicide did not prevent the law enforcement authorities from trying to punish Kevorkian. Within a week of Mrs. Adkins's death, the Oakland County prosecutor went to court to ask for a temporary restraining order to stop him from using his suicide machine. In his defense Kevorkian argued at length that his service was essential to stop suffering, and that if the medical profession had any real compassion it would support him. Questioned about his medical ability to make judgments on all types of diseases and conditions, Kevorkian responded that he always first consulted with the patient's own doctor about the diagnosis and prognosis. He denied the prosecutor's claim that he intended to set up "pizza parlors of death"; he had only helped Mrs. Adkins to die in his camper because there was nowhere else to go.[9]

The temporary restraining order was granted. Kevorkian said he would obey it. When next month it became time to consider whether to make the order permanent, Kevorkian tried to submit to the court a rambling, twenty-page statement, which included the views of Aristotle, Pliny the Elder, Saint Thomas More, Thomas Jefferson, and Albert Einstein. It outlined his plan for the medical practice of a "rational policy of planned death" for patients with physical diseases.[10] The court would not accept the document. The judge told Kevorkian he ought to have a lawyer and adjourned the case to give him time to find one. Kevorkian telephoned Geoffrey Fieger, a lawyer whom he had read about and admired. Aggressive both in court and in public, then unknown but with an impressive pedigree of legal victories, Fieger was the right lawyer for Kevorkian, whom he agreed to represent free of charge because the case interested him.

At the end of 1990, the day before the civil trial was due to begin, the local prosecutor, Richard Thompson, announced at a press conference that Kevorkian would be charged with first-degree murder: the prosecutor stated,

> Dr. Kevorkian was the primary and legal cause of Janet Adkins's death. He cannot avoid his criminal culpability by the clever use of a switch. For me not to charge Dr. Kevorkian under these circumstances would be a corruption of the law and turn Oakland County into the suicide Mecca of the nation. . . . Janet Adkins was not terminally ill. She was not in any pain. Dr. Kevorkian's sole interest in her was to put her to death and use that death to advance his cause and his machine.[11]

This statement touched off a new and unusual debate in the United States about the ethics of assisted death. Was the switch on the suicide machine a legal maneuver that would hold up in court? How much responsibility lay with Kevorkian through use of his machine, and how much with the user? Is Alzheimer's a terminal disease? (Its normal course is to weaken a person over many years to the point where he or she is susceptible to other fatal illnesses, such as pneumonia. Many would therefore argue that Alzheimer's is a terminal illness.)

More frightening to many lawmakers across the country was the thought that Kevorkian might visit their state and help local people to die; this touched off legislative efforts by some right-wing politicians to pass clearer laws forbidding assisted suicide; in four states they succeeded. A maximum of eight years in prison and a fine of ten thousand dollars now became the penalty in Indiana for providing the means to commit suicide. In 1996 the state of Iowa passed a new law making it a Class C felony to assist a suicide, either by providing the means or actually helping. Later the same year in Rhode Island, too, the legislature passed a bill punishing doctors with up to ten years' imprisonment for assisting a suicide. During the debates in both legislatures, Doctor Kevorkian's name was bandied about as the reason for introducing the sanctions. In Virginia the General Assembly passed a bill, which took effect in June 1998, levying a civil fine of up to one hundred thousand dollars for "any person who intentionally and knowingly" helps another to commit suicide. The law also revokes the license of any health care worker who helps someone commit suicide. Oklahoma passed a law in May 1998 strengthening existing penalties for assisting a suicide.

For right-to-die groups, this embodied the dark side of Doctor Kevorkian's campaign. Doctors in these states were now more nervous of these laws, which, being new, had high public visibility and were therefore more likely to be enforced. These laws will eventually have to be repealed before more compassionate choices in dying laws can be introduced.

The deeper issue of Mrs. Adkins's death was whether people with degenerative diseases—especially one like hers, which produces mental incompetence—have a right to commit suicide before they lose control or the quality of their lives is destroyed. Or were they "checking out" so as not to be a burden over the years to their family? Because of the understandable desire not to be burdened, was the family pressuring this course of action, sometimes crudely called "the push-Granny-into-the grave syndrome"? A significant section of the American public is sympathetic toward a very sick but not immediately dying person who is helped to die. A poll conducted by the Institute of Social Inquiry at the University of Connecticut in December 1996 found that 42 percent of Americans thought that a patient with Alzheimer's should be allowed PAS before he or she becomes completely helpless, with 14 percent saying that they did not know. Asked whether such assistance was appropriate for a patient with a physically very painful but not terminal illness, 38 percent agreed that it was, with 12 percent not knowing how to answer.

Almost immediately, as the civil judge was discussing an order to Kevorkian to desist from using his suicide machine, the doctor was arrested and charged with the murder of Janet Adkins. Kevorkian told reporters: "I don't take this seriously. This is all immoral anyway. What happens to me is immaterial. The time has come for this thing."[12]

In 1991 Kevorkian helped two people to die, and they remain among his most controversial cases. Sherry Miller had multiple sclerosis (MS), and Marjorie Wantz had severe abdominal pain. They died in the same place at the same time, Mrs. Wantz using the suicide machine while Mrs. Miller, whose veins were too difficult to find, died by the inhalation of carbon monoxide gas.

Neither woman could be ruled as "terminally ill" by the customary criterion of death being likely within the next six months. Mrs. Miller's MS was far advanced, and she was in a pitiful state which would have led to her eventual death. Mrs. Wantz suffered continual and unrelievable pelvic pain, apparently as the result of previous surgeries. There can be no doubt that both women were determined to die and easily persuaded Kevorkian to help. Whereas most people thought of euthanasia in terms of patients close to death and in great pain, Kevorkian was advancing the debate by demonstrating that there was a broader need for assisted death. He was arguing that in some cases of degenerative illness the suffering justified a hastened death because the mental distress equaled that of the physical pain of, for instance, cancer.

His argument contrasted directly with the citizens' ballot initiative, which that year was being conducted in Washington State to address legislation that would allow doctors to help the terminally ill to die either by prescribing lethal drugs or by direct injection. (Irreversible illness was not included.) This was the first time in the world that voters were being asked their opinion on such a law. The proponents looked set to win—opinion polls showed a substantial margin of support—until about two weeks before voting day on November 4.

On October 23 Kevorkian helped Miller and Wantz to die. The double suicide attracted enormous publicity, which the sponsors of the ballot measure claimed was extremely hurtful, raising the specter that Kevorkian would extend his operations across the nation and also visit Washington State. This alone, they argued, could cost them their predicted victory. But other observers noted that the sponsors had run out of money for media advertising during the last two weeks of the campaign, while the opponents in this vital period saturated the airwaves with an effective campaign emphasizing that the proposed law had no clear protections against abuses. Kevorkian himself regarded the Washington law reform campaign with disdain, believing that in its efforts to be extremely dignified and responsible, it was too wishy-washy to be effective in the real world. A little more than three months later Kevorkian was charged with murdering the two women.

In his first year of activity, Kevorkian helped only one person to die; he assisted two in his second and six in his third. But in 1993, even as legal pressures on him escalated, he helped twelve people. The next year he helped only one person to die, and then five the year after that. In 1996 he was extremely busy helping nineteen people to their ends. His activity increased in 1997 to twenty-nine people. In the early months of 1998, eighteen people received his help to die, making a total then of ninety-three recorded deaths. He had a waiting list of hundreds of patients.

Three times he faced trial for murder or assisted suicide, and on each occasion the jury acquitted him. His lawyer found the argument that Kevorkian was not actually killing people but relieving suffering to be the most persuasive in court. To a policeman or a lawyer this was a phony argument, an escape from reality, but it appealed greatly to juries who in any case did not wish to convict Kevorkian, whom they viewed as a humanitarian. A fourth trial in 1997 was declared a mistrial before it properly started. There was little point in the law enforcement authorities continuing to prosecute him because public sentiment was clearly on his side.

In late 1991 Kevorkian's Michigan medical license had been suspended by the Michigan Board of Medicine in an 8–0 vote. After his appeal against the decision was rejected, he took no further notice of the suspension—and neither did the people who wanted his unique services. In 1992 the Michigan Legislature passed a law making assisted suicide a felony for a two-year period, during which a commission would investigate the problem and offer a legal solution. Kevorkian declared the new statute "immoral" and said he would not obey it. In the end the commission could not agree on an answer, and the law, which was never used against Kevorkian—for whom it was intended—expired.

By early 1998 Kevorkian had helped at least 93 people to die. Twenty-five of those had cancer and twenty suffered from MS, eleven from ALS, three from arthritis (and other problems), and one each from AIDS and Alzheimer's (Mrs. Adkins). Of the 93, 63 were women. He came in for heavy criticism when he helped a woman suffering from chronic fatigue syndrome who also had been suffering marital difficulties. But the most severe attack came when he helped a woman named Rebecca Badger who claimed she had MS. The autopsy showed no signs of the disease and it appeared that Ms. Badger had fooled both her own doctors and Kevorkian. Here Kevorkian had fallen into a trap caused by his limited medical knowledge combined with a complete lack of modern medical technology, which is poor at curing but superb at diagnosis. But, given his ostracism by the medical profession, how could his safeguards be other than inadequate?

The majority of Kevorkian's patients were people with serious health problems, often terminal, who had made a conscious decision that because of their suffering they no longer wished to live. Dr. Ljubisa J. Dragovic, a Michigan coroner who performed autopsies on forty-six of Doctor Kevorkian's cases, said that four of them showed no physical evidence of any disease, and only eleven were terminally ill.[13] Kevorkian's credo seemed to be that to wish to die because of acutely poor health provided sufficient justification for his help. This policy contrasted with the rest of the right-to-die movement, which was campaigning with more limited goals—for PAS for only the advanced terminally ill. While the Hemlock Society had throughout the 1980s embraced the irreversibly ill in its credo, when the political realities of getting such a law passed became evident, the society modified its mission statement to involve only the terminally ill, calculating that the American voter was barely ready even for this smaller step.

Challenging even his fellow supporters of the right to die, Kevorkian is a rebel with a cause. His chief enemy is old-fashioned, head-in-the-sand medicine, as personified chiefly by the AMA, which he has called "dishonest and disingenuous."[14] Also in his sights is the powerful element of organized religion, which wants to control public and medical policy to prevent both a woman's right to choose an abortion and a dying person's right to opt for a quick death. He has said that the Pope "has a grip on our government. I know he has a grip on the Michigan Supreme Court. Grip! He owns it! I know he got a grip on our Supreme Court. Therefore I don't care what any legislature does. Pass any law you want, I don't care."[15]

The Michigan doctor has scant use for law reform through the legislature or the ballot box. He attacked the citizens' ballot initiatives backed by Hemlock in Washington and California: "The California bill, the initiative, is wrong on several points. No law is needed for medical practice, provided the profession itself sets down its guidelines based on proven medical procedures, and only doctors can determine that."[16] In 1994 he had a change of heart and briefly worked with friends in Michigan to gather signatures to get a law on the election slate. This failed through lack of money and supporters, after which he resumed his normal derisory attitude toward law reform via the democratic political process. Given the great difficulty Hemlock and its satellite organizations had in finding sympathetic politicians throughout the state legislatures, his pessimism was justified, at least in the short term.

Most of the publicity on Kevorkian has consisted of criticism, direct or implied; mockery (in cartoons and late-night TV comedy shows); or ponderous judgments according to the personal values of the critic. Little has ever been mentioned about the importance to the dying of Kevorkian's special services. Essentially these services were sought after by individuals who wanted an end to their suffering. They heard about him through the extensive media coverage; he no longer advertised after that brief—and unproductive—attempt in 1989.

Patients turned to Kevorkian not only because their own doctors refused to help them die, but as a form of personal empowerment at the close of their lives. It gave them control and choice, exactly what the Hemlock movement had always been campaigning for, without success except in the "do-it-yourself" manner explained in its literature.

In one of a handful of supportive articles published over eight years, George Kovanis, a writer for the *Detroit Free Press*, explored the patient point of view and, in this instance, ignored that of physicians, philosophers, and theologians. Kovanis quoted Franklin Curren, a psychiatrist whose wife turned to Kevorkian, as saying that patients felt: "I'm master of very little, but this is one way I can be master of my final fate." Another relative of a patient who died with Kevorkian's help stated: "There's more doctor in Dr. K's little pinkie than all the doctors put together. He just came across as caring." In case after case investigated by Kovanis, the theme of patient control comes through. For instance, the Reverend Ken Phifer says of his longtime friend, Merian Frederick, who had ALS and finally went to Kevorkian to be helped to die: "I think that if Merian could have found . . . a way to live longer without the fear of not being given what she wanted—release from her suffering—when she wanted it, she would have chosen that."[17] The same worry had plagued Kevorkian's first patient, Janet Adkins, who, like millions of others, dreaded slipping into the netherworld of mental incompetence.

"Humanitarian," "hero," "messiah," "saint," "weirdo," "nut," "zealot," "death-obsessed crusader:" Kevorkian has been called all these names and more. Had he possessed a gentler, more lovable personality, he might have achieved a much greater effect on public and medical opinion. His mockery of the establishment, such as dressing up for television in cardboard stocks, with ball and chain on one leg, mimicking medieval justice, was often both daring and funny, amusing some and provoking the scorn of others. Satire may not have been the way to achieve social change in so serious a subject as dying, but it cannot be denied that his has been the most significant impact on death in the United States in this century. Few others have possessed the courage, determination, and integrity to accomplish what he has done.

His reception by the American right-to-die movement has been mixed. Some praised him unreservedly. Others, such as Hemlock, have mixed praise with criticism. Those supporters linked to the health care professions, trained to pay close attention to medical details, have tended to be critical, even hostile. Kevorkian's slender qualifications as a physician troubled serious medical people who might otherwise have applauded him. While the right-to-die groups maintained the high ground over the 1990s, concentrating on law reform, Kevorkian was setting the pace, even the agenda, and constantly keeping the issue in the forefront of the public's eye. Hardly any book or article, scholarly or otherwise, on the subject was published without some reference to the impact of his constant stream of assisted deaths. By the end of 1997 the authorities were admitting, albeit grudgingly, that he had in effect created a "free suicide zone" in Michigan by escaping prosecution on four occasions. Law professor at the University of Detroit Mercy School of Law, Larry Dubin, commented: "It does appear as if Jack Kevorkian has been granted the implicit authority to be able to assist in suicides in southeastern Michigan under the current state of law."[18] Never slow to put the boot in, Kevorkian's feisty lawyer Fieger declared: "They're afraid. They're never going to prosecute."[19] Thus, unless and until the Michigan legislature found the courage and the skills to pass a definitive law criminalizing assisted suicide, Kevorkian would remain free to help Americans from all over the country to die peacefully, provided they could travel to him.

After eight years of Kevorkian, many in Michigan were getting tired of his behavior. It was not so much that he helped people to die—he had many supporters—but his cocksureness and his rude rebuttal of other people's viewpoints were upsetting. Additionally, the almost weekly reports of Kevorkian strolling down the sidewalk pushing dead bodies in wheelchairs to the medical examiner's office was nobody's idea of death with dignity. Commented the *Detroit Free Press* in November 1997:

> Dr. Kevorkian is scarcely the poster boy for the right to die movement. His behavior has often been bizarre, and his sneering contempt for anyone who disagrees with him has not made him an ally to be sought. . . .

So this state is trapped in a no-man's land on assisted suicide, taunted by this man who makes himself judge, jury and executioner for any who say they need to die. He sets his own rules and then does not follow them.

The newspaper staunchly endorsed a petition campaign by a political group called Merian's Friends to get an Oregon-type law on the Michigan statute books. The group is named after Merian Frederick who, unable to get her own doctor to ease her suffering, reluctantly went to Dr. Kevorkian to be euthanized. While her family and friends were grateful to him for helping Mrs. Frederick escape further suffering, they felt that a state law should be introduced so that people could die at home with the help of their own doctor, provided he or she was willing. In 1998 they succeed in getting 250,000 signatures so that a PAS law could be put before the electorate. A 1997 opinion poll showed that 59 percent of registered voters would support it, replicating the level of support in Oregon.

Going completely against the climate of public opinion in the state and, indeed, the whole of the United States, at the end of 1997 the Michigan Senate passed a law banning PAS. Offenders would be liable for up to five years' imprisonment. It was expected to pass easily in the House of Representatives, and the governor was willing to sign it. With his customary intrepidity Kevorkian instantly announced that he would welcome prosecution under the new law, and that if convicted he would starve himself to death in prison.

Fortunately for the right-to-die movement, within a year of Kevorkian's thunderbolt appearance on the scene in 1990, another doctor surfaced who mitigated much of the deleterious effect of the Michigan pathologist. Dr. Timothy Quill, a tall, kindly-looking internist on the staff of the Genesee Hospital, in Rochester, New York, confessed in an article entitled "Death and Dignity" that he had assisted the suicide of one of his patients, whom he referred to only as "Diane."[20] Explaining "Diane's" decline from leukemia, Quill emphasized that he had been the woman's doctor for nearly eight years and was well aware of the difficulties she had endured in her life.

Diane refused chemotherapy on the grounds that its benefits were marginal and the side effects usually distressing. Quill wrote that he did not tell Diane that "the last four patients with acute leukemia had died very painful deaths in the hospital during various stages of treatment."[21] Quill and Diane discussed the diagnosis, prognosis, and all her options over several days, and she shared this information with her husband and son. Diane broached the subject of assisted suicide, and Quill at first neither acquiesced nor refused. Having been involved for many years in hospice, he arranged home hospice for her in case she changed her mind and wanted that service.

"It was extraordinarily important to Diane to maintain control of herself and her own dignity during the time remaining to her," Quill wrote:

> When this was no longer possible, she clearly wanted to die. As a former director of a hospice program, I know how to use pain medicines to keep patients comfortable and lessen suffering. I explained the philosophy of comfort care, which I believe in. Although Diane understood and appreciated this, she had known of people lingering in what was called relative comfort and she wanted no part of it. When the time came, she wanted to take her life in the least painful way possible. Knowing of her desire for independence and her decision to stay in control I thought this request made perfect sense.[22]

To test her resolve and independence of action, Quill put Diane in touch with the Hemlock Society, from which she ordered *Let Me Die Before I Wake* and a chart giving lethal dosages of drugs. (*Final Exit* had not yet been published.) After reading this material, Diane telephoned Quill asking for a prescription for a large amount of barbiturates, which indicated to him that she had read the Hemlock literature, for these were their drugs of choice. Diane offered Quill the protection, suggested by Hemlock, that they have a discussion about insomnia as a pretext for the lethal prescription, but Quill rightly regarded this as superficial. He was more interested in being sure that she was not depressed. "It was clear that she was not despondent and that in fact she was making deep, personal connections with her family and close friends. I made sure that she knew how to use the barbiturate for sleep, and also she knew the amount needed to commit suicide."[23]

Quill reported that he wrote the prescription with uneasy feelings about the boundaries he was exploring—spiritual, legal, professional, and personal. At the same time he felt it right to "set her free to get the most out of the time she had left." Three months passed, during which Diane had painful emotional episodes and also needed blood transfusions, but her determination to kill herself at a certain point never wavered. As the end approached, Diane said good-bye to her friends and to Quill. Her family called to say they found her dead on the couch, wearing her favorite shawl, and asked how to proceed. Quill went to the house and called the medical examiner to advise him that a hospice patient had died. Asked for the cause of death Quill replied, "Acute leukemia." Quill well knew that if he had breathed a word about suicide, paramedics would have rushed to the scene and tried to revive his patient, the police would have launched investigations, and probably an autopsy would have been ordered.

In his article Quill wrote:

> Although I truly believe that the family and I gave her the best care possible, allowing her to define her limits and directions as much as

possible, I am not sure the law, society, or the medical profession would agree. So I said "acute leukemia" to protect all of us, to protect Diane from an invasion into her past, and her body, and to continue to shield society from the knowledge of the degree of suffering that people often undergo in the process of dying.[24]

Quill wrote that although pain management was available, it was an illusion to think that people do not suffer in the process of dying. He pondered how many severely ill or dying patients secretly take their lives, dying alone in despair. Toward the end of his impressive article, Quill reflected on whether he should have been with Diane as she killed herself, but it seems that he did not feel able to go that far, given the state of the law.

Quill's confession, and the fact that it appeared in the world's most prestigious medical journal, burst upon a grateful public desperate for an antidote to the seemingly perfunctory, speedy, back-of-the-van methods of assisted death as practiced by Kevorkian. Yes, Quill's article cried out, it *could* be done at home with caution, love, justifiability, and finality.

At first the law enforcement authorities decided not to investigate Quill's actions. There was, after all, no body. Only he knew that lethal drugs had been prescribed and a person cannot be convicted on his or her evidence alone. But a few weeks after the article appeared a tipster told the district attorney's office that Diane's cadaver was in cold storage at a local community college awaiting dissection. The tipster said the body was that of Patricia Diane Trumbell, forty-five, of Pittsford, New York. Although the body had been embalmed, an autopsy showed that it still contained a lethal dose of barbiturates. The Rochester district attorney now felt he had no choice but to put the matter before a grand jury. "The grand jurors," said John J. Regan, professor of criminal and health care law at Hofstra University School of Law, Long Island, New York, "will have to use their own value systems to decide: do we want to send a signal that doctors will not be prosecuted if they help their patients commit suicide?"[25] For his part Quill welcomed the opportunity to explore the legal boundaries of his action; also to get a deeper understanding of the sufferings of dying people.

Quill never disguised the fact that he had made his action public partly as an answer to Kevorkian's "distressing arrogance and superficial approach."[26] Preferring to put his views cautiously on paper rather than in sound bites on television, Quill wrote: "We should all be troubled that he helped put to death eighteen people whom he barely knew, and did so evidently without doubt or personal struggle. We should also wonder about a medical and legal system that could leave suffering patients so desperate [as to go to Kevorkian]."[27] Quill received more than a thousand letters from the public in response to his article, 99 percent of which supported his action. A number of physicians contacted him to say they had acted similarly.

Quill went before the grand jury on July 21, 1991, and spent several hours telling the jurors the details of Diane's suffering, and her independence of spirit, carefully explaining his motives for assisting in her suicide. Grand jury hearings are confidential, so we do not know exactly what was said. In an interview two weeks later, Quill commented: "The saddest part of the story . . . is that Diane had to be alone at the end of her life. She wouldn't have had to be alone had it not been for the law in New York State. I think she felt she had to. That to me is a very sad thing."[28] The grand jury refused to indict Quill, and he continued practicing medicine; still, the experience turned him into a determined campaigner for law reform, developing into the most convincing and persistent medical advocate for the procedure to appear so far.

In the following years Quill wrote two books on the subject that were more about patient decision making than assisted suicide, and—collaborating with medical colleagues—wrote a series of articles in medical journals exploring the issue. The year following his original article, Quill and two other doctors outlined in the *New England Journal of Medicine* a six-point series of tests a doctor should make before assisting a suicide:

1. The patient must have a condition that is incurable and associated with severe, unrelenting suffering, and must understand the problem;
2. Doctors must be sure patients are not asking for death only because they are not getting treatment that would relieve their suffering;
3. The patient must clearly and repeatedly ask to die to avoid suffering without making the patient beg for assistance;
4. A doctor must be sure a patient's judgment is not distorted or resulting from a treatable problem like depression;
5. The doctor who assists in the suicide should be the patient's physician unless he or she has moral objections;
6. An independent doctor should give a second opinion in the case, with all three each signing a document showing informed consent.[29]

Quill and his colleagues said that they wanted family members involved, but in no circumstances could family wishes override those of a patient who was competent to think for him- or herself. The doctor should be present at the suicide. "It is of the utmost importance not to abandon the patient at this critical moment."[30] In everything he has said and written, Quill has emphasized that PAS remains the option of last resort after treatment, comfort care, and palliative care have been shown to be of no avail.

Quill has never said whether he has helped a patient other than Diane to die, preferring to confine his campaign year after year to lectures, addressing conferences, writing articles, and serving as the plaintiff in a court case that reached the U.S. Supreme Court before losing (*Quill v. Vacco*, NY 95-7028). He typifies the medical profession's disgust with Kevorkian's methods. "Jack Kevorkian is on a rampage," Quill and Betty Rollin wrote in the *New York Times* in 1996. "Many who believe in doctor-assisted suicide are as horrified by what he is doing as those on the other side of the debate."[31] Touching off this attack was the news, disturbing to many, that Kevorkian had assisted the suicide of Judith Curren, a forty-two-year-old nurse with chronic fatigue syndrome, a history of psychiatric problems, and a troubled marriage. Even Kevorkian admitted that if he had known more about the domestic problems he might have been slower to help. Quill and Rollin contended: "It takes time for a careful assessment of a patient. Dr. Kevorkian seems to be the sole proprietor of a quick-fix death store. His expertise is in methods of death, not in managing pain or in considering the wish to die."[32]

By this time Kevorkian had been acquitted of murder and assisted suicide three times by Michigan juries, convincingly demonstrating to many people that the law needed to be changed and safeguards promulgated. But, as we report in later chapters, although the Ninth and Second Circuit Courts of Appeals—arguably two of the most important courts in the nation— recommended changes, the U.S. Supreme Court lacked the mettle when confronted with the issue in 1997. It would not be in good taste for lawyers to argue so in court, but the effect of the judges' obstinacy was to drive the practice of medically and privately assisted suicides further underground. One indication of the extent of this covert behavior was that *Final Exit* was selling a thousand copies a month even six years after bursting onto the scene, and 1997 saw the publication of a revised second edition, which sold at an even higher rate. Moreover, a clear demonstration of public opinion—other than opinion polls—were the two occasions over three years in which Oregon voters insisted on reform, as we shall report in later chapters.

Kevorkian's essential contribution to the right-to-die movement was the enormous scope of the publicity he attracted. At times he was on every radio and television bulletin. The Hemlock Society, through its books, conferences, and appearances on serious television like *60 Minutes* and *Nightline*, had alerted the better-educated section of the American public to the issue, but Kevorkian reached everybody, regardless of their education and interests. He was a household name in the English-speaking world and also famous in other countries. Humphry believes that Kevorkian's role in making all Americans aware of the right-to-die issue was a crucial factor in the ballot initiative victories in Oregon, even if the new law lacked the scope they both wanted. Quill presented the gentle, thoughtful face of compassionate medicine, but, even though he never approached Kevorkian's level of public visibility, his philosophy seemed to be the one most likely to succeed in the long term in the United States.

The Dutch Experiment

The universal test laboratory for euthanasia has been the Netherlands, making U.S. efforts look like mere baby steps. First moves toward permitting assisted deaths were taken there in the early 1970s, were sanctioned by the Supreme Court in 1984, and finally approved by Parliament in 1993. The rules are refined constantly. No one could accuse the Dutch of rushing covertly into the practice of euthanasia: Over some thirty years they have called numerous commissions of inquiry, held conferences, carried out academic studies, taken doctors to court to ascertain whether they broke any rules, and made themselves available for critical studies by visiting foreign medical experts and writers.

Termination of life is now in three categories:

- termination of life at the request of the patient (euthanasia);
- assisted suicide: The doctor supplies a drug which the patient administers to himself or herself;
- termination of life without a request from the patient.

All three actions are felonies under the criminal code, with penalties ranging from a fine to life imprisonment for murder. But doctors in the Netherlands are for the most part not prosecuted, under a doctrine called *force majeure*—necessity or duress—because of the conflict between their duty to preserve life and their duty not to allow the patient to suffer. There must be clear exonerating circumstances before immunity from prosecution is granted, and even then the doctor must have obeyed preordained criteria, and also made the statutory notification of an unnatural death, giving full reasons for the action taken.

The criteria a doctor must observe are:

- The patient must have made voluntary, carefully considered, and persistent requests [to his doctor] for euthanasia.
- The attending physician must know the patient well enough to assess whether the request is indeed voluntary and whether it is well considered.
- A close doctor-patient relationship is a prerequisite for such an assessment.
- According to prevailing medical opinion, the patient's suffering must be unbearable and without prospect of improvement.
- The doctor and the patient must have considered and discussed alternatives to euthanasia.
- The attending physician must have consulted at least one other physician with an independent viewpoint who must have read the medical records and seen the patient.
- Euthanasia must have been performed by a doctor in accordance with good medical practice.

In a country with a total population of fifteen million, and about 130,000 deaths a year, surveys ordered by the government indicate that 2,300 people annually die via euthanasia, with a further 400 dying by assisted suicide.

The essential difference between how the Dutch have handled the debate in comparison to the Americans is that, early on, the Dutch government and medical and legal institutions recognized the extent of public sympathy for euthanasia, proceeding immediately to examine the situation and seek solutions. In the United States—as well as in most other Western countries—the government and institutions have instinctively and immediately opposed dealing with the subject, except when forced to by the pressure of events, such as the new Oregon law, Doctor Kevorkian's actions, or some legal cause célèbre such as *Quinlan* or *Cruzan*, which aroused public awareness. Once those matters were dropped from the headlines, it was back to the status quo. The knee-jerk reaction of the establishment has been to say that any form of assisted death is never acceptable, thus stifling inquiry into ethical and practical problems, and development of safeguards.

In contrast, the Dutch personality generally is one that likes to solve problems, not avoid them. Their history as a great international trading nation obligated them to develop a sense of fair play and tolerance of contrary views in other countries or else they would not have prospered as they did. Atheism and agnosticism are not only tolerated but widespread in the Netherlands. The Roman Catholic Church in that country is the most liberal and freethinking internationally, with some Catholic priests occasionally in supportive attendance at instances of voluntary euthanasia by doctors. It is a nation that has legalized, supervised voluntary female prostitution, in contrast to the United States, where it remains a severely punishable crime. Small amounts of recreational "soft" drugs, such as marijuana, are permitted to be sold under controlled conditions in coffee shops. Judges, appointed for life, cannot be removed except in the most exceptional circumstances; thus they are able to render unpopular judgments without fear of losing their positions. Parliament is elected by proportional representation—political parties get legislative seats according to the amount of votes received—a system which allows members with unorthodox viewpoints to win seats, and sometimes access to political power.

A significant factor separating the United States and the Netherlands is the quality, extent, and availability of health care. The Dutch have one of the best systems in the world, free to rich and poor alike, and funded by all taxpayers. No one is deprived of appropriate medical care. By contrast, the United States has an estimated thirty-seven million persons without health-care benefits.[1] This brings up the troubling argument, frequently made by critics of euthanasia, that the uninsureds are vulnerable to having their deaths hastened because there may be no one to foot the bills for expensive or long-term care. Proponents of assisted dying answer that death cannot be induced without first obeying strict legal safeguards, including examinations by two doctors; thus persons without doctors will not be eligible. With a socialized medical system, which eliminates any criticism that they hasten deaths to save money, the Dutch have never hesitated to institute acceler-ated death procedures that include both voluntary euthanasia and PAS. Most of those who get hastened deaths (2.3 percent of all deaths) opt for euthanasia—injection of lethal drugs—to take advantage of its quickness and certainty. Only 0.4 percent choose assisted suicide—drinking a lethal elixir—because it is sometimes slower.[2]

In the process of euthanasia the doctor physically administers the coup de grace with a hypodermic syringe, so the ultimate power lies with the physician. This control could, some argue, be abused. With assisted suicide the doctor agrees to provide the drugs, leaving the patient to make the final decision whether and when to ingest them by mouth, reducing the likelihood of abuse. (Dutch doctors supply the actual drugs in the form of an elixir; in the United States the plan appears to be that the doctor will provide a prescription only, not the drugs, although some Oregon doctors are arguing for close and continuing supervision, which that law permits.) For these reasons—the doctor distancing him- or herself from the act, the patient making the final decision—it is likely that the United States will legalize assisted suicide many years before voluntary euthanasia. The two serious drawbacks to this limited form of hastened death are that patients unable to ingest oral drugs must unfairly continue to suffer, and unless the patient takes adequate antiemetics beforehand, the lethal drugs may be vomited.

Many Dutch medical practitioners of hastened death, like Dr. Pieter Admiraal and Dr. Herbert Cohen, who for thirty years have each helped up to a hundred people die, urge that the United States should not copy their system. Chief among their arguments is the very different operating methods of health care in the two countries. The Netherlands being a small country both in population (fifteen million) and geographical size, possessing fairly stable and homogenous communities, doctors and patients tend to come to know each other over many years, often a lifetime. When death is approaching, the matter of how it shall eventually take place is more like a shared decision between friends than the relative coldness and brevity of the American doctor-patient relationship. The United States (population 265 million), has a geographically scattered, culturally diverse population, affording the opportunity to become acquainted with doctors only when sick, and then only cursorily because of time and money pressures. Additionally, a terminal patient is likely to be in the care of several specialists, with none as the familiar friend and counselor.

Particularly distinguishing the Dutch approach to hastened death from the American way is that, from the beginning of its development in the 1970s, organized medicine and pharmacology in the Netherlands were willing to join the debate. The turning point came in 1984 when the Royal Dutch Medical Association announced its sympathy with accelerated death, provided there were sensible guidelines. The Royal Dutch Society for the Advancement of Pharmacy soon followed. The medical professionals' group acknowledged that euthanasia was already taking place covertly, making it necessary to define its legality and guidelines immediately. Within a few months the Dutch Supreme Court ruled in the so-called *Alkmaar* case, taking the view that the appeals court that had convicted a doctor for helping a ninety-five-year-old woman in poor health, with a fractured hip, had not properly considered whether he had any alternatives. The judges in an unusual move ruled that the primary judgment in a hastened-death case should rest with doctors, while the judgment as to whether it was lawful remained the duty of society. Where there was a conflict of facts in a case, they ruled that criminal courts should decide the issue.[3] Between 1981 and 1995, twenty-nine doctors were prosecuted either for flagrant violation of the criteria rules (outlined earlier in this chapter), or to establish a better legal and practical understanding of how the rules should be implemented. Most were acquitted, while six received suspended sentences, four were acquitted with a fine, and one was found guilty but not punished. None went to prison.[4]

Dutch people and doctors appear, in general, to be satisfied with the way euthanasia currently operates. *U.S. News & World Report* in a January 1997 article that tended to be more critical than sympathetic, reported that "Dutch faith in euthanasia remains strong. Polls consistently show that about 80 percent favor it, up from 44 percent in the early 1970s." But there have been problems, which, to their credit, the Dutch have made public and been willing to work to rectify. Foremost among the problems discovered by researchers was that about a thousand patients a year were helped by doctors to die without the explicit request of the patient.[5] This procedure was not included in the guidelines given to doctors. Opponents of euthanasia around the world were quick to pounce on this statistic as proof of the "slippery slope"—permitting some kinds of euthanasia inevitably leading to doctors using the practice more extensively, most likely with comatose patients. But the researchers replied that a breakdown of the thousand cases showed that half of such patients had requested euthanasia before they became incompetent, while in the other half the termination of life was discussed with family, friends, and other medical staff.

Right-to-die spokespeople pointed out that the same sort of "mercy killing" went on in other countries but went unnoticed because nobody looked for it. They claimed that if American doctors were given confidentiality and indemnity from prosecution, similar to Dutch doctors, research would find the same statistics. Over the next few years, more intensive research was done in the Netherlands into what the Dutch call "Ending of Life Without Explicit Request." A report that studied the situation from 1990 to 1995 found that, among physicians interviewed, "23 percent said that at some time they had ended a patient's life without his or her explicit request, and 32 percent said they had never done so but that they could conceive of a situation in which they could, whereas 45 percent said they had never done so and could not conceive of a situation in which they would."[6] The amount of life lost by these patients, mostly cancer sufferers, was not large. "In 33 percent of cases life was shortened by 24 hours at the most, and in a further 58 percent it was shortened by at most one week," said the researchers, who concluded that, while requests for euthanasia and assisted suicide had increased slightly in the previous five years, this was due to a growth in the aged population.[7] The Dutch had lifted a stone in a gray area in the practice of medicine that not only they, but medicine worldwide, should address seriously. In 1998 the Dutch were planning to issue new guidelines to cover the cases of unrequested accelerated death.

Reporting how many deaths were hastened has been another problem in the Netherlands. How well or how badly the guidelines work cannot be assessed unless the authorities know to what extent the practice takes place, by whom, and in what type of cases. Here again, when they realized how few cases were coming to the attention of the coroners or the prosecutors, the Dutch took administrative steps to improve this. Notification of cases of euthanasia and PAS were a mere 18 percent in 1990, but rose to 41 percent in 1995 as new reporting requirements were introduced. This was still not good enough. The willingness of doctors to take part in surveys and answer detailed questions demonstrated that they wanted something done to improve reporting, but finding the answer was difficult.

Some doctors did not report such cases through fear of prosecution and of being subjected to a possible court trial in the unwelcome glare of publicity. Others either did not want the trouble of being examined by officials or felt it was an intrusion into the privacy of the patient-doctor relationship. Not a few argued that the appropriate time for review of whether a person should be helped to die was before the act, not after. There was another serious division of opinion between coroners and public prosecutors as to which body of officials should be the reviewers of cases. In 1996 the government suggested a system of medical panels should do the reviewing, but this was met without enthusiasm when the administrative time and effort was calculated. From November 1998 the Dutch government ordered doctors to report all hastened death cases to one of five regional committees. The committees, made up of legal, medical, and ethics experts, will ensure that proper criteria are observed and investigated if they are not.

Does a mentally ill person have as much right to assisted suicide as a physically ill person? That question has always dogged the right-to-die movement. Some argue that psychic suffering is just as, or more, painful and distressing than the physical suffering from a disease of the physical body. Therefore, such persons deserve help to die if, after careful assessment, there is no cure or satisfactory treatment. Anyway, the argument goes, they will often end up killing themselves in a messy way, perhaps hurting others in the act of self-destruction.

The contrary argument is that most mental illness, including depression, can nowadays be treated with therapy or drugs, or both. There is always an outside chance of recovery; perhaps a cure lies in the future, whereas a person suffering from, say, advanced cancer, will be deteriorating as the body ceases to function properly, and is certain to die in the not too distant future. Moreover, do we yet know enough about the human mind to sanction assisted death for those with poor mental health? As a last resort, if their suffering is so severe that they are suicidal, they have the physical ability to kill themselves, whereas the terminal patient is frequently too weak or bedridden.

It will not happen any time soon that the United States sanctions assisted death for mentally troubled people. It is not part of the American right-to-die movement's credo to fight for such a procedure, absorbed as they are with the complex task of getting help for the obviously dying person. People on both sides of the argument—except for the deeply religious—generally agree that a person has a moral right to suicide, an act that is no longer against the law.

But the Dutch are forever pushing the ethical boundaries, regardless of what the rest of the world thinks. From the very beginning of the development of procedures for hastened death, they have included mental suffering in their parameters, although the predominant emphasis has been on physical illness. In a series of 1970s lectures, Dutch experts frequently addressed the mental health issue in euthanasia, saying that it was rare but permissible legally and morally. A landmark court case in Rotterdam in 1981 laid down ten rules for noncriminal assistance in dying which included the provision:

"There must be physical *or mental* suffering which the sufferer finds unbearable." The court also said that a person seeking aid in dying "need not be a dying person. Paraplegics can request and get aid in dying."[8] When the Dutch Parliament in 1993 approved guidelines for physicians to report assisted deaths to the coroner, it included a clause posing the question: "Was the patient's mental and/or physical suffering so great that he or she perceived it, or could have perceived it, as unbearable?"[9] The Royal Dutch Medical Association in its policy statements has also stated that mental health may be taken into consideration.

But such cases were few and at first received no public attention. A Dutch psychiatrist writing in 1994 in the *Journal of Crisis Intervention and Suicide Prevention* let drop the little-known fact that, "Recently, some cases have been brought before court where psychiatrists have assisted with suicide by psychiatric patients, or by persons where there was uncertainty about their status as psychiatric patients."[10] But no evidence has emerged that these cases are growing in number.

The focus of this particular debate became the case of *The State* v. *Chabot*, which concerned a psychiatrist named Dr. Boudewijn Chabot who in 1993 had provided lethal drugs to a troubled woman so that she could kill herself. He reported it dutifully to the coroner as an unnatural death. The woman was fifty-year-old Hilly Bosscher, a severely depressed woman who had good reason to be tired of life. Her husband was an alcoholic, and they separated after a miserable marriage. In 1986 one son shot himself, and in 1991 her second son died of lung cancer. The night of the second death Mrs. Bosscher tried to kill herself with drugs. She had spells in the hospital and extensive counseling, but they did not help her. Mrs. Bosscher was convinced that she wanted to die, and that drugs were the only acceptable method. She arranged for her own burial plot between her two sons. When she approached the Dutch Society for Voluntary Euthanasia for help about drugs, the staff referred her to Doctor Chabot. He saw her several times over a month in 1991, kept extensive records of the consultations, and submitted his notes to seven other experts in psychiatric disorders. Five of them agreed with Chabot that the woman's situation was hopeless, one opining that her eventual suicide was inevitable. Slightly more than a year after their first meeting, Doctor Chabot agreed to help Mrs. Bosscher die, taking lethal drugs to her at home, where she died in his presence, as well as in the presence of a colleague and one of her friends. Before he handed over the drugs he asked her if she wished to change her mind, but she replied that she remained firmly resolved to die.[11]

Here was an example of the type of case that the Dutch authorities decided, in order to get clarification, must go for trial by judge. There is no jury system in the Netherlands. In the regional court in Assen, Doctor Chabot argued that he was faced with conflicting duties—to save her life on the one hand, and to respect her wishes on the other hand. In his opinion his was a reasonable choice that was scientifically and medically acceptable. The court felt that the crucial issue was whether Mrs. Bosscher's suffering was unbearable and hopeless, thus an "emergency situation." It concluded from the facts that it was. Treatment would have lasted three to five years, and could only be expected to have limited benefit. In addition, the patient's refusal of treatment made complete or partial recovery impossible. The court agreed with Doctor Chabot that if he had not helped her, Mrs. Bosscher would have killed herself in a horrible manner.

The court regarded Doctor Chabot's consultation with seven other experts as adequate and rejected the prosecution's contention that he had not deliberated long enough over this patient's consultations. Chabot's decision to help Mrs. Bosscher commit suicide was regarded as reasonable under the circumstances, so the court freed him from the indictment.[12] Still not satisfied, the prosecution took the case to the Leeuwarden Court of Appeals, which confirmed the lower court's decision.

The case moved up to the Dutch Supreme Court, in The Hague, which was more critical. The judges here found him guilty of the criminal offense of assisted suicide because they felt he had not followed the rules for careful practice of the procedure by arranging personal contact between Mrs. Bosscher and another psychiatrist. Yet they imposed no penalty. Legal observers considered the fact that Doctor Chabot was not punished in any way as being tantamount to the court's approval of assisted suicide in severe psychiatric cases.

Another step. But was it down the notorious slippery slope or toward more progressive medical understanding of and dealing with suffering?

Published opinions in the United States—the few that there were—were critical. A physician who supports assisted suicide for a dying person, Dr. Samuel C. Klagsbrun, said in a letter:

> Even in this age of biological psychiatry, I feel very strongly that giving up on human beings, with respect to psychiatric treatments, and helping them to die, is unacceptable. We have to continue to reach every individual even in the face of major obstacles. That is not to say that some individuals, because of personality disorders, are not committed to a need to defeat treatment. The obstinate symptoms of these individuals, frequently presenting themselves as depressed, can frustrate the efforts of a physician. Assisted suicide, however, is not an option.[13]

In his nationally syndicated ethics column, Arthur Caplan, director of the Center for Bioethics at the University of Pennsylvania, commented: "The Dutch have now slipped down the slope to the point where mental suffering is a sufficient basis for allowing a doctor to kill. It is a morally frightening place for the public policy of any nation to be." Doctor Caplan claimed that Doctor Chabot agreed to help Mrs. Bosscher to die "less than 24 hours after meeting her," but this does not jibe with the court evidence that they had known each other for fourteen months. And, as reported earlier in this chapter, from the outset the Dutch standards have always included mental suffering as justifiable, which fact denies any claim of the slippery slope.

It is one thing for ethicists to pontificate from their desk or in the media about theoretical standards and practices, but another for a treating physician to be faced in the consulting room with a desperately ill patient. "I do not know if I made the right choice," Chabot was quoted as saying, "but I believe I opted for the lesser of two evils."[14] While his was the test case, further proof later emerged that it was not a solitary occurrence. In a survey carried out in 1997 by the Dutch Department of Public Health of Dutch psychiatrists, twelve (or 6 percent) admitted that they had agreed to help a person with a mental disorder to die, although in some of the cases the person also had a terminal disease. While two-thirds of the polled psychiatrists said that assisted suicide was acceptable for some severe cases of mental disorder, most said that treatment was preferable.[15]

The Dutch government, irked by uninformed foreign criticisms, supplies its embassies around the world with clarification documents on euthanasia. These documents are available to the public in many languages. A web page on the Internet in English briefs visitors with the same materials. Dutch experts on euthanasia—doctors, philosophers, and academic researchers—regularly attend international conferences to explain what is happening in their country, to be questioned, and to hear criticisms. When one listens to their quiet, deliberate, self-effacing talks at seminars, it seems that the Dutch do not realize how unique and pragmatic they are. That they have done something courageous and quite exceptional in the world apparently does not occur to them. Regulated, justifiable, voluntary euthanasia is, they consider, the only human approach, but the concept was proving to be a hard sell in other parts of the world.

Chapter 11

The World's Problem

Whether or not there is a right, when terminally ill, to be able to die with medical help either by voluntary euthanasia or PAS is by no means a purely American or Dutch debate. It has its own peculiarities in the United States, connected to the lack of homogeneity in a huge population of 265 million, absence of universal health care, and a daunting number of states with a complex variety of laws governing the subject. But there are also some forty organizations around the globe fighting in their respective nations to educate and legitimize aid in dying. With the exception of India, Colombia, and Zimbabwe, they are all located in highly developed countries.

A few fortunate nations do not have the problem—at least legally. Switzerland's laws have permitted assisted suicide since 1937, provided it is for the relief of terminal suffering and carried out for compassionate and altruistic motives. The Swiss Academy of Medical Sciences opposes doctors actively helping patients to die, but it nevertheless supports the principle and practice of "double effect"—administering morphine to relieve all pain despite the risk of accelerating death. In a population of seven million, there are between 100 and 120 cases of hastened death every year. Doctors carry out some 20, the rest are effected by family and friends. There has never been a prosecution.[1] Although discretion on this matter has been around in their country for a long time, many Swiss realize that they possess a precarious right that opponents would not hesitate to strike down. Consequently, in the last twenty years, two right-to-die organizations have sprung up; the largest, EXIT, has more than sixty thousand members—three times the size of Hemlock in the United States.

Japan is a contradiction. As most people know, past and present, suicide is neither forbidden nor a taboo. While the act no longer has the official and religious sanction—even glorification—it had in ancient times, or even in World War II, the Japanese people generally understand and tolerate self-destruction by an individual. As a society they no longer promote it. Strange as it may seem, given this tolerance, voluntary euthanasia and PAS for the terminally ill are veritable taboos. Worse, many people still are allowed to die without being told that they are terminal, although this practice is declining. Heart transplants are rare. Overuse of life-support systems for the hopelessly ill is a major problem. To the horror of much of the public, Emperor Hirohito in 1989, at the age of eighty-seven, suffering from advanced pancreatic cancer, was kept alive by machinery and drugs for 111 days after he would have died naturally.[2] Every medical procedure carried out on the old man was reported in detail in the daily newspapers and on television. This protracted and macabre medical death of so highly respected a figurehead produced a national revolution in attitudes to dying: For instance, within a short time the membership of the Japan Society for Dying with Dignity had leaped from three thousand to eighty thousand.

Voluntary euthanasia has been legal in Japan since 1962. That year the High Court of Central Japan, located in Nagoya, issued a ruling in the *Yamanouchi* case in which a son had killed his suffering father. The three judges ruled that death by euthanasia was lawful if these six conditions were met:

1. The patient's condition must be a terminal one (meaning incurable) with no hope of recovery and death imminent;
2. The patient is being forced to endure unbearable pain (to look at the patient suffering from that pain is totally and utterly unbearable for others);
3. Euthanasia must have the purpose of alleviating the patient's suffering;
4. Euthanasia can only be undertaken at the request or with the permission of the patient (the patient's genuine request or permission should be provided);
5. A doctor must perform the task of euthanasia;
6. The method of euthanasia must be ethically acceptable. It is concerned with the legality or ethical acceptance of methods of euthanasia.

The conditions set out here are taken verbatim from a talk given by one of the three judges in the *Yamanouchi* case, Kaoru Narita, now retired from the bench, to the ninth international conference of the World Federation of Right to Die Societies, held in Kyoto, Japan, in October 1992.

Judge Narita commented that "It was the first case in the world where the court actually enunciated the legality or legal acceptability of euthanasia." He pointed out that even thirty years later the Japan Medical Association did not support active euthanasia. Euthanasia, he continued, was "very closely intermingled with the issue of life, and therefore there is some risk and danger of misuse or abuse. While admitting such risks and dangers, we need to make

the utmost effort for establishing the most stringent requirement for euthanasia. When it comes to the implementation of the requirements, humanity
should not be forgotten since it is the very foundation."[3]

It is completely unknown how often euthanasia takes place in Japan.
Given the ethical and religious rules and taboos that govern that society, it
probably happens very rarely, and then only in great secrecy. What is known
from several well-publicized prosecutions is that doctors who accelerate a
death without clear permission from the patient quickly find themselves in
trouble with the law.

Not unlike Japan, Germany has legal procedures allowing hastened
death, but the taboos are so strong that they are rarely used. There has not
been a law forbidding assistance in suicide in Germany, provided the motive
was altruistic, for more than two hundred years. It was decriminalized by
Frederick the Great in 1751, given the conditions that the person seeking
assisted death must be rational and acting out of free choice. (Direct killing
by euthanasia is a crime in Germany.) But getting PAS remains a forbidding
task. The combination of strong religious opposition and the haunting legacy
of the genocidal Nazi "euthanasia program" during World War II renders it
virtually unobtainable unless privately negotiated in great secrecy. One man
who tested the law was the late Professor Julius Hackethal, a cancer specialist. On several occasions he announced that he had provided cyanide to
people suffering from cancer, on one occasion issuing a video of a woman
dying in this manner. Attempts by law enforcement authorities to stop him
failed completely.

Elsewhere in the world, notably Australia and Colombia, the struggle to
legalize and regulate assistance in dying has so far been a stuttering process.
Australia has shown remarkable involvement and progress in securing the
right to choose to die. From the early 1970s—a decade before the United
States and Canada—it had small but dynamic voluntary euthanasia groups
struggling to educate its population with a view to law reform. This special
interest in dying apparently stems from the toughness of much of Australian
family life; with huge distances in the Outback separating homes and hospitals, the people have been forced to deal themselves with the death of
loved ones instead of—as so often occurs in the United States—shipping
them off to nursing homes and hospitals. Second, the pioneering, "handle-
problems-yourself" spirit of the vast Outback generated an interest in knowing how to kill oneself if terminal suffering became unbearable.

So it was no surprise to many people when Australia became the first
country in the world actually to legalize euthanasia by statute, albeit in one
small territory that had not yet qualified to be a full state. The nation comprises a federal government, five full states, and three territories that will

eventually become states. These territories have their own elected legislatures and are largely self-governing, but—as the Northern Territory was to find, to its chagrin—the federal government can override some of its decisions.

Although the Northern Territory is twice the size of Texas, its population is a mere 170,000, of whom 27 percent consists of Aboriginal people. On an average, death comes earlier here than in the rest of the country—at fifty-three for men and sixty-four for women—while infant mortality, at 11.3 deaths per 1,000 live births, is nearly twice the national rate. Thus in terms of quality health care and longevity, particularly lacking for the Aborigines, it was not the ideal place to start.

As is often the case, the impetus for reform came from one person who gathered support among colleagues for a universal idea—the right to choose to die if suffering unbearably. Marshall Perron, the chief minister of the territory, had no personal experience of painful death to influence him when he made the first moves to change the law; he was impressed by the intellectual arguments put forward in a paper by Dr. Helga Kuhse, published by the Australian Medical Association (AMA), "Medically Assisted Dying for Competent Patients."[4] The paper had been given at a conference called by the AMA on August 11, 1994, in Canberra, the capital. Perron also read the papers arguing against any form of euthanasia. The one in favor that impressed him most was the paper by Kuhse, director of the Center for Bioethics at Monash University, Melbourne. "[It was] so compelling, so absolute in its logic and good sense, it motivated me to try and do something about it," he has said.[5]

In a mere seventeen pages, Kuhse, with a clarity and rationality befitting her training in philosophy, surveyed the arguments for and against doctor-assisted death, concluding:

What is to be done? It seems that at least one option is open to us: to adopt a public policy approach that is based on mutual respect of freedom or autonomy. This is not a morally arbitrary approach. Personal autonomy or freedom is a very important moral value, and central to what it means to be a person and a moral agent. It follows from this acceptance of the value of autonomy that persons should be free to pursue their vision of "the good life" and that it is inappropriate for the state to either adopt a paternalistic stance towards its mature citizens, or to restrict their freedom through the enforcement of a particular moral point of view. Only if one person's actions cause harm to others will it be legitimate for the state to step in, and to bring in laws that restrict individual liberty. . . . It is inappropriate that the law or the policies of medical associations should enshrine a particular moral point of view. Public policies should be based on respect for autonomy, where people who approach questions of the good life from different moral, cultural, and religious perspectives are provided with a moral space that allows them to live their lives in accordance with their values and beliefs.

Perron personally wrote the first draft of the Rights of the Terminally Ill Act, then showed it to his staff. To his delight he found they were totally supportive and eager to get it passed. Perron shrewdly planned a step-by-step campaign in order to keep misreporting and misunderstandings to a minimum. First, in February 1995, he released a draft bill accompanied by detailed notes explaining every clause. This went to the media, all the territory's politicians, and some three hundred organizations and individuals. The recipients were not merely medical people but a broad band of public-interest organizations. Perron was seeking an informed public debate once the controversy broke; to a large extent he succeeded.

Horrified, the AMA, church groups, and right-to-life organizations reacted strongly. Within days euthanasia became the foremost news topic in the nation, continuing as such for the next two years.

"When the campaign was at its peak, they [opposing groups] resorted to dishonest claims and statements which probably worked against their interests, because by this time the community was well versed in the issues," says Perron. "The initial public reaction was somewhat as I had anticipated although the expressions of support were in stronger terms and more voluminous than I expected. I have letters from people who, through love and compassion, have killed a parent to free them from a tortuous existence, regretful only that they did not respond to the pleas to die earlier."[5]

Next, a parliamentary committee was established to receive submissions, for and against euthanasia, from anyone who cared to come forward. But Perron has said that he does not think a single member of the committee underwent a change of mind on the subject despite the voluminous evidence of hundreds of submissions and questioning dozens of witnesses from either side: "There are not a lot of 'swingers' in this debate, and I also believe that almost all those who oppose the decriminalization of voluntary euthanasia are religiously motivated. While people will give you all the hypothetical slippery slope reasons for their opposition, the facts are that they will never agree to voluntary euthanasia even if you suggest an absurd level of safeguards."[6]

As the bill reached the territory's parliament, Perron, anxious to gain as much consensus as possible, accepted amendments that he saw were needed to gain a sufficient number of "yes" votes. The elected members were now confronting the same dilemma as politicians all over the world when faced with a highly controversial issue: Many won their seats with a majority of 30 or 50 votes, which could vanish with even a minor church boycott if they supported law reform. Dogging the whole effort was "the race card." Perron did not have a great record in Aboriginal affairs, while those opposing euthanasia made great play with the perceived fears of the native people that this was a dangerous piece of law for them. Support began to slip away.

When the crucial vote came to the floor of the Parliament, it was left to a conscience vote, with no party restrictions or personal loyalties involved. It squeaked by 13–12 on May 25, three months after its introduction. Soon after, it was amended to require a psychiatrist to be formally involved in the euthanasia decision-making process. The law required a working group of officials to draw up regulations for the implementation of the new act, to ensure that adequate hospice facilities were available to those who wanted them, and to draft education programs for the public, the medical profession and the sizable Aborigine population.

The first person to request death under the new act was Bob Dent, who had suffered from prostate cancer for five years, had undergone numerous surgeries, was impotent, unable to urinate, and losing bowel control. Despite heavy analgesic medication, he still suffered considerable pain. Dr. Philip Nitschke, a local doctor, offered to help Dent die.

Having satisfied detailed and complex legal conditions for assisting a suicide, Doctor Nitschke then connected Dent to an apparatus comprising a bottle of lethal drugs linked to a laptop computer. The computer asked him three questions, all restatements of the same question, "Do you know what you are doing?" This was to demonstrate that the patient was conscious and able to interact, demonstrating informed consent. The last message on the little screen warned that if the patient pressed the spacebar the drugs would kick in automatically and he or she would die. Dent chose death.

Doctor Nitschke's apparatus was a more sophisticated version of Doctor Kevorkian's machine, substituting computer-asked questions for verbal ones and a keyboard spacebar for a button. Both doctors found helping people to die emotionally draining, but were helped to cope with the stress by the remote mechanisms (Kevorkian's a button, Nitschke's a laptop) that forced the patient to make the final decision to die.

Always something of a rebel against the establishment, Doctor Nitschke came onto the euthanasia scene as a result of a challenge. He heard on the radio that the AMA claimed that no doctor in the Northern Territory would implement Perron's new law. Not only did he step forward, but he encouraged twenty other doctors to join him in making a statement of support for the principles behind the law. The twenty placed a newspaper advertisement proclaiming their support for the new law.

The Vatican soon described Dent's death as "an absurd act of total cruelty." Cardinal Edward Clancy, head of the Roman Catholic Church in Australia, said: "This first case of legalized euthanasia in all the world is an act of reckless disregard for the convictions of people around the globe, and will be widely condemned."[7] The territory's Catholic bishop said it was immoral. Mrs. Dent said it was what her husband wanted.

In the battle to get it passed, the law had undergone several changes. For instance, it allowed dying people from other parts of Australia to come to the Northern Territory to avail themselves of the procedure, yet only the four hundred-odd doctors based in the territory could carry it out. Then it was realized that there were so few psychiatrists in the territory that an amendment had to be made to allow psychiatry professionals from outside to be used, or the law would never work. One of the arguments against the passage of the law was that, since it allowed dying people from other states to travel to the Northern Territory to die, it was in effect legislating euthanasia for all of Australia, for which, of course, it had no mandate.

The whole country soon became embroiled in the euthanasia controversy. In October of the same year, the New South Wales Parliament had a "conscience debate" on the topic—without an actual bill before it—which resulted in forty speakers against, and ten in favor. "Not one of the [Labour] party's dominant Catholic Right broke ranks," reported the *Weekend Australian* on October 19, 1996. "If they were inclined to do so, they had the good sense to keep their mouths shut."

In the South Australia Parliament a month later, private members' bills were introduced. One would permit voluntary euthanasia, and the other sought a referendum on the principle. These began to wend their way through the labyrinth of state politics.

An opinion poll in the Northern Territory found that 46 percent of the public supported their new right to choose to die, compared to 14 percent of doctors and 33 percent of nurses. Disapproval rate for doctors was 28 percent against 8 percent of the public.[8] The AMA surveyed its three thousand doctors, of whom almost two thousand responded, to see if its strong opposition to euthanasia was supported. "Doctors overwhelmingly believed that existing laws [prohibiting euthanasia] rarely interfered with the best management of dying patients," said Dr. Keith Wollard, the AMA president.[9]

The battle to make or break the Northern Territory's vanguard law now shifted to Canberra, Australia's federal capital. Church groups intensified their objections, chiefly on the grounds that hastened death defiled the sanctity of life. The AMA branded it as totally unethical and destructive of the traditional truthfulness between doctor and patient. "Voluntary euthanasia is simply legalized killing," the AMA said in a statement. The fires of the controversy were constantly refueled by the highly publicized deaths under the act, all carried out by one doctor, Philip Nitschke, and the pathetic stories of other people who wanted to use the law but could not, for one reason or another.

A fundamentalist Christian faction, the Lyons Forum, which had played a significant part in the total rejection by the New South Wales Parliament of a similar euthanasia plan, now approached right-wing federal MPs offering to help pass a national law nullifying the Northern Territory's action. They found not only sympathy but a willingness to act immediately from Senator Kevin Andrews, a practicing Roman Catholic, father of five children, and a lawyer specializing in bioethics. Andrews was a stalwart of the Liberal Party, which believes the opposite of what it does in most other countries. Also throwing their weight publicly and politically behind the drive to destroy the law were the federal Prime Minister, John Howard; his deputy, Tim Fisher; and the leader of the Labour Party, Kim Beazley. With such powerful enemies the law was doomed.

Andrews introduced into the Australian federal parliament in September a private members' bill that overrode the two-month-old Northern Territory law. This set off a second debate across the nation: Should the federal parliament interfere with a law passed by a territory, even if the former clearly had the constitutional right to do so? It had never been done before, but then none of the three territories had previously passed a law that offended the ethical and religious sensitivities of so many across the country. The Andrews bill originally contained a draconian clause which would punish doctors retroactively if they had hastened a death before the federal bill was passed. After it was pointed out to him that this was not only unfair but also unconstitutional, Andrews removed the clause.

Addressing the House of Representatives in Canberra, Andrews criticized the Northern Territory for not introducing modern "refusal of treatment" legislation, and he declared that palliative care there was also totally inadequate. "Instead, the Northern Territory chose to bypass a caring response of all dying people and to legalize assisted suicide for a few," stated Andrews.[10] In fact, the law stated that no doctor must help a patient to die if palliative care options "were reasonably available," and the Northern Territory had hurriedly stepped up the availability of hospice care to comply with the law.

Andrews's supporters organized massive letter-writing campaigns to all MPs in both houses deploring the euthanasia law. This paid off handsomely when the House of Representatives voted by a margin of 91 to 38 for the Andrews bill in a "conscience vote"—one with no party restrictions. The representatives were told by Nick Dondas, member for the Northern Territory, that "The debate, in terms of amending the Self-Government Act, has really been driven by the Catholic society and the Catholic community of this country."[11] Other MPs asked why the federal parliament had given the territories self-government only to take it back after eighteen years.

By contrast with its opponents, the supporters of euthanasia were poorly organized and underfunded. Some of Australia's older voluntary euthanasia organizations, in New South Wales and Victoria, had spare funds but were not willing to use them to defend the Northern Territory's law, preferring to hoard the money for their own future campaigns. Better funding might have made a big difference to the federal Senate campaign. The right-to-die groups lacked the political experience and expertise needed to fight such an intensive, insider political battle, in which money talks and political trade-offs are made. Their only avenue for making their points against the Andrews bill was the news media, which reveled in the combat with scant regard for the serious nature of the debate.

Before the Senate took its all-important vote, a Senate committee began gathering evidence. It received an estimated ten thousand written submissions, far more than ever received by a parliamentary committee, demonstrating that the whole of Australia was involved in this debate.[12] The vast majority of the evidence was in fact personal opinions and individual experiences; what the debate shrieked out for were solid facts and figures. These were forthcoming from one source only, fortuitously arriving before the crucial Senate debate.

In February 1997 the *Medical Journal of Australia* published a paper, "End-of-Life Decisions in Australian Medical Practice".[13] The paper presented the results of a survey whose objective was to estimate the number of medical end-of-life decisions in Australia, to describe the characteristics of such decisions, and to compare these with medical end-of-life decisions in the Netherlands. The participants were a random sample of active medical practitioners across the country whose practices were likely to be dealing with nonacute patient deaths, and hence to be making medical end-of-life decisions. There was a good response rate of 64 percent from doctors, a section of the population known for its reluctance to reply to surveys.

The survey found that the percentage of all Australian deaths that involved a medical end-of-life decision were:

- Euthanasia, 1.8 percent (including physician-assisted suicide of 0.1 percent)
- Ending of a patient's life without patient's concurrent explicit request, 3.5 percent
- Withholding or withdrawing of potentially life-prolonging treatment, 28.6 percent
- Alleviation of pain with opioids in doses large enough that there was a probable life-shortening effect, 30.9 percent

The report went on to say that in 30 percent of all Australian deaths, a medical decision was made with the explicit intention of ending the patient's life, of which 4 percent responded directly to a request from the patient. Overall, Australia had a higher rate of ending life than did the Netherlands. The authors' conclusions were that Australian law had not prevented doctors from practicing euthanasia or making medical end-of-life decisions explicitly intended to hasten the patient's death without the patient's request.

Dr. Robert Marr, spokesman for the Coalition for Voluntary Euthanasia, commented: "I think the study shows that there is secret voluntary euthanasia going on in Australia, and what we need to do is bring this out into the open and have safeguards as the Northern Territory law allows."[14]

Around the same time, the Royal Australian College of Practitioners took a survey of 1,108 of its 10,000 members, which revealed that 56 percent supported euthanasia provided it was restricted to "the terminal stage of terminal illness." Some 68 percent said they felt euthanasia was an act of caring on the part of the doctor, and 45 percent declared that they wanted it for themselves if they were dying.[15] None of these surveys appeared to have any influence on the politicians who were intent on stopping euthanasia regardless of the arguments in its favor.

When the Andrews bill finally reached the parliamentary floor on 24 March 1997, the issue had been thoroughly thrashed out all across Australia, in public and in private. A last-minute attempt to get a national referendum on euthanasia was lost in the Senate, 56 votes to 15, setting the stage for the inevitable victory for the repeal bill. The final vote—again according to conscience, not party lines—was fairly close: 38 for the Andrews bill and 33 against. It was a clear victory for the opponents, but it also demonstrated a strong political support for legal euthanasia. For the first time it was obvious to the public where each politician stood on the issue. The long and bitter controversy had focused and educated many minds not hitherto cognizant of the euthanasia issue.

During the nine months of the implementation of the Northern Territory Rights of the Terminally Ill Act, four people were known to have chosen death under its terms, all helped by Doctor Nitschke, who was about the only doctor in the territory willing to treat drug addicts, who some thought would be better off dead. Like Doctor Kevorkian in the United States, Nitschke disliked the established medical profession, but, unlike Kevorkian, he meticulously obeyed the law with the goal of securing its wider and long-term acceptance. As the law did not obligate people to report assisted deaths, it is possible that other deaths took place, but this is not likely, given the intense scrutiny of the subject at the time, and the timidity of all doctors except Nitschke. More than fifty people were frustrated in their wish to make use of the law, sometimes because they could not travel the huge distance to the Northern Territory; often because they were very sick but not terminally ill; usually because they could not find the cooperative two doctors and the psychiatrist needed to qualify. Nitschke says: "Of the 50, one third were unhelpable because they would not have qualified; a third received some assistance, either by the law when it was in place, or illegally either before or after the law when it was in place; the last third either died or changed their minds during negotiations."[16] Given the intense spotlight and the brief period of the operation of the law, it was difficult to assess its true worth and feasibility.

The world was once again without any statutory euthanasia laws. Yet the fierce debate had shaken Australia, motivating many to try to get similar laws passed in their state, where the federal parliament did not have the power to nullify them. By the end of 1997 there were proposed laws before the parliaments of Tasmania, South Australia, and Western Australia, while in Victoria, considered to have one of the more progressive state parliaments and many socially conscious doctors, some of whom were openly practicing euthanasia, the chances of introducing and passing such a bill were considered good.

Thwarted by the repeal of the law, and steadfastly refusing to break the old existing laws, which, given his visibility in the campaign, would soon land him in legal trouble, Doctor Nitschke continued speaking out for the right to choose to die. "We emerged briefly into a period of light in the Territory, but thanks to the Kevin Andrews Bill, it seems we've been pushed back into the jungle," he said.[17]

While it was no surprise that some people in Australia had legalized euthanasia, if only briefly, the biggest shock of 1997 came with the announcement that the highest court in Colombia had also approved it. On May 20 the nation's Constitutional Court announced that by a vote of 6–3 it had ruled that "no person can be held criminally responsible for taking the life of a terminally ill patient who has given clear authorization to do so." The court defined "terminally ill" as a patient with cancer, kidney or liver failure, or AIDS, at the same time excluding patients with Lou Gehrig's, Parkinson's, or Alzheimer's diseases. Comatose patients were specifically ruled out, as were physically healthy people. Up to that point anyone killing a patient who was terminal had been liable for between six months' and three years' imprisonment.

Ironically, the change in the law came about because an individual went to court to try to strengthen the penalties for mercy killing. Jose Euripides Parra, a Bogotá lawyer, objected to a 1980 penal code mandating lesser prison sentences for mercy killing than for murder. His argument was not so much against euthanasia as that the Constitutional Court had no right to change laws, only to interpret them.

The Roman Catholic Church, to which the overwhelming number of Colombians belong, was staggered at the court's decision. Gino Concetti, a Catholic theologian said to be close to Pope John Paul II, wrote in the Vatican's semiofficial newspaper, L'Osservatore Romano, under the headline A PERVERSE HYPOCRISY: KILLING FOR MERCY, that the ruling that freedom from prosecution applied only to dying people able to make the request did not make it any more morally acceptable: "The fact that euthanasia would be carried out in a terminal stage and with consent of the patient does not change the nature of the act which is intrinsically perverse."[18]

Carlos Gavira, the chief justice of the court, said that the ruling was consistent with reforms passed by the national legislature in 1991, when the constitution was altered to give individuals more freedom of choice. He explained: "What the court did was simply to recognize what is already consecrated in the constitution: the autonomy of a person to decide whether to opt for euthanasia. What it means is that if a person has religious beliefs and regards this as reprehensible, he will have the liberty not to partake. But if the person doesn't have these kinds of beliefs, he can observe his rights legally."[19]

The surprise court ruling triggered a sudden discussion of the rights and needs of the dying, an issue which had remained dormant in predominantly Catholic Colombia (population 36 million). Civil divorce had been legalized only in the 1980s. The nation has had a right-to-die organization—the only one in South America—since 1972, the Foundation for the Right-to-Die With Dignity, but the group had no part in the court case. A delighted Beatriz Kopp de Gomez, the president, said: "At first we couldn't believe it. It was a real bombshell." Bogotá's main newspaper, *El Espectador*, carried out a poll in the country's four main cities and found that 53 percent of Colombians agreed with the court's ruling.[20]

Immediately, the Roman Catholic Church lodged an appeal against the decision of the court, calling it, in the words of Monsignor Dario Molina, bishop of Montería, "an attack on life which is especially monstrous in a society where we've lost all sense of direction because of so much violence."[21] The bishop was referring to the long-running battles between police and drug runners, and between the army and guerrillas. Once more the question arose of whether a nation may decently introduce euthanasia while there are other, more pressing problems, such as appalling violence in Colombia, lack of universal health care in the United States, and grinding poverty in India. Must the dying wait for a perfect society before they can obtain compassionate and lawful relief from their suffering?

Undeterred, on October 3 the Constitutional Court judges, by exactly the same margin, 6–3, affirmed their earlier decision. The court directed that the law should now go to the congress for detailed study and regulations to be adopted. How long this will take is not known; some cynics have said years, given the powerful opposition to its implementation. Until then, euthanasia in Colombia remains lawful in theory but not in practice.

All other nations retain criminal sanctions against voluntary euthanasia and PAS. Since 1986, France has even had a law forbidding the publication of literature giving advice about any form of suicide. It caused the French right-to-die organization, Association pour le Droit de Mourir dans la Dignité, to destroy its own literature on the subject. *Final Exit* remains on the list of banned books.

The biggest division between public opinion and establishment power, however, is in Britain, said to be the fountainhead of democracy, where a massive contradiction exists:

- Eighty-two percent of the public would like some form of lawful euthanasia to be available.[22]
- Seven times in sixty years, when presented with bills, Parliament has refused to legislate.

So great is the power of the Church of England, the official religion of the state since the time of King Henry VIII, that a few hours' polite debate on a bill is permitted in Parliament to keep up appearances of fairness to all, but the matter is then quietly dropped. Aiding and abetting the rejection of voters' opinions on this issue is the Roman Catholic Church in England, and much of the British Medical Association (BMA). Similar to the blanket opposition in the American Congress, it makes no difference which political party is in power in Britain, the answer is always negative. Timidity in tackling moral issues seems to be universal among politicians.

Like many others, the British establishment prefers to allow assisted deaths to be carried out covertly. A survey of physicians published in the *British Medical Journal* in 1994 showed that nearly a third of the nation's doctors who had been asked for active euthanasia gave lethal injections. A larger proportion—46 percent—would consider taking active steps to bring about a patient's death if it were legal to do so.[23]

Commented the Voluntary Euthanasia Society, founded in London in 1935 and still vainly laboring to change the law: "Voluntary euthanasia in Britain today takes place in a shadowy criminal world. Patients cannot always be sure they will get what they are asking for, and doctors are denied the open advice and support of their colleagues."[24]

Underlying almost all the opposition to euthanasia throughout the world is the Christian religion, in particular the hierarchies of the different denominations. Clearly their congregations are more divided, or the opinion polls could not show a majority of people supporting it. Consequently, the theological reasons for Christian opposition are worth examining.

PART THREE

Opposition
from the
Establishment

Religion Resists Change

Just as the right-to-die movement has been propelled forward by developments in American culture, backed by popular support, so have the forces of restraint provided a formidable check on the evolution of public policy. The institutions that have historically opposed an assisted death are arguably the most powerful in the nation—religion, the medical profession, and the government. Yet these institutions, the very core of the American establishment, are losing their grip on public opinion as the forces of activism begin to dominate the debate. Though weakening however, the establishment must never be underestimated. It is determined to prevent mentally competent terminally ill patients from enlisting the help of a physician in order to hasten their inevitable death. Each institution has its own agenda to promote and its own territory to protect, and combined they have the economic and political power to shape minds and issues.

Populist activism is largely propelled by the will and convictions of the people. These powerful restraints on the autonomy of the individual are weakening, says Hoefler, and death is now on the public agenda. Private individuals, medical professionals, hospital administrators, members of the clergy, and state legislators will have to find a way to cope. Moreover, forces of activism are combining to "slowly overcome countervailing pressures of restraint that have helped to keep the right to die off the agenda until recently. Currently, the forces of restraint are strong enough only to limit the scope of right-to-die policy and slow its development."[1]

Two clauses of the First Amendment deal with the subject of religion: The amendment mandates that "Congress shall make no law respecting an establishment of religion, or prohibiting the free exercise thereof." The first clause is referred to as "the establishment clause"; the second is the "free exercise clause." These clauses apply to state governments as well.

The tension between these two clauses often leaves the Court having to choose between competing values in religion cases. The general guide here is the concept of "neutrality," which requires that the government act to achieve only secular goals and that it achieve them in a religiously neutral manner. Unfortunately, situations arise in which government may have no choice but incidentally to help or hinder religious groups or practices.

Although the historical meaning of the clauses is unclear, the majority of Supreme Court decisions during the past sixty years have been consistent, holding that the "values protected by the religion clauses are fundamental aspects of liberty in our society and must be protected from both state and federal interference."[2]

Religious beliefs have had an impact on the right-to-die movement since well before the movement officially began with the *Quinlan* case in 1976. And when restrictions on religious beliefs exist, U.S. constitutional issues are raised automatically. The legal questions in these pre-*Quinlan* cases involved primarily the religious beliefs of Jehovah's Witnesses and Christian Scientists, long at odds with traditional medicine. The Jehovah's Witnesses religion forbids blood transfusions, whereas members of the Christian Science church refuse all medical treatment. The questions raised in these cases were: Is a court authorized to step in and stop a Jehovah's Witness from refusing blood transfusions or a Christian Scientist from refusing medical treatment, both of which may result in their deaths? Do people have a right to die for their religious beliefs?

Ever since the Christian Science Church was founded more than a century ago by Mary Baker Eddy, Christian Scientists have been in conflict with the medical profession and, more recently, the law. They believe in the power of prayer as the answer to all physical ailments, since the origin of such ailments is really mental in nature. Christian Scientists consider it hypocritical to place faith in prayer *and* medicine. There have been more than a few convictions of involuntary manslaughter, primarily against Christian Science parents, who relied on spiritual beliefs instead of medical treatment for children who subsequently died.

In these cases the pertinent clause of the First Amendment is "the free-exercise clause." The Supreme Court, since its inception, has consistently reaffirmed the absolute prohibition against government interference in religious beliefs. The individual must be left free to exercise his or her religious preferences as conscience dictates. In its free-exercise clause decisions, the Court has ruled that in cases of childless adults, the Jehovah's Witness could refuse the blood transfusion, since there was no threat to the morals, welfare, or health of society and no minor children were involved. On the other hand, where minor children have been involved, the Court has determined that the state has an interest, and often a compelling one, to protect the health and safety of minor children over the religiously based objections of the child or parent. The lesson of these cases is that while parents are free to die for their religious beliefs, children cannot be allowed to die for their *parents'* religious beliefs. Also, when a pregnant woman refused medical treatment that would save her life, the Court ordered the transfusion for the mother, taking precedent over her religious beliefs. The state, as *"parens patriae* (father of the country), would not let the mother die because death was the ultimate abandonment."[3]

The other prong of the First Amendment, "the establishment clause," has only recently come into the right-to-die dialogues, as a result of certain religious groups' dogmatic intent to impose their beliefs on the rest of the nation. This clause in the Constitution prohibits government sponsorship of religion, mandating that federal and state governments neither aid, promote, nor formally establish a religion. While at its inception the clause might not have been intended to prohibit governmental aid to all religions, the accepted view today is that it also prohibits a preference for religion over nonreligion.

The bedrock American concept of separation between church and state is often the focus of an argument by those who believe that the Roman Catholic Church, in particular, oversteps its bounds by campaigning against PAS, thereby blurring the distinction. So firmly planted is the freedom of religion in our national heritage that Americans can react from a gut level when they sense that religion is being imposed on them. Many of the original colonists had fled European religious persecution, and certain regions, notably the Virginia Commonwealth, argued "for a complete separation of religious matters from secular government. In Virginia, Jefferson and Madison led a continuing battle for total religious freedom and an end of government aid to religion."[4] Describing the purpose of the establishment clause in 1802 letters to the Danbury Community Baptist Association in Virginia, Thomas Jefferson wrote that the First Amendment built "a wall of separation between church and state." And thus the phrase was born.

In some instances it is relatively easy to determine that a governmental action violates "the establishment clause" if it either delegates governmental power to a religious group in a manner that allows for excessive entanglement between the government and religion, or if it constitutes a preference for certain religions. It can and has been argued that the Roman Catholic Church, predominant among other churches, is attempting to impose its religious beliefs prohibiting assisted suicide on Catholics as well as non-Catholics, and that any law forbidding the practice concedes religious preference to that church's dogma over other religious beliefs. Moreover, if a law regulating private sector activity, such as assisted suicide, favors people with religious beliefs over people *without* religious beliefs, it may have the primary effect of advancing religion, and such a law would again violate the establishment clause.

Most Christian and Jewish groups approve of the withholding and withdrawing of life-sustaining treatment, as do most Eastern religions, although the latter are less specific about it. Allowing a hopelessly ill person to die by not introducing medical technology is widely accepted today by a broad

range of faiths. Only Mormons, Evangelicals, and other strict Gospel denominations are opposed to this practice in the West, while Islam is opposed
in the East.

Pope John Paul II's 1995 encyclical, *Evangelium Vitae*, noted that Roman Catholic teaching allows the ending of "aggressive medical treatment"
for terminally ill people—treatment that would buy negligible extra life at
exorbitant cost to the dying person's family. "To forgo extraordinary or disproportionate means is not the equivalent of suicide or euthanasia," John
Paul wrote. "It rather expresses acceptance of the human condition in the
face of death."[5]

However, taking one's own life or helping another to die is a different
matter. Major faiths have historically opposed suicide and assisted suicide.
Pope John Paul II has attacked the "culture of death," and calls euthanasia
"a grave violation of the law of God." Although liberal Protestants and Reform Jews tend to believe that this most personal and intimate decision is
best left to the individual conscience, traditional Catholic, Protestant, Jewish, and Muslim teachings on suicide—and by extension, on assisted suicide—have run close to parallel for centuries. With few exceptions they
oppose the ending of one's own life as well as assisting in ending the life of
another.

Contrary to popular belief, the Bible contains no condemnation of suicide
(except in a literal application of the Sixth Commandment, "Thou shall not
kill"). In its reporting of seven suicides that took place, the Bible speaks of
them as part of the struggle and tragedy of life. The Greek and Roman
approach to suicide (as a rational and humane choice under certain circumstances, such as intolerable pain) still seems to have influenced the Bible's
authors.

By the fifth century, however, Saint Augustine (A.D. 354–430) had developed a strong philosophical bias against suicide. He denounced suicide
as a "detestable and damnable wickedness." Life is a gift from God and not
man's to give away. Self-destruction was as much a sin as homicide. He
presented arguments: First, taking one's own life defied the Sixth Commandment. By committing suicide a person was usurping the functions of
church and state. Finally Augustine held that life and its sufferings are
divinely ordained by God and must be borne accordingly.

Intolerance toward suicide culminated in the thirteenth century with
Saint Thomas Aquinas (1225–74). He reinforced Augustine's arguments,
saying that suicide was a mortal sin, contrary to natural law, damaging to
the human community, and symbolic of humans assuming divine prerogatives concerning decisions of life and death. The Augustine-Aquinas view
has prevailed in church dogma ever since.

The Roman Catholic Church has been the sternest, most vigilant, and most effective opponent of PAS and voluntary euthanasia. Its position—the acceptance of forgoing treatment but the rejection of an assisted death—is the most clearly articulated of any faith, beginning with the Vatican's 1980 Declaration on Euthanasia, which said, in part:

1. No one can make an attempt on the life of an innocent person without opposing God's love for that person, without violating a fundamental right, and therefore without committing a crime of the utmost gravity.
2. Everyone has the duty to lead his or her life in accordance with God's plan. That life is entrusted to the individual as a good that must bear fruit already here on earth, but that finds its full perfection only in eternal life.
3. Intentionally causing one's own death, or suicide, is therefore equally as wrong as murder; such an action on the part of a person is to be considered as a rejection of God's sovereignty and living plan. Furthermore, suicide is also often a refusal of love for self, the denial of the natural instinct to live, a flight from the duties of justice and charity owed to one's neighbor, to various communities or to the whole of society—although, as is generally recognized, at times there are psychological factors present that can diminish responsibility or even completely remove it.
4. However, one must clearly distinguish suicide from that sacrifice of one's life whereby for a higher cause, such as God's glory, the salvation of souls or the service of one's brethren, a person offers his or her own life or puts it in danger.[6]

The Orthodox Jewish position regarding an assisted death as well as forgoing treatment appears equally clear. Immanuel Jacobovits, a religious leader whose work is frequently cited, writes:

It is clear then, that, even when the patient is already known to be on his deathbed and close to the end, any form of active euthanasia is strictly prohibited. In fact, it is condemned as plain murder. In purely legal terms, this is borne out by the ruling that anyone who kills a dying person is liable to the death penalty as a common murderer. At the same time, Jewish law sanctions, and perhaps even demands, the withdrawal of any factor—extraneous to the patient himself or not—which may artificially delay his demise in the final phase.[7]

Many leaders of the predominant strands of Christianity and Judaism believe that the absolute master of life and death is the Creator and that any choice between life and death is not in the hands of humans. Because life is given by God, it is a sin to end it—the life of an unborn as well as that of the terminally ill. It is God's right to determine the beginning and the end of life, not ours. And since life is on loan to us from God, "one's passage from this life is subject to the will and power of God." Therefore, "suicide represents a rejection of God's absolute sovereignty over life and death."[8]

Strength is found in the doctrine of the sanctity of life. Simply stated this doctrine holds that it is *always* wrong intentionally to take an innocent human life. Central to the Judeo-Christian ethic is the belief that our humanity, the greatest creation of God, is "intrinsically holy and worthy of respect because of its connection with God. Our mere existence is proof of that sacredness. . . . Our lives are sanctified because we are alive, all because of God's greatness." God controls our life just as He controls the rest of the universe. Says the 147th Psalm, God " 'covers the heavens with clouds, prepares the rain for the earth, makes grass grow upon the hills. . . .' We do not have the ability to rule such things because it is not in our nature. Our everyday, mundane decisions may be our own, but it is God's Will that will be done."[9]

The sacredness of life gives rise to its inviolability, wrote Pope John Paul II in his *Evangelium Vitae*: " 'Human life is sacred because from it involves the creative action of God, and it remains forever in a special relationship with the Creator, who is its sole end: no one can, in any circumstance, claim for himself the right to destroy directly an innocent human being.' With these words the Instruction *Donum Vitae* sets forth the central content of God's revelation on the sacredness and inviolability of human life."[10]

In its "application to the medical context, it has been put like this: 'It is absolutely prohibited to either intentionally kill a patient, or intentionally to let a patient die, and to base decisions relating to the prolongation or shortening of human life on considerations of its quality or kind.' " For those who subscribe to this doctrine, the taking of an innocent human life is absolutely forbidden and it is "not a principle to be balanced against conflicting considerations. . . . They really do mean never."[11] This doctrine, known as "vitalism," maintains that human life is of absolute value and must be preserved at all costs. Chief Justice Hughes specifically rejected vitalism in the *Quinlan* case. Hughes concluded that under certain circumstances, an individual's right to privacy is greater than the state's interest in the preservation and sanctity of life.

The life-is-sacred argument may be extended to "suggest that suffering is redemptive, that suicide is never rational, and that killing (assisted suicide) is intrinsically wrong."[12] The *Declaration on Euthanasia*, issued in Rome in 1980, acknowledged the desire to remove suffering at all cost, but stated: "According to Christian teaching, however, suffering, especially suffering during the last moments of life, has a special place in God's saving plan; it is in fact a sharing in Christ's passion and a union with the redeeming sacrifice which He offered in obedience to the Father's will. Therefore, one must not be surprised if some Christians prefer to moderate their use of painkillers, in order to accept voluntarily at least a part of their sufferings and thus associate themselves in a conscious way with the sufferings of Christ crucified."[13] Rev. John Lanzrath, vice chancellor of the Catholic Diocese of Wichita, Kansas, counsels people to "remember that suffering is part of the human condition; that it has redeeming value."[14]

The church dogma of vitalism is carried out by individual Roman Catholic bishops. In a unique move in 1997, Bishop Fabian Bruskewitz of Lincoln, Nebraska, ordered Catholics to resign from twelve proscribed groups, including the Hemlock Society, or else face excommunication.

The Hemlock Society, which actively supports assisted suicide, was joined on the list by such groups as Planned Parenthood, a pro-choice abortion organization; Call to Action, a group that wants the church to discuss allowing women and married men to become priests, issues that Pope John Paul II has said are closed; Catholics for a Free Choice; and Masonic organizations like Rainbow Girls, whose teenage members volunteer in hospitals, perform community service, and read Scripture at meetings. The diocese itself has about 85,000 members, and while no exact number was known to be affected by the excommunication order, it is believed that hundreds of Catholics had belonged to the banned groups. Bishop Bruskewitz said that his order "succeeded in 'unmasking some people who previously had a very questionable relationship with the Catholic Church.' "[15]

John Cardinal McGann, Long Island's Catholic bishop, released a pastoral letter in 1997, in which he advocated "a letting go with the true dignity that comes with adequate treatment of the physical, emotional, social and spiritual suffering of the dying person."[16] That letting go may include the withholding or withdrawing of life-sustaining technology that offers no hope of improvement. It may also be the administering of pain medication with the intent to ease suffering, even if the medication shortens the patient's life. The latter method, known as the "double effect," is approved of by virtually all groups, including the Roman Catholic Church and the AMA. Also acceptable is "terminal sedation."

Pope John Paul II, in *Evangelium Vitae*, quotes Pius XII's affirmation "that it is licit to relieve pain by narcotics, even with the result being decreased consciousness and a shortening of life, 'if no other means exist, and if, in the given circumstances, this does not prevent the carrying out of other religious and moral duties.' In such a case, death is not willed or sought, even though for reasonable motives one runs the risk of it: there is simply a desire to ease pain effectively by using the analgesics which medicine provides."[17]

This philosophical principle of the "double effect," a distinction used by theologians, ethicists, physicians, and courts to differentiate permissible from impermissible conduct by physicians is that between "intended" consequences and "unintended but foreseeable" consequences. It is also a distinction that advocates of PAS call hypocritical. Originating in Roman Catholic moral theology, it states that there can be a situation in which it is morally justifiable to cause evil in the pursuit of good. In the context of the right-to-die, the double effect is invoked when a doctor administers painkilling medication, and the patient dies as a result of the medication. This can happen quite easily, since a medication that reduces or eliminates pain, usually morphine, also serves to depress the patient's respiration, sometimes causing death. Under these circumstances the *intent* is to relieve the pain, and so is morally justifiable.

On the other hand, if a physician administers a larger-than-necessary dose to control pain, or a lethal dose, to a patient not suffering from pain, and the intent is to cause death, the legal, theological, and medical powers that be consider such conduct to be immoral, unethical, and criminally homicidal. In other words, "actions taken with the intent to cause death are culpable, whereas actions taken with some other legitimate purpose in mind—such as the elimination of pain—are not, because the patient's death was the unintended consequence."[18]

Another religiously and medically acceptable way of letting go is the procedure known as "terminal sedation." In this procedure the physician, with the help of barbiturates, puts the patient suffering from intractable pain into a coma. The doctor then removes the artificial nutrition and hydration sustaining the patient, and after roughly ten days or so, the patient dies of starvation and dehydration.

While starvation is indeed an option that the desperate can pursue, Faye Girsh, executive director of Hemlock USA, questions the logic of allowing starvation while prohibiting assisted suicide. "Why take ten days when you can take ten minutes? I mean, what's the point?" she asks. Referring to a seventy-eight-year-old woman who lasted forty-two days without food and twenty-nine days without fluids, Girsh quite correctly comments, "If prisoners on death row were sentenced to die this way, the ACLU would file suit so fast it would make your head spin."

The religious reasoning does not stand up under principles of criminal or tort liability. The principle of double effect overlooks the fact that an individual is not only liable for the intended consequences of his or her actions, but also for those actions that are reasonably foreseeable under the circumstances. Most physicians would agree that it is reasonably foreseeable that a large dose of morphine or another analgesic medication will cause death even if the intent is to relieve suffering. However, in the eyes of the Roman Catholic Church and the law, the distinction lies in the intent alone. And, unlike other penalized actors in a courtroom, physicians who administer lethal doses of morphine to eliminate pain are free of criminal or civil liability unless another party questions the exact intent. This fine line of intent has, and will increasingly, cause legal difficulty for physicians who attempt to ease terminal suffering in this litigious society, where assisted suicide is such an emotionally charged issue.

Margaret P. Battin and Arthur G. Lipman, joint editors of *Drug Use in Assisted Suicide and Euthanasia*, include case commentaries of professional caregivers to illustrate not only different perspectives on euthanasia, but also to provide insight into how people define their positions. One such commentary, written by a nurse, Barbara Jeanne McGuire, involves a terminally ill AIDS patient named Donald. He had reached the stage in his disease where he was blind, seriously impaired in his ability to communicate, confused and forgetful, and in apparent pain. Bret, his lover, understanding that his health would not improve, asked the hospice team to facilitate a speedy and dignified death for Donald. The health care professional writing the case commentary recommends against either Bret or the hospice team intentionally causing Donald's death. She then attempts to explain her recommendation and, in so doing, comments on Donald vis-à-vis the concept of the double effect:

> Most people would agree that to adequately control Donald's pain, the possibility exists that the morphine might hasten or cause his death. For me, this result does not fall into the category of euthanasia. First of all our intent is to control Donald's pain—a morally good action. Secondly, we foresee, and even permit this administration of morphine to cause or hasten death, but death is not our intent. Thirdly, it is the morphine that we anticipate will control the pain—not Donald's death. And finally, adequate control of Donald's pain is important enough to outweigh the possibility, or even probability, of hastening or causing his death. Therefore, all four conditions specified by the principle of double effect have been met to my satisfaction.[19]

Proponents of aid in dying, on the other hand, view this emphasis on intent as "smoke-and-mirrors" logic. They see no ethical or moral difference between the accepted practices of administering the morphine drip used in the double effect, terminal sedation, and foregoing life-sustaining treatment on the one hand, and prescribing or injecting lethal medication on the other. What we have in practice now is voluntary euthanasia, even if the establishment denies it. The Ninth and Second Circuit Courts of Appeals agree.

Peter Singer, author of *Rethinking Life and Death*, comments: "The idea that it is always wrong intentionally to end an innocent human life is often seen as the one moral commandment that we must never violate. In extreme situations, however, it has always been difficult to defend. Therefore, those who claim to uphold it resort to strange distinctions in order to reach a reasonable outcome without appearing to break the absolute commandment." Singer also questions the assumption that we are responsible for what we intentionally do in a way that we are not responsible for what we deliberately fail to prevent. He asks: "Can doctors who remove the feeding tubes from patients in a persistent vegetative state really believe that there is a huge gulf between this, and giving the same patients an injection that will stop their hearts beating? Doctors may be trained in such a way that it is psychologically easier for them to do the one and not the other, but both are equally certain ways of bringing about the death of the patient."[20]

In a *New York Times* article in November 1994, Thomas A. Preston, a cardiologist and professor of medicine at the University of Washington, explains the distorted thinking that allows the morphine drip used in the double-effect principle while at the same time condemning euthanasia. In his words, the

> morphine drip is euthanasia by another name. . . . The Catholic Church sees nothing wrong with such procedures: "It is not euthanasia to give a dying person sedatives and analgesics for the alleviation of pain," says a 1975 directive from the National Conference of Catholic Bishops, "even though they may deprive the patient of the use of reason, or shorten his life." But the morphine drip is undeniably euthanasia, hidden by the cosmetics of professional tradition and language. Americans had better wake up to that fact if we are ever to approach a national consensus on the issue of euthanasia. When physicians secretly and silently adapt a normal medical practice to hasten dying, we are on shaky ground indeed if we say that they may not do so openly and honestly.[21]

The New York State Task Force on Life and the Law concluded in 1994 that assisted suicide should not be legalized, partially because it could never be adequately regulated. This is a common complaint about assisted deaths. The panel, however, failed to mention that physicians routinely end lives with the morphine drip. Moreover, says Preston, this covert form of assisted death empowers physicians to initiate and carry out the ultimate act of medical paternalism. Preston believes that physician-assisted suicide rightly gives the decision to the patient, where it belongs. "The necessary regulation will be possible only if we admit that euthanasia is widespread now," he says. "Only then can we turn the debate to the real issue: specific guidelines on who qualifies for aid in dying—and how to be sure that the decision is made by the patient, not just for the convenience of the family, the doctor or the hospital."[22]

The hypocrisy of the distinction does not escape Laurence H. Tribe, the Harvard Law School constitutional expert who argued the New York assisted suicide case before the Supreme Court. Interviewed on *60 Minutes* and responding to a physician who said that terminal sedation was not killing, it is only relieving a patient's pain, Tribe remarked: "The state, though it doesn't advertise this, makes it possible for doctors to give what is called terminal sedation; that is, basically, to chemically knock out your mind and at that point they just don't feed you, they don't give you water and you starve and dehydrate to death as your family watches your body decay. That, the state says—'Oh, that's fine because they're not killing you.' "

Later in the program Tribe refuted the argument that in terminating life-sustaining treatment, doctors are not causing the patient to die. This is a line of reasoning backed by religious groups, who claim that doctors are merely allowing nature to take its course. "I don't know whether to call it self-deception or just silly," says Tribe. "We know it's not true. We know that if they did that without the consent of the patient, then we're prosecuted for homicide and—said, 'Oh, my defense is I didn't kill the patient; nature did it.' And that—that wouldn't even pass the straight-face test. The cause of death when a respirator is disconnected is not nature. It's the disconnection of the respirator."

The Roman Catholic Church is not alone in regarding human life as sacred and in making a distinction between active physician-assisted suicide and the cessation of futile medical procedures. Traditional Jewish and Muslim teachings espouse the same philosophies. Because there is no possibility of repentance for self-destruction, Orthodox Judaism considers suicide a sin worse than murder; therefore active euthanasia, voluntary or involuntary, is forbidden:

> While Jewish law rates the mitigation of a patient's suffering, especially in the ordeal prior to death, above virtually any other consideration, if necessary even his ability to make his spiritual and temporal preparations for death, what it cannot do is purchase relief from pain and misery at the cost of life itself. This is based on Judaism's attribution of infinity value to human life. Infinity being indivisible, any fraction of life, however limited its expectancy or its health, remains equally infinite in value.[23]

Anyone who assists in the dying process has committed "a capital offense" of murder, wrote Maimonides in the *Mishne Torah*, a code of Jewish law compiled in 1168. Orthodox and Conservative Jews tend to stay close to the law when considering such questions.

Muslim teaching on suicide closely parallels Roman Catholic and Jewish thought. Dr. Maher Hathout, a cardiologist and spokesperson for the Islamic Center of Southern California in Los Angeles, says claiming that assisted suicide is acceptable incorrectly implies "that we're more merciful than God. It's a false assumption that death ends suffering." His brother, a teacher of Islam, says that the Koran, the Islamic scripture, and the teachings of the prophet Muhammad deny salvation to anyone who commits suicide. "Do not kill yourself or destroy yourself, for verily God has been to you most merciful," the Koran dictates (4:29). "Take not life which God made sacred, otherwise than in the course of justice," Hassan Hathout says, quoting from the Koran (6:151). The positive value of suffering in Islam derives from the belief that "when pain cannot be avoided, to endure the pain patiently is a rewardable charity." For one who dies after enduring great suffering, he adds, quoting from the prophet, "God shed off his sins like a tree shedding its leaves." Also, warns Saleh Saleh, of the American Muslim Council, if a Muslim should, under any circumstances, take his life by his own hand, "he will be punished in the hereafter."[24]

Unlike Roman Catholicism and traditional Jewish and Muslim teachings, the Eastern religions are divided in their beliefs. A study by the Beijing Society Investigations Institute in April 1996 revealed that 78 percent of Chinese interviewed think that people should have the right to choose whether to live or die. Suicide is not considered a sin according to traditional Chinese or Taoist beliefs, but many Chinese, particularly those living in rural areas, believe that helping a person to die is taboo. Hindus and Sikhs favor individual choice and conscience, while orthodox Buddhists condone foregoing medical treatment but not assisting in someone's death.

Orthodox Jewish law prohibits suicides, but the Reform Jewish community frequently favors euthanasia when all medical attempts at recovery have failed and the patient's suffering remains unabated. Rabbi David Saperstein, Director of Reform Judaism's Religious Action Center in Washington, D.C., emphasizes "the reality that often the best way to protect the right of people to live in accord with their own religious dictates is to keep the Government out, which is the attitude of many Jews on the abortion issue."[25] That more liberal view is echoed by other Jewish leaders. Although finding doctor-assisted suicide and euthanasia sharply at odds with Jewish tradition, they seem content with—or resigned to—having the courts dismantle barriers to these practices. Another rabbi in the Reform community parted with tradition as he faced the issues with acceptance: "Why expend our energies in fighting something that will come anyway and doesn't affect me directly because I am not obligated, in a country with separation of church and state, to do something against my scruples."[26]

Protestants differ widely on the subject of assisted suicide. There is not one overall Protestant view of assisted suicide. While many traditional Protestant denominations, such as the Baptist Church, the Lutheran Church, and the Church of Jesus Christ of Latter-Day Saints (Mormons), oppose aided suicide, others, like the Unitarian Universalists, the United Church of Christ, and the Methodist Church, opt for freedom of individual conscience. In fact, the Unitarian Universalists have been among the right-to-die movement's closest allies for years, and most Hemlock chapter meetings are held in UU facilities.

Perhaps no denomination reflects the angst, anguish, and dissension in the controversy more than the Episcopal Church. Officially the Episcopal Church is against assisted suicide. In 1991 the Episcopal General Convention approved a resolution saying that "it is morally wrong and unacceptable to take a human life in order to relieve the suffering caused by incurable illness."

On the other hand, in early 1996, a majority of the two hundred delegates to the annual convention of the Episcopal Diocese of Newark, New Jersey, adopted a resolution declaring that committing suicide or aiding someone else to commit suicide is morally acceptable under certain circumstances. The Newark resolution, the result of a yearlong study by a diocesan task force, decided that suicide may be acceptable for a terminally ill patient when "pain is persistent and/or progressive; when all other reasonable means of amelioration of pain and suffering have been exhausted; and when the decision to hasten death is a truly informed and voluntary choice, free from external coercion." Under these circumstances, said the resolution, suicide is a "moral choice" for the terminally ill.

There is no real consensus about aid in dying among people of faith, even if their official religious creed forbids it. Within Judaism, Christianity, and Islam the traditional rule is not to kill yourself and not to help anyone else do it either. However, within these groups, there are people who are willing to exercise the freedom of thought and practice that belongs to individuals who believe in liberty and autonomy while refusing to judge their fellows. In his probe of fifty religions around the world on their attitudes toward the right to die, Larue writes:

> The differences in points of view . . . make it clear that no one can claim that "this is what a Christian believes concerning euthanasia," or, "this is the Jewish position on physician-assisted euthanasia." Even as a denomination may produce a statement outlining its position opposing physician-assisted euthanasia, the clergy in the field may argue that men and women in terminal pain and suffering have the right to choose for themselves their way of death without condemnation.[27]

Some denominations produce official statements that describe either the position held by the majority in that particular religious group, or the opinions of those at the top. Of these denominations some give the individual the leeway to follow his or her conscience; the Roman Catholic Church does not. Larue writes:

> Such [official] statements tend to be products of long and careful study, analysis and reflection on the relationship between faith positions, scrip-

tural interpretations, or traditional patterns of thought and the problems raised by modern medicine and the efforts to legalize physician-assisted death. These documents are designed to provide guidelines as opposed to must-be-followed orders. On the other hand, the guiding and authoritative statement produced in Rome, in May 1980, by the Sacred Congregation for the Doctrine of the Faith is to be followed and adhered to by all Roman Catholics.[28]

Given their formal and informal policies, how do these religious groups operate to restrain policy favorable to the right-to-die-movement? How do they limit the scope of the emerging public policy allowing a physician's aid in dying?

One example came in November 1994, when 51 percent of Oregon voters approved Measure 16, a ballot initiative allowing doctors to prescribe lethal medication for mentally competent, terminally ill adults who choose to shorten the dying process. The win, however, came about despite the stiff opposition of most religious faiths. In a rare meeting, several groups, ranging from Buddhists to Baptists, united behind the Roman Catholic Church to fight against the passage of Measure 16. Jewish and Muslim leaders, along with sixteen other Christian denominations, also opposed the measure. Among the latter, the Mormons, the state's second-biggest denomination, with ninety thousand members, lent their support.

In September, two months before the election, and for the first time in Oregon's history, money was collected in Roman Catholic Churches for a political cause. Priests asked the state's 297,000 Catholics to make a political donation to defeat the assisted-suicide initiative in the next election. A special collection was taken up and turned over to a political committee organized to ensure that sanctity of life was preserved.

In the end the Catholic Church contributed a million dollars in a losing effort to defeat the initiative. Theirs was a war chest three times that of the winning pro-16 campaign. The church had underestimated Oregonians' support of Measure 16. Three years later, in an attempt to get the law repealed, Catholic Church groups provided some 80 percent of the five-million-dollar campaign expenditures. They lost again.

The 1994 Oregon victory woke people up to the realization that PAS was no longer an unattainable goal. If it was legal in Oregon, it could be legal elsewhere. Cases had been filed earlier in 1994 in Washington and New York challenging the constitutionality of the existing statutes prohibiting PAS. Rarely has an issue found itself so squarely at the intersection of private faith and public values as did PAS in the spring of 1996, when both the Ninth and the Second Circuit Courts of Appeals struck down the two states' laws making assisted suicide a felony. It was now legally possible for doctors in twelve states, Guam, and the Northern Marianas to prescribe lethal drugs for the mentally competent terminally ill adult who wished to hasten his or her death.

Implementation of these new laws was almost immediately halted by court challenges. Nevertheless, the court decisions ignited a firestorm of protest from religious leaders, as well as from doctors and hospitals, even as supporters of assisted suicide applauded the decision as an act of compassion that allowed the terminally ill to die without prolonging pain and suffering. Said Richard M. Doerflinger, associate director of the Secretariat for the Pro-Life Activities of the National Conference of Catholic Bishops, "This [Ninth Circuit] decision is so sweeping in its assault on numerous traditional legal distinctions that it truly demands appeal."[29] With renewed vigor, some of the nation's most powerful religious organizations, including the National Conference of Catholic Bishops and the National Association of Evangelicals, reaffirmed their vows to file their own briefs with the U.S. Supreme Court, if and when it decided to hear the cases.

The Supreme Court *did* decide to review the cases, and the conflict intensified. In a continuing interfaith partnership, the Roman Catholic bishops and the Muslim leaders, joined by the Southern Baptist Convention, the Lutheran Church–Missouri Synod and the Evangelicals, submitted legal briefs attacking PAS in the two cases before the Court.

In characteristic form, Geoffrey Fieger, Kevorkian's outspoken attorney, did not let the thirty-page religion-based brief to the Court go by unnoticed. "They should keep their religious noses out of secular business. . . . If they want to inflict suffering on their followers, then that's fine. But they shouldn't inflict their religious precepts on others," he declared.[30]

And so, mounting a campaign against assisted dying that appears to be more extensive than the one waged against abortion, the nation's Roman Catholic bishops quickly galvanized themselves into devoting new energy and resources to opposing such suicide in the courts and the legislatures. Bernard Cardinal Law of Boston, who heads the National Conference of Catholic Bishops Committee on Pro-Life Activity, revealed the church's intent to form alliances with hospitals and doctors, as well as with other religious groups to achieve its goal. Cardinal Law said the bishops themselves would act primarily "in our role as teachers," addressing "underlying cultural issues." However, compromising the whole notion of separation of church and state, and violating the First Amendment's establishment clause, Law added that "anything as critical as this would be grist for this year's political campaigns. I don't see any way we can avoid full public discussion, including in the political arenas."[31]

In an unprecedented religious foray into politics, and again in violation of the constitutional clauses that prohibit both promoting or establishing one religion over another and favoring religious over nonreligious beliefs, the late

Joseph Cardinal Bernardin, the Roman Catholic archbishop of Chicago, writing as a man approaching death, sent a personal letter directly to the Supreme Court asking the justices not to find that terminally ill people have a constitutional right to PAS.

Dated November 7, 1996, and attached to the Catholic Health Association's appeal to overturn bans on assisted suicides in New York and Washington, the letter stated:

> I am at the end of my earthly life. There is much that I have contemplated these last few months of my illness, but as one who is dying I have especially come to appreciate the gift of life. I know from my own experience that patients often face difficult and deeply personal decisions about their care. However, I also know that even a person who decides to forgo treatment does not necessarily choose death. Rather, he chooses life without the burden of disproportionate medical intervention. . . .
>
> There can be no such thing as a "right to assisted suicide" because there can be no legal and moral order which tolerates the killing of innocent life, even if the agent of death is self-administered. Creating a new "right" to assisted death will endanger society and send a false signal that a less than "perfect" life is not worth living.

In their relentless pursuit to put the brakes on any advancement of the right-to-die cause, Doerflinger said the National Conference of Catholic Bishops would launch a three-pronged offensive that would include education, public policy advocacy—including lobbying on both the state and federal levels and involvement in court cases—and pastoral care that would include promoting efforts to improve care of the dying. Doerflinger compared the bishops' efforts to combat the legalization of assisted suicide with efforts to fight legal abortion, another area of political entanglement. When asked if their opposing efforts would be more successful against aid in dying, he said, "obviously the *Roe* v. *Wade* of euthanasia has not been handed down by the Supreme Court. One reason for getting organized now is to prevent that from happening."

John Cardinal O'Connor, the Catholic archbishop of New York, interrupted the Easter celebration to utter strong disapproval of the circuit courts' rulings. Consistent with his religion's staunch opposition to abortion and euthanasia and a mighty foe of both himself, O'Connor decried as "unspeakable" the recent federal Appeals Court ruling permitting PAS suicide in New York State. He warned that this "new, latest horror" could be a harbinger of worse to come. Reading a statement by Pope John Paul II, the cardinal said, "Euthanasia is a crime in which no one should cooperate or even consent." He urged physicians to not assist in a suicide even if the law should permit it. "There can be no excuse," the cardinal reprimanded. "Only the Lord has power over life and death. No one should take it away from Him."[32]

Not all of the religious community is opposed to PAS, as evidenced by an amicus (friend-of-the-court) brief of thirty-six religious organizations, leaders, and scholars in support of physician-assisted suicide, also submitted to the Supreme Court. This facet of the religious community views state bans on assisted suicide as violations of the First Amendment's two guarantees of freedom of religion.

The free-exercise clause prohibits the government from interfering with the individual's right to exercise, live by, and practice his or her religious beliefs. While some religious denominations adamantly oppose aid in dying in all instances, still others affirmatively support the right to self-determination in dying. To stifle the latter is to violate the First Amendment.

At the core of the establishment clause is a prohibition on governmental favoring of a particular religion or of religion in general. By adopting a view of PAS that is sponsored by the Roman Catholic Church but not accepted by, for example, the Unitarian Church, Reform Jews, or by those with no religious affiliation, the Washington and New York assisted-suicide bans, in essence, endorse the Roman Catholic religious viewpoint to the exclusion of all others.

The bottom line of the thirty-six religious leaders' petition to the Court was: To prohibit assisted dying for the terminally ill is to legalize one religious view and to criminalize others, impermissible under the First Amendment and in violation of the separation of church and state.

Seemingly oblivious to concerns about constitutional infringements, religion may tighten its restraint on individual rights. Three phenomena quietly bode even greater resistance to ideas based on a credo of self-determination and autonomy. First, the former cultural divide between Roman Catholics and Protestants has been shrinking for years, and with it has emerged the growing influence of the Christian right on American politics. The "moralist Catholics and evangelical Protestants have discovered more and more that they share a natural affinity of ideas, and they have been moving steadily closer together," says Jacob Heilbrunn in *The New Republic*.[33] The first giant step toward closing the gap took place in the early 1970s, when religious right leaders such as Jerry Falwell adopted the right-to-life stance so favored by the Catholic Church. Falwell "declared that Protestants had 'joined the fight' and lauded Pope John Paul II as the 'best hope we Baptists ever had.' It was a little noticed but important moment in political history: Northern Catholics and Southern Baptists—two powerful blocs that had traditionally shared an allegiance to the Democratic Party but had also traditionally viewed one another with cultural suspicion—had joined hands in cultural conservatism."[34] In fact, the Catholic conservatives are providing the brainpower for the Christian Coalition.[35]

While the alliance may have begun on the common ground of abortion, it has now broadened to include assisted suicide and homosexuality as well. This growing convergence and cooperation between Roman Catholics and Evangelicals is a combined force to be taken seriously. The central point of agreement is grounded in the concept that the United States government (in particular the judiciary) has become so debased—so essentially un-Christian and therefore illegitimate—as to threaten the existence of the United States as a nation under God, a crisis that might require a revolutionary response.

In remarks delivered privately but made public by Americans United for Separation of Church and State, a liberal watchdog group, Pat Robertson offered a rare glimpse into the Christian Coalition's political objectives, despite its insistence that the group does not engage in activities to elect candidates. He spoke in detail about how his organization needed to increase precinct-level political efforts and suggested that Tammany Hall, the former New York City Democratic political machine, should serve as a model. Robertson took credit for the Republican Congress of 1994 and declared his intent to select "the next President of the United States."[36]

These opinions and goals are backed by great financial strength and must not be taken lightly. Not only does the Roman Catholic Church have unlimited wealth to finance its projects, but the Christian Coalition, in a record-breaking 1996, generated more than $24.9 million through fundraising. This amount represents a 17 percent increase over the $21.2 million the organization raised in 1994.

Second, a survey by the Pew Research Center for the People and the Press found that white Evangelical Protestants are emerging as a cohesive political force shaping American politics and holding more conservative views than other groups on gay marriage, gun control, immigration policy, abortion, and allowing public schools to provide birth control information. Andrew Kohut, director of the Pew Research Center, said: "The conservatism of white evangelicals is the most powerful political force in the country." In 1978 a *New York Times*/CBS News Poll found that only 16 percent of the population identified themselves as white Evangelicals. In 1987 the number had risen to 19 percent. Then, in 1996, the Pew survey found that their strength had increased to 23 percent of the population.

While the survey did not raise the issue of assisted suicide, it does not require a giant mental leap to surmise that assisted death would have been included, if the question had been asked. Suffice it to say that the religious right, in combination with the Roman Catholic Church are, and will continue to be, formidable opponents of the right-to-die movement.

Third, surprising to many is that religious involvement in political and societal issues is currently *approved* of by the American public, the reversal of an ideology fought for so fiercely by the Founding Fathers. A striking change in American attitudes about religion and politics is taking place. A majority of the public now believes that churches should be allowed to express political views, a reversal from what a majority believed a generation ago. A survey by the Pew Center found that, when asked whether churches should keep out of political matters or whether they should express their views on day-to-day social and political questions, 54 percent said churches should express their views, while 43 percent said they should keep out of politics. These public views are almost the exact reverse of those reflected in a Gallup survey done in 1968. At that time 40 percent said churches should express their views, while 53 percent said they should keep out of political matters. While the political attitude of religious groups varied somewhat, all of them were relatively high. The highest, however, were the white Evangelical Protestants, 70 percent of whom believed it acceptable for churches to express political views.

While there is no real consensus about aid in dying among people of faith, the traditional, official creeds generally forbid it, and they are the part of the religious community with access to the media, with the money to sway opinions, shape minds, and often distort the facts. Religion's resistance to assisted death appears to be impenetrable, especially as the Roman Catholic Church and the religious right join numbers, finances, and political clout. With the rising number of conservative Evangelicals being the most powerful political force in the United States today, and with their support for church entanglement in political activities, chances of success of the right to die appear much slimmer.

However, the two Oregon initiatives prove that money, with its ability to buy television airtime, does not always determine the outcome. Indeed, many believe that the Catholic Church's overt campaign against PAS, especially in the second election, actually turned people toward supporting the practice. Without doubt, it is an idea whose time has come and a majority agree. For those who favor assisted dying, it is a matter of personal choice, the ultimate human right in a society where people should be free to determine their fate. Opponents of the practice, however, define a civilized society as one in which life is sacrosanct at all times. Trespassing into God's domain is absolutely forbidden. Religious resistance is joined in intensity by the hierarchy of the medical profession, as the two institutions battle to keep the practice illegal.

Chapter 13

Medical Hierarchy Opposes Reform

Much like the religious organizations, the medical profession is seriously divided over the issue of assisted deaths. The hierarchies of both, however, are opposed. Tension exists between the AMA and state medical organizations, between the AMA and practicing physicians, among individual physicians, and between doctors and patients. Study after study offers many examples of PAS and euthanasia, with high physician approval for the legalization of the practice, yet the AMA and other professional associations remain militantly opposed. The pattern is familiar.

The medical profession has a history of resistance to change and its opposition to an assisted death is no exception. Between 1920 and 1965 the AMA opposed the following: compulsory vaccination against smallpox and diphtheria; mandatory reporting of tuberculosis cases to public health agencies; establishment of public venereal disease clinics; establishment of Red Cross blood banks; federal grants for medical school construction; federal scholarships for medical students; Blue Cross and other private health insurance programs; free centers for cancer diagnosis; and Medicare and Medicaid.

The pattern is familiar. The medical hierarchy opposes an innovation, aggressively fights to maintain the status quo, eventually loses, and then acquiesces in the practice of whatever was so objectionable. As long as it opposes an innovation, however, the medical profession is a formidable restraining force on change. The forces of activism—manifested in the general public and physician approval rating as well as legalization in Oregon—are overtaking, once again, medicine's resistance to innovation and change.

The AMA's opposition to these earlier innovations was based on its belief that these measures constituted "bureaucratic interference with the sacred rights of the American Home," with a "tendency to promote Communism and socialized medicine." Prepaid group health plans, it was argued, destroyed the "sacred doctor-patient relationship," a common AMA criticism of PAS.[1]

The AMA's conservatism surfaced again when it became apparent that more and more women were choosing medicine as a career. Objecting to women physicians, and especially to women surgeons, the AMA effectively barred the door to medical school through the 1950s, when only a trace of females could be found practicing medicine. The AMA issued the following statement in defense of its position that only men should be trained as physicians: "When a critical case demands independent action, and fearless judgment, man's success depends on his virile courage, which the normal woman does not have, nor is expected to have."[2] The medical establishment built on this and other Hippocratic stereotypes by suggesting that women were unfit to be doctors because menstrual cycles caused emotional instabilities that were incompatible with the practice of medicine. Others worried that if women were admitted to the profession, female patients would prefer female physicians to their male counterparts, thereby diverting business from the men.

The AMA also resisted the legalization of abortion and was notoriously slow in approving the withholding and the withdrawing of unwanted life-support treatment. Changes occurred only over the strenuous objections of organized medicine. A combative spirit—similar to what we now see with PAS—gave each successive innovation an adversarial quality.

A few specialized groups, including the Euthanasia Educational Council and the Euthanasia Society of America (after 1975 called the Society for the Right to Die), had long promoted public awareness of the right-to-die. The first living will legislation was proposed and defeated in the Florida legislature in 1970, but there were signs that the issue was receiving growing public support. In 1973 the bill was again defeated in committee, but this time, the vote was markedly closer. Aware of the real possibility that living wills might become legal, the AMA announced its opposition to the medical directives, encouraging instead traditional doctor-patient interactions as the proper setting for making treatment decisions. Several years later the AMA officially opposed any judicial or legislative right-to-die policy and refused to issue its own guidelines for termination of treatment.

The *Quinlan* case in 1976 was the first of many to expand the direct involvement of law in medical decision making. The medical profession was stridently opposed to the New Jersey court's decision granting Julia and Joe Quinlan's request to disconnect Karen's respirator. How dare the court have the audacity to overrule the medical profession and have treatment discontinued?

The following year a Massachusetts decision represented all-out war on physicians' authority by limiting not only the individual physician but the medical ethics committee as well. The court's decision, said an editorial in the *New England Journal of Medicine*, left "[no] doubt of its total distrust of physicians' judgment in such matters. . . . Physicians must not be allowed to use their own professional judgment, but should be guided instead by government regulation. . . . This astonishing opinion can only be viewed as a resounding vote of 'no confidence' in the abilities of physicians and families to act in the best interest of the incapable patient suffering from terminal illness."[3]

Even though the first living will legislation was passed in California in 1976, it was not until 1986, following profound resistance, that the AMA endorsed the withholding or withdrawing of all life-sustaining treatment from patients who were permanently unconscious or dying, if discontinuance of treatment was what the patient would have wanted. The medical hierarchy did not reach this decision graciously or voluntarily. Pressure to reduce physician discretion and to enhance patient autonomy was so intense that they were left with virtually no choice but to concede. Therefore, in 1986, the AMA issued a statement concluding that "Whenever the doctor's duties conflict with the choice of the patient, or the family or legal representative, the patient's choice should prevail."[4]

Although many physicians have moved comfortably into the employee role and follow their patients' wishes, acceptance is far from universal. Official AMA policy notwithstanding, many doctors have yet to accept a change in their status. At a 1995 conference sponsored by the Harvard Medical School's Division of Medical Ethics entitled "Care Near the End of Life," Dr. Ruth L. Fischbach, assistant professor of social medicine, revealed that 66 percent of all physicians interviewed in a recent study believe there is nothing wrong with overriding a patient's advance directive, even if the directive "unambiguously" states the conditions for withholding treatment.[5]

There are also the disastrous SUPPORT study results mentioned previously. Patient end-of-life requests were summarily ignored, as patients were kept on life support long after any quality of life existed and far past what they had explicitly requested.

A nurse at the Harvard Medical School conference told a story portraying the kind of behavior that severely undermines confidence in medicine and trust in the doctor-patient relationship. The incident also shows the profession's strong resistance to patient autonomy, regardless of what laws are on the books. Christine Mitchell, RN, an ethicist at the medical school, told of another nurse who had, with all good intentions and with the promise that the doctor would not amputate her leg without her consent, encouraged a diabetic woman to return to the hospital for an office visit with her physician.

The physician believed that amputation was the only way to save her life. The woman refused the operation, but the physician would not accept the AMA's own 1986 statement that the patient's choice should prevail or that the statement was in response to a need to reduce physician discretion and enhance patient autonomy. Realizing that he was unable to change her mind, the surgeon called in a psychiatrist to talk with the competent woman. The surgeon pressured the psychiatrist to declare the women incompetent, freeing the way for the surgeon to assume the role of decision maker and thus amputate her leg. As the doctor wheeled the diabetic woman toward the operating room, with all her senses intact and aware of her dilemma, she began to cry hysterically, shouting and pointing at the nurse: "You tricked me. You lied to me!"[6]

Even though the AMA, if not all individual physicians, eventually permitted the patient to refuse unwanted treatment, it continues to remain staunchly opposed to hastening death with a prescription for lethal drugs or by means of a lethal injection. Virtually every major medical organization in the nation, from the AMA to the National Hospice Organization (NHO), is opposed to an assisted death. State medical associations do not automatically agree, and individual doctors—like the medical profession as a whole—are currently divided on the issue, but the side with the money, the political clout, and the access to the media, the AMA, is lobbying hard to keep the practice illegal.

The AMA's current guidelines, updated in 1993, are, in summary: PAS is fundamentally inconsistent with the physician's professional role; it is critical that the medical profession redouble its efforts to ensure that patients are provided optimal treatment for their pain and discomfort; physicians must resist the natural tendency to withdraw physically from their terminally ill patients; requests for PAS should be a signal to the physician that the patient's needs are unmet and that further evaluation to identify the elements contributing to the patient's suffering is necessary; and further efforts to educate physicians about advanced pain management techniques, both at the undergraduate and graduate levels, are necessary to overcome the shortcomings of this area.[7]

Not even legalization would make the practice acceptable to the AMA. Physicians participating in assisted suicide, even if legal, would be performing an unethical act, said AMA board chair, Lonnie R. Bristow, M.D.: "The House of Medicine has spoken very clearly on the matter and has stated that to prescribe a medicine and to knowingly inform a patient of the lethal dosage so that a patient can in effect plan their own suicide is unethical behavior. And even if a state passes a law making it legal, it won't make it ethical."[8] The doctor continued that ethical standards are higher than legal standards, and the fact that the law condones particular activity "fortunately does not guide the profession."[9]

The "House of Medicine" may have spoken, but its tenants did not necessarily listen. State medical associations are not required to accept the position of the national AMA, but it is generally expected that "the company line is going to be similar between the national and state organization,"[10] said an Oregon surgeon. There was no united party line on Oregon's Measure 16, however, as two state medical associations disagreed with the powerful AMA. The Oregon Medical Association refused to affirm the national organization's opposition to Measure 16, maintaining a neutral stance through that 1994 election.

The Michigan State Medical Association, propelled largely by the spotlight on Kevorkian, voted in favor of taking no position on supporting or opposing assisted suicide. However, as a physician and member of the MSMA's board of directors said: "This is not a no-policy decision. We have a very strong policy on doctor-assisted suicide. . . . I think the House of Delegates very unanimously expressed the feeling that this is an individual-conscience-decision between doctors and patients."[11] In a statement directed at both the Oregon and Michigan Medical Associations, the AMA president remarked that "it doesn't make either the OMA, the MSMA, or the AMA comfortable to be disagreeing with each other. It's sort of unprecedented."[12]

Discomfort was relatively short-lived, however. After three years and before the 1997 second initiative vote in Oregon, both state associations succumbed to pressure from their parent group, the AMA, as well as from the Roman Catholic Church and the right-to-life movement. After considerable arm-twisting and infiltration by these religious organizations and months of intensive lobbying by Dr. William Toffler, an ardent Roman Catholic with an obsession to overturn the state's right-to-die law, the Oregon House of Delegates overwhelmingly voted to reject physician-assisted suicide.

In both Oregon initiatives the majority of the public favored PAS. The people, it appears, were not listening to the "House of Medicine" any more than they were responding to the "House of God." Approval rating for the 1994 initiative had been 51 percent. By the time these two powerful groups had finished their less-than-persuasive campaigning in 1997, support for PAS had reached 60 percent.

In the spring of 1996, between the two Oregon votes, the medical establishment received another blow. The Ninth and Second Circuit Courts of Appeals, finding that the laws banning PAS in New York and Washington were unconstitutional, also rejected organized medicine's long-held distinction between withholding and withdrawing treatment and PAS, and gave patients the means to end a life of suffering. The courts found no ethical distinction between assisted suicide and the medical profession's common practice of giving large doses of morphine for pain with the "unintended" consequence of hastening death (known as "the double effect"), and no ethical distinction between assisted suicide and the medical profession's common practice of using large doses of barbiturates for pain to put the patient in a deep coma, followed by removing artificial food and water ("terminal sedation"). The AMA and other health organizations lost no time in combining forces to dissuade the Supreme Court from upholding these unorthodox opinions.

Even though the AMA was convinced that the bicoastal courts had "clearly erred" in their analysis, they also realized the urgency of articulating a new strategy that would rely "upon reason and scholarship" to support their position. In a memo to the board, in his capacity as AMA executive vice-president, Dr. John Seward, "said that the AMA would continue to stand by its ethical prohibition of assisted suicide, but 'it is imperative,' he added, 'that we engage in constructive debate and not project an image of stridency or arrogance.' "[13]

To this end, forty-six medical groups, including the NHO and the American Psychiatric Association (APA), the AMA and the American Nurses Association (ANA), filed a joint amicus brief, urging the Supreme Court to uphold the state bans on assisted death. They maintained that making PAS a legal right throughout the country would "create profound danger" for terminally ill patients. AMA Vice Chairman Thomas Reardon, said that his members think "it is unethical for physicians to hasten death or actively participate in the killing of patients," a practice he argues health care providers do not want and cannot control.[14]

In a surprising move, 30,000 medical students filed their own brief, sending a clear signal to the Court that attitudes about treatment of the dying are changing within the medical community. The American Medical Students Association (AMSA), which describes itself as "the future of medicine in the United States," rebuffed its elders at the AMA by declaring its support for legalizing PAS: "We recognize that, for most patients . . . a physician can adequately ease a patient's suffering even when there is no cure for the patient's underlying condition," the brief said. "When appropriate palliative care is adequate to relieve the patient's pain and suffering, we do not believe that physician-assisted suicide is an advisable option. However," the brief continued, "we also recognize that even the highest quality palliative care will not always adequately ease a patient's suffering. In such exceptional circumstances, mentally competent terminally ill patients should have the option of a safe, legal and state-regulated means of hastening death with the assistance of a physician."[15]

The medical students sided with the Ninth and Second Circuit Courts, which saw no difference between an assisted suicide and the withdrawing of life-support treatment. Organized medicine maintains that there *is* a difference—withdrawing treatment requires no "affirmative action" to cause the patient's death, whereas writing a prescription *does* require such action.

The students agreed with Tribe and other advocates of PAS who see the hypocrisy of differentiating the two procedures: "This contention simply ignores the clinical reality of life-sustaining technology. For example, to disconnect a respirator, a physician or nurse must take each of the following steps: 1. Turn off the respirator; 2. Disconnect the machine from the tube that goes to the patient's lungs; 3. Remove the tube from the patient's lungs; 4. Administer morphine or barbiturates to ease the patient's sense of suffocation; and 5. Monitor medication levels to ensure that symptoms of severe air hunger do not arise. . . . There can be no question that if a physician performed . . . these actions without the patient's consent, she would be legally responsible for causing the patient's death just as surely as if she had shot her patient," the brief concludes.[16]

Executive Director Girsh of Hemlock USA commented on the medical students' brief: "Younger physicians grew up with a sense of the importance of patient autonomy. Older doctors grew up with the sense that the doctor is always right. These doctors growing up now know that patients want to decide about how they want their treatment and how they want to live and die. They probably just see aid-in-dying as an extension of refusal of treatment."[17]

At the AMA's annual meeting in Chicago during the summer of 1996, two brave, lone physicians urged the association to reconsider its long-standing official opposition to PAS. "What business is it of organized medicine to require the continuation of agony when the result is imminent and inevitable?" asked Dr. David Carter, a family doctor from Pawtucket, Rhode Island, during an hour-long debate on the first day of the meeting. "Is this caregiving, when healing is impossible? Is there no room for patient choice if death is the only therapeutic alternative? Is this cruel and paternalistic?"[18]

A second physician, retired Illinois radiologist Ulrich Danckers, asked the AMA to be neutral on the issue until public opinion, courts, and state legislatures had decided which way to go. "I may have heard the question a hundred times: 'Why doctor, am I not allowed to die? Why will you not help me?' Danckers said. Do I tell the patient, 'Please respect my pledge to be a healer, not a killer?' Do I say, 'My medical society does not want me to help you die?' " The patient's response to that, said Danckers, is usually: " 'Damn your medical society with its doctor-knows-best attitudes that tries to substitute its own moral judgment for . . . my own.' "[19]

Carter and Danckers were the only two doctors, out of 430 delegates representing approximately 350,000 physicians nationwide, who supported changing or staying neutral on the AMA's official policy. A final report by the Board of Trustees of the American Medical Association, however, left no doubt about its position: "Physician-assisted suicide is fundamentally incompatible with the physician's role as healer, would be difficult or impossible to control and would pose serious societal risks."[20]

Regardless of what the hierarchies of national medical associations espouse, there is ample evidence that a significant number of physicians support the practice of hastening death in certain situations—both in theory and in practice. A 1961 national survey found that only 34 percent of the internists and surgeons questioned would support legalization.[21] A 1996 survey published in the *New England Journal of Medicine* found that 56 percent of responding doctors in Michigan preferred legalizing assisted suicide to an explicit ban.[22] A 1996 survey of Oregon doctors, published in the same journal, showed 60 percent of the responding doctors supporting legalization of assisted suicide for terminally ill patients.[23] (Not surprisingly, perhaps, a 1974 survey had revealed that 86 percent of the doctors interviewed wanted assisted suicide for themselves if the need arose.)[24]

Physicians tend to mirror the general public. Both populations are divided, but approval of assisted suicide is gaining ground in both. Existing surveys show the trend among physicians has been to lag behind public opinion on the issue of legalizing PAS. A recent poll conducted by NTN Communications, Inc., determined that 78 percent of adults surveyed believe that PAS for the terminally ill should be legalized by the federal government.[25] A Michigan poll showed 80 percent support for Dr. Jack Kevorkian. The only other place with approval this high is England, where an equal 80 percent support PAS.[26]

As the general population's approval has climbed to a level between 65 and 78 percent, so too is the physician approval rating on the rise. Recent surveys have shown that as many as 60 percent of American doctors now support PAS.[27] The public, the churches, the legal community, and the physicians—all of two minds on the subject—are struggling to cope with societal changes that are slowly overwhelming opposition to assisted suicide.

Although 54 percent of the doctors randomly selected in Washington State thought voluntary euthanasia should be legalized in some circumstances, only 33 percent said they would be willing to inject a lethal dosage of a drug. While 53 percent thought that doctor-assisted suicide should be legal, only 40 percent said they would write a lethal prescription for a patient to self-administer. The research team found that blood and cancer specialists, the doctors most likely to be exposed to terminally ill patients, were also the strongest opponents of voluntary euthanasia. By contrast, psychiatrists, who had the least contact, were the strongest advocates of the two practices.[28]

The same survey found women significantly more likely to support PAS than men, but both genders have similar attitudes towards euthanasia. In addition the numbers showed that 91 percent of the physicians supporting suicide and euthanasia believed the two practices to be consistent with the doctor's role of relieving pain and suffering, while 74 percent of those against the practices cited the same reason for the opposition. The researchers concluded that "the polarized attitudes of physicians will make it difficult to formulate and implement laws and policies concerning assisted suicide."[29]

In a nationwide survey of neurologists released as recently as the spring of 1998, 14 percent of the doctors said they would consider prescribing medication to shorten the dying process if it were illegal. This statistic jumped to 43 percent if PAS was legalized. One-half of the neurologists supported such legalization. Predictably, the American Academy of Neurology, the organization that represents them, has a strongly worded policy opposing an assisted death.[30]

Some physicians are helping their patients achieve a dignified death with a lethal prescription or injection despite the law. The risks are high. Legal and professional pressures require the procedure to be carried out covertly. Patients fear involuntary commitment to prevent their suicides, and physicians fear criminal prosecution. Doctors rarely seek advice from colleagues, forgoing valuable information and support. The situation also forces many patients to conspire with their loved ones, who have reason to fear prosecution as a result of their assistance in the death.

Many doctors have the courage of their convictions, and risk loss of license, career, income, and personal freedom. A study showed that 16 percent of physicians polled in Washington State reported having been asked by their terminally ill patients for either PAS or euthanasia. Of the patients who requested PAS, 24 percent received prescriptions, and of those who requested euthanasia, another 24 percent received lethal injections.[31]

A study of Michigan oncologists reported that 18 percent of those who responded reported active participation in PAS; 4 percent reported participation in voluntary euthanasia: That is a total of 22 percent of Michigan's oncologists surveyed who complied with requests to hasten death.[32] In another study of cancer specialists, 57 percent had been asked for help in ending their life, and 13.5 percent of them had complied.[33]

People with AIDS often attempt suicide, and doctors appear increasingly willing to help them. More than half (53 percent) of San Francisco AIDS doctors surveyed admitted having helped at least one patient commit suicide. One doctor admitted to having assisted one hundred patients. "Everyone knows this occurs," says Thomas Mitchell, a public health specialist.[34]

These figures show the high percentage of physicians who operate outside the law and the purview of the national and state medical organizations. The conventional wisdom that the AMA is "against assisted dying" belies the number of health care professionals who disagree enough with the law and the AMA to risk being charged with murder.

Physicians fall into basically three categories, claims a *New England Journal of Medicine* editorial. Those in the category that supports the practice of hastening a death see it as a "compassionate response to a medical need, a symbol of nonabandonment, and a means to reestablish patients' trust in doctors who have used technology excessively. They argue that regulation of physician-assisted suicide is possible and, in fact, necessary to control the actions of physicians who are currently providing assistance surreptitiously."[35]

The two remaining groups of physicians oppose legalization. One group is not ethically, morally, or religiously opposed to the practice and views it, in fact, as justifiable under certain circumstances—even participating in the practice. However, these physicians do not want it legalized and thus regulated. The third group, including the AMA, is morally opposed to hastening death. They believe physicians should not be executioners—should not endorse justified killing.

Medical professionals, attending a conference to honor the Quinlan and Cruzan families, derided the Ninth and Second Circuit Courts of Appeals decisions legalizing assisted suicide. It is a known fact, however, that many of them support assisted death for the suffering, therefore the contradiction was confusing and unsettling. Had they changed their minds? When one of the medical participants was privately questioned, the doctor gave an astonishingly honest and forthright answer—but asked for confidentiality. "Most of us medical people here are personally in favor of assisted suicide, and many have helped patients die. One helped yesterday, but—heck—we don't want the law involved. We can do this on our own. We want to do it on our terms, and we don't want no one, no how, looking at us and regulating our behavior. There is so much regulation now. It's easier for us this way," he said.

This attitude is eerily reminiscent of the 1960s and 1970s, when the medical profession viewed external interventions as unnecessary, insulting, and, frankly, nobody's business but their own. This autonomy continued until they abused their discretion to such a degree that state and federal authorities declared that playtime was over. The practice of medicine subsequently underwent a remarkable transformation, as the previously unfettered profession gradually came to be dominated by regulations, peer review, and monitoring. History has demonstrated physicians' clear and repeated inability to regulate themselves. Whether a similar result will take place with assisted suicide remains to be seen.

It appears, therefore, that many health care providers oppose legalization but support the practice. Being opposed to the former, with its rules and regulations, does not necessarily translate into being against hastening the death of a mentally competent terminally ill adult. Many doctors simply do not want the regulation and the loss of control that legalization would bring, while at the same time aiding patients if it can be on their own terms.

An increasing number of doctors are breaking silence about their participation, in order to spark discussion about assisted suicide and to help patients. Every doctor's style and approach is different. Richard MacDonald and Bry Benjamin are just two of many doctors who are quietly going about the business of putting patients out of their misery. MacDonald has helped end the lives of the terminal and those in pain as well as the lives of patients who were not in a great deal of pain but who were physically incapacitated and suffering the discomforts and indignities of being totally dependent. Says MacDonald: "If I were convinced that their request was rational, that the patient was mentally competent, and I were convinced that the disease was indeed without any possibility of improvement, I would—and I have done so—assist my patients to die prematurely by a few days or a few weeks."

MacDonald, a Canadian practicing in California, reviews methods with the patient and often the family. "I think everything should be openly discussed," he says. The compassionate doctor helps patients end their lives "several different ways: by dripping, or helping family members drip, liquid morphine under a patient's tongue, by administering morphine through a vein, by removing breathing tubes, and by giving patients high doses of barbiturates, such as Seconal, that they could drink themselves."

Benjamin, a specialist in internal medicine and geriatrics in New York City, also says he has helped patients to end their lives, but that he always tries to cover his tracks. "Usually I'm pretty careful to give any medication in limited amounts," he says. "And patients themselves want to protect those connected with their deaths, so they switch bottles and change labels." Benjamin does not administer the medication, but instead makes it clear to the patient that misuse will result in death. "The way around the law is saying, well, the person was suffering a great deal and so I gave it to them to end their suffering, not their lives. It was they who were willing to take more and risk their lives. There's a lot of purposeful ambiguity," he says. Doctor Benjamin does not like writing the prescriptions, but he is clear in his determination not to abandon his patients. "This is not something that I wanted to do," he admits. "But I do not close doors on my patients. And this is about listening to patients when they say, 'I've had enough.'"

Doctors are not the only health care professionals who hasten the death of a suffering patient. Acting on their own, or with at least the tacit consent of doctors or families, one in five nurses in intensive care units reported deliberately hastening a patient's death. In a national survey of 850 nurses who practiced exclusively in intensive care units, 141 said they had received requests from patients or family members to engage in euthanasia or assisted suicide, 129 said they had carried out these practices at least once, and 35 said they had hastened a patient's death by only pretending to carry out a life-sustaining treatment that was ordered by a doctor. The usual method was a high dose of an opiate, like morphine. Dr. John W. Hoyt, president of the International Society of Critical Care Medicine, said he was "shocked" by the findings because the actions to which these nurses admitted "violate the ethical norms of our profession."

The ANA and the American Association of Critical Care Nurses (AACCN) immediately and flatly denied the results of this research. The organizations jointly expressed concern "about the negative impact this article will have on patients who are dependent on nursing care and would have hoped for more responsible action from both the physician researcher and the New England Journal of Medicine."[36]

Why is the medical establishment so averse to PAS when so many of its members favor it? Its history is to resist change, but what is the reasoning on this issue? What is it so afraid of?

Some doctors automatically object for religious reasons. There is also the generic concern that voluntary PAS will progress to eventually include killing people against their wishes or without their consent. Other than these general concerns, the most frequently raised objections are: (1) pressure would be put on elderly and infirmed patients by family members who do not want the burden but do want the inheritance; (2) there would be reduced incentive to improve palliative care, especially pain control; (3) helping patients die would taint the integrity of the medical profession; (4) ignorance of effective methods might lead to botched suicide attempts; (5) the practice would be dangerous for patients with undiagnosed depression; (6) it is unethical for physicians to hasten death or actively participate in the killing of patient; (7) doctors are healers, not murderers; and (8) the practice would destroy the "trust factor" of the doctor-patient relationship.

The all-encompassing reason most frequently offered, however, is that any assistance on the part of the doctor in hastening a patient's death is in violation of the ethics and tradition of the medical profession. To this end the Hippocratic Oath is often cited. Yet the Oath has been selectively cited over time both in support for and against the matter.

The Oath of Hippocrates reads as follows:

> I swear by Apollo Physician and Asclepius and Hygeia and Panacea and all the gods and goddesses, making them my witness, that I will fulfill according to my ability and judgment this oath and this covenant:
>
> To hold him who has taught me this art as equal to my parents and to live my life in partnership with him, and if he is in need of money to give him a share of mine, and to regard his offspring as equal to my brothers in male lineage and to teach them this art—if they desire to learn it—without fee and covenant; to give a share of precepts and oral instruction and all the other learning to my sons and to the sons of him who has instructed me and to pupils who have signed the covenant and have taken an oath according to the medical law, but to no one else.
>
> I will apply dietetic measures for the benefit of the sick according to my ability and judgment; I will keep them from harm and injustice.
>
> I will neither give a deadly drug to anybody if asked for it, nor will I make a suggestion to this effect. Similarly, I will not give to a woman an abortion remedy. In purity and holiness I will guard my life and my art.
>
> Whatever house I may visit, I will come for the benefit of the sick, remaining free of all intentional injustice, of all mischief and in particular sexual relations with both female and male persons, be they free or slaves.

Whatever I may see or hear in the course of treatment on regard to the life of men, which on no account one must spread abroad, I will keep to myself holding such things shameful to be spoken about.

If I fulfill this oath and do not violate it, may it be granted to me to enjoy life and art, being honored with fame among all men for all time to come; if I transgress it and swear falsely, may the opposite of all this be my lot.

Conventional wisdom says that physicians are bound by the Hippocratic Oath. This is not the case. It is ironic that the profession, which prides itself on the Oath, does not require its members to take it. Indeed, physicians who have actually taken it are few and far between. Many physicians have never even read it, much less sworn to it. Few medical schools require its reading at graduation ceremonies. At the most, and even this is uncommon, medical school commencements include a rote and ritualistic recitation of the Oath, but it is usually a sanitized version that "omits references to sensitive subjects like euthanasia and abortion. Ignorance of the Hippocratic Oath's actual content is perhaps best exemplified by the frequent references to the maxim *Primum non nocere*, or 'First do no harm.' The precept is indeed Hippocratic, but it does not appear in the Oath."[37]

Those who argue against physician assistance quote the phrase, "I will neither give a deadly drug to anyone, if asked for, nor will I make a suggestion to this effect." It also forbids performing an abortion, receiving money for teaching medicine and performing surgery. What makes all the difference, and what is frequently overlooked, is that the Oath's first sentence affords room for "ability and judgment."

It is thus more of a guiding tradition to provide ethical guidelines than a literal promise to do or not do something. Physicians are free to rely on their own interpretation of the Oath—if they choose to rely on it at all. An elderly physician who had taken the life of a dying patient the previous day with an injection of morphine had this to say about his actions: "I don't believe I broke my Hippocratic Oath. Part of that Oath is not to do any harm to people and try to help people. I thought I was not doing harm but good in this case. I thought it was colleagues who were doing harm in prolonging his pain and suffering. The Hippocratic Oath in spirit is what I was doing. It will depend on your interpretation."[38]

Except in its broadest sense, the Oath has little relevance today. "A literal interpretation of the Hippocratic Oath in the twentieth century would be contrary to the very principle of application of fact that was so important to Hippocrates," writes John H. Leversee, physician and author of *Hippocrates Revisited: A View from General Practice*. "Time does change most things, if not all things. The passage of twenty-four centuries certainly changes the circumstances under which one must interpret facts. . . . Thus, it seems to me, we must see his principles in their broadest sense and not be bogged down by literal interpretations."

By 1948 the World Medical Association (WMA) issued a more current version of the Oath. It became known as the Geneva version of the Hippocratic Oath, or the Geneva Oath, because leaders of the medical profession accepted it at a meeting in Geneva. It contains no direct reference to abortion, to surgery, to payment, to educating the children of one's teachers or to assisting in a suicide. The revised Oath reads:

> Now being admitted to the profession of medicine, I solemnly pledge to consecrate my life to the services of humanity. I will give respect and gratitude to my teachers. I will practice medicine with conscience and dignity. The health and life of my patient will be my first consideration. I will hold in confidence all that my patient confides in me.
>
> I will maintain the honor and the noble traditions of the medical profession. My colleagues will be as my brothers. I will not permit consideration of race, religion, nationality, party politics or social standing to intervene between my duty and my patient. I will maintain the utmost respect for human life from the time of conception. Even under threat I will not use my knowledge contrary to the laws of humanity.
>
> These promises I make freely and upon my honor.

Physicians opposed to PAS ignore the existence of the Geneva Oath. They quote the 2,500-year-old version, even though the WMA has deemed it outdated. Nevertheless the original version serves as a convenient justification to support the claim that an assisted death should remain prohibited. It is similar to quoting a legal decision that was subsequently overturned by a higher court, knowing that the public is not sophisticated enough to see through the deception. An even more updated version of the Oath is under consideration by the WMA. There is no reason to expect, however, that selective reference to the ancient Oath will cease as long as it substantiates what benefits the physician.

There exists a truth far more subtle than the party-line talk of legalization's endangering patients and violating health care's mission to heal. The public debate obscures private concerns about legalization: regulations, red tape, and loss of control, which is, perhaps, the real issue here. Legalization would give patients more control, as *Quinlan* and its progeny empowered the patient—a fact the profession still resents. Measures 16 and 51 in Oregon were about the empowerment of patients, not doctors. The initiatives were fueled by the realization that physicians often ignore patient end-of-life wishes and appear uninterested in dealing with patient pain and emotional issues.

Charles Baron, professor of constitutional law and bioethics at the Boston College Law School, explains that physicians are concerned that legalizing assisted suicide would lead to stricter oversight of *other* end-of-life decisions, such as removing patients from ventilators. "I think it is truly motivated by the fear that doctors will lose their totally unsupervised autonomy when it comes to making decisions about their patients."[39]

While struggling to retain some control, the AMA knows that its public and private image needs improvement. Membership is dropping. In the beginning of 1997 the association represented just under 40 percent of the nation's 700,000 physicians, down from 51 percent nine years earlier, and down from its high of 75 percent in the 1960s. Being so out of sync with physicians over current issues, such as physician participation in the death of a terminal patient, contributes to its immateriality. The AMA's irrelevancy has hurt it badly; membership dues dropped $2.1 million from 1995 to 1996, a shortfall of $1.3 million.[40]

The medical establishment is beginning to concede physician assistance in dying. Similar to the way in which it eventually agreed to living wills, women surgeons, Red Cross blood banks, and Medicare, this compliance has not been voluntary or without a fight. The Oregon Medical Association, the organization that remained neutral for the first Oregon initiative, but then opposed the practice in the 1997 initiative, is cooperating with the state's new law—even if without enthusiasm.

Faced with mounting evidence that PAS will one day be legal throughout the nation, other regional medical communities are taking tentative steps toward setting professional standards for helping people die. The Michigan State Medical Society, a group of California health care providers, and Stanford University Center for Biomedical Ethics are working independently on proper ways to handle patients who want to die.

The AMA, however, continues to take a hard line. Dr. Charles Plows, chairman of the AMA's Council on Ethical and Judicial Affairs, said after a recent meeting, "We did talk about it, and decided this was not the proper time to consider guidelines. My own opinion is if we produce guidelines, we are indirectly offering some credence to physician-assisted suicide. It gives more fuel to the fire."[41]

Bioethicist Caplan reacts to Plows's and the AMA's ostrich approach to the growing issue: "Dr. Plows is, if not standing in front of a steamroller, he's at least got a rapidly moving train headed straight at him. I'm on his side. I oppose legalization right now. But I believe if you can't win your argument, your next obligation is to make sure as few people as possible get hurt."[42]

It has been said that the dinosaur became extinct because it could not adjust to a changing environment. Only time will tell if the same adage holds true for the medical establishment. Instead of being in the forefront of implementing workable guidelines for the inevitable legalization, the AMA is fighting fiercely to maintain its diminished reputation and authority.

By contrast a solid majority of practicing physicians believe in the need to alleviate pain and suffering under certain circumstances by hastening an approaching death. A substantial number practice what they believe, at considerable risk. Unfortunately this polarization will make it difficult to reach a consensus that will benefit the American people. Yet with 60 percent of the nation's doctors supporting aid in dying, they join the rest of the communities struggling to cope with societal changes that are overwhelming resistance to assisted suicide.

In a rare strand of liberal thinking, the usually conservative *British Medical Journal* has praised the renegade, Doctor Kevorkian, as a "medical hero." It quotes the *Oxford English Dictionary*: "A hero is a man of action rather than thought and lives by a personal code of honour that admits of no qualification. His responses are usually instinctive, predictable and inevitable. He accepts challenge and sometimes even courts disaster."[43] To be a hero, the *Journal* continues, "means being honest with yourself and acting on your own morality, risking the fall from the pinnacle."[44] The health care professionals who confront the issues, take the risks, and attempt to stop the hypocrisy, are the real heroes of today's right-to-die movement. Meanwhile the AMA complacently issues press releases, attempts to polish its tarnished image, and struggles to maintain the status quo, with apparent dismissal of the inevitable.

Chapter 14

President and Government Resist Reform

While it is true that government has introduced advance directives and the Patient Self-Determination Act, and has generally supported the forgoing of futile medical treatment, the government is also a powerful restraining force on the PAS and voluntary euthanasia planks of the right-to-die movement. All branches—executive, legislative and judicial—on both the state and federal levels, have had a hand in limiting the scope of this populist, grass-roots movement.

The Ninth and Second Circuit Courts of Appeals, in the spring of 1996, struck down criminal prohibitions against assisted suicide in Washington and New York States. These cases, the first appellate rulings on the subject, were subsequently appealed to the U.S. Supreme Court. In October of the same year, the Court agreed to consider the issue of PAS. When the Supreme Court agreed to take the states' appeals, it entered one of the most controversial social debates to arise in recent years.

On the final day for filing a brief, the Clinton administration, for the first time, voiced its official opposition to an assisted death. Walter E. Dellinger, acting solicitor general, filed briefs representing President Clinton's point of view, and would later argue the cases before the Supreme Court.

The solicitor general is the attorney appointed by the president who argues the government's position before the High Court. Although the government was not a party to the suit, the Federal Rules of Civil Procedure allow the solicitor general to intervene and argue a case where the government believes it has an interest. This was the first indication that the government would join the restraining forces of religion and medicine in opposing PAS.

The government's position, similar to that of other opponents, emphasized the potential for error and abuse. It also distinguished between assisting a death and allowing a death to occur by forgoing life-support treatment. In his legal briefs on behalf of the Clinton administration, Dellinger argued that the state has a legitimate interest in upholding the value of human life and in protecting sick, depressed, mentally ill, or otherwise vulnerable people from themselves and others. Dellinger noted that the government's interest derives from its ownership and operation of health care facilities, including 173 veterans' medical centers and 126 nursing homes, and he stressed the need to protect sick people at a vulnerable time in their lives. "The difficulty that physicians have in determining whether requests for assisted suicide come from patients with treatable pain or depression, the vulnerability of terminally ill patients to subtle influences from physicians and family members . . . and the continuing possibility that someone can be misdiagnosed as terminally ill, all support a state's decision to ban all assisted suicides," he said.[1]

The solicitor general concluded: "There is an important and common-sense distinction between withdrawing artificial supports so that a disease will progress to its inevitable end, and providing chemicals to be used to kill someone." The laws should therefore continue "to preserve the distinction between killing a patient and letting a patient die."[2]

Dellinger acknowledged that the cases before the Court concerned only mentally competent terminally ill people who want to end their intolerable suffering. However, a ruling in their favor, he said, could result in many others being "steered toward suicide by family members or their doctors." Because this practice could be so easily abused, wrote the administration's chief attorney, it is wiser not to allow it for *anyone*, including those patients only hours away from death. This innate suspicion of family, a result of the *Cruzan* decision, provides the basis for the "slippery slope" argument that opposes PAS under any and all circumstances.

The family, rather than seen as supportive and caring, is now perceived as a vaguely evil entity with sinister intentions, plotting to end the lives of its weakest members. It was not always this way: Judges and society alike used to praise the family. Chief Justice Hughes recognized, in *Quinlan*, the important principle that right-to-die cases are family matters that do not belong in court unless there is a disagreement amongst family members. The advances made in *Quinlan* and its progeny underwent a decided shift in *Cruzan*. Indeed, what *Quinlan* gave to the family, *Cruzan* took away. There is no rational basis for this greedy-family-killing-its-sick theory. No one has *ever* brought a charge against a family member or a doctor for inappropriately withholding or withdrawing life support. If no abuse has been uncovered in these sensitive scenarios over the last twenty years, there is absolutely no reason to believe it would happen with PAS, where the patient has even more control over life's final moments.

In *Washington* v. *Glucksberg*, the appeals court equated the right to hasten a death with the right to an abortion. The Clinton administration, now positioning itself on the other side of a civil rights issue, wanted to preserve its pro-choice stance on abortion. Not wanting to provide the Court with the opening to remove abortion from the protection of the Fourteenth Amendment, Dellinger emphasized the difference between an abortion and an assisted death. He attempted to persuade the Court, therefore, that

> while both are associated with pain and suffering, . . . "A prohibition on abortion interferes with personal autonomy in an extremely consequential way: by forcing a woman to continue an unwanted pregnancy, the state requires a woman to undertake the birth of, and responsibility for another person in a way that has no counterpart in our laws." While the Constitution does give some protection for the kind of pain and suffering experienced by terminally ill patients, said the government, those rights do not rise to the same level as women seeking abortions.[3]

While the government acknowledged that individuals have a significant constitutional interest in controlling their fate, it concluded that the government's interest in prohibiting suicide is greater than the terminally ill patient's right of self-determination:

> A competent, terminally ill adult has a constitutionally recognizable liberty interest in avoiding the kind of suffering experienced by the plaintiffs in this case. That liberty interest encompasses an interest not only in avoiding severe physical pain, but also the despair and distress that comes from physical deterioration and the inability to control basic bodily or mental functions in the terminal stage of an illness. . . .
>
> Nevertheless, overriding state interests justify the state's decision to ban physicians from prescribing lethal medication. The state has an interest of the highest order in prohibiting its physicians from assisting in the purposeful taking of another person's life.

Not long after the oral arguments before the Court, the House of Representatives voted to bar the federal government from paying for doctor-assisted deaths. The practice was illegal in all fifty states at the time, and no federal funds were being used. Nevertheless, the bill, sparked by concern over the increasing acceptability of the practice and fear that the Supreme Court might legalize it, passed by a whopping 398–16. Passage ensured that, regardless of what happened in the Supreme Court or in the states, no Medicare, Medicaid, or other federal funds would be used to pay for assisted suicide. This barring of federal money was, paradoxically, a testimony to the increasing support for PAS and anticipated its inevitable legalization.

Rep. Ralph Hall (D., Tex.), a sponsor of the bill, warned that the courts would "get the last guess as to what the law is. If they guess wrong on this, you can open up the Treasury to every Dr. Kevorkian all across the country."[4]

While few lawmakers were officially willing to oppose the bill, numerous Democrats spoke out against it, deriding it as a meaningless political stunt:

"This bill does nothing," said Rep. Pete Stark (D., Wash.) "It just addresses a problem that does not exist. It eases some pseudo-religious wackos. It is a sham, it is a shame, we are a sad, sad, Congress if we pass this bill." "This is nothing more than a hollow exercise probably designed to fill a massive hole in this do-nothing Congress," said Rep. Sherrod Brown (D., Ohio).[5]

At the committee level, Democrats pressed for amendments that would have at least provided counseling and guidelines for those physicians treating terminally ill patients. Even though the goal of these amendments was to have fewer people attempting to end their lives, the politicians rejected the proposals. The legislation did, however, authorize the government to develop programs designed to reduce the rate of suicide.

Not long after the House vote, the Senate followed with a bill that again barred the federal government from ever financing PAS. The same measure that had cleared the House by a 398–16 vote, passed the Senate with a staggering 99–0. Senators and representatives alike voiced many of the same reasons, pro and con. However, there was one difference. The Senate Democrats pressed through measures authorizing the secretary of health and human services to fund research in pain treatment and suicide prevention, and a federal study on how health care professionals are trained in end-of-life care.

Even though the legislation focused on federal funding and not on whether PAS should be legalized, the passage of the bills in both houses of Congress dramatically shows just how wide the gap is between politicians and the electorates. With national opinion polls consistently showing that between 63 to 78 percent of Americans support the right of terminally ill patients to end their lives, how could the Congress elect, by a combined vote of 497–16, to deny that right? There is a reasonable expectation that congressional support should mirror the percentage of public support—unless, that is, other affluent restraining forces are pressuring the politicians with threats of withholding financial contributions to campaigns if the politicians vote otherwise.

Bill Clinton again threw his political weight against the right to an assisted death by declaring his intention to sign the legislation into law. At a White House press conference, Michael McCurry, the presidential spokesperson, confirmed the president's support of the bill. The press conference went on to discuss human rights in China. Why Clinton doesn't see the suffering of the terminally ill as a human rights or civil rights issue is unclear. Generally speaking, those people in favor of abortion are in favor of assisted suicide, and those opposed to one tend to be opposed to the other. While Clinton personally supports a pregnant woman's right to choose, he does not support the suffering patient's right to choose. For whatever personal reason, Clinton made the decision to intervene in restraining a national movement that has been called the "ultimate civil right."

For a long while, all that was known was that Clinton was against PAS. He gave no explanation. Ultimately the White House released a statement from President Clinton:

> Today I am signing into law H.R. 1003, the "Assisted Suicide Funding Restriction Act of 1997" which reaffirms current Federal policy banning the use of Federal funds to pay for assisted suicide, euthanasia, or mercy killing.
>
> This is appropriate legislation. Over the years, I have clearly expressed my personal opposition to assisted suicide, and I continue to believe that assisted suicide is wrong. While I have deep sympathy for those who suffer greatly from incurable illness, I believe that to endorse assisted suicide would set us on a disturbing and perhaps dangerous path. This legislation will ensure that taxpayer dollars will not be used to subsidize or promote assisted suicide. The Act will, among other things, ban the funding of assisted suicide, euthanasia, or mercy killing through Medicaid, Medicare, military and Federal employee health plans, the veterans' health care system, and other Federally funded programs.
>
> Section 5(a)(3) of the Act also assures that taxpayer funds will not be used to subsidize legal assistance or other forms of advocacy in support of legal protection for assisted suicide, euthanasia, or mercy killing. The restrictions on the use of funds contained in this section, properly construed, will allow the Federal Government to speak with a clear voice in opposing these practices. The Department of Justice has advised, however, that a broad construction of this section would raise serious First Amendment concerns. I am therefore instructing the Federal agencies that they should construe section 5(a)(3) only to prohibit Federal funding for activities and services that provide legal assistance for the purpose of advocating a right to assisted suicide, or that have as their purpose the advocacy of assisted suicide, and not to restrict Federal funding for other activities, such as those that provide forums for the free exchange of ideas. In addition, I emphasize that section 5(a)(3) imposes no restriction on the use of nonfederal funds.[6]

The same day that the Supreme Court ruled against a constitutional right to PAS, the White House issued the following statement by a satisfied President Clinton:

> I am very pleased with today's Supreme Court decision which accepted my Administration's position that states may ban PAS. The decision is a victory for all Americans—it prevents us from going down a very dan-

gerous and troubling path on this difficult and often agonizing issue. With today's decision, the Court voices its concern that there is a significant distinction between assisting in death and allowing a death to occur. Not only is this an important legal distinction, it is also a distinction of deep moral and ethical implications. I have a great deal of sympathy and a profound respect for those who suffer from incurable illnesses, and for their families. I have had a number of family members die from painful and protracted illnesses. Even so, I have always expressed my strong opposition to PAS. I believe that it is wrong and have always believed it to be wrong. This issue is unavoidably heartrending, and we must never ignore the agony of terminally ill patients, but the Supreme Court made the right decision today. The risks and consequences of PAS are simply too great.[7]

A dangerous trend in this country bears watching: The government is not listening to the people. Ever since President Ronald Reagan resurrected the debate over states' rights in the 1980s, and particularly since the Republicans took control of Congress in 1994, power seems to be flowing out of Washington and into the hands of the states. Authority is not, however, reaching the people. Public input is ebbing from the voter into the hands of both state and federal officials. Voters are becoming angry, insulted by, and resentful of recent paternalistic power plays by the Clinton administration, state lawmakers, and state and federal judiciaries.

This is the pattern: State voters approve an issue by ballot, referendum, or initiative. Shortly thereafter the government ignores the voters' decision by extinguishing their mandate, saying, in essence, that the voting public either did not understand what it was voting for or voted incorrectly. The government steps in on the basis that it is protecting the public from itself. In other words, the vote stands if the government agrees with the people, but if the powers that be disagree with how the vote turned out, then the public is proclaimed ignorant or uninformed, and the ballot, referendum, or initiative is discounted.

Federal judges are coming under increasing attack for overturning controversial new laws passed by grassroots voters in initiatives or referendums. Numerous measures, ranging from term limits to assisted suicide, have been delayed or rebuffed entirely by federal courts. Critics say the federal judges are thwarting the will of the people. Endorsers say the judges are fulfilling their duty of enforcing the Constitution and checking the tyranny of the majority.

It can fairly be said that the three branches of state and federal government are asserting an authority often associated with a police state. A federal judge blocked California from cutting back on affirmative-action programs, even though a majority of voters in a November 1996 referendum had required state officials to do precisely that. A three-judge panel reversed the lower court's ruling with a warning: "A system which permits one judge to block with a stroke of a pen what 4,736,180 state residents voted to enact as law tests the integrity of our constitutional democracy."[8]

California residents cast their votes for term limits. Federal Judge Claudia Wilken said Proposition 140 violated the U.S. Constitution by imposing lifetime term limits on state legislators. Wilken's decision "fuels the frustration citizens harbor toward a judiciary that all too often extinguishes their mandates," said California Attorney General Dan Lungren.[9] California's Proposition 187, which cut off certain state benefits to undocumented aliens, has been tied up in federal court since voters endorsed it in 1994.

Residents of Arizona have had their vote overturned twice since 1988. That was the year they endorsed English as the official language for all state business, but a challenge by a state worker continues to halt implementation of the new law. Then, in 1996, Arizona voters, by a substantial majority, approved ballot initiatives legalizing certain drugs for medicinal use. The state legislature invalidated the vote on the pretext of protecting the public from its own poor judgment. Critics of the reversal called it a "slap in the face of the voters. 'It seems to me, we're saying to the voters that you're smart when you vote for us but we don't trust you when you vote on other important issues,'" said a member of the legislature.[10]

The list of government reversals of public decisions grows longer, and certainly extends to the right to die. Oregon's 1994 winning initiative declaring an individual's right to PAS under prescribed circumstances was held up in federal court *by one judge* for almost three years. The Oregon legislature put the same issue back on the ballot in 1997, in essence saying to voters, "Let's vote again and see if you can get it right this time." Efforts by the legislature to repeal Measure 16 were met with resistance and outrage. Said Jim Moore, a political scientist from the University of Portland, "People are looking at . . . the state legislature mucking around with this measure as an attack on the initiative system. That has hit a wellspring of resentment."[11]

The second time around, the percentage favoring a physician's help in dying was considerably higher than three years earlier. Although the Roman Catholic Church spent five million dollars on the campaign, the AMA and the Oregon Medical Association opposed the practice, and the state government did its best to derail the issue, the assisted suicide law prevailed partly because Oregon voters were angry they had to pass judgment again on something they had already decided. Said Barbara Coombs Lee, who with Eli Stutsman helped write the 1994 initiative and led the antirepeal campaign: "This is a turning point for the death-with-dignity movement nationwide, not because we won but because we've proved the citizens of a state can band together and beat the political machine."[12]

Even though Oregon citizens twice voted the same way, the government still did not want to respect the will of the people. The difference this time was that a federal agency was blocking implementation. The federal Drug

Enforcement Administration (DEA) warned Oregon doctors that prescribing drugs to help terminally ill patients kill themselves could force a physician to face severe sanctions. Prescriptions for assisted suicide would violate federal narcotics law because assisted suicide does not fit "under any current definition [of] legitimate medical purpose."[13]

Attorney General Janet Reno, on March 5, 1998, removed the last legal obstacle—or so it seemed—to the full operation of Oregon's landmark assisted suicide law, declaring that doctors who use the law to prescribe lethal drugs to terminally ill patients will not be prosecuted. While Oregon is the only state to currently legalize such a law, Reno's ruling signals that other states may enact similar laws without interference from the federal government.

Within hours of Reno's announcement, however, Rep. Henry J. Hyde (R., Ill.) and Rep. James L. Oberstar (D., Minn.) introduced legislation in Congress that would ban doctors from using medication to assist in a suicide. Although the early votes seem to be in favor of the Hyde and Oberstar bill, it is doubtful that the Supreme Court would let the Congressional legislation stand. The Court gave to the states the power to legalize PAS and a Congressional revocation would be pointedly contrary to the Court's previously articulated position.

It is quite remarkable that a populous, grassroots movement could withstand the slings and arrows of the combined forces of religion, medicine, and the government and then come out on top. It is more than remarkable—it is almost miraculous. Those advocating physician assistance for the mentally competent terminally ill adult who wishes a shortened dying experience may have felt like they were swimming upstream for many years. Indeed they were, for the prevailing establishment forces of American culture were flowing against them. These forces still are. The difference is that the right-to-die movement is gaining momentum, leaving the Goliath forces without a foundation of popular support.

PART FOUR

Into
Action:
The Battle
for Rights

Chapter 15

The West Coast Resorts
to the Polls

History was made in Oregon in 1997 when its citizens became the first community to confirm by popular vote the legalization of PAS for the terminally ill. Through a political miscalculation by its opponents, this was the second vote within three years on an identical law by the same electorate. On the first occasion the law passed by a mere 2 percent margin, but the second time around it succeeded by a 20 percent. A more thorough and democratic demonstration of the public will could hardly have been deliberately orchestrated; the fault lay with opponents, who, overzealous in their desire to destroy the 1994 law, ended up greatly increasing the mandate for its implementation.

There were many reasons why public support increased so dramatically, not least that it demonstrated that the more the public knew about choice in dying, weighing the pros and the cons, the greater their willingness to vote for a law regulating it. It was a landmark decision for the euthanasia movement in the United States denoting a turning point in public acceptance as well as a major setback for its chief opponents, the National Right to Life Committee and the hierarchy of the Roman Catholic Church. For years the proponents of the euthanasia movement had suffered from a lack of political experience, in contrast to its enemies, who had spent a quarter of a century in the legislatures and the courts contesting a woman's right to an abortion. Now, with the Oregon result, the movement had matured and entered the corridors of political power.

The Oregon results showed that a movement, though small in membership and funding, can—provided that it has deep-rooted, general public support—succeed over much bigger opponents. The fragmented euthanasia movement in the United States has fewer than 75,000 combined active supporters, whereas the National Right to Life Committee claims 15 million in 3,000 chapters. The Hemlock Society of Oregon had only 600 members in a state of more than 3,181,000 people. Some idea of the extent of the organized opposition is revealed in the statistic that the forces seeking repeal of the law managed to install 100,000 campaign lawn signs in the state and outspent the right-to-die group by more than four dollars to one.[1] The euthanasia parent organization, Hemlock USA, had a mere 25,000 members in a nation of 265 million people. Clearly, with their lopsided 60–40 percent victory in the face of powerful, well-funded opposition, Oregon Right to Die (the state political action committee spun off from the local Hemlock Society) was tapping into a vein of public opinion that was extremely uneasy about how Americans meet their ends.

The law passed in Oregon was not as broad as that permanently sanctioned in the Netherlands since 1984, or that which operated in the Northern Territory of Australia for nine months in 1996–97. It was a law tailored both for the shortcomings in the American health insurance system, and the puritanical streak that permeates a good deal of American morality. While the two other countries simultaneously introduced both active voluntary euthanasia (death by injection) and PAS (death by taking lethal drugs prescribed by a doctor), Oregon chose PAS alone as the best hope of getting a law onto the statute books. Ballot initiatives introducing both methods of assisted dying had previously failed in Washington State (1991) and in California (1992), each getting 46 percent of the popular vote.

What the Oregon law (see Appendix C for full details) permits is for a terminally ill adult, close to death, who has made a competent and consistent request for drugs with which to kill him- or herself, to have that request considered by a doctor. Before that can happen there are many precautions against mistakes, hastiness, or abuse, such as a fifteen-day waiting period, a second opinion by another doctor, investigation of whether pain control is adequate, and assessment of possible depression. Provided members of the medical staff obey the law meticulously, they are free from criminal prosecution and administrative or professional punishment. A "conscience clause" allows health professionals and hospitals to decline to participate in a hastened death; the patient must then seek an alternate doctor. Any coercion, forgery, or fraud resulting in an untimely death is punishable as a serious felony. This law, unique in United States, first took effect on October 27, 1997. It was the end of a seventeen-year struggle to legalize a concept, and the start of a drive to make it available across the country.

Predictably, reception to the Oregon result was mixed. Dr. Peter Goodwin, a Portland internal medicine physician who had been a fighter for law reform for many years, commented: "It's a huge step forward for the care of the dying, and a powerful message to the rest of the country. Legislatures throughout the country are going to have to look at this vote and realize that if this is what the people are saying, we better respond more positively than we have in the past."[2]

The U.S. Catholic Conference of Bishops issued a statement calling the vote "a tragedy for seriously ill patients who deserve better care for their real needs, not an invitation to suicide."[3] Boston's Cardinal Law weighed in with the oft-repeated warning that "a right to die" easily becomes a "duty to die" once society labels some lives as not worth living.[4]

Public response could be gauged by the impassioned letters to the editors of newspapers. A man in Tualatin wrote: "The winning side believed in the best of the judgment of individuals and their caretakers. The losers were trying to convince us that doctors were at best incompetent and at worst evil, and we as individuals are completely unable to take care of ourselves . . . We are a society of intelligent and well-meaning citizens, not idiots or kids."[5] A reader from Eugene complained: "Our beautiful state will now be known as the 'death state' and being old, ill and living in Oregon will be detrimental to one's life."[6] The *Eugene Register-Guard*, the second biggest paper in the state, which had long supported PAS, rejoiced under a headline GOOD SENSE ON SUICIDE: "The majority, including ourselves, see assisted suicide as a rational choice that ought to be accessible to the dying. The availability of the choice, not the desirability of suicide, is the crux of the matter—just as with abortion."[7] The state's largest newspaper, *The Oregonian*, which had furiously resisted both ballot measures, moaned in an editorial entitled "The abyss": "With their reaffirmation of the state's 1994 assisted suicide law, Oregonians have officially surrendered the state's sole authority to use lethal force, and turned a small part of that power over to a profession—doctors. No other government in the world has gone so far. That's our idea of an abyss."[8] But the people had spoken through the democratic process, and, despite some rear-guard actions by opponents, the law went into effect, slowly and cautiously, as a divided medical profession considered its newly appointed responsibility.

As we have seen, the struggle to change the law had begun seventeen years earlier, when Derek Humphry founded the Hemlock Society with the dual goals of legalizing assisted dying and helping, through information and moral support, the dying who could not wait for legal reforms. Aware that education comes before reform, the Hemlock leadership made the latter their main focus throughout most of the 1980s. Halfway through the decade, two Los Angeles law partners, Robert Risley and Michael White, began constructing a law for assisted dying that they called the "Humane and Dignified Death Act." The idea had come to Risley while nursing his wife through a long terminal illness. She had not actually asked him for assisted suicide or voluntary euthanasia, but he wondered what he would have done if she had done so. He recognized the need for such a law, and with his colleague began to draft one. Risley and White had nothing to build on—this had not been attempted in any other country in the world—so they were forced to rely purely on common sense against a background of what they, as attorneys specializing in medical malpractice cases, knew of existing laws on health, treatment, informed consent, and definitions of death.

The *Quinlan* case (1976) was fresh in their minds, as was California's Natural Death Act of the same year, which introduced the concept of Living Wills, more practically known as advance directives making doctors aware of the patient's wishes regarding end-of-life care. This is known both as "passive euthanasia" and "allowing to die." But the two lawyers were taking the advance directive a major step further into the realm of active voluntary euthanasia and PAS. They, and others in the so-called right-to-die movement, were to learn that this was a morally contentious and legally rocky road, requiring many serious refinements to their ideas before an electorate would sign on.

Risley and White lacked both knowledge of the international history of euthanasia and experience with its practical difficulties. To remedy this they approached the Hemlock Society for collaboration on framing a new law. It was at this point, in the latter half of the 1980s, that Hemlock was beginning to emerge from its intellectual wilderness; the taboo on talking about assisted death was breaking down; Humphry knew it was now time to begin crafting a law for use in the near future. Curt Garbesi, a member of Hemlock's board and a professor at Loyola Law School, Los Angeles, was attracted to the idea of constructing a totally new law. The four men began meeting on Saturday mornings to hammer out a fresh draft based on what Risley and White had done so far. For a year revision followed revision, until it was ready to be published in *Hemlock Quarterly* for public scrutiny.[9]

Looked at today from the vantage point of ten years' distance, in terms of political viability, the Humane and Dignified Death Act model law published in 1986 was more suitable to the next century than this one. But the quartet of reformers did not know this. The law for which they sought approval, with many built-in safeguards, permitted active voluntary euthanasia for the terminally and irreversibly ill, PAS for the same patients, and advance directives allowing patients with Alzheimer's disease to nominate a person who would end their lives even though they were incompetent.

Risley resolved to start a political action group to press for the new law. Hemlock, being an educational organization under the tax codes, could not do so. Thus the new organization, Americans Against Human Suffering (AAHS), was in a way the political arm of Hemlock. The latter lent AAHS its mailing list, by now some twenty thousand names and addresses, provided minimal funding within the tax restrictions, and exchanged a couple of directors. Risley tried to interest California politicians in pushing the law in the legislature in Sacramento, but none would do so. A couple of state senators who were mildly interested because they had been instrumental in getting the Natural Death Act passed ten years earlier remarked encouragingly that such a law would eventually get on the statute books, but they had been so bruised by the 1976 fight that they were not prepared to endure another bitter right-to-die battle against the powerful and vocal groups of the religious right.

California and twelve other states have the "initiative system" of passing laws. This form of democracy began in the pioneering days at the end of the previous century, when West Coast politics was extremely corrupt and almost entirely beholden to big business. The only way the federal government could find to break the stranglehold was to permit these states to pass—or undo—laws by popular vote, thus circumventing the legislatures.

Sometimes this method of government is called "citizens' referendum," but it is more than that; it is direct lawmaking. Every state has different rules on exactly how the vote shall be conducted, but all require a large number of signatures of registered voters on petition forms asking for a vote to be taken on a certain issue. In California, for instance, the sponsors of a new law must secure signatures equal to 5 percent of votes cast for all candidates for governor of the state in the last election. In the largest state in the union this amounts to some four hundred thousand signatures needed to qualify a law for the next ballot—a daunting task for small organizations, but no hindrance for large organizations with money to pay professional signature gatherers.

AAHS, working closely with Hemlock's members and chapters, began the huge task of gathering signatures in early 1988. The unusual nature of the proposed law attracted considerable media attention, beyond that drawn by several more "respectable" issues on the same ticket. In the course of events the law itself was subjected to minute examination by friends and foes, making it obvious to the sponsors where their political weak points were. Major criticism focused on the safeguard that the patient must be "likely to die, within reasonable medical judgment, within six months." How could any person, medical or otherwise, predict this? But AAHS refused to concede this point, pointing out that admission to a hospice program required the same time prognosis. Another criticism was that pregnant women were not allowed to make use of the new law, upsetting feminists and advocates for women at the American Civil Liberties Union (ACLU). Most controversial of all was the wording allowing people who became incompetent with Alzheimer's disease to have their lives ended by another provided that they had signed an advance directive. Although this feature enjoyed significant public support, it was withdrawn from subsequent versions of the law as being both unworkable and too controversial.

So extensive was the publicity for the act that the "bandwagon effect" began to give people the impression that it was certain to qualify for the main vote. Hemlock had arranged for the international congress of the World Federation of Right to Die Societies to be held in San Francisco in the middle of the signature-gathering campaign, so that maximum public attention would be drawn to the issue. The conference's keynote speaker was Willie Brown, then speaker of the California legislature and, after the governor, the most powerful man in the state. In 1997–98 he was the mayor of San Francisco. He told the audience that "the Humane and Dignified Death Act is going to pass." This made banner headlines in the next day's newspapers, but it was an illusion. AAHS and Hemlock leaders knew that the qualification drive was doomed but decided to let it proceed because the new law was being taken seriously by legal experts and considerable political experience was being acquired. By the time the five months allowed for signature gathering was up, AAHS had collected only 129,764 of the 372,000 certified signatures needed to qualify for the ballot.[10] All the signatures had been garnered by Hemlock supporters, but they were physically incapable of getting a sufficient number by standing on street corners and outside supermarkets. A professional signature-gathering firm had midway through the campaign tested the public response to the law and found it was a shoo-in. It immediately offered to get the necessary remainder for a payment of $300,000, pointing out that no volunteer organization, even the PTA, was capable of gathering the necessary signatures. But AAHS had to decline because it was broke. AAHS had used up the $195,000 supplied by Hemlock in an expensive fund-raising campaign that failed completely because the theme used by a hired mailing firm was too brash and sentimental. Feedback showed that the public would be more likely to donate if the approach combined realism and practicality with compassion. It was another learning experience for the young movement, which immediately set about refining the law and replacing the money spent. The latter was no problem, Hemlock found, because the public now saw that an organization once derided as a flaky California suicide club was extremely serious in pushing a law that had considerable moral and practical merit. Over the next year membership doubled, and finances were recouped for the next battle. The model act was further polished, and the problematical clause giving help to die for Alzheimer's victims was deleted. The problem of the incompetent patient would have to be addressed sometime in the future, when more experience had been gained with the law on assisted death.

From the day Hemlock started chapters across the United States, it had given them autonomy and recommended their incorporation as individual entities. National Hemlock could never dictate to its chapters; it could merely make suggestions. In this way if the chapters broke any law or brought the movement into disrepute, the national group could disclaim responsibility. None ever did get into trouble, but the freedom to act as the local group thought fit brought failure in Washington State, when the next initiative campaign started in 1990.

At first the Washington campaign got off to a tremendous start, raising $200,000 in its first year and gathering nearly double the number of signatures needed to qualify—150,001. The next year, when the balloting was due, the campaign raised $1,657,650 by soliciting thousands of donors across the country, chiefly from the Hemlock Society's mailing list, which was expanding at the rate of one thousand new members a month. Advance polling in the state indicated a firm victory on November 4.

But as the Death with Dignity Act—as it was now called—came under scrutiny, it was apparent that it lacked many of the kinds of safeguards the Hemlock leadership had advocated publicly for years. The Washington chapter had argued that they knew best about politics in their state and drew up their own law. Examination showed that Initiative 119 (its official name) was too loosely drawn. It had no special protection for nursing-home patients who are trapped in extremely vulnerable situations, requiring extra safeguards against possible abuse. Requests to die from residents of nursing homes should have mandatory monitoring by an ombudsman or a review committee. Initiative 119 contained no mention of psychological evaluations so that depression could be detected, a feature specially requested by the mental health profession. There was no reporting requirement to enable the number and place of assisted dying to be monitored. The most serious omission was the absence of any waiting period between the request to die and its fulfillment. On top of this the law proposed to improve Washington's advance directives, which were badly flawed. This addition confused the issues of passive and active euthanasia, which experts on both sides agree should legally be dealt with separately, although the ethical issues might be similar.

The opponents of 119 were quick to spot the poorly drafted act, instantly setting up an effective campaign around the slogan No Safeguards. They raised $1.9 million and shrewdly spent almost all of it in the final month of the campaign on radio and television advertising campaigns slamming a law that would allow widespread abuse because of the lack of safeguards. While the "No on 119" campaign easily gathered the bulk of its money from large contributors in lump sums, the Yes campaign had to spend large sums on begging letters across America to raise funds. They allocated too much of their money to education, staff, offices, embossed coffee mugs and printing and only $660,000 to television, which they began too soon with insufficient money left for the vital last weeks. In the final month, when their campaign should have been at its most intense, they were broke, and the ten-point lead in the opinion polls slipped away. Defeat was inevitable. Despite the strategic blunders and the flawed law, however, they did well at the polls, demonstrating that the public wanted improved choices in dying and was not too fussy about the details.

The final count on Initiative 119 on November 4, 1991, in Washington defeated the new law. Those voting yes numbered 701,818 (46.4 percent) while the no vote came to 811,104 (53.6 percent). The Yes campaign spent $1,800,000 and the opponents $1,900,000.

The disappointed leadership of the Yes campaign blamed two factors for the sound defeat: Two weeks before polling day Dr. Jack Kevorkian made national headlines and television by helping two people die in Michigan. The No campaign quickly spread the rumor that he would be bringing his famous "suicide machine" to Washington if the law was passed. (In fact he has never helped people to die except in his home state, Michigan, which then lacked any law prohibiting assisted suicide. Nor did he come to Oregon when that state approved the assistance.) Second, a month before polling day, Ann Wickett, Derek Humphry's second wife, who had been a cofounder of Hemlock, committed suicide in a highly publicized manner. She was not terminally ill but had serious, enduring problems of emotional instability and depression. Their divorce two years before her death had also been painful and public. Opinion was divided as to whether the electoral defeat was in any way due to Kevorkian and Wickett, or to an inadequate law and poor campaign strategy. The latter seemed more likely.

All the while planning was going ahead for another initiative drive in California, regardless of whether the Washington one succeeded or failed. Unfortunately, some sections of the right-to-die movement were anxious to be the first to get a law for assisted dying passed without paying sufficient attention to fund-raising. Considering the almost unlimited financial strength of their main opponent, the Roman Catholic Church, this was a serious omission. To have a good chance of being successful with a ballot initiative in a state the size of California (population 36 million), about $3 million is needed, at least $1 million of it at the beginning of the campaign. AAHS, after modifying its name to Californians Against Human Suffering (CAHS), launched its drive with almost no money in its bank account and no professional fund-raiser on board. CAHS was relying on the alluring situation that the right to die was an extremely hot topic in America in 1991–92, mainly due to the high level of publicity accorded to the actions of Dr. Jack Kevorkian and the continuing position at the top of the best-seller list of Humphry's *Final Exit*.[11] The work of these two men was the subject of many heated dinner table conversations at that time: Why was Kevorkian "getting away with it," and how could it be that a book on how to commit suicide could be the most desirable nonfiction reading in the United States?

The law being offered to voters in California was better drafted than the Washington version but still wide open to criticism. In every state where assisted dying laws have been offered, the local organization has formulated its own law, containing some elements that are either new and useful, or learned from previous campaigns.

Intrinsically in a movement comprising educated, strongly opinionated people, each constituent group thinks it is coming up with the best solution to the intricate problems of voluntary euthanasia and PAS, heedless that some of the best legal minds in the United States are immediately going to tear it to pieces. Neither the state groups, national Hemlock, nor a panel of experts at Harvard University have yet come up with the ideal law. PAS law in its nature embraces all aspects of human life, behavior, and death—personal, family, and community responsibilities and religious and medical ethics—which makes it perhaps the most difficult statute law ever to be drafted. Differing opinions of how it should be worded become divisive debates and heated arguments.

CAHS was led by the two lawyers, Risley and White, whose legal minds assumed that a phrase like "an enduring request" was good enough for what lay people call "a waiting period." They defined "enduring" as "a request for aid-in-dying expressed on more than one occasion." But what if the first request was followed by another ten minutes later? This was not time enough for thoughtful reflection or careful examination of the circumstances on the part of those involved. Risley and White countered that if too many conditions were inserted into the protocols, it could cause unnecessary suffering while they were sorted out. But the absence of a waiting period was a weakness in the law on which opponents effectively capitalized. The Risley-White law stipulated that when a patient signed the Voluntary Directive to Physicians asking for accelerated end of life, this signing had to be witnessed by two persons not related to the patient and not beneficiaries of his or her estate. The patient must not owe them money. Neither witness could be the treating doctor or the owner of the health care facility where death was to take place. But these witnesses were only to the authenticity of the signature. No witnesses were required to be physically present at the actual negotiations between doctor and patient. Who was to check whether the doctor was trying to influence the patient's decision, or, conversely, if the doctor was ethically opposed to the procedure and unreasonably trying to persuade the patient not to do it? But would the presence of witnesses interfere with the confidentiality of the doctor-patient relationship? One solution only seemed to breed another problem.

As in Washington, the California proponents ran afoul of the "likely to die within six months" provision. It is a sensible provision but is also wide open to legitimate jeers from opponents that exact times of death can be predicted by no one. Trying to frame a law covering all eventualities was a nightmare. There was a provision in this proposed law that a doctor "may request a psychiatric or psychological consultation if that physician has any concern about the patient's competence," but the entirely voluntary nature of this clause triggered the demand from the opposition for the evaluation to be mandatory. Supporters of the law countered that this could be an infringement of civil liberties—it was Soviet Russia that used psychiatrists to incarcerate troublesome dissidents—to force a patient to see a mental health professional. It was argued that the doctor had sufficient leverage over a reluctant patient by declining to help with dying unless an evaluation was carried out.

Even more tricky was trying to explain the complexities of an entirely new law to ordinary people whose only interest, at bottom, is not to suffer when their life is ending. Most voters either do not understand, or care nothing about, the legal language that surrounds this most controversial and sensitive set of circumstances. They simply want the right of choice in their own dying process. The opponents of Proposition 161, as the California initiative was now officially named, had the simple task of slamming the law by repeating that it was "poorly drafted," rarely specifying what they meant. Because it was an improvement on Washington's version, they could not claim that it had "no safeguards," so they campaigned on a slogan of No Real Safeguards, which was just as damaging.

The proponents of 161 found that one simple question at public debates with opponents reached the essential truth of the battle: "If we made all the modifications to the law which you recommend, would you then vote for it?" The answer was always in the negative, revealing the opposition's hidden agenda—ethical/religious opposition—which will never accept as public policy any form of hastened death, however perfect the law that ensures that it is death by choice. The incessant carping criticisms of the right-to-life movement are pure political theater from those who are determined not to let other people have choices in both abortion and euthanasia.

When the campaign opened in the summer of 1992, CAHS was broke, a hopeless way to win a political campaign. At least this time they had secured the 385,000 certified signatures needed to qualify for the ballot, but only by paying a professional signature-gathering firm $286,354 for most of them. Up to that point CAHS fund-raising had been fairly successful, with the largest sum, $100,000 coming from the Hemlock Society. But Hemlock refused to contribute to the actual voting campaign, saying that CAHS should not have started down this road unless it could find its own financing. It was a totally one-sided fight, with the opponents spending nearly $3.5 million on the "No on 161" campaign, which was efficiently run by political professionals. Effective television advertising flooded the screens. One commercial trumpeted the apocryphal information: "Even those who believe in euthanasia don't like this law," seizing on critiques by academics, supporters in principle of assisted death, but with varying ideas as to how the law should be drafted. Even more effective as negative propaganda was a famous television advertisement that showed an old lady in an armchair shrinking in terror as her doctor approached, carrying a huge syringe and needle. A voice-over said that people would not be able to trust their doctors if 161 passed into law. Just as in Washington, the sponsors of 161 had very little money for advertising to counter such claims.

The No campaign raised a total of $3,510,215 in the last half of 1992. Remarkably, 172,500 people gave a total of $1,489,430 in sums of less than $100. Most of this was money collected at Sunday services in Roman Catholic churches, where the cash flow was so huge that $16,185 had to be spent on armored cars to transport it to campaign headquarters. The Knights of Columbus gave $209,733, and other Catholic organizations gave $178,991, the biggest of these contributions being $83,529 from the California Association of Catholic Hospitals. The U.S. Catholic Conference gave $76,768, and the California Catholic Conference $16,686. The bishops of Oakland, Stockton, Sacramento, Monterey, all in California, and Spokane, Washington, gave a total of $182,079, with the archbishop of Los Angeles adding $45,000. Twenty Catholic churches and religious orders gave a total of $54,546. Four non-Catholic churches contributed a paltry $1,236. Thirty-one medical groups and hospitals contributed $343,300, and twenty of these donors were identifiable as Catholic.[12] The No campaign spent $763,694 for television and radio advertising, while the Yes side spent $68,870. The impetus of campaign fervor helped the Yes side raise a grand total of $1,704,607 over two years, but much of this went into the long grind to raise the qualifying signatures, a task in which the No campaign, of course, did not need to be involved. In addition to the original $100,000 from national Hemlock to help secure the signatures, seven Hemlock chapters contributed a further $20,585. Expenditures on printing and mailing begging letters to thousands of people swallowed large sums. Unsurprisingly no churches gave any money.[13] Despite this extreme difference in funding, the final result on November 3, 1992, on California's Proposition 161, was remarkably close. Those voting yes amounted to 4,562,010 (46 percent) while those against the law amounted to 5,348,947 votes (54 percent). The sponsors of the law spent $1,704,607 and its opponents had an outlay of $3,510,215.

In the counties in and around liberally inclined San Francisco, 161 had passed easily, 60–40, and all eleven counties were in favor, with five tied at 50–50. But the largest county in the nation, Los Angeles County, with some five million electors, and a bastion of Catholic strength among the Latino community, affected the result drastically by voting 45 percent for and 55 percent against. The voting appeared to depend on the contrasting social and religious demographics of a county. For example, in little Mono County, mainly dependent on tourism, 161 passed 63–37 percent, while in Tulare County, home to ultraconservative, wealthy dairy and citrus farmers, combined with a large Catholic Latino worker population, it lost 35–65 percent.

The right-to-die movement took some comfort in their defeat in the support of 4,500,000 voters for their cause despite the campaign of denigration run by the other side. As had their opponents, the movement had called on the financial resources of its supporters all across the nation. But California is no longer the socially conscious, reformist state it was back in the 1960s and 1970s. The breakthrough was to come not in sunny California but in the wet and forested state to its north, which had already gotten a proposed law in front of its legislature through the determination of a senior state senator who was dying of cancer.

Chapter 16

Oregon Breaks Through

It has always been the policy of the right-to-die movement to try to achieve law reform through the elected representatives in state legislatures. As we have said, in Washington and in California approaches by advocates were quickly rebuffed by even liberal-minded politicians, who felt such a law had no hope, at least for many years. The vocal and bellicose tactics of the right-to-life movement, so well demonstrated in the abortion controversy, made many politicians nervous. Opinion polls consistently showing 60 percent public support did not imbue them with the courage properly to represent their electorates. So the right-to-die movement was thrown back on citizens' ballot initiatives, which, while being the last word in democratic government, require huge amounts of physical and mental effort, plus millions of dollars, to succeed. Yet, as the Oregon experience shows, the right-to-die movement had no alternative but to take this difficult route.

The Hemlock Society of Oregon was started in 1987 by Derek Humphry, when he moved his home and office to the state to benefit from cleaner air and lower living and working costs than in Los Angeles, where he had spent the previous ten years. Contrary to the often-expressed views of opponents, he did not relocate because he had targeted Oregon as politically vulnerable. For him it was a quality-of-life decision, linked to the financial reality that the rapidly expanding national Hemlock Society could be more economically run from the small university town of Eugene. At the time of the move, Humphry knew nothing of Oregon's politics or social and religious demographics.

By pure chance, as the state's young Hemlock chapter grew, its leaders came in touch with State Senator Frank Roberts, a Democrat from Portland, whose long political experience gave him considerable clout in the legislature in Salem. He was president pro tem of the Senate and chaired the subcommittee on human resources. His wife, Barbara, was soon to be elected Oregon's governor. Roberts, seventy-six, had cancer, was confined to a wheelchair, and knew his time was short. Quite naturally he not only approved of euthanasia intellectually, but he wanted it for himself. Hemlock redrafted refinements into what it now called the "Death With Dignity Act," and Senator Roberts and colleagues introduced it in the 1991 session. Roberts also found representatives in the House who would introduce it, and himself spoke eloquently at public meetings for the concept. This public acknowledgment of the need for law reform by an elected representative was in itself a first in 1990. Still, despite the respect in which Roberts was widely held, the attempt at legislation failed miserably.

The proposed law was granted one "courtesy hearing," which can best be described as pure theater. Committee members hearing evidence from sponsors set the tone by asking a Hemlock representative if her organization was a religion. The committee room was thronged with men, clad in the black garb of their various religious ministries, all of whom—except for one Unitarian minister—spoke trenchantly against Senate Bill 1141. Committee members talked about disabled persons and senior citizens being killed under the act, completely ignoring the absence of any such provision in it. The act did not get out of committee, and a frustrated Senator Roberts dropped his effort. He died two years later.

Yet the first step had been taken. Over the next two years Hemlock's Oregon leadership, who had watched their bill cast out like unwanted rubbish, monitored developments as the states north and south of them, Washington and California, starting to chart a new strategy. By 1993 there was plenty of evidence on what worked with the voters, the tactics and strengths of the opposition, and the Death With Dignity Act was considerably refined. To modify it any further risked creating more hoops than the dying patient would be able to jump through. The Hemlock leaders realized that the opposition to the act came almost entirely from the religious right, which was making a lot of noise picking technical holes in the law as a means of avoiding saying that really they opposed it on theological grounds. To admit publicly that they were opposed for this reason would smack of the imposition of their religious views on others. Instead they played the "not good public policy" card to the hilt. When pressed, spokespersons for the religious right usually contend that laws are based on moral precepts; that in the United States these are the result of the predominance of the Judeo-Christian religion—"one nation under God," as the Pledge of Allegiance puts it. Similarly, a great deal of the opposition from the medical profession is in truth not based on the specious "loss of trust" or "the doctor is a healer, not a killer" arguments but on the individual religious beliefs of doctors and on their desire not to be regulated. Even academics in their ivory towers, who profess neutral investigation and independence of thought, cannot—on this one issue—escape the certainty that their personal views on euthanasia must color their research and the learned papers that follow.

Oregon is the birthplace of voters' initiatives. In 1902 the state's electorate overwhelmingly approved a ballot measure that created the initiative and referendum, a system of direct legislation by the people. The initiative and referendum became nationally known at the time as "the Oregon system" and many other states, mostly in the West, followed their example. The federal government approved because of the widespread political control then held in certain western state legislatures by a few rich politicians, mostly concerned with furthering their own commercial interests.

To qualify an initiative in Oregon is easier than in most states because of the small population. Qualification for the ballot requires proponents to gather signatures equal to six percent of the total votes cast for all candidates for governor at the last election. Only 66,700 were needed in 1994, yet 95,000 signatures were turned in, enough to guarantee qualification even if there were a number of spoiled signatures. Paid petitioners were used to gather the signatures.

To launch an initiative, Hemlock of Oregon, a nonprofit, educational organization, needed to form an independent political action committee. Oregon Right to Die (ORTD) was set up to plan and conduct the initiative. Eager to spearhead the political campaign, a burly young Portland attorney, Eli Stutsman, extremely bright and a glutton for work, gave up the presidency of the Hemlock chapter, which he had held in 1992–93, to take charge. Coming into ORTD soon after it was formed was a tough-minded political professional, Barbara Coombs Lee, who at the time of the debacle of the Roberts bill in the legislature had been a legislative aide working on advance-directive issues. She then saw firsthand the hatchet job the right-wing politicians carried out, but she also knew from her study of the subject that most of the American public opinion favored choice in dying. Coombs Lee brought to the ORTD skills both as an attorney and a nurse. The voluntary services of relatively young professionals like Stutsman and Coombs Lee were now making the difference to the practical quality of planning in the right-to-die movement.

They retained a young but experienced political consultant, Geoff Sugerman, to handle the political strategy. The old guard—all determined crusaders but not too politically smart—was giving way to the "foot soldiers" of the baby-boomer era, who were now itching to take over. This triumvirate masterminded the two initiatives that were to follow: Stutsman, guarding the law and raising funds; Coombs Lee, a handsome woman with considerable presence, served as the front person at press conferences and on television; Sugerman monitored the political nuances and legislative actions.

They looked to see if they could do something to get the percentage of the vote up from the customary 46 percent to above the 50 percent needed to change the law. Why in both the previous initiatives had the reformers started out with clear victories indicated by opinion polls, only to drop some 10–15 percent over the last months and lose? Was the opposition's sharp and extensive television advertising, styled to induce fear of the new law in the voter, the real culprit? Or perhaps the movement was going too far too fast? Would a modified, less contentious law surmount the "fear and abuse factor" the opposition had so brilliantly exploited? A pointer favoring minimizing the proposed law came in a Roper Poll done for Hemlock in Oregon in 1991. When people were asked if they supported "aid-in-dying" for terminally ill people, 63 percent approved. When the question was put to the same sample as to whether doctors should be allowed to give lethal injections, the approval rate dropped to 53 percent.[1]

Another Roper poll, done in 1993, showed how wording influenced public thinking about choice in dying. When researchers asked one thousand Americans: "Would they vote for or against a law allowing people to choose *euthanasia?*" 55 percent were in favor. But when the question was put to a different one thousand people: "Would you vote for or against a law allowing people to choose to *die with dignity?*" the favorable response rate shot up to 65 percent.[2]

Removing voluntary euthanasia from the law, and using euphemisms—clearly more popular where the threatening subject of one's own death is concerned—seemed like it might be enough to stop the hemorrhaging of electoral support in the final month that occurred in Washington and California.

One person with influential views was Doctor Peter Goodwin, who argued trenchantly that doctors instinctively opposed inducing deaths by injection because this act too closely resembled killing. Even the word "euthanasia" had sinister connotations, dating back to the Nazi era in Germany when the word was misused by the Hitler propaganda machine to legitimatize the mass murder of more than one hundred thousand mentally and physically handicapped German citizens. Many of Goodwin's colleagues, he felt, would support PAS if it meant that the patient administered the drugs to him- or herself. The final responsibility for inducing death would thus lie with the patient.

This ultimate responsibility of the patient in choosing whether to commit suicide also, to a certain extent, reduced the effectiveness of the fears expressed by some doctors and ethicists that those Americans who were poor, without health insurance, or disabled—the vulnerable in society—could be "gotten rid of" by unscrupulous doctors with syringes full of lethal drugs. The action of injecting a poison, the argument went, would be a crime under all circumstances in this type of law—even the most compassionate—whereas death by prescription, surrounded by a bodyguard of guidelines and safeguards, would be more acceptable to doctors and voters alike. The universal dread of death via a stealthy needle into a vein would be eliminated. If that happened, it was murder, and punishable as such.

This argument prevailed in the inner councils of ORTD. Sugerman, a newcomer to the right-to-die scene, was convinced that they could stop the late loss of votes by emphasizing the "patient control" issue. It would not be the doctor in command at the deathbed but rather the patient. This would reassure the many Americans who see doctors—fairly or unfairly—in the same class as they see lawyers—self-centered, arrogant, and financially on the make.

Opinion was hardening among the leadership that victory could be achieved if voluntary euthanasia, or death by injection, was outlawed in the initiative. It would be what was known as "a prescribing bill"—terminally ill people received the prescription for lethal drugs from their doctor under certain conditions, filled it at a pharmacy, and took the drugs home to kill themselves if they still wished to. The newly appointed campaign director, Sugerman, gave the first public clue to the new policy when he admitted to a medical newspaper: "Certainly from a political standpoint only, there's a lot of merit to limiting the proposal to physician-assisted suicide."[3]

Humphry and a few others at first vigorously resisted this reduction in the scope of lawful assisted dying, feeling that it was a sellout after the fourteen years the movement had spent building up its membership with a manifesto promising that laws would be sought for both methods of ending death. Humphry argued that the people who most needed assistance in dying—those who could not put the drugs in their mouths or could not hold them in their stomachs—were being left out. Victims of ALS were the most obvious example of this discrimination because they lose control of all limbs toward the end. Literally and figuratively such patients could not put hand to mouth. There were also, Humphry contended, problems with the occasional protracted lethalness of oral drugs, sometimes causing a few patients to linger for many hours, in rare cases for days. To eliminate the chance of delay, Humphry had written in *Final Exit* that patients might consider using a plastic bag in addition to lethal drugs, and many fearing delay or failure did so. In the Netherlands the delayed cases are helped to die after five hours with a lethal injection, an action to be specifically outlawed in the proposed Oregon law.

Those favoring a "prescribing bill" argued that the two previous initiative defeats indicated that:

- The United States lacking universal health insurance, was not yet ready for voluntary euthanasia of the type practiced in the Netherlands, which has 100 percent health insurance for all;
- the medical profession had a history of being resistant to change and was always afraid of malpractice suits, the chance of which would be reduced in the watered-down type of law;
- when doctors became accustomed over time to PAS, with the knowledge that it was successful, and that any administrative flaws had been eliminated, they would eventually come around to the additional need for justifiable voluntary euthanasia;
- the thirty-seven million uninsured patients, also the disabled and the

elderly, would not fear doctors killing them because, if they wished to die, they had to be terminal patients to qualify for help, and then had to do it themselves;

- the argument that those without health insurance would be vulnerable would be answered by the requirement that two doctors rule that they had a terminal condition;
- the patient would be in ultimate control of life; and
- it was wise strategy to go step-by-step because the movement could not afford a third defeat at the polls and still remain credible."

It has been said that politics is the art of compromise. Realizing this, Humphry and those who thought as he did gradually came around to the idea of the "prescribing bill." In the election battle he worked behind the scenes, using his influence to raise substantial campaign money. Still, when asked, Humphry would always quietly reaffirm his belief that society would one day realize that it was fair and humanitarian also to legalize voluntary euthanasia for the dying who wanted and needed it. He was in this movement for the long haul, and prepared to wait.

The Measure 16 campaign opened with the customary lead in the opinion surveys. A poll done four weeks before election day showed that six in ten voters supported it. Already religion was at the core of the issue. The poll showed that the strongest opposition came from those describing themselves as "very religious" (62 percent), while 82 percent of those who described themselves at "not at all religious" supported the proposed new law.[4] Pivotal to this campaign, or so many thought, was the official attitude of the medical profession. The Oregon Medical Association (OMA)—the state branch of the AMA—met in conference in Eugene to settle the issue. A week previously the AMA had warned that any Oregon doctor carrying out PAS would be performing an unethical act. Under this dark cloud they debated all day one Sunday, tossing around one resolution after another. The chairman of Oregon Right to Die, Doctor Goodwin, had deliberately joined OMA in order to speak at its delegates' meeting. He pleaded for a neutral stance to allow the people to decide the issue for themselves. "Doctors were saying, 'What is our role' and there was a hell of a lot of soul searching," said OMA's executive director.[5] At the end of the day's debate, OMA decided to take a neutral stance on Measure 16, which Goodwin praised as the most rational thing to do. It was a significant victory for ORTD to be able to keep the doctors on the sidelines. Furious, the AMA national leaders took over the campaign in Oregon and publicly pounded the medical point of view that doctors must not hasten the death of their patients, pointing to a 1993 opinion issued by the AMA Council on Ethical and Judicial Affairs, adopted as AMA national policy, that "Physician-assisted suicide is fundamentally inconsistent with the physician's professional role."[6] Many Oregon doctors were furious that their neutral stance had been overridden by their national leaders. The Catholic lobby was also angry. "What other profession would not stand up for its own ethics?' asked Robert J. Castagna, head of the state public policy arm of Oregon's Roman Catholic Church.[7]

The opponents of Measure 16 used a different strategy from those used in the fights in Washington and California. Living among the vast forests and snowcapped mountains, the state's residents are famed for their independence of political spirit and social awareness. Attempts to pass laws that restrict their freedoms—ranging from how bears are hunted to what books can be read in public libraries—are always defeated. Homophobes who try to restrict the rights of gay people are excoriated. Crucially, Oregonians resent outsiders, particularly those from the East Coast, trying to tell them how to think and act. The "No on 16" campaign relied on less aggressive advertising techniques than had been used in the two other states. The appeal was more to the emotions, depicting people who had beaten cancer and lived, who might have died had they used PAS. As expected, it cynically attacked the law as poorly drafted, unsafe, and open to abuse.

ORTD, learning from the miscalculations in Washington, hoarded its money up to the last month, spending nothing on meetings, publications, posters or yard signs. Most of the the budget went for last-minute radio ads, with some also on television. For its part ORTD campaigned on the issue of choice in decision making, something dear to the hearts of Oregonians. A serious blunder was made by ORTD with one of its television advertisements which opponents were quick to spot. The ad showed Patty Rosen, a retired nurse from Bend, Oregon, talking about how she had helped her terminally ill daughter who was asking to die. She told viewers: "So I broke the law and got her the pills necessary." What was not taken into account by the producers of the ad was that right-to-life observers attend every Hemlock Society conference. They had noted that when speaking to a meeting in 1992 Rosen had said that she gave her daughter an injection—"hit a vein." Immediately *The Oregonian* newspaper was alerted to the conflicting stories. A front-page article pointed out the crucial omission, embarrassing to ORTD, which wanted to keep talk of lethal injections completely out of the battle. ORTD replied that if a doctor could have helped the young woman to die with pills alone, Rosen would not have panicked and used the injection to save her daughter further suffering. Opponents retorted that the story modification was done to make PAS sound like a benign and easy process. In a counterpunch ORTD pointed out to the media that a No television advertisement was questionable because the man pretending his father had beaten cancer was an actor performing a script. Both sides were trying, with scant regard for the truth, to tap into people's emotions in a war of words. Gaining even the most minor public understanding of this remarkable piece of law took second place.

Governor Barbara Roberts gave her endorsement to Measure 16. It was a backing probably no other governor would have given at the time. Her husband, who as a state senator tried in vain to get a PAS law passed in 1991, had died in considerable pain the year before. Governor Roberts said that her husband would have "given very strong consideration" to ending his life if that option had been legal when he was in the terminal stages of prostate cancer. Nevertheless Governor Roberts said that she was not openly campaigning for PAS because she considered it a personal issue for voters.[8] The man who was to succeed her as governor, John Kitzhaber, a physician who in his long service in the Oregon legislature had worked diligently for both end-of-life advance declarations and the state's experimental health-rationing scheme, would not back Measure 16 because he felt that it was a subject which the legislature was better suited to deal with. But he would not campaign against the ballot initiative.

Nearly all of Oregon's newspapers supported Measure 16. In Eugene the *Register-Guard*, which has the second largest circulation, consistently endorsed PAS but warned: "This is an area in which society should move with deliberate caution, not speed. By that standard Measure 16 deserves approval."[9] The largest newspaper in the state, *The Oregonian* consistently opposed the measure. Reporting in its news columns was sometimes slanted, and its editorials bordered on the hysterical. For example, under the headline NO LICENSE TO KILL the papers' editors fulminated: "Oregon's assisted suicide measure is grotesquely wrong headed . . . it yells that the measure unfairly exploits fear of pain, suffering, indignity, abandonment and loss of control . . . even if you favor assisted suicide—it cynically protects doctors while putting patients in peril."[10]

From the other side of the country, the more sober *New York Times* thought the Oregon law reform commendable. An editorial headlined MERCY FOR THE DYING, argued:

> The best approach to assisted suicide is to do it openly, requiring doctors to follow codes of conduct designed to minimize mistakes and abuses. . . . There is no need to plunge ahead all at once. Surely one or more states should start gingerly down the road of assisted suicide and monitor whether it leads to widespread abuse—or to a new frontier of freedom of choice for the desperately ill.[11]

As in Washington and California, the Roman Catholic Church led the battle against legalizing PAS. In the month before the election, all its priests were ordered by Archbishop William J. Levada and other bishops in the state to condemn the practice in their sermons, following this the next week with a request for campaign funds from every parishioner. Normally the total Sunday offerings at mass from the three hundred thousand or so Catholics in Oregon amount to approximately one hundred thousand. Given the controversial high visibility of this measure, this time it may have been more. Several other churches in the state also joined the fight against Measure 16, including the Church of Jesus Christ of Latter-Day Saints (Mormon), the Evangelical Lutheran Church in America, the Assemblies of God, the Southern Baptist Convention, the Episcopal Church, the Missouri Lutheran Synod, the Church of the Nazarene, and Muslims in Oregon.

Four churches with small congregations supported Measure 16, arguing that PAS was a matter of individual freedom and responsibility. These were the Unitarian Universalist Association, the United Church of Christ, the United Methodist Church, and the Presbyterian Church.

Leaders of the Ecumenical Ministries of Oregon, representing seventeen denominations, held a press conference to say that it was unfair to single out the Roman Catholic Church as the only religious opponent of the initiative. They particularly objected to a Yes television advertisement in which a woman asked if the voters were going to allow one church (implying the Catholic Church) to make rules for everyone.[12] The Christian Coalition, based across the nation in Virginia, sent 650,000 voters guides to Oregon for distribution in Christian bookstores and churches. The guides called not only for a No vote on Measure 16, but a Yes vote on Measure 13, which would restrict gay rights and Measure 19, an antiobscenity measure. (Measures 13 and 19 ultimately failed.) The group most notorious in Oregon for trying to pass laws discriminating against gays and lesbians, the Oregon Citizens' Alliance (OCA) joined the fray late in the campaign by publishing 200,000 copies of a "Christian Voters Guide."[13] A newspaper advertisement appeared, paid for by the Believers in the Lord Jesus Christ, which quoted Scriptures and ended with the words: "We would urge you to reject Measure 16 which is against God and his absolute rights over us."

At the election on November 8, 1994, Measure 16 received more votes than any of the eight other ballot measures—1,223,998. It scraped to victory by a 2 percent margin. But it was enough to change the law. And against the current trend in the rest of country, a Democratic governor—John Kitzhaber, M.D.—was elected. Oregon remained freethinking, liberal, and independent.

The "Yes on 16" campaign secured 627,980 votes (51 percent) while the Nos gained 596,018 (49 percent). Voter turnout was 57 percent. The sponsors of the law spent $547,592 on their campaign (including signature gathering), against $1,517,179 by their opponents.

Once again support had dropped seriously in the final month, but this time by only about 10 percent instead of the 15 percent in the two previous campaigns. Most ballot initiatives lose much of their early support as the novelty wears off, criticisms became effective, and big-money advertising influences the undecided voter. What had made the difference in saving Measure 16? Stutsman, the attorney who represented ORTD and directed most of its political strategy, is convinced it was the elimination of the voluntary euthanasia clause in the law. "We aren't legalizing suicide or legalizing mercy killing," Stutsman kept propounding. "The patient is taking control. They can't control the disease or the outcome, but they can control the timing and their dignity. That's the one part they can keep—and that's very important to them."[14] Another factor was the all-too-obvious involvement of the churches in the campaign, in response to which he and his colleagues were able to play on the traditional Oregon philosophy of independence. The churches chose to have the election turn on religious and family values, citing the commandment: "Thou shalt not kill." In a letter to the state's Catholic flock asking them each to contribute fifty dollars, the bishops said: "A euthanasia initiative permitting physician-assisted suicide would cross the moral boundary by legalizing intentional acts to end life."[15]

Religious surveys have repeatedly shown that fewer people in Oregon go to church than in any other American state, which Oregon natives like to explain as meaning not that they all are irreligious, but that they prefer to think independently.

Humphry believes that the law would have passed, even containing voluntary euthanasia availability, basing his conviction on the timing of the election. By the end of 1994, he believes, the right-to-die issue had received huge exposure, particularly on the West Coast, thereby educating the public. The ordinary man and woman are not too bothered about the finer details of the law, but want a generalized right of choice to be able to avoid terminal suffering. And while ORTD fought hard to distance itself from Dr. Jack Kevorkian, vast numbers of ordinary people admire him, and speak of going for his services if they needed to. Farmers and farm workers, who frequently have to induce the death of sick or injured animals to prevent suffering, can relate to Doctor Kevorkian's actions. Through his extensive exposure in the early 1990s in the news media, he brought awareness of the hastened-death issue to people who previously had not thought about it, let alone considered it as an option. Additional factors contributing to the public's greater awareness were that the Hemlock Society had been around for fourteen years, the fame of the best-selling *Final Exit*, and the screening on network television of such films as *When the Time Comes* and *Last Wish*. These dealt honestly with assisted suicide, making people much more comfortable with the subject. The taboo on talking about how we die was fast diminishing, replaced by a healthy realism.

More than $1 million of the opposition's campaign funds came from Catholic sources—churches, church groups, Catholic hospitals and medical groups, and religious institutions, while the Yes campaign's biggest contributor was the Hemlock Society, with $175,000, whose political arm, USA Patients' Rights Organization, gave another $72,629. Although they were not anxious to tell the average voter so, both sides raised most of their campaign money from out of state, and in a few instances from other countries, although these amounts were small.

The law was due to take effect one month later, on December 5, 1994. In a display of legal brinkmanship, lawyers for the National Right to Life

Committee flew on December 4 to Eugene from Terre Haute, Indiana, and went before Judge Michael Hogan, in the federal district court, asking for a temporary restraining order preventing implementation on the grounds that it was unconstitutional. The visiting attorneys' request was immediately granted by Judge Hogan, stopping the implementation of the law six hours before it would have taken effect. Then began an expensive, much-publicized three-year battle in the courts. The injunction is an instance of lawyers shrewdly getting their case heard before a judge who they know is in sympathy with them. Hogan, forty-eight years old, became a U.S. magistrate in 1973 after an extremely brief career as an attorney. Colleagues attributed his appointment, fairly or unfairly, to his father's big contribution to Republican Party funds when Nixon was president. Under President Bush he was given the lifetime appointment in 1991 as a U.S. district judge. More pertinent, Hogan was known in the small city of Eugene to be a deeply religious man—an Evangelical—who often held lunch-hour prayer meetings for his staff.

Prior to this, Hogan's most publicly visible case had been a suit claiming that a concrete cross on a hill overlooking Eugene was on city property and thus infringed the doctrine of separation of church and state under the Constitution. Hogan ruled for the retention of the cross on the grounds that it was really a memorial to war veterans. The Ninth Circuit Court of Appeals overruled him and the cross was removed to church land.

James Bopp, chief attorney for the National Right to Life Committee, asked Judge Hogan to stop the law on the grounds that it was unconstitutional. Bopp, a shrewd, highly intelligent, and resourceful lawyer, has specialized for more than twenty years in inserting himself into abortion and right-to-die cases around the United States, always seeking to stop the practice of individual rights. For instance, where families have sought to allow a brain-damaged member to die, he had been in court to oppose. Using a Eugene attorney, Bopp brought into court two physicians, Gary Lee and William Petty, vocal opponents of PAS, and five individuals. All said that they were being hurt by the passage of Measure 16, but attorneys for the state of Oregon (which is obliged under the Constitution to defend a law), ORTD, and the ACLU argued that these plaintiffs had "no standing" to bring the case. People are not supposed to be able to launch lawsuits unless it can be shown that they have been hurt in some way—morally, physically, or financially—by a law. "Standing" has been defined for the purposes of the Oregon PAS law as "a person who is in imminent danger of having the Act inflicted upon them; a relative would have standing if the steps [towards PAS] had been started."[16] The defending lawyers argued that on two grounds these plaintiffs could not bring a case: (a) the law was not yet in effect; and (b) even when it was, seeking and getting PAS was a purely voluntary action, and you cannot be hurt by a law you need not obey. Judge Hogan gave short shrift to the "no standing" argument and allowed the arguments to proceed claiming that the Death With Dignity Act was unconstitutional. On August 4, 1995, Judge Hogan struck down the law, saying that it denied residents of Oregon who are terminally ill the protection of laws intended to prevent suicide—a violation of the equal protection clause of the Fourteenth Amendment to the Constitution. ORTD and the ACLU appealed Hogan's ruling to the Ninth U.S. Circuit Court of Appeals, and it was apparent from the moment the appeal hearing opened in Portland before a panel of three judges that they were going to address only the question of the plaintiff's qualifications to bring such a case. The court declined to hear the merits of the case for unconstitutionality.

On February 28, 1997, in a 3–0 decision, the appeals court threw out the case, saying that the plaintiffs failed to show that they would be harmed if the law took effect. The judges added that it was pure speculation to claim that a doctor or a patient might participate in a suicide against his or her will. Bopp immediately appealed this finding to the U.S. Supreme Court and won a stay of the law until the court decided whether it would hear the case. Another six months passed. In September the Supreme Court said it would not hear Bopp's appeal, and the law came into force for the first time on October 27, 1997, almost three years after it could have taken effect.

Right-to-die supporters were angry that freedom of choice in dying for many people had all this while been frustrated; right-to-life advocates were happy that they had frustrated Measure 16 and no one had yet died from lawful PAS. Delay had all along been the game plan of Measure 16's opponents; they had other strategies ready to destroy the law if Hogan's opinion was overruled. Legal scholars—even some opposed to PAS—knew all along that his rulings were on shaky constitutional grounds and unlikely to survive. After all, his interpretations of constitutional law were different from those of many other judges—he had been overturned on the cross dispute involving the Fourteenth Amendment. Opponents of choice in dying had needed three years in which to develop other ways to destroy a law that was morally anathema to them—and they got it from their coreligionist on the bench. But 1997 was to turn out to be their Waterloo, when going to the polls for a second time badly backfired on them.

Chapter 17

Oregon Gives a Second Mandate

As if one citizens' ballot measure were not enough, the opponents of PAS were determined to have a second in Oregon. Despite spending $3,000,000 on the first one in 1994, they confidently assumed that with a higher-powered campaign they could overturn the 2 percent majority by which it had succeeded. They cleverly manipulated the political scene in the state to place the act before the electorate again in 1997, refusing all pleas, including the governor's, to present the voters with an improved version of the Death with Dignity Act. To ask people to vote twice on exactly the same law was insulting, the governor and others felt. The anti-PAS lobby refused all appeals to modify the law for two reasons: first, so that they could campaign on the issue that it was "a flawed law" (as they had in Washington and California); second, by sticking to the alleged flaws in the law it could avoid getting into the theological ethics of PAS, which would instantly label them as religious zealots.

Once the Ninth Circuit Court of Appeals had thrown out the case without even going into the dubious claim that it was unconstitutional, ruling that the plaintiffs had not been harmed and could not therefore bring a suit, the religious right swung its attention to the Oregon legislature. Traditionally a Democratic stronghold with marked liberal tendencies, the legislature—and specifically the key committees—at this time was controlled by the Republicans, a sprinkling of them Catholics.

At the beginning of 1997, immediately after Judge Hogan was ordered by the appeals court to lift his injunction, no fewer than seven bills were introduced in the legislature, all aimed at repealing, delaying, or severely altering the act. One bill prohibited the use of state funds for assisted suicide, another did the same under the Oregon Health Plan, while others sought to define wording of the act in ways that would handicap the law's practical operation. Passing laws that destroy the original intentions of a law's drafters is a common political tactic, known by insiders as "gutting and stuffing."

For weeks the House Committee on Judiciary's subcommittee on family law held hearings on the pros and cons of the Death With Dignity Act, listening to evidence from lawyers, doctors, ethicists, and lay people. In reality it was all theater, and informed people knew this, because it was clear from the start that the Republicans intended to try to kill the law.

Ever present at committee hearings was Robert J. Castagna, general counsel and executive director of the Oregon Catholic Conference. In part of one statement offered to a committee, Castagna said: "The Conference has particular interest in the issue of physician-assisted suicide. Catholic Church teaching is well articulated on this issue: the Church supports the dignity of the individual throughout life's journey from conception until natural death. Accordingly, the Conference opposes physician-assisted suicide and has been engaged significantly in the public debate in Oregon on this issue."[1]

The Catholics were not the only people out to destroy the law. Spokespersons for the disabled always claim that they represent everyone who is handicapped physically and mentally, which is obviously not the case because disabled persons also belong to the Hemlock Society and attend its meetings. They are divided on issues, like any other human community. A spokesperson for the Oregon Advocacy Center, working for the rights of individuals with disabilities, Bob Joondeph, told the legislative committee: "People with disabilities have a well-founded fear of euthanasia. Historically, people with disabilities have been the first to be sacrificed to social imperatives of purity or utility." Joondeph did not explain to whom or what he was referring here, but presumably it was the Nazi so-called euthanasia program in the 1940s. He continued: "From a disability advocacy perspective, assisted suicide accentuates the tension that always exists in our role: to protect those who need protection while also asserting the right of individuals to make their own decisions."

A note of practicality entered the proceedings with the evidence of oncologist Peter Rasmussen, founder of a local hospice and an active member of the ethics committee of his hospital, Salem General. He surprised the committee, which was working on the assumption that almost nothing had been done about the Oregon Death With Dignity Act, now nearly three years old, by revealing that eighteen months previously he and other doctors had formed the "Mid-Willamette Valley Assisted Suicide Interest Group." Rasmussen said that they had realized that they would be confronted with PAS before long and needed to know how to handle it.

The interest group had developed these guidelines for the time when people began asking, within the law, for a hastened death:

On the day of the suicide:

1. Review the checklist to be sure all the entries are completed and that consents and consultations are within the appropriate time limits.
2. The prescription should not be written until the day the patient plans to take it. Once written, the prescription should be promptly filled. Two specific statements should be written on the prescription. Firstly, writing "If not filled on this date, this prescription is invalid" reduces the chance that the drugs could be taken without a physician present. Secondly, writing "This is a Chapter 3, Oregon Laws of 1994, prescription," alerts the pharmacist to the purpose of the prescription so she may decline to fill the prescription and/or will not ask a lot of unnecessary questions about the prescription.
3. Ideally, the prescription should be dispensed to the attending or another physician.
4. Before handing the drugs to the patient, the physician should check one final time to be sure that the patient still is competent and wants to proceed. The doctor or nurse may assist in preparing the drugs, and may assist in bringing the drugs to the patient's mouth, but the act of ingestion by the patient must be voluntary.
5. If the patient develops distressing symptoms during or after taking the drugs, the physician may, and should, use good medical judgment to relieve those symptoms. This might include administration of antiemetics, antianxiety agents, oxygen and/or antiseizure medications. These drugs may be given by injection as appropriate. The dose and method of administration must be consistent with an attempt to control symptoms rather than an attempt to hasten death. Intravenous medications such as narcotics that have been used for control of symptoms may be continued and even increased during the suicide process, but the doses must be consistent with an attempt to control symptoms rather than to hasten death.
6. During the early years of assisted suicide, physicians must be present to observe the effects of our treatments if we hope to improve them. For several reasons, the physician should remain near the patient at least until unconsciousness occurs. Once the patient is unconscious, the physician should leave only if another physician or an RN remains. The physician and nurse should be prepared to provide interventions to relieve uncomfortable symptoms.
7. If at any time in the suicide process the patient changes his mind, every reasonable effort should be made to recover him, but any existing DNR (do not resuscitate) request should be honored.
8. Should the attempt at suicide fail, the patient should be allowed to recover naturally from the effects of the drugs. If once the patient regains consciousness he still requests assisted suicide, another attempt can be made if he consents and consultations remain timely.

Patiently and professionally Doctor Rasmussen steered the committee members through the ethical and medical matters the interest group had thought about. He was firm that doctors should be in attendance between the time the patient ingested the lethal drugs until death took place, chiefly to learn about the effects but also to be on hand if anything went wrong. As to whether there was one universal drug or drug combination that would be used in all cases, he replied that "in actual practice the doses would be modified for patients. For instance, morphine would be effective in some cases but not for patients who had developed tolerance to it."

On the troublesome issue of depression affecting a patient's judgment, Doctor Rasmussen agreed that this was not taught in medical schools, but there was "a difference between depression in connection with terminal illness and clinical depression." On whether there could be a firm prediction of death within six months, he agreed that there was no reliability in that, but "in the last months it becomes clear that the patient is dying." He did not like the idea of certain doctors specializing in PAS—like Doctor Kevorkian; it made sense to him to have all physicians in general practice able to carry out the procedure. Asked how many dying patients at present, with the law in Oregon on hold, were now committing suicide with the help of their doctors, Rasmussen thought it was "small, under 1 percent" and mostly, so far as he could tell, among AIDS victims. He attributed this to the state's availability of good palliative care.

As the committee strayed further into matters of medical practice, Doctor Rasmussen responded: "It should be left to doctors to establish good medical practice. . . . Each doctor will have his or her own ethical standards." Asked if he had ever done PAS, he replied: "I might have done it had it been lawful." Rasmussen said that sometimes taking lethal drugs orally failed to work quickly and "the prohibition of injectable drugs may cause a lot of patients a lot of grief. But I understand that it was a political decision." To the final question by those committee members as to whether he had ever seen families pressure people to hurry up and die, Rasmussen declared: "I have not. Usually it's the patient who is keen [to die] and the family which is against it."

A spokesperson for the Oregon State Medical Examiner's Office asked the committee to amend the act so that the physician who was both treating the patient and supplying the prescription for lethal drugs would also be the one who signed the death certificate. As the law in Oregon on suicide stood, only a medical examiner (known as a coroner in some states) could sign the death certificate. Changing this would save the taxpayer the cost of a medical examiner's investigation and allow the family to avoid emotional stress. Asked if his office looked into instances of patients dying through the "double effect" of excessive pain medication, the spokesperson replied tartly: "We don't charge into hospitals and investigate those deaths."

Dr. Scott Franklin, president of the Oregon Psychiatrists' Association, an organization representing three-quarters of the state's 325 psychiatrists, told the committee that opinion among members was split on PAS. "Some will help, some not, but psychiatry should be part of the process," he claimed. "We are the best people to evaluate. . . . Psychiatrists used to stand aside on such social issues, but we can no longer do that because the issues are in the public arena."

Oregon's pharmacists were caught flat-footed by the passage of Measure 16. Their leaders had been asked to take part in the drafting of the law and declined, convinced it would not become law. When it did so, they belatedly saw what they considered gaps in the law as it affected them. The term "health care provider" was meant by the drafters to include doctors, nurses, mental health workers, and pharmacists, but pharmacists had considered themselves "health care contractors"—somewhat hairsplitting, many believed. The drafters of the act stuck to their belief that the prescription-filling profession was definitely included. An even bigger complaint was that a pharmacist who was ethically opposed to PAS might fill the prescription not knowing what it was intended for. Their representatives pointed out to the committee that the pharmacist must know the intent of the prescription, because he or she might be the last person to see the patient alive. The pharmacist might need to confer with the doctor about the most effective lethal dosage.

Under questioning, the pharmacists' representatives seemed to think that there was no problem with the effectiveness of a lethal overdose provided it was taken properly. The committee was surprised when Joe Schnabel, president of the Oregon Board of Pharmacy, questioned about the effectiveness of drugs to kill a patient quickly, pulled from his jacket pocket a plastic device. "It could be easily done with this, a midflow home infusion pump which injects over 100 ml. of drugs over thirty minutes," said Schnabel. He argued that this was not a doctor using a syringe, as prohibited by law, but self-administration. The needle might have already been inserted in a vein by a doctor or a nurse for the infusion of other drugs, such as chemotherapy, and kept closed by a screwtop. (After the committee hearing, the law's drafters, Stutsman and Lee, challenged the use of a home infusion pump as a superior way of administering the drugs. They feared that the mere mention of the dreaded needle might blight their political campaign, which was exclusively for oral PAS.)

Crucial to the whole debate was the position of Oregon doctors. They were the ones who had to operate the new law; equally, they had the same right to personal ethical standards as everyone else. Dutch doctors constantly expressed surprise that the Oregon law had gotten so far without the official and extensive cooperation of the medical profession. Doctor Goodwin, who had been an inspiring leader of the campaign for Measure 16 and had played a significant part in getting the OMA to take a neutral position on the law in 1994, was still leading the charge. But his medical opponents had in the meantime become better organized.

Immediately after the success of Measure 16, a group of Catholic doctors got together under Dr. William Toffler and resolved to destroy the law. Calling themselves Physicians for Compassionate Care, founded in early 1995, they spent the next three years lobbying for support for abolition. They had an uphill task getting commitments because a study published in the *New England Journal of Medicine* in early 1996 showed that 60 percent of Oregon doctors who answered an academic survey said they thought that PAS "should be legal in some cases." Nearly half (46 percent) might be willing to prescribe a lethal dose of medication if it were legal to do so, while 31 percent of the respondents would not do so on moral grounds.[2]

By the time the OMA met in Eugene on April 27, 1997—in the middle of the legislature's committee hearings in Salem—the Physicians for Compassionate Care had their strategy ready. First they distributed statewide one hundred thousand pamphlets, many left in doctors' waiting rooms, urging a Yes vote on Measure 51. By now the group claimed between eight hundred and one thousand doctors as members.[3] The opponents hammered away for most of the day, claiming that everyone receiving the dosage did not die immediately. As with the committee hearings, everybody quoted other people or news reports; nobody had firsthand experience. Reporting on the proceedings of the OMA was *The Oregonian's* specialist on the subject, Mark O'Keefe. Both he and the publisher of the newspaper, Fred Stickel, happened to be Catholics.[4] The next day's *Oregonian* carried the shattering headline: DOCTORS CONDEMN SUICIDE INITIATIVE. The report credited Doctor Toffler's group with helping persuade delegates, and said that the vote against Measure 16 was an overwhelming 121–1.[5] If this was true, it was an amazing turnaround. The proponents of Measure 16 said that the lopsided vote did not seem to reflect the views of Oregon's seven thousand doctors, quoting the aforementioned study as evidence.

But four days later a correction appeared in the same newspaper, which said: "The House of Delegates of the OMA used a voice vote of 122 members present in Eugene on Sunday to denounce Oregon's doctor-assisted suicide law. A Monday story cast the vote as tallied. There was one oral dissenting vote. Some members may have abstained." It was a case of wishful thinking on the part of a newspaper that had from the start screamed its opposition to the PAS law. O'Keefe had heard one voice shout no and forgot about the abstainers.

In fact, even at this heavily lobbied meeting of representatives of Oregon's medical profession, one small ray of liberalism emerged. They accepted an amended resolution that "acknowledges a patient's legitimate right to autonomy at the end of life." "We said we're against Measure 16," said Dr. Leigh Dolin, a former OMA president who had supported neutrality in

1994. "We did not say we're against PAS in general. We're still deeply divided on that."[6]

The House Judiciary Committee hearings resumed with the members focused on the OMA's meeting. Giving testimony as president of the OMA, Dr. Charles Hoffman sounded a more conciliatory note. "With a due respect to Mr. O'Keefe, I did not see a vote of 122–1," he said. "I personally did not hear the one nay vote. There may have been others. There may have been nay votes that were not voiced. In 1994, the decision was made to establish neutrality on Measure 16. It is my opinion that the votes were similar." In another part of his evidence, Doctor Hoffman stated: "I feel very, very strongly that no matter how well our profession provides end-of-life care there will always be those individuals who, for whatever reason, desire PAS. What about them?"

On the vexed question of the delayed efficacy of lethal doses, State Rep. George Eighmey argued that the law should be amended to inform a patient of this fact. "The figure of 25 percent is misrepresented," he declared. "The truth is, all patients who take the medication die. In 75 percent of cases, the death takes less than three hours. But in 25 percent of cases it takes longer than three hours for the patient to die."

At times the committee hearings were enlivened by right-to-life zealots who gave shrill testimony that Oregon was about to become known as "the suicide state," and predicting that abundant dead bodies would be found in motels and in public parks, similar to the Kevorkian syndrome in Michigan. One of them told the committee: "Measure 16 is a dangerous measure— similar to the Nazis. We lobbied against Living Will legislation because we knew it would lead to this."

Among the right-to-die supporters who traveled to Salem to testify before the committee was Penny Schlueter. She told the committee that she was suffering from ovarian cancer and did not expect to live much longer. By this stage of the hearings it was obvious to all observers that the controlling Republican Party intended either to repeal the Death With Dignity Act itself or return it to the voters asking them to do so. Schlueter complained: "I had hoped that the Act would be in place when I might need it. Now, not only do I have to worry about unwarranted court delay, I feel that other people, including myself, have been stabbed in the back . . . I would like to be proud to say that I live in a state that recognizes the ultimate civil right."

In her evidence the main sponsor of Measure 16, Barbara Coombs Lee, reminded the committee that there had been no call for repeal except from the Oregon Catholic Conference and from Oregon Right to Die, a consortium of religious right organizations. No one else had gone on record as opposed. "If you overturn Measure 16 after the citizens have voted for it, it is sham democracy," she proclaimed. A gynecologist, Dr. Richard Thorn, insisted to the committee that "Measure 16 was vaguely and imprecisely written," but when asked by a member if he would still be opposed if they corrected the law, he said he would. Representative Ron Sunseri, who was leading the effort against the law, told his colleagues that there was no way to amend Measure 16 to cover the issue of the estimated 25 percent failure rate. "We cannot amend that flaw. People should vote again because this is a very serious issue," he said. Representative Eighmey, a Democrat, countered by saying that it was not "a failure rate; the person dies later on." Eighmey argued unsuccessfully that it was their duty as legislators to amend a law they saw as flawed, and he was willing to make concessions. By now all the bills trying to neutralize the Death With Dignity Act had fallen away, leaving only HB 2954, which sought its repeal. The bill spent one morning in front of the full House of Representatives. As hard as the Democrats fought for the law to be amended before sending it back to the voters, it was a hopeless task. The House was told that Governor Kitzhaber opposed its being sent back to the voters. His message was: "The issue will not go away by repeal. The House is being cowardly by not continuing the debate on the flaws and fixing them."

By now the debate turned entirely on the issue of whether everybody who took a lethal dose died. Some evidence had emerged from the Netherlands that in one study 25 percent were found not to have died immediately, but over the following three days. They were in a coma throughout this time, and nobody suffered. Opponents of the law insisted that this was "a failure"; supporters responded that the 25 percent could more accurately be described as "a delay rate." Representative Eighmey introduced a minority report that if accepted, would make psychological counseling mandatory instead of by consent; specified six months as the minimum period of residency; dealt with the pharmacists' ethical and legal concerns; and called for stronger penalties for a doctor who infringed the law. As the debate grew more heated, Rep. Floyd Prozanski said that the House had never before sent an unchanged law back to the voters. "We shall be remembered as the legislature which stuck its finger in the eye of the voters," he said. Representative Sunseri acknowledged that he was a Catholic: "It's part of me," he declared. "We must send it back to the voters and the Measure 16 people [who drafted it] are responsible." Sunseri repeated the usual arguments of the disabled being vulnerable to being killed off, and old and sick people having "a duty to die" if the law took effect. Rep. Cynthia Wooten retorted: "You may be imposing your personal religious beliefs on others. Measure 16 is being intentionally left flawed. Sending it back will, I think, shatter the trust of us with the voters."

Once again the euthanasia question was demonstrated to be an issue about which people are not likely to change their minds. By lunchtime on May 13, HB 2954 sailed through by 32 votes to 26. The debates in the legislature had achieved nothing—except to warn the voters of what was coming in the fall.

A month later, when the bill to repeal was before the Oregon Senate, the debate had the same partisanship, plus a heavy dose of myths and legends about assisted suicide. The dramatic mass suicide in March of the same year of thirty-nine people in Rancho Sante Fe, California, belonging to the "Heaven's Gate" cult, was introduced into the debate, although its relevance to the wishes of terminally ill people was not addressed. Apocryphal stories were told about failed suicides, people choking on their own vomit, and families having to put plastic bags over the heads of a loved one to finish off what the drugs had failed to do. No case of assisted suicide by an actual doctor was mentioned. At the end of an emotional morning's debate on June 9, the bill asking the voters to repeal Measure 16 swept through by a vote of 20–10. It broke an eighty-year-old Senate tradition of not sending the same law back to the public for a second vote. The politicians' blindness to the effect this would have on voters' opinions would prove disastrous for them.

During the three years that the act was on hold, it benefited from a great deal of study not previously possible because no such law was on the books anywhere else in the United States. It was a rich field for medical academics to harvest. One study, "Attitudes of Oregon Psychiatrists Towards PAS," was carried out by a group of academics in Portland. It found that two-thirds of the state's psychiatrists endorsed the view that "a physician should be permitted, under some circumstances, to write a prescription for a medication whose sole purpose would be to allow a patient to end his or her life." Psychiatrists, who are also M.D.'s, have prescribing rights, whereas psychologists do not. More than half the psychiatrists surveyed said they supported the Death With Dignity Act. There was, however, a note of warning in the report, which was seized upon by the opponents of PAS: "Only 6 percent of psychiatrists were very confident that in a single evaluation they could adequately assess whether a psychiatric disorder was impairing the judgment of a patient requesting assisted suicide." Of the rest, 43 percent were "somewhat confident" that they could do so, with 51 percent "not at all confident." A revealing sidenote to the survey was that when the psychiatrists in the survey were asked what they would want if they themselves were terminally ill, 74 percent said that they would want PAS.[7] Of course, the law does not confine the evaluation to one consultation; it would be common sense, if the psychiatrist was doubtful after one session, to insist on another.

"Depression" and "drug failure" were to become the key terms in the frantic battle for votes that followed, and the opposition needed every scrap of ammunition it could gather. This was because opinion polls were, once again, showing that public support was no longer a slender majority but had increased considerably.

In February 1997, when GLS Research asked six hundred Oregon voters for their current opinions, 63 percent said that the act should definitely not be overturned, with another 14 percent saying it probably should not be overturned.

When asked if a terminally ill patient's decision about when to end his or her own suffering was an individual one, 60 percent of those surveyed answered positively. Those who believed that human life was sacred and only God should make life-ending decisions amounted to 30 percent. The Oregon character showed itself significantly when people were asked if the government should keep out of the time and manner of a person's death. Those who "strongly agreed" totaled 77 percent, with another 11 percent "somewhat agreeing." This poll was distributed in the spring to all Oregon legislators, but the majority party chose to ignore it.[8] In May, GLS Research again surveyed the voters of Oregon. The message, similarly ignored by most politicians, was clear: 67 percent said they would vote against repeal of Measure 16, and 65 percent said they were less likely to vote to reelect a legislator who asked them to vote on Measure 16 a second time.

ORTD circulated these poll results among all the state's elected representatives, but they in no way affected the opponents' final decisions. Although few expressed it publicly, they were faced now with serious moral decisions instead of the usual, lighter-weight political ones involving roads, education, and taxes. Euthanasia in any form is an issue about which politicians are inexperienced and naive. It was this "morality barrier" and ignorance that had prevented right-to-die groups for years from interesting politicians in progressive law-reform ideas. Always in the back of most elected representatives' minds is the matter of reelection. What if the Catholic hierarchy called for a boycott of pro-euthanasia politicians?

Then, in September, with the election only two months away, the archenemy of PAS, *The Oregonian*, polled voters. The results merely confirmed the two earlier polls. Those who wanted the 1994 law repealed amounted to 32 percent, while those in favor of retaining it amounted to 64 percent.

The voters' penchant for individual choice was clearly illustrated by this poll's supplementary questions about who was influencing their thinking. Eighty-two percent said the Catholic Church's desire for repeal did not affect them, while 76 percent said they were indifferent to the negative vote of the doctors in the OMA.[9] With these battle lines drawn, there was a widely canvassed view that big-bucks spending could turn it around. The man who ran *The Oregonian*'s poll, Tim Hibbitts, said that the repeal campaign obviously had problems. In reporting this pessimistic view, the newspaper, desperately looking for a brighter picture, went on: "Despite the underdog position, the repeal campaign could change public opinion if efforts are well-organized and well-financed, Hibbitts said. Supporters' best chance . . . might be to overwhelm the opposition [to repeal] with money and a sharply focused ad theme."[10]

The beleaguered repeal campaign sent down to California for a political "gunslinger" with a reputation for defeating euthanasia ballots. Chuck Cavalier, a Sacramento political consultant, claims to have taken a leading hand in defeating the Washington and California ballot initiatives, and even advised on the defeat of the Northern Territory law in Australia. Certainly his heavy hand was obvious in the California campaign in 1992, and he "dined out" on this victory, neglecting to point out that it was a one-sided campaign, as the competition was almost bankrupt and unable to buy any network television advertising. Cavalier had engineered come-from-behind ballot victories in Washington and California, but Oregon was different: Opinion in the other two states was, especially in those early days, more fluid. In Oregon the people had been pummeled by the issue for five years; opinions had been formed and hardened. Millions of dollars' worth of television advertising was less likely to change attitudes on a gut issue like euthanasia. There is very little middle ground and few floating voters in so crucial a moral topic. Moreover, the law was well drafted in language that was fairly easily understood by nonlawyers. In California, Cavalier's advertisements constantly referred to the opportunities for abuse of the law, and liberally used such violent words as "murder," "homicide," and "kill." On this issue the better-informed Oregon voters would have laughed had such emotive language been used.

Describing Cavalier at work in a studio, a *Wall Street Journal* reporter wrote: "Mr. Cavalier interrupts the narrator to suggest he put a little more oomph behind words like 'dangerous' and 'botched suicides.' 'Alarm is what we're trying to convey here,' he urges." And later in the same article, "Mr. Cavalier builds his campaigns around ominous TV and radio ads suggesting that right-to-die laws will lead to widespread killing of the elderly, infirm and merely confused. In California, for instance, he created an ad portraying a physician about to plunge a presumably lethal syringe into an uncomprehending old woman."[11] With some $4 million to spend, Cavalier created advertisements around the two-word theme that the Death With Dignity Act, 1994, was "fatally flawed," fastening on to the claims that lethal drugs did not always work. As with the state politicians, the true position, that in some cases lethal drugs do take *longer* to work but still are lethal, was conveniently ignored. With his first advertisement—known as "the Billy ad"—Cavalier ran into trouble.

The advertisement featured a youthful actor of unspecified age walking into what was apparently a doctor's waiting room and taking a seat. A voice-over explained that the patient, who had been told that he had less than six months left to live, was about to receive a lethal drug prescription from his doctor. The tone soon turned ominous:

But what Bill doesn't know is that he won't die right away. He'll choke on his own vomit, in painful convulsions, and linger for days. That isn't a bad dream. It's a nightmare. Because Measure 16 isn't about dying. It's about killing. And only you can stop it. Vote Yes on Measure 51.

The ad omitted mentioning all the hoops a person like Billy would have to jump through before getting a lethal prescription—being over eighteen, seeing two doctors, making written and oral requests, waiting fifteen days, and the ability to change his mind. Unquestionably, suicide attempts by mentally troubled people who hastily and indiscriminately ingest any drug they can secure to self-destruct show a pattern in medical literature of distressing suffering and ugly deaths. This was the misinformation the opponents of Measure 51 were relying on. Properly planned PAS, with advance use of antiemetics, and huge overdoses quickly taken, bring about quick death in the vast majority of cases. Some 2 to 4 percent might linger for a few hours or up to four days for unknown reasons, but these unlucky few are unconscious and in no pain.

With polling day less than a month away, Portland's three big network television stations refused to screen the Billy ad. A day earlier smaller stations in Eugene, Medford, and Klamath Falls, concerned about the inaccuracy of the ad, had announced that they would not accept it. One television station manager, Bruce Liljegren, of KEZI in Eugene and KDRV in Medford, said: "It crosses the line of just good, plain decency. I don't want that on our stations."[12] Other stations did not take the same attitude and continued to run the ad for the next month, but the well-publicized objections to it had cast a pall over all the Yes on 51 advertisements.

The No on 51 campaign ad featured three real physicians. An announcer described politicians and the Catholic Church, claiming that a new medical study had been conducted which exposed flaws in Measure 16. After several doctors appeared on-screen, asking to see the study, the voice-over continued:

The truth is, you could look forever and you won't find that study—because it doesn't exist. It's simply not true. And any campaign not based on the truth is fundamentally and fatally flawed. Vote no on 51. We were right the first time.

Now the No campaign supporting the PAS law was also using the phrase "fatally flawed," which appeared on thousands of billboards and lawn signs across the state. The Portland pollster Tim Hibbitts, according to *The Oregonian*, called the tactic "one of the cleverest moves in politics in a long time." The dueling slogans could confuse voters and "confused or uncertain voters almost inevitably vote no."[13]

The hierarchy of the Catholic Church was annoyed by the inclusion of their church's views in the "No Repeal" advertisements. "It's popular to bash Catholics," said Auxiliary Bishop Kenneth Steiner of the Archdiocese of

Portland. "If they did it with any other minority, they wouldn't get away with it."[14] It was no mystery even to people poorly informed on current affairs that the Catholic hierarchy was the financial powerhouse behind the repeal drive. The frequent listing in the news media of the main contributors to the campaigns made it abundantly clear to the general public that this repeal effort was being driven by the churches. Around the week they were filling out their ballots, voters were reading that the Catholic Church and Catholic organizations were prominent contributors of huge sums. Allegations of "anti-Catholic bigotry" flew wildly whenever people remarked on the sources of most of the money for repeal. But was it bigotry to take note of, and have a view on, who was funding a particular political campaign? Providing such information is the purpose of the laws governing publication of campaign funding. While most of the money came from Catholic sources, the Church of Jesus Christ of Latter-Day Saints, based in Utah, also weighed in with a solid contribution of $100,000 to fight for repeal.

As well as giving $125,000 to the repeal campaign, the Providence Peace Health System, run by Catholic nuns, took out quarter-page advertisements headlined COMPASSION in many newspapers, asking for a yes vote on 51. "We do not believe that PAS is necessary," said their ad. "Why? Because advances in pain management and the widespread availability of hospice care and other support services mean that we can meet the needs of dying patients. No patient needs to suffer intolerable pain." Apart from their adherence to Catholic religious doctrine opposing any form of suicide, to support PAS might, of course, imply that they were failing in their medical and nursing services. Catholic hospitals have been some of the biggest financial supporters for rejection of all the campaigns for assisted dying of the terminally ill. That the two failed laws and the successful one have always contained a "conscience clause" allowing hospitals and medical staff to decline to participate has never deterred the Catholic health groups from fighting against a law that would not have to affect them. The only logical inference to be drawn from this partisanship is that Catholic hospitals, for reasons of dogma, do not wish people outside of their faith to have it either.

Also throwing its considerable weight for repeal was the extremely wealthy AMA which, for example, gave $2.8 million to national political parties and candidates in 1995–96, of which 77 percent went to Republicans.[15] A series of full-page ads appeared in newspapers throughout the state, saying, in part: "Measure 16 is dangerous. It does not safeguard against the possibility that a request for assisted suicide is driven by other treatable causes, like depression or severe pain. People seek PAS when they fear indignity, abandonment and suffering."

But for the first time in all these electoral battles, a sizable section of the medical profession came out openly in favor of PAS. An organization sprang up in opposition to Physicians for Compassionate Care, calling itself Physicians for Death With Dignity. By the time of the election the pro-PAS

M.D.'s numbered 396 out of a total of 7,000 licensed Oregon doctors. The most radical part of the new group was in Lane County, where doctors, under the initiative of internist Glenn Gordon, inserted a quarter-page ad in Eugene's *Register-Guard* informing the public that not all doctors supported the AMA. The ad ran:

> Lane County Physicians urge you to vote No on Measure 51. . . . Dying patients who are suffering at the end of life have the right to make their own choices as to how end-of-life care is given.[16]

It continued on to attack the legislature for usurping the power of doctors' initiatives by forcing them to vote on the same measure they had approved in 1994.

The ad was signed by fifty-four physicians, including two past presidents of the OMA, putting on record for the first time—and all time—where they stood on the issue. While a few bold physicians had in the past individually gone public with theoretical support for PAS, never before had so large a group put their names to a public declaration of sympathy. They were not only contradicting the almighty AMA but also implying that they would carry out the procedure if circumstances were appropriate. It was a breach in the hitherto solid phalanx of medical indifference to, opposition to, or fear of PAS. Although not as large as the prorepeal doctors' group claimed to be, the doctors who wanted the law maintained significantly helped ORTD to retain its electoral support in the last few weeks under enormous pressure from expensive advertising.

For the first time the international financier and philanthropist George Soros stepped into a euthanasia campaign. In 1993 in New York he had established Project on Death in America with a grant of $15 million, with the mission to improve the quality of dying through study and education about palliative care and pain control. The executives of the project were mostly hostile to PAS, confident that palliative care was the complete answer. His contribution of $250,000 to the No on 51 campaign was a welcome surprise, yet Soros has a penchant for giving generously to campaigns which are underfunded without necessarily committing himself personally to that particular issue.

The second biggest contributor was Loren Parks, a manufacturer of hospital medical equipment in Portland who feels strongly—almost to the point of obsession—that religious organizations should stay out of the lives of people who are not their adherents. In the 1994 campaign he gave $75,000, and in 1997 he supplied a further $150,000 on condition it was entirely spent on hard-hitting radio advertisements with the theme of the separation of religion from politics. The political action committee to which Parks contributed was bluntly named: "Don't Let Them Shove Their Religion Down Your Throat."

The Oregon campaign received support from philanthropists as no right-to-die campaign had ever done. This alone signaled the topic's turning point from one of isolated crusading by a few pioneers—Joseph Fletcher, Derek Humphry, Jack Kevorkian, and Timothy Quill—to a sweeping societal controversial issue now bigger than the protracted abortion rights battle.

The biggest institutional contribution to the antirepeal campaign total of $966,000 was $142,000 from the Hemlock Society through its political arm, the USA Patients' Rights Organization. Eighteen chapters of the Hemlock Society gave a total of $23,400, with $6,200 of it coming from the Oregon chapter. The Oregon ACLU added another $4,000. Alvin Sinnard, a retired Portland businessman, whose terminally ill first wife, unable to secure lethal drugs from a doctor, killed herself with a plastic bag rather than continue to suffer, gave $10,000 and lent the campaign another $40,000. Donald Pels, a New York businessman, gave $100,000. Contributions of huge sums from capitalist entrepreneurs were a new development in the political struggle for the right to die, marking its change from a marginal to a major societal issue.

The person who provided the driving force behind the whole crusade, Portland attorney Stutsman, had sufficient confidence in the campaign to lend it $70,000 in addition to his modest gifts of cash. The only faintly religious contributions to help retain the law came from the Unitarian Universalist Fellowship, in Corvallis, Oregon, with $500; a man who said he was the organist at a United Methodist Church in North Carolina; and a professor of religious studies at a California State University (both $100).

Whereas in 1994 Catholic groups contributed about half of the campaign funds, this time the figure was nearer two-thirds. The top repeal contributors were Oregon Right to Life, $416,350; U.S. Catholic Conference, $350,000; Catholic Archdiocese of Portland, $340,000; Archdiocese of Oregon, $200,000; Catholic Health Initiatives, Colorado, $250,000; Knights of Columbus, $251,003; Catholic Health Association, $200,425; Association of California Catholic Hospitals, $175,000; Peacehealth, $150,000; Providence Health System, $100,000; Oregon Catholic Conference, $103,966; Mormon Church, $100,000; and Tom Monaghan (Domino's Pizza), $50,000.

Illustrating just how intensive was the nationwide Catholic involvement with the campaign to repeal the Oregon law, records show that 136 of the church's dioceses across the country contributed a total of $968,104. Additionally thirty-seven archdioceses collectively gave $862,239. Thirty-seven priests gave $11,425, and four bishops gave a total of $2,000. Altogether more than 350 contributions came from groups or individuals identifiable by their names as being associated with the same church.

As a beautiful summer drew to a close in Oregon, an essentially modern political campaign opened quietly. There were almost no public meetings, only an occasional tiny street rally, and there were of course no candidates to meet. At issue was a fundamental moral choice to be made in every voter's soul. Both sides tried to reach that soul with television and radio advertising, but to many it seemed that the real intellectual battle was being fought out in the scores of poignant letters to the editors published in the state's twenty daily newspapers. Hardly a day passed without strong letters arguing for and against Measure 51 filling the correspondence columns. The ones planted by the advocates for the respective campaigns could easily be spotted by their repetitive natures, in contrast to the genuine cries for approval or disapproval of the law, which were human and fascinating.

Those correspondents favoring retention of the 1994 law concentrated on issues of personal choice, told harrowing stories of witnessing a loved one's suffering, or warned people who held different views to stand aside in the name of religious freedom. A recurring theme was anger at the state legislature's questioning the honesty of their first vote.

An eighty-year-old Eugene man with terminal cancer wrote that he prayed several times daily for God either to cure him or take him away. Only thoughts of his loved ones and friends kept him from committing suicide. The man wrote, in part:

> Now that we have the legal right to die, I have thought that now I can die with dignity. If you have never walked in my shoes, and I pray to my Lord that you never have to, then please don't condemn the people who voted for it. It is fair and just, and I believe God would vote to make it a law also.

Another Eugene man described the terminal suffering of his brother and begged: "Such medieval barbarism, typified by the inquisition and arising from medieval religion, must stop." A woman writing from the town of Lebanon described her husband's terminal agony toward the end: "I miss him terribly but that last six months with him was not worth the misery he was put through. Can anyone really say an extra month or two of this kind of life is really worth going against a vote for relief and closure. I can't."

A Portland woman took exception to a columnist's comment that the opposition many people felt toward the Catholic Church's involvement in the campaign amounted to "anti-Catholic bigotry." She replied that she and many of her fellow Catholics opposed the church's position and its intrusion into the referendum process.

> Those of us who follow our hearts and conscience in these matters are not heretics but people of faith with individual hearts and minds. We

remain God's children within the fold of the church but excluded from its decisions.

A man in Langlois wrote: "The measure is not so much a debate over the ethicality of physician-assisted suicide as it is a debate over freedom of choice. This measure comes down to the very principle upon which this country was founded: individual rights."

Newspapers appeared to be scrupulously fair in balancing the letters from either side. How a dying person dealt with terminal pain was a recurring theme, with contradictory interpretations and experiences. For instance, a Eugene woman wrote: "I am reminded of the final days of my uncle, age 59, who was dying of cancer. His demeanor was peaceful, yes, even joyous in spite of extreme pain. He showered love on all who came near his bedside. His last days taught a lesson about death with dignity, death without fear." A Springfield man strongly against abortion wrote:

> It appears this holocaust of well over 30 million unborn children sacrificed on the altar of personal convenience isn't enough. Now we must take more life away, starting with the terminally ill.

Calling Oregon a death camp, he went on to warn senior citizens and the disabled that these policies would unfairly target them. Father Timothy Mockaitis, of Saint Paul Catholic Church in Eugene, in a letter to *The Oregonian*, claimed: "The purely secular movement towards euthanasia is based on control and financial efficiency. Such a 'choice' cannot be forced upon an uninformed population." A Portland woman wrote to the same newspaper: "To put into law that a doctor may assist a person to commit suicide establishes a precedent far beyond the first few deaths. Once it is legal, a doctor may suggest suicide as an option to patients diagnosed as terminal. Many lonely elderly people, with or without a caring family, could be easily influenced to see a bottle full of pills as the best way to avoid expense or the fear of being a burden."

The Oregonian, by far the state's largest newspaper, editorialized energetically for repeal of the law, consistent with its 1994 position opposing its passage. Conscious now that much of its readership strongly disagreed with its stance, the reporting was markedly fairer during the second campaign.[17] After the campaign it summarized its coverage via letters and opinion columns this way: "In the five weeks before the election, the paper published 56 letters and four reader columns favoring the assisted-suicide law, and 45 letters and one reader column opposing it. It published three reader columns supporting Measure 51." A lesson to newspapers that their views are not necessarily swallowed by their readers is clear in the poll results because in the Portland conurbation, by far *The Oregonian's* strongest circulation area, the vote was approximately 64–32 percent against repeal.

Given the weight of the churches, the AMA, and the OMA; their spending superiority of 4–1; and the experienced political operatives they brought into the state, the measure to repeal the PAS should have won easily. But, just as the jury system can often produce surprising trial verdicts, so can the democratic vote.

The vote was entirely postal, another feature being pioneered in Oregon, which is not only cheaper than the traditional way of asking people to visit a school, church hall, or other public place and enter a polling booth, but also produces higher turnouts. Oregon had 1,888,976 registered voters, of whom 1,108,052 returned their envelopes, a turnout of 58.66 percent. The final result was that 40 percent wanted the law repealed (445,830 votes) while 60 percent (666,275) did not. The campaign for repeal of the law spent $4,077,882, against $966,000 by those for its retention.

Between 1994 and 1997 the pro-PAS vote increased by 38,295 votes, while the anti-PAS vote dropped in the same period by 150,188, despite the more-than-doubled spending by the repeal campaign. The turnout at the first election was higher because it was a standard general election with many contests, including governor, on the ballot. "The weakness of the pro-51 vote reinforces our impression that the most recent outcome strongly affirmed general support for the assisted-suicide law," commented Eugene's *Register-Guard*.[18] An Oregon ethicist consistently opposed to PAS blamed the defeat on religious timidity. The *Washington Post* reported:

> In 1994, when advocates of assisted suicide prevailed in Oregon by 51 percent, religious arguments were strong on both sides of the issue, said Courtney Campbell, an ethicist at Oregon State University. The same was true earlier this year when religious groups pushed successfully for a new referendum. But in the weeks leading to this month's vote, the religious voices against suicide were virtually silent, Campbell said. Instead, he said, opponents focused their television ads and other campaign efforts on more concrete issues—such as the horror of failed suicide attempts—out of a concern that branding anything "a religious issue" could be what he called "almost the kiss of death," especially in a state that has one of the lowest per capita rates of church attendance in the nation. The result, Campbell said, "was that explicit religious commentary on the ballot measure was almost nonexistent, and because of that explicit ethical commentary was also absent."[19]

The Oregonian newspaper, in its commentaries, had carefully avoided bringing religion into the debate when it was in fact the catalyst—though virtually ignored—of the whole controversy. It only addressed the issue after the election in an extensive article in its Forum section headlined "Freedom from religion." Commenting on the reactions to the amount of money poured into the campaign by Catholic groups, William Lunch, a political science professor at Oregon State University, said: "Having stepped into the ring of politics, they have to expect to duke it out."[20] A hint that the Catholic hierarchy had caved in to the arguments of Chuck Cavalier can be seen in the post-election comment of Bishop Steiner, the church's top administrator overseeing the campaign, that he regretted putting moral values on the shelf as if they were something to be ashamed of. "These values are not only Roman Catholic, they're not only religious. They are human values, the values of life and freedom and true rights that aren't selfish rights."[21] The same article was illustrated by a large picture of Doctor Toffler, the determined anti-PAS campaigner, kneeling at prayer in a Catholic church.

David J. Garrow, a professor at Emory University, Atlanta, Georgia, and author of several major books on civil liberties, remarked that there was great irony in how the victory occurred:

Right to die advocates owe their opponents a big "thank you." Had Oregon voters not had the opportunity to speak, or had they not spoken as decisively, aid in dying activists would have kept licking their judicial wounds [from the US Supreme Court] and pondering what their next court suit ought to be. Now, however, they can lay claim to a powerful popular mandate that otherwise would not have come within their grasp.

He pointed to the almost ritual opposition of "elite" opinion makers such as editorial writers and legislators, which flew in the face of a Harris poll of ordinary Americans showing 68 percent support for PAS.[22]

When the advance opinion polls are compared to the final vote, the combined $5 million lavished by both sides on trying to influence electoral decisions through the media seems not to have affected the outcome at all. In the week after the vote the U.S. Catholic Conference commissioned an opinion poll to find out what had gone wrong for them. Again this poll confirmed the approximately 60 percent support for the law but also revealed that 83 percent of people had made up their minds on the proposal *before* the final weeks of the campaign.[23] The advertising blitz had been a dud. The price of voters' souls in Oregon concerning a fundamental issue like dying was too high for anyone to pay.

How the Oregon Law Works

The Oregon Death With Dignity Act permits qualified patients to "legally request and obtain medication from a physician to achieve a humane and dignified death."[1] The two cases heard in 1997 by the U.S. Supreme Court, as well as all legislation proposed on a state level, asked for the same rights to be granted. Generally, the same safeguards against possible abuses found in the Death With Dignity Act (DWD Act) are also found in any proposed legislation. So, when assessing the scope of PAS in the United States—what it allows, what it excludes, who is eligible, issues for health care professionals and how it works—the Oregon Act (Appendix C) is a generic blueprint of how different state laws will probably operate. While every state may vary in detail, any deviations from the DWD Act are minimal and unimportant in the overall understanding of how PAS works.

THE EFFECT ON THE PATIENT

The DWD Act allows a capable (competent) adult, who is a resident of Oregon, and has been determined by the attending physician and the consulting physician to be suffering from a terminal disease, and who has voluntarily expressed a wish to die, to request medication for the purpose of ending his or her life in a humane and dignified manner. The patient must request suicide assistance by two oral and one written requests. At least fifteen days after the initial oral request, the patient must reiterate the oral request to the attending physician. An additional forty-eight hours must elapse before the written request, which the patient must sign, date, and have witnessed by at least two individuals who attest that the patient is capable, is acting voluntarily, and is not being coerced to sign the request. The physician may write the prescription for the lethal drugs only after these requirements have been satisfied.

One witness must not be a relative, an heir, or an owner, operator, or employee of a health care facility at which the patient is receiving care. The patient's attending physician at the time of the request may not be a witness. If the patient is a resident of a long-term care facility at the time the written request is made, one of the witnesses must be an individual designated by the facility and have the qualifications legally specified by the Department of Human Resources. The attending physician must request that the patient notify his or her next of kin, but such notification is not a prerequisite for physician assistance. The patient may rescind the request at any time and in any manner.

Once the patients receive the prescription for the lethal dose, they take the prescription to the pharmacy to be filled. Then, at their discretion, they decide when, where, in what manner, and with whom present, to self-administer the lethal dose. Or they may decide to hold the medication for future use when the suffering becomes intolerable. Sometimes it is never used. There is, therefore, no need for the physician to be present, and the ingesting of the medication is one hundred percent within the control of the patient.

Now that the law is in effect, however, those doctors who are willing to use it in justifiable circumstances have announced that they prefer to be with their patients as they die.

The attending physician must make the initial determination of whether the patient has a terminal illness, is competent, and has made the request voluntarily. The physician must inform the patient of the medical diagnosis and prognosis, as well as the probable risks and results of taking the prescribed medication. In addition to discussing feasible alternatives, the physician must also explain the options of comfort care, hospice care, and pain control. The physician must refer the patient to a consulting physician who confirms, in writing, the attending physician's assessment that the patient is suffering from a terminal disease, is competent, is acting voluntarily, and is making an informed decision. If either the attending or the consulting physician suspects that the patient may be suffering from a psychiatric or psychological disorder, or depression causing impaired judgment, that patient must be referred for counseling. The doctor cannot prescribe the medication until the counselor determines that the patient is not suffering from such a disorder.

Physicians who comply in good faith with the provisions of the act are granted legal immunity from criminal, civil, and professional disciplinary actions. No liability attaches to anyone, family and friends included, being present when a qualified patient takes the prescribed medication to end his or her life. No health care organization may subject a health care provider to discipline or loss of privileges for participating or refusing to participate in the act. Most important, no health care professional is *required* to prescribe medication to a qualified patient. *The choice to participate is left totally*

to the physician and his or her conscience. As with the patient, the decision
to participate is one's own choice. Also, deliberate ingestion of a lethal dose
of medication by a qualified patient will not affect life, health, or accident
insurance or annuity policy.

Attending physicians are required to document all oral and written requests, their own and the consulting physician's agreement that the patient
complies with the requirements of the act, and all reports of any counseling.
The Oregon Health Division is required to collect information regarding
compliance with the act and publish an annual statistical report.

But what exactly do some of these key words mean? What is a mentally
competent, terminally ill adult? How is *voluntary* assessed? These are not
random words. Each word has a very specific meaning and is used for a very
specific purpose. For example, the patient must have the capacity to make
the decision to terminate his or her life. The patient must be competent.
(*Competent* and *capacity* are used interchangeably in this context.) What is
meant by *terminal*? Aren't we all terminal, in that, eventually, all of us will
die? And when does someone become an adult? Eighteen? Twenty-one?

The law pertains to a very narrow group of people, since *all* of these
requirements must be satisfied in order for the patient to be eligible for
PAS. Indeed, the *Oregonian*, using statistics and academic surveys, tried to
determine how many terminally ill persons might actually hasten their death
each year with the new DWD Act. The conclusion: "Fewer than 100 will
ask for lethal prescriptions under the new law. . . . About 50 of them will
take the medicine and die."[2] As of June 1998, at least forty-two people have
requested assisted suicide since Oregon's DWD Act took effect in October
1997, although only four have reportedly used lethal prescriptions to end
their lives.[3] The law allows such deaths to be carried out in private, however,
so there is no definitive way of knowing how many have died under the law.
Deaths must be reported to the Oregon Health Division, but the agency
plans to make no statistical report on the incidents until the end of the year
or until ten PAS deaths have occurred.[4] The patient must clear four hurdles
before the physician is allowed to prescribe a lethal dose of medication to
hasten death. The patient must be mentally competent, terminally ill, adult,
and voluntarily seeking the help of a willing physician.

The first hurdle is the requirement that the patient be *mentally competent.* The *American Heritage Dictionary* defines competent as: "1. Properly
or well qualified. 2. Adequate for the purpose. 3. Legally qualified to perform
an act." *Black's Law Dictionary*, the world's most widely used and recognized
authority for definitions of legal words and terms, generically defines
competence as being: "Duly qualified; answering all requirements; having
sufficient ability or authority; possessing the requisite natural or legal qualifications; able; adequate; suitable; sufficient; capable; legally fit."

None of these words or terms, however, gives anything near sufficient
guidance to the physician who must determine the patient's rational ability

to act in this irreversible manner. More specifically, the general law incorporates the word into such phrases as "the competency to stand trial," "the competency to execute a will or enter into a contract," and "the competency to make medical decisions about forgoing life-sustaining treatment." These and many other types of competency have individual legal standards and criteria which the individual must not fall below, or a determination of incapacity will be found. A declaration of incompetency for one task does not automatically mean that the patient is incompetent for another task, since the level of astuteness and ability needed differ according to the task.

The DWD Act defines "incapable" as meaning that "in the opinion of a court or in the opinion of the patient's attending physician or consulting physician, a patient lacks the ability to make and communicate health care decisions to health care providers, including communication through persons familiar with the patient's manner of communicating if those persons are available." While the law clearly gives the attending and consulting physicians the power to decide and no judicial hearing is necessary, it is not settled whether, for practical purposes, the final determination of incompetency must be made by a court or whether it may be made in the clinical setting without judicial participation.

An adult is presumed competent for purposes of medical decision-making, unless proven otherwise. There is no single, accepted definition of what constitutes a capacity to make medical decisions. The case law is unclear on the meaning of an incapacity to make medical decisions in general, an ambiguity that carries over into the removal of life-support treatment: "The search for a single test of competency is a search for a Holy Grail. Unless it is recognized that there is no magical definition of competency to make decisions about treatment, the search for an acceptable test will never end," write Roth, Meisel, and Lidz in the *American Journal of Psychiatry*.[5] The main reason for the absence of any agreement is that only rarely do the courts directly address this issue, despite the fact that competency is a central concern in medical decision-making. The actual meanings of competency and incompetency are usually taken for granted or dealt with in a cursory way by the courts. Few, if any, courts have meaningfully grappled with the concepts.

It is well accepted that for patients to participate effectively in making decisions about their health care, they must possess the mental, emotional, and legal capacity to do so. A competent adult may choose to forgo medical care, even if that choice results in death. This follows from the principle of autonomy and informed consent that underlies the doctor-patient relationship. Since physician-aid-in-dying has been illegal and therefore provides no precedent to guide physician or court decisions, it is necessary to rely on judicial interpretation of incompetency in the context of forgoing life-support treatment.

There is guidance in the DWD Act's definition of "informed decision."

To quote precisely: " 'Informed decision' means a decision by a qualified patient, to request and obtain a prescription to end his or her life in a humane and dignified manner, that is based on an appreciation of the relevant facts and after being fully informed by the attending physician of: (a) his or her medical diagnosis; (b) his or her prognosis; (c) the potential risks associated with taking the medication to be prescribed; (d) the probable result of taking the medication to be prescribed; (e) the feasible alternatives, including, but not limited to, comfort care, hospice care and pain control."

Questions about a patient's capacity do not arise in most cases. Most people clearly possess the capacity to make medical decisions; others just as clearly lack it. For the most part, the patient is mentally alert and capable of making decisions by any standard. On the other end of the spectrum lies the patient in a coma or persistent vegetative state, obviously unable to reach a reasoned conclusion about anything. It is, therefore, the gray area between the obvious that draws judicial and medical attention.

Since there is a legal presumption of competency, some event or circumstance must trigger the suspicion that decision-making capacity does *not* exist. Alan Meisel, professor of law and right-to-die expert, elaborates: "The patient's general demeanor, difficulty in communicating, or overall medical condition are such conditions. Clinicians also tend to treat patients who are delirious, demented, intoxicated, obtunded, or stuporous as lacking decision-making capacity. These conditions alone are not the same as incompetency. Neither, however, should their existence be ignored; they serve as signs to alert both clinical personnel and family members to the need to inquire further about the patient's competence."[6]

For many years, physicians were likely to find a patient competent to make a serious medical decision only when that patient agreed with the physician. When the patient disagreed with the physician—especially if that disagreement would lead to the death of the patient—the physician, and subsequently the court, would likely declare the patient incompetent and then search for some surrogate decision-maker who was more likely to agree with the physician.[7] This bias began changing in the 1970s. Courts now consistently recognize the right of a competent individual to refuse treatment, even if that decision will hasten death, and declining medical care is not considered an indication of incompetency. As a result, the law protects a person's right to reject treatment, no matter how wise or unwise another individual might view it. Beliefs that are "unwise, foolish or ridiculous" do not render a patient incompetent.

One of the arguments against legalizing PAS is that depression is the cause of the request for drugs, that depression can be treated or cured, and that the patient may end his or her life because of a condition that could have been corrected. Psychiatrists point out that depression can be difficult to detect. Most patients in such a condition are profoundly sad, and their sorrow can be difficult to distinguish from clinical depression. Others see depression as perhaps being warranted given the circumstances that would motivate someone in the last days of life to hasten death. Certainly some terminally ill patients do benefit from treatment with antidepressants. However, the DWD Act recognizes that not all suicidal thoughts are evidence of mental illness and that some requests are based on a rational thought process. Furthermore, in the Oregon act and in other state proposals, if either the attending or the consulting physician believes, or even suspects, that the patient is suffering from psychiatric or psychological illness, or depression causing impaired judgment, they *must* refer the patient for counseling.

If the patient's capacity is already questionable, ambivalence or vacillation can trigger an assessment of possible incompetence. Hence the 15-day waiting period in the Oregon act, to ensure an enduring state of mind. A momentous decision of this finality would naturally generate inconsistency in a person's thinking, yet in the extreme such vacillation can trigger an inquiry into the patient's competence. Patients who are about to refuse life-sustaining treatment and those requesting an assisted death usually do not have a specific intent or wish to die. Rather, they may desperately wish to live, but only if life exists free of unwanted medical technology, surgery, or drugs, and without protracted suffering. As one perceptive judge wrote, "The testimony of Mr. Perlmutter . . . is that he really wants to live, but . . . under his own power."[8]

There are two ways of assessing (though not defining) incompetence: the general competence approach and the specific competence approach, although the former is being replaced by the latter in most jurisdictions. Under the general approach, incompetence is viewed as a characteristic of a person. In particular, an individual's overall ability to function. Under this approach, people are either competent or incompetent. There are no degrees of incompetency.

A consensus is emerging in right-to-die cases, however, that incompetence should be viewed as an inability to perform a specific task. Specific incompetence rejects the idea of the all-or-nothing approach, focusing instead on a person's capacity to perform the particular task in question. That is, a person is competent or incompetent to do "x"—sign a will, enter into a contract, forgo life-sustaining treatment, or ingest lethal medication that will result in a hastened death. There is no blanket condemnation of the individual's mental capacity, only a disqualification from performing a particular task. For example, a patient may be competent to sign a living will, but not competent to be the guardian of someone else's child.

The approach to assessing specific incompetence, and the approach most consistent with the law of informed consent, is the ability to understand. This test—the ability of the patient to understand the risks, benefits, and alternatives to treatment (including no treatment)—demands that the patient understand this information about treatment. How the patient weighs these elements, values them, or puts them together to reach a decision is not important. Consistent with the standard of "understanding," the Hastings Center defines decision-making capacity as: "(a) the ability to comprehend information relevant to the decision; (b) the ability to deliberate about the choices in accordance with personal values and goals; and (c) the ability to communicate (verbally or nonverbally) with caregivers."

Even though the courts have failed to enunciate this standard as authoritative, the requirement that the patient "understand" can be inferred from various decisions. What the patient *must* understand, naturally, is "information necessary to make the relevant treatment decision," says Meisel. "This, of course, is information of the type a physician is required to give the patient under the informed consent doctrine: material information about the potential risks and benefits of treatment, the nature and purpose of the treatment, and the available alternatives. More particularly, an incompetent patient is one who lacks 'a clear understanding of the nature of his or her illness and prognosis, and of the risks and benefits of the proposed treatment, and [lacks] the capacity to reason and make judgments about that information.' In right-to-die cases, patients should also understand their prognosis, that is, that they are terminally or incurably ill and that the treatment or treatments in question will possibly prolong life but not restore health," he concludes.[9]

In addition, when a patient is contemplating ending his or her life with assistance from a physician, the patient must fully understand the finality of the decision. The prognosis of the disease, the probable result of ingesting the lethal drugs, and the alternatives to assisted suicide must be explained, a discussion should ensue, preferably with physician and family, and the patient must come to a firm decision with as clear a mind as the physician is able to promote.

The understanding approach sounds simple enough, yet it leaves many questions unanswered: What level of understanding must the patient have? How can the doctor determine whether the patient does or does not understand? To what length must the attending physician go to probe the patient's understanding? Should the physician be confident if the patient says or signs that he or she understands? Not necessarily, say the courts.

Understanding should not be measured solely by cognitive skills. It may not be adequate that a patient can recall information, repeat it, and intelligently answer questions about it. For example, a court found a cancer patient incompetent to make her own medical decisions even though she understood the life-threatening nature of the disease and the myriad array of treatments with different levels of risks and benefits. The court believed that even though "she was fully alert and could respond directly to questions, she suffered from delusions regarding the cause of her illness. She could not comprehend that her condition did not arise from a corroded or otherwise bad heater in the apartment she had been occupying."[10]

Finally, some patients may be fully competent, yet may have lost the physical ability to speak or to write. Patients with Lou Gehrig's disease or victims of a paralyzing stroke come to mind. Therefore, the courts have determined that a patient may be able to signify a choice through conduct as well as through verbal communication. A positive or negative shake of the head, patient interference with a particular procedure, and eye blinking in response to questions with a predetermined meaning assigned to different numbers of blinks, have all manifested evidence of a legal choice by the patient.

With this requirement that the patient have decision-making capacity, the availability of physician-assisted suicide begins to narrow. No one in a coma, in a persistent vegetative state, unconscious, or with any kind of dementia, including Alzheimer's disease, is eligible to receive a prescription for lethal medication. Critics complain that doctors, egged on by the family, will "kill" unconscious or demented individuals with legalization. Not so, unless they want to be found guilty of first-degree murder. The requesting patient must be fully competent, as described above. Competency or capacity is the first hurdle. This is only the first requirement of eligibility.

The next word that needs clarification is the word *terminal*. In order to qualify for PAS, the patient must be *terminally ill*. This is the second hurdle. The DWD Act defines *terminal* as an incurable and irreversible disease that has been medically confirmed and will, within reasonable medical judgment, produce death within six (6) months. A special communication in the *Journal of the American Medical Association* warns physicians against manipulating the word *terminal*:

> Physicians should not misrepresent the medical situation to implement their personal views on assisted suicide. Compassion may move some physicians to help patients who present compelling requests for suicide assistance but are not terminally ill. However, it would be dishonest to certify that a patient with early Alzheimer's disease has a projected prognosis of less than six months. In the opposite situation, opponents of assisted suicide may wish to avoid an overt disagreement with the patient by stating that they cannot be sure of the prognosis, even though they would be willing to certify prognosis when referring patients to hospice care. Opponents may also delay certification until the patient's disease has robbed him or her of decision-making capacity and made the patient ineligible for assisted suicide under the act. Honesty is important in all social relationships, and honesty is particularly important in the physician-patient relationship because patients depend on their physicians for complete and truthful information.[11]

This second hurdle eliminates more people from coverage under the act. Physician assistance is not available to patients who suffer from nonterminal illnesses, even progressively debilitating and chronic conditions such as ALS (Lou Gehrig's disease) or multiple sclerosis. Paraplegics and stroke victims are also not covered, nor is anyone whose predicted time of death is incalculable. Patients in the early stages of a disease are usually not eligible, since the law defines a terminal disease as one leading to death in six months.

The third hurdle to clear: the mentally competent, terminally ill patient must also be an *adult*. The definition of an adult is determined by individual state law. In most states, the minor becomes an adult at age eighteen, although several states have set the age limit at twenty-one. In Oregon, an adult is a person eighteen years of age or older. PAS, therefore, does not apply to the teenagers, jilted by their sweethearts, as those opposed to the practice would often lead us to believe. Aside from being below the age of consent for something as serious as ending their lives, love-struck teenagers are also not terminally ill, even if mentally competent. There is much misinformation bantered about on this subject. Those groups that seek to restrain the progress of the right-to-die movement deliberately and calculatingly try to deceive and confuse the unknowing public in a desperate attempt to gain support for their losing battle.

There is one more hurdle to pass over in order to arrive at the final group of individuals who are permitted to hasten their inevitable death. The patient must make the decision *voluntarily*. Those who wish to discredit the right-to-die movement warn that the state, the hospital, the insurance company, or the family will be keen to kill the disabled, the elderly, or the terminally ill if the practice of an assisted death is legalized. This could not be further from the truth. Quite to the contrary, the basis for the movement is the furthering of individual autonomy, the freedom to form, to revise over time, and to pursue one's own particular plan of life and death—in other words, the freedom to die.

A choice is voluntary when it is selected freely in accordance with the values and goals of the individual. A patient's permission is not legally effective unless it is voluntary, freely given, without duress, undue influence, or coercion. Selecting options for health care must not be so influenced by others that free choice is precluded. Of course, patients do not make decisions in isolation from others. Most people would probably be unable to do so even if they tried. Complex networks of relationships and interdependence make it almost impossible.

Drawing the line between influence that is legitimate and that which is not is difficult in both theory and practice. The difference between legitimate influence and "undue influence" is not always certain. Distinctions are often made between "coercion," "duress," and "manipulation"—all of which are unacceptable and illegal—and "advice," "persuasion," and "influence"— which are expected, desired, and often requested. These words convey a judgment call on whether an action interferes with voluntary choice or not, but the words are too poorly defined and the nuances too subtle to provide an automatically recognizable basis for judging the difficult cases. Obviously, permission extracted by the use, or the threatened or attempted use, of physical force is not legally binding.

How information is communicated and how continuing care is provided can induce a patient to make certain choices. The physician, therefore, has an enormous responsibility when helping to shape the deliberations and decisions of a patient who is facing choices relating to the duration of his or her life: "Letting a patient know that his or her death is now seen by others to be appropriate—or at least not unexpected—may be 'giving permission to die' to a patient who no longer wishes to struggle against overwhelming odds. On the other hand, it may encourage overly rapid acceptance of death by a patient who feels rejected and unimportant," says the 1983 President's Commission for the Study of Ethical Problems in Medicine and Biomedical and Behavioral Research, Deciding to Forgo Life-Sustaining Treatment.[12]

There is no evidence of family members coercing terminally ill patients to end their lives by forgoing medical treatment and there is no reason to expect family members suddenly to begin exerting undue influence on patients to end their lives with the assistance of a physician. Certainly, where human nature is involved, abuse will occur, but to predict widespread coercion of dying patients to hasten their deaths is to say that the elderly should not have money because unscrupulous characters might try to take it away from them. Reasoning in both instances is faulty.

Only after patients clear these four hurdles are they allowed to receive a prescription of lethal drugs with which to end their life. If one hurdle is missed, the doctor is prohibited from prescribing the medication. Moreover, the courts have suggested, even invited, the legislatures to step in and make regulations for PAS. It is very important that these guidelines be carefully crafted. Similar to Oregon, most states will probably include: a waiting period between the time that the drugs are requested and the time that the drugs are prescribed; consultation with a second physician to corroborate that the patient is, in fact, terminally ill; and mandatory evaluation by a psychiatrist if depression is suspected.

The Oregon act specifically prohibits voluntary euthanasia. With voluntary euthanasia, the physician ends the patient's life by the administration of a lethal injection at the request of the patient. Lethal injections are nowhere on the table for discussion in the United States. The patient must get the prescription filled and then self-administer the medication—that is, the patient swallows the pills at a time of his or her choosing. No lethal injection and no carbon monoxide is administered, as in a death with Dr. Kevorkian. PAS is only for the patients who are able to fill the prescription and swallow the pills or elixir on their own. Many people at the end of life are unable to coordinate this action, which logistically must also include liquid or soft food to accompany the medication. Patients near death are often unable to even swallow, much less pour juice and hold the glass. These people are not able to end their lives under the Oregon act.

To summarize, PAS applies only to the mentally competent, terminally ill adult: (1) mentally competent (able to understand the prognosis, alternatives, risks and consequences of his or her actions); (2) terminally ill (in all likelihood the patient will die within six months); and (3) adult (in most states, at least eighteen years old); who (4) voluntarily requests medication from a doctor, whose presence is not necessary when the drugs are ingested. This method of dying is purely voluntary for everyone involved—a matter of individual choice. Neither the doctor nor the patient is forced to do anything against their will or conscience. This is not a law that *makes* anybody do anything. Patients need not fear that someone else will make a judgment call about their pain and suffering or their quality of life. If doctor or patient disagree religiously or morally, PAS has nothing to do with them. It simply opens up end-of-life alternatives for those who wish to take advantage of them. The law does not allow patients to request suicide assistance through advance directives or surrogate decision-makers.

With all of these groups excluded, it is appropriate to ask exactly who *is* covered by the DWD Act and by legislation currently proposed in other states. The act applies primarily to individuals with cancer and AIDS, a narrow group of suffering people. These patients are usually conscious and capable of making medical decisions. They satisfy the terminally ill requirement in that the medical profession can fairly accurately predict how long the patient will live, particularly in the last hours, days, and weeks. The adult requirement is obvious. Furthermore, unless the patient has waited too long, these patients are generally not too incapacitated or physically restricted to go to the drugstore, have the prescription filled, and take the lethal medication on their own. They can fill a glass, raise the pills to the mouth, and swallow them. Not everyone in the final stages of a terminal illness can do this.

Furthermore, nonresidents are excluded under the DWD Act, although the act fails to define the residency requirements. Generally, residence is defined by a person's dwelling and determined by his or her intent to reside in the state, or if the person is absent from the state, the intent to return. How residency is defined for purposes of the act will determine whether there will be an influx into the state to obtain suicide assistance.

PAS is only one way of shortening the dying process. The characteristics of the different methods of speeding up an imminent death can be confusing, yet they all fall under the umbrella of the right-to-die. There is the use of advance directives, the best known being the Living Will and the Health Care Proxy. Advance directives come into play only when the patient is:

(1) *incompetent, unconscious* or otherwise unable to make medical decisions. If competent, he or she would personally convey decisions to the doctor; 2) incurably or irreversibly mentally or physically ill; and 3) on some kind of life-support system. Advance directives are legal in all states. The suffering patient is, from the standpoint of hastening death, better off being on life-support, conscious or unconscious, since removal of life-sustaining treatment is routine, lawful practice. Fully 80 percent of all Americans die in health care institutions today—65 percent in hospitals, 15 percent in nursing homes. Roughly 70 to 90 percent of institutional deaths in the United States are right-to-die cases, with death occurring after a decision has been made to forgo treatment. Some 17.5 percent of all U.S. deaths are preceded by the use, for pain relief, of life-shortening quantities of opioids, usually morphine.

There is a tendency for people to think that Dr. Jack Kevorkian's assistance and PAS are one and the same. They are not. Dr. Kevorkian's patients are mentally competent and adult, but here the similarity ends, since his patients, while physically and emotionally suffering individuals, are not necessarily terminally ill. Many had Lou Gehrig's disease, multiple sclerosis, or other disorders, and could have lived for well over six months. Moreover, Doctor Kevorkian is present at the time of the patient's death and assists by lethal injections at the patient's voluntary request. This procedure is different from PAS, which forbids lethal injections or carbon monoxide.

Experience will tell whether the waiting period of fifteen days between the first request for assisted death and the writing of the prescription is too long or too short. Many think it is too long, and could cause unnecessary suffering. The law proposed in Michigan in 1998 requires a seven-day wait, which seems more practical, quite long enough for further investigations or a change of mind.

THE EFFECT ON PHYSICIANS, NURSES, AND PHARMACISTS

The legalization of PAS also poses difficult questions for health care providers. Physicians, who are given wide discretion under the law, need to examine their own ethics to decide in advance how they will respond to requests from patients. Expertise and data must be gathered in an area where both are lacking. The majority of terminally ill patients who consider, or openly discuss, suicide do not kill themselves. Nevertheless, doctors can expect patients to inquire about or request aid-in-dying. The first task of the physician, therefore, will be to discuss the patient's concerns, the reasons for considering suicide, and then to attempt to relieve them. This conversation should occur whether the physician supports or opposes assisted suicide. Physicians can often provide better relief of symptoms, allay fears, and offer support and suggestions for ongoing care. While the Oregon act recognizes that, for some patients, suicide may be the least worse death, physicians must not substitute high-quality care for the ease of the written prescription. Regardless of their position, doctors must continue to improve their care for and understanding of the dying patient.

Until recently, a physician could respond to a request for PAS by acknowledging the appeal but dismissing even the possibility as illegal. While the DWD Act eliminated this easy response, and while it sanctions assisted suicide, it also explicitly states that no physician is required to assist a patient who requests medication for purposes of committing suicide. The act is based on individual choice. It states: "No health care provider shall be under any duty, whether by contract, by statute or by any other legal requirement to participate in the provision to a qualified patient of medication to end his or her life in a humane and dignified manner. If a health care provider is unable or unwilling to carry out a patient's request, the health care provider shall transfer, upon request, a copy of the patient's relevant medical records to the new health care provider."

An article in the *Journal of the American Medical Association* offers recommendations.[13] Physicians should examine, they suggest, whether the issue of assisted suicide should be raised with patients. The act does not forbid physicians from doing this, but, given the psychology of the doctor-patient relationship and the ill and weakened patient's dependence on the physician, the patient may interpret the doctor's introduction of the topic as an encouragement to end his or her life. Consequently, the *Journal* recommends that physicians should generally discuss their willingness to help only after the patient has raised the issue.

Another issue for physicians is whether to assist new patients. Many terminal patients do not have long-standing relationships with their health care provider. A growing segment of the population lacks health insurance, people change health care plans, and our society is a mobile one. Therefore, doctors will be faced with the decision of whether to provide assistance to new patients basically unknown to them. The *Journal* recommends that doctors who write prescriptions based only on brief encounters do so in combination with a commitment to provide necessary ongoing care and support.

Physicians will be faced with the dilemma of whether to assist a patient who has no access to hospice care, no caregiver at home, and perhaps even no home. They may feel that prescribing medication makes them accomplices to society's refusal to care properly for its dying members and the nation's lack of universal health insurance. Don't get mired in guilt, advises the *Journal*. There are strong arguments in favor of PAS in such cases: "No individual physician can correct the shortcomings of the health care system or society as a whole. Also, it would be unfair to allow PAS for well-off patients, while denying it to patients who are not only socially disadvantaged but who also suffer unrelieved symptoms. It is our society's tragedy that PAS may be the least bad option for such patients. Regardless of whether a physician chooses to assist a suicide in the absence of good supportive care, he or she must commit to serving as an advocate for such patients and fighting to obtain better support for them."[14]

Physicians who choose to prescribe lethal drugs need to know what they are doing so that the terminal patient does not wake up in the emergency room. The suitability of lethal doses of medication is not something discussed in medical literature or taught in medical school. A guidebook aimed at steering health care providers through the practical, ethical, and bureaucratic maze surrounding the state's landmark law has been completed by a panel of twenty-five mainstream health care organizations, lawyers, doctors, nurses, pharmacists, ethicists, and members of the clergy in Oregon. The guidebook mentions what drugs may be used but stops short of providing recipes for lethal drug cocktails. For that, physicians may contact Compassion in Dying Oregon.[15]

Nurses also have a part in the hastening of a terminal patient's death. Like physicians, their participation is voluntary. If willing, they can play a valuable role, possessing more regular contact with the patient and the family than do the physicians. This familiarity can be helpful in decision-making conversations as well as in their comforting physical presence at the time the patient brings life to an end. The DWD Act exempts all persons from civil and criminal liability and professional disciplinary actions for being present when a qualified patient takes the prescribed medication to end his or her life. At the same time, the Oregon law prohibits nurses from administering lethal medication or taking direct action to end a person's life.

Institutions, including hospitals, nursing homes, and hospices, are also under no duty to participate in an assisted death. They can give prior notice to patients of their official policy or mission statement, allowing patients to choose a facility with an outlook compatible with their own. Institutions can also ban their pharmacies from filling prescriptions for PAS. Although they may prohibit the practice of PAS within their facilities, the DWD Act forbids them from revoking medical staff privileges from physicians who provide such prescriptions. Pharmacists are also not required to participate in an assisted death over their moral and religious objections.

The Oregon Health Services Commission has voted to include physician-aided deaths on the prioritized list of health services available to the state's 380,000 Medicaid recipients. Because federal financing for PAS is prohibited, the state will bear the entire cost for terminally ill poor Oregonians. The complete procedure, which includes doctor office visits, psychiatric and psychological assessment, and lethal prescriptions will rank 260th of 745 services on the list. It will be included with comfort care as a treatment for "terminal illness, regardless of diagnosis."[16]

With the passage of Measure 16, and its overwhelming confirmation with Measure 51, the debate over PAS enters a new phase. The issue no longer is *whether* assisted suicide should or would be legalized, but *how* this act will be implemented, and whether other states will follow Oregon's example. Theory has now given way to practice.

Chapter 19

On the Way to the Supreme Court

Compassion in Dying is a unique nonprofit organization formed in Seattle, Washington, in April 1993. It is the first right-to-die group to provide open and direct assistance to people who are considering ending their own lives. The group acknowledges that it is operating in an uncertain legal environment, yet it claims not to intentionally violate a Washington State statute that prohibits "promoting a suicide attempt."[1]

There have been no court proceedings in Washington under this statute, and prosecutors have been reluctant to comment on the likelihood of an inquiry. Compassion in Dying defines assistance with suicide as "providing information, counseling, emotional support, and personal presence at the time of death."[2] The group believes that by placing control in the hands of terminal patients, and assuring them of assistance with rational suicide as an option, they help prevent or postpone suicide, especially suicide by violent means.

Compassion limits its assistance to persons who are physically suffering in the last stages of terminal illness and who can self-administer their drugs, either orally or intravenously. It will not become involved in the suicides of persons who are depressed or unable to accept full responsibility for their actions. It is totally opposed to suicide as a means of dealing with depression, emotional illness, or family difficulties. Compassion attempts to ensure that suicide is not a consideration because of financial problems or inadequate health insurance.

Compassion in Dying serves terminally ill patients in two ways: First, the organization provides specific details on preparing for dying and how death can be accomplished. It does not administer lethal injections or "kill" anyone, but instead helps patients obtain barbiturate prescriptions from their primary-care physicians. It also attempts to persuade physicians to make these drugs available. For dying patients who decide to hasten death, and who meet their guidelines and safeguards, Compassion offers counseling and emotional support for them and their families. To this end the group has physicians and other trained personnel willing to sit with dying patients and family members at the time of the suicide. It believes that people with terminal illnesses who seek to end their suffering should not have to die alone, which often happens because their family and friends fear prosecution.

Second, Compassion in Dying's National Litigation Project challenges the constitutionality of state laws that prohibit dying patients from receiving prescription medications that they may self-administer to hasten death. It was through this project that the U.S. Supreme Court came to decide whether mentally competent, terminally ill patients have a constitutional right to receive assistance from their physicians to shorten the dying process by committing suicide, and, if so, whether the state has a sufficient interest so as to prohibit the exercise of this right.

Before the formation of Compassion in Dying and prior to the first Oregon initiative, the Washington State chapter of the Hemlock Society sponsored a statewide Death with Dignity initiative in 1991. A young attorney, Kathryn L. Tucker, with Seattle's prestigious Perkins Coie law firm, volunteered to help the sponsors with the initiative. After a hard-fought battle, Washington voters defeated the measure by 54 to 46 percent. In the wake of this defeat, Hemlock's top Washington State activist, Unitarian minister Ralph Mero, stepped forward to establish Compassion in Dying. Fearing that the newly founded organization might be vulnerable to prosecution under Washington's assisted suicide statute, Kathryn Tucker called Mero with advice: Actively challenge the constitutionality of the law instead of waiting to defend against a possible prosecution. Out of Tucker's advice to Mero came the first of two cases that the Supreme Court would hear on January 8, 1997. Kathryn Tucker would eventually argue this challenge before the Court in *Washington* v. *Glucksberg*,[3] originally styled *Compassion in Dying, et al.* v. *Washington*.

Turning the issue of PAS away from the legislatures and placing it in the judicial arena instead, *Compassion in Dying, et al.* v. *Washington* was filed in the U.S. District Court for Western Washington on January 24, 1994. Compassion in Dying was joined by four physicians, Drs. Harold Glucksberg, Abigail Halperin, Thomas A. Preston, and Peter Shalit. The physicians alleged that the statute violated their right to due process of law in that it limited their ability to practice medicine consistent with their best professional judgment. None of their patients was currently suicidal, but all wanted lethal drugs they could take if their suffering became intolerable. The plaintiff-physicians were unable to comply with the patients' requests because of the law against assisting in a suicide.

One of Dr. Harold Glucksberg's patients, not wanting to spend his last days in a drug-induced stupor, asked for his physician's help. Glucksberg, citing the Washington statute prohibiting physician aid in dying, refused. A family member subsequently helped the dying man climb over a bridge railing, so he could jump to his death. Doctor Shalit refused an AIDS patient's request for lethal drugs, leaving the man in excruciating pain and with lesions that prevented him from walking and urinating. After Doctor Halperin refused a patient's request for drugs to hasten her death, the woman killed herself by tying a plastic bag over her head.

Three terminally ill patients, using pseudonyms, also joined the lawsuit. One of them, identified as "Jane Roe," a bedridden doctor, was dying from rapidly spreading breast cancer, causing chronic, severe pain, anemia, and incontinence. Another patient, "John Doe," an artist dying of AIDS, had lost 70 percent of his eyesight and suffered severe seizures. The third, "James Poe," a salesman, was dying from emphysema. He was permanently connected to an oxygen tent.

These physicians and mentally competent, terminally ill patients asked the court to declare unconstitutional Washington's penal statute prohibiting suicide assistance to the extent that it prohibited physicians from prescribing death-producing drugs for mentally competent terminally ill patients to self-administer. The plaintiffs raised two main issues. First, they argued that the statute in question violated the due process clause of the Fourteenth Amendment of the Constitution because competent terminally ill patients have a fundamental liberty interest in ending their lives in the time and manner of their choosing. Because the statute prohibits *all* suicide assistance, they argued, state interests were not sufficient to justify such total prohibitions as imposed by state laws. Plaintiffs cited previous decisions of the Supreme Court that found, for example, "It is a promise of the Constitution that there is a realm of personal liberty which the government may not enter."[4]

Alternatively, the plaintiffs argued that the statute was invalid under the equal protection clause of the Fourteenth Amendment. Through a series of statutes and court decisions, including *Cruzan*, competent terminally ill patients on life support are permitted to choose death by refusing, or authorizing the withdrawal of, life-sustaining treatment. The Washington statute, however, prohibits those who do *not* depend on life support from similarly choosing death to end *their* suffering. Plaintiffs claimed that when this opportunity to hasten death is denied to mentally competent terminally ill patients *not* being maintained on artificial life support, a discriminatory class is created that violates the equal protection of the Fourteenth Amendment.

On May 3, 1994, federal District Court Judge Barbara Rothstein declared the Washington State law unconstitutional.[5] She held that state laws which totally prohibit assistance with hastening death for the terminally ill person violate both clauses of the Fourteenth Amendment—the fundamental liberty interest of the due process clause and the equal protection clause. Based on the reasoning set forth in *Casey*, which affirmed *Roe* v. *Wade* and

Cruzan, whereby a competent person has a protected liberty interest in refusing unwanted medical treatment, even if the refusal means certain death, the court concluded that like the abortion decision, the decision of a terminally ill person to end his or her life "involves the most intimate and personal choices a person may make in a lifetime" and constitutes a "choice central to personal dignity and autonomy." Rothstein concluded "that the suffering of a terminally ill person cannot be deemed any less intimate or personal, or any less deserving of protection from unwarranted governmental interference, than that of a pregnant woman."[6]

In addition to finding a due process violation, the court found no distinction between refusing life-sustaining medical treatment and physician-assisted suicide by an uncoerced mentally competent terminally ill adult. Allowing one practice and prohibiting the other for suffering terminal patients thereby violates the equal protection clause as well. While the interests of a state may justify regulating this activity, Rothstein ruled that a state may not totally prohibit this assistance to patients dying in acute suffering.

Washington State appealed, and the Rothstein decision was overturned by a 2 to 1 decision of the U.S. Ninth Circuit Court of Appeals. The author of the decision was Judge John T. Noonan, Jr., a former leader of the U.S. antiabortion movement. Noonan, who has a doctorate in scholastic theology from the Catholic University of America, was a consultant to the U.S. Catholic Conference and a former director of the National Right to Life Committee. Judge Diarmuid F. O'Scannlain joined him in the 2 to 1 decision.[7] However, citing religious bias on the part of two of the judges, the plaintiffs petitioned for a rehearing. In an unusual move, a majority of the *entire* appeals court, citing previous lack of objectivity on the part of Noonan and O'Scannlain, voted to refer the case to an eleven-judge panel for the requested rehearing.

On March 9, 1996, in a landmark 8 to 3 *en banc* ruling (one in which the entire membership of the court participates, as opposed to the regular quorum), the Ninth Circuit Court of Appeals overruled its previous decision and overturned the Washington law on physician-assisted suicide.[8] The Ninth Circuit was the first federal appellate court to rule on assisted suicide by affirming the courageous 1994 decision of Judge Rothstein. It thus became unconstitutional to ban PAS in the jurisdictions where the Ninth Circuit's opinion is applicable: Alaska, Arizona, California, Hawaii, Idaho, Montana, Nevada, Oregon, Washington, Guam, and the Northern Marianas.

Judge Stephen Reinhardt wrote the 112-page majority decision, which focused on the "liberty interest" inherent in the due process clause of the Constitution. The Ninth Circuit had no illusions about the legal and ethical complexities of the issues in this seminal case. As Judge Reinhardt stated, the decision "requires us to confront the most basic of human concerns—the mortality of self and loved ones—and to balance the interest in preserving human life against the desire to die peacefully and with dignity."[9]

In a ringing statement directed at those who would allow their religious views to dictate their interpretation of the U.S. Constitution, Judge Reinhardt declared: "Those who believe strongly that death must come without physician assistance are free to follow that creed, be they doctors or patients. They are not free, however, to force their views, their religious convictions, or their philosophies on all other members of a democratic society, and to compel those whose values differ with theirs to die painful, protracted, and agonizing deaths."[10]

Bowing to the concept of the autonomy of the patient, Reinhardt then issued his frequently quoted statement:

A competent terminally ill adult, having lived nearly the full measure of his life, has a strong liberty interest in choosing a dignified and humane death rather than being reduced at the end of his existence to a childlike state of helplessness, diapered, sedated, incontinent. How a person dies not only determines the nature of the final period of his existence, but in many cases, the enduring memories held by those who love him.[11]

Finding a substantive due process link between the issue before the court and those in so-called right-to-privacy cases, the court reasoned that assisted dying, like abortion and the right to refuse medical treatment, is an intimate personal choice protected by the due process clause of the Fourteenth Amendment.

Concluding the court's lengthy and sensitive opinion, Reinhardt wrote: "In this case, by permitting the individual to exercise the right to choose we are following the constitutional mandate to take such decisions out of the hands of the government, both state and federal, and to put them where they rightly belong, in the hands of the people."[12]

The second of the two cases that would eventually be heard before the Supreme Court in January 1997 came about in part as the result of a gubernatorial New York State Task Force on Life and the Law. In 1994 it unanimously rejected proposals to legalize PAS. Tucker had already filed the first case in Seattle in 1994 and had won the stunning victory from Judge Rothstein. Disappointed by the results of the task force, and hoping to get another case before the Supreme Court, Tucker filed a companion lawsuit in New York's federal court.

The statute prohibiting assisted suicide in New York is similar to Washington's law, so Tucker used essentially the same arguments but a different set of plaintiffs. *Quill* v. *Vacco* was therefore filed in the U.S. District Court for the Southern District of New York on July 29, 1994. The plaintiffs sued the New York attorney general on the grounds that the New York statutes penalizing assisted suicide were unconstitutional.

Though it was not a plaintiff in this second case, Compassion in Dying sponsored the litigation and assumed certain financial responsibilities for the plaintiffs' legal expenses. The plaintiff-patients were "Jane Doe," a seventy-six-year-old woman suffering from cancer; George A. Kingsley, a forty-nine-year-old publishing executive with AIDS; and William A. Barth, a twenty-eight-year-old fashion editor with AIDS. All three died in the months following the filing of the case. They alleged, as had their counterparts in Washington, that the penal laws denied them due process of law and the equal protection of the laws by precluding their right to choose a hastened death.

The plaintiff-physicians were Drs. Timothy E. Quill, Samuel C. Klagsbrun, and Howard A. Grossman—all highly regarded and licensed to practice medicine in New York State. Tucker employed another clever strategy when she recruited as her lead plaintiff the respected Doctor Quill, whose name the case bears. As in the Washington case, the doctors alleged that they were prohibited from exercising their best professional judgment, which was to prescribe the requested drugs.

Doctor Quill is a professor of medicine and psychiatry at the University of Rochester, associate director of medicine at the Genesee Hospital on the edge of downtown Rochester, and a general practitioner. He had stumbled into the assisted-suicide spotlight quite by accident when, in 1991, the *New England Journal of Medicine* published his account of helping a woman with terminal leukemia end her life by swallowing an overdose of barbiturates he had prescribed. Because the story flouted the central medical ethic of keeping people alive, and because what he did was highly illegal, it sparked wide publicity and deep debate. A grand jury was empaneled, and Doctor Quill waived immunity from prosecution to testify, against his lawyer's advice. The state pursued misconduct charges, but the grand jury chose not to indict him. After his "legal adventure," as Quill calls it, he embarked on another crusade. He challenged the law that banned assisted suicide.

Quill exudes reliability, and even the fiercest critics of assisted suicide say his approach is thoughtful and his credentials impeccable. His insistence that aid in dying is a rare, last step in a long, rich doctor-patient relationship makes him a perfect plaintiff for a case on the frontier of social change. Also, there is little about him to criticize: "I realize I've become probably the most vocal physician in talking about this, but I'm not really an advocate of assisted suicide. I'm an advocate of not abandoning people," says Quill.[13]

On December 15, 1994, the constitutionality of the New York law banning PAS was upheld by Judge Thomas Griesa of the U.S. District Court for the Southern District of New York. Judge Griesa ruled that the statutes in question did not violate the due process clause because patients have no fundamental liberty interest in engaging in a physician-assisted death. Moreover, he argued that the statutes did not violate the equal protection clause because even if there were similarities between terminally ill patients wishing to commit suicide and those wishing to forgo life support, the state of

New York had legitimate interests, and thus a rational basis for distinguishing between the two groups.

Griesa declined to extend the rulings in the Supreme Court's abortion and right-to-die cases to assisted suicide. "The Supreme Court has been careful to explain," he maintained, that those decisions "are not intended to lead automatically to the recognition of other fundamental rights on different subjects."[14] As a consequence he recognized no fundamental liberty interest in PAS. Predictably his decision was appealed.

On September 1, 1995, three judges of the Second Circuit Court of Appeals heard oral arguments in New York City. On April 2, 1996, within weeks of the Ninth Circuit's favorable decision, all three judges reversed Judge Griesa's decision on equal protection grounds. They reached the same result as did the Ninth Circuit, but they employed a different legal theory. While they agreed with the district court with regard to the asserted fundamental liberty interest in PAS, the judges ruled that New York law violated the equal protection clause by treating similarly situated groups in a dissimilar fashion without a rational reason for doing so. New York, the court said, "does not treat equally all competent persons who are in the final stages of fatal illness and wish to hasten their deaths."[15]

Judge Roger J. Miner wrote the decision.[16] The other two judges on the panel were Judge Guido Calabresi, former dean of Yale Law School, and Judge Milton Pollack. Equating the forgoing of life-sustaining treatment with physician-assisted suicide, Miner wrote:

> The writing of a prescription to hasten death, after consultation with a patient, involves a far less active role for the physician than is required in bringing about death through asphyxiation, starvation and/or dehydration. Withdrawal of life support requires physicians or those acting at their direction physically to remove equipment and, often, to administer palliative drugs which may themselves contribute to death. The ending of life by these means is nothing more or less than assisted suicide.[17]

Moreover, in answer to the state's contention that its principal interest is in preserving the life of all its citizens at all times and under all conditions, the court responded:

> But what interest can the state possibly have in requiring the prolongation of a life that is all but ended? Surely, the state's interest lessens as the potential for life diminishes. And what business is it of the state to require the continuation of agony when the result is imminent and inevitable? What concern prompts the state to interfere with a mentally competent patient's "right to define [his or her] own concept of exis-

tence, of meaning, of the universe and of the mystery of human life," when the patient seeks to have drugs prescribed to end life during the final stages of a terminal illness? The greatly reduced interest of the state in preserving life compels the answer to these questions: "None."[18]

Although decided in New York, the Second Circuit's ruling also applied to Connecticut and Vermont. The decision of the Ninth Circuit, combined with the Second Circuit decision, made PAS available to the qualifying people of almost one-quarter of the United States. "I have always thought that society would move toward some sort of legalization of assisted suicide, but I thought it would take the better part of a decade, not the better part of a year," said Arthur Caplan. "You're talking about a sea change—overnight—in public policy on this issue."[19]

There *was* a change of public policy in theory if not in practice. Not long after the two decisions legalizing PAS, Supreme Court Justice Sandra Day O'Connor blocked doctors in the applicable states from helping any terminally ill patients end their lives until the justices decided whether to hear the case. Consequently neither court ruling took effect, as both were put on hold by the Supreme Court.

New York and Washington petitioned the Supreme Court to settle the matter of the constitutionality of a physician-assisted death. "The Justices clearly thought they could no longer avoid the euthanasia question, which is under debate in many legislatures and is beginning to become the subject of crusades, both for and against," reasoned an article in the *Economist*.[20] Do mentally competent, terminally ill adults have a constitutional right to receive lethal medication from physicians for the purpose of hastening their inevitable death? Would the Court agree to consider the issue? If it refused, PAS would be implemented in all the states and territories under the jurisdiction of the two appellate courts.

On October 1, 1996, the first day of its new term, the Court agreed to decide whether states might ban doctor-assisted suicides, setting the stage for a momentous ruling in the national debate over the right-to-die. Supreme Court orders granting review of the cases also said they would be heard "in tandem"—meaning that each would take up a full hour of argument, and that one argument would immediately follow the other. The two assisted-suicide cases brought the Court to a place where the current justices, by all indications, would rather not be: "visibly, singularly, on the frontier of social change."[21]

Linda Greenhouse, veteran legal analyst for the *New York Times*, observed that the cases would provide not only the answer to the constitutional issues raised, but also a window into how the Court sees its role:

Certain outlines are clear enough. The epic era of *Brown* v. *Board of Education*, of the Court dragging the country out of the moral wilderness, has long been over. While the Court recently reaffirmed the constitutional right to abortion, its opinion rested more on loyalty to precedent than on enthusiasm for *Roe* v. *Wade*. There is not a sitting Justice committed to a view of the Constitution as an engine of social change. Nor is it a Court given to sweeping invocations of doctrine. . . . If the distance from the *Cruzan* case to the right to assisted suicide was a small step for the appeals courts, it may be a wide gulf to the Justices, for reasons due only in part to constitutional doctrine.[22]

The Economist saw a ruling for or against physician aid in dying as a complete disaster, preferring legislative debate, referendums, and perhaps in the end a constitutional amendment as the way to sort out the matter. Explaining why the Court should remain neutral, the magazine considered not only the current Court, but also the less-than-perfect judgment of the Court throughout its history:

> The Supreme Court has an unimpressive record in dealing with highly divisive social issues. The *Roe* v. *Wade* decision of 1973, which established a constitutional right to abortion, has brought America strife ever since. Long before that, the *Dred Scott* decision of 1857, which attempted to settle the issues of slavery and race by denying citizenship "forever" to blacks, did much to precipitate the Civil War. These rulings caused grief not because they were bad in themselves; indeed, Roe was on balance a good decision. They caused grief because a handful of unelected justices short-circuited democratic debate by ruling one side of the argument out of order.

November 12 was the deadline for all amicus briefs on the side of New York and Washington States defending their laws prohibiting assisted suicide—December 10 for those who supported the right of a PAS. Dozens and dozens of groups representing a myriad of religious faiths, medical interests, and state governments filed with the Supreme Court during this period.

The complexity of the issue was illustrated by the diversity of views within individual organizations. Religious groups, medical ethicists, medical associations, philosophers, hospice associations, and lawmakers were unable to agree among themselves. It became clear, however, that for the most part, the big guns—the religious, medical, and government hierarchies—opposed the legalization of an assisted death. The Roman Catholic Church, the AMA, and the Clinton administration all submitted briefs in opposition to an individual's right to a chosen death with dignity.

The Catholic Medical Association (CMA), the Lutheran Church in

America, and an Orthodox Jewish group opposed constitutional protection for assisted suicide. "Weighing against any interest in assisted suicide is the state's compelling interest in protecting, indeed its obligation to protect, the lives of its citizens," the CMA told the Court.[23] "Both lower courts trivialize the enormous complexity of the issues underlying the social experiment they find imbedded in the Fourteenth Amendment. They make unfulfillable promises and they grossly underestimate the peril to liberty and equality inherent in a scheme of physician-assisted suicide," wrote the Lutherans.[24] Agudath Israel of America, an Orthodox Jewish group, pointed to the Holocaust in urging the Supreme Court to overturn the appellate courts' decisions. "Agudath Israel is particularly sensitive to the legal assignment of diminished levels of life 'quality,' " the group wrote.[25]

Countering these groups, a coalition of thirty-six religious organizations, leaders, and scholars urged the Justices to allow the controversial practice. They called the right of terminally ill patients to avoid a protracted death with the help of a doctor, "one of the most important liberties protected by the Due Process Clause, implicating as it does the right to define one's own concept of the mystery of human life. Our long tradition of individual religious liberty and government noninterference with religious decisions, exemplified by the religion clauses of the First Amendment, serves to confirm that the 'perplexing question' of physician-assisted suicide with its 'unusually strong moral and ethical overtones,' is an intimate, personal, and ultimately spiritual decision appropriately reserved to the individual's own conscience," the coalition added.[26] Included in the group were reverends, bishops, rabbis, and an assortment of Protestant and Jewish groups.

The healing profession, as previously discussed, is divided, yet the most powerful and influential organizations uniformly resist giving control of the individual's life to the individual. One of the strongest foes of an assisted death is the AMA, which joined forty-five other medical societies asking the justices to see it their way. "The power to assist in intentionally taking the life of a patient is antithetical to the central mission of healing that guides both medicine and nursing," they wrote.[27]

The American Association of Homes and Services for the Aging (AAHSA), a religion-sponsored national organization representing five thousand not-for-profit nursing homes, continuing-care retirement communities, assisted-living residences, senior housing facilities, and community service organizations for the elderly, is unequivocally opposed to legalization: "It would inexorably move homes and services for the aging away from a culture of life, caring and trust, to a culture of death and distrust," their brief stated.[28]

On the other hand, the younger American Medical Students Association members and a coalition of medical professions have a more realistic view of "harm" than do their elders. "[Opponents of assisted suicide] argue that the principle that doctors should not intentionally harm their patients trumps all the other ethical consideration that support physician-assisted suicide," they wrote to the Supreme Court Justices.[29] "This takes an unreasonably narrow view of what may constitute harm for a patient suffering irremediable and severe pain and confronting an imminent and unavoidable death. For such a patient, death may constitute not harm but the only available relief; the true harm may lie in being compelled either to continue unnecessary suffering or to end one's life in a lonely and violent manner," they declared.[30]

Hospice professionals also cannot achieve unanimity, but, again, the national organization is opposed. The NHO, like the AMA, supports the status quo of state law. It maintains that hospices provide a middle ground between dying in pain and committing suicide with the help of a doctor, making the need for an assisted death unnecessary. "The decisions below failed to appreciate that the final stage of life presents opportunities that could be lost without the state's protection of life and prevention of assisted suicide even among the terminally ill," the organization told the Supreme Court.[31]

On the other hand, the Coalition of Hospice Professionals emphasizes individual choice. The coalition believes its job is to respect the wishes of terminally ill patients, even those who seek a doctor's assistance in speeding the death process. For one thing, not everyone's pain can be eliminated:

> The medical profession and policy makers should enhance the availability of comfort care and establish it as the standard of care for dying patients. However, hospice and palliative care does not always relieve suffering. For some patients, the pain can be so overwhelming that they cannot focus on anything beyond their unremitting suffering, and "life" becomes nothing more than their pain. Other patients appear to attain relief only with sedation so heavy that they cannot function, cannot interact with anyone, and "life" consists merely of lying inert, which some patients reject as intolerable. The Coalition's members have treated patients whose distressing physical symptoms were too severe to be managed and have observed such patients wishing to hasten death. The Coalition believes that those desires can be fully competent and rational choices.[32]

In another brief, three powerful Republican members of Congress[8] urged the Court to find no constitutionally protected liberty interest in physician aid in dying, and to leave this decision to the seasoned judgment of the legislature. "Whatever one may think of legislators as moral deliberators, few would dispute that they have the expertise and incentive to resolve social conflict in a way that minimizes political opposition and resistance," they wrote.[33]

Another group of legislators from sixteen states disagreed. Seeing the issue as a constitutional one that properly belonged in the judiciary, these state legislators wrote: "The right of a mentally competent, terminally ill adult to the assistance of a willing physician in carrying out a decision about how to live life's final days is an essential aspect of liberty protected by the due process clause of the Fourteenth Amendment."[34]

In another brief, nineteen states and the Commonwealth of Puerto Rico urged the Justices to reject the idea that any form of suicide could ever be constitutionally protected. The signatories were Alabama, California, Colorado, Florida, Georgia, Illinois, Iowa, Louisiana, Maryland, Michigan, Mississippi, Montana, Nebraska, New Hampshire, New York, South Carolina, South Dakota, Tennessee, and Virginia.

The distinction between withdrawing life support and acting directly to cause death is itself subject to disagreement. A brief filed by surviving family members in support of physician-assisted dying reads:

> The distinction in the law between withdrawal of life support and physician-assisted suicide makes no sense to those who are suffering while dying or to the families and loved ones who watch them suffer. . . . How "natural" is it to die of convulsions and dementia? Similarly, how "natural" is death by starvation and dehydration, or an induced coma, both legal in Washington and New York? The Second Circuit concluded these deaths are no more "natural" than a doctor prescribing medication to hasten death.[35]

On the other hand, the Solicitor General's Office, on behalf of the Clinton administration, saw a definite distinction. "There is a very significant distinction between removing artificial supports—and thereby allowing the underlying disease to progress to its inevitable end—and providing chemicals to kill someone," the United States wrote. "In one case, the cause of death can reasonably be viewed as the underlying disease; in the other, the cause of death can only be viewed as the lethal medication."[36]

Legal philosophers Ronald Dworkin, Thomas Nagel, Robert Nozick, John Rawls, Thomas Scanlon, and Judith Jarvis Thomson all credit the terminal individual with more intelligence and perception than do the leaders of many national organizations. They told the Court:

> Even people who are dying have a right to hear and, if they wish, act on what others might wish to tell or suggest or even hint to them, and it would be dangerous to suppose that a state may prevent this on the ground that it knows better than its citizens when they should be moved by or yield to particular advice or suggestion in the exercise of their right

to make fateful personal decisions for themselves. It is not a good reply that some people may not decide as they really wish—as they would decide, for example, if free from the "pressure" of others.[37]

The American Civil Liberties Union, the Euthanasia Research and Guidance Organization (ERGO!), Hemlock Society USA, and nine other like-minded organizations said that based on the Supreme Court's previous decisions on personal autonomy, terminal patients have a right to choose suicide and to have a doctor help them. Such a ruling would be a natural extension of the Court's other findings. In addition, the brief pointed to the hypocrisy of prohibiting aid in dying, since "assisting the terminally ill who wish to hasten their deaths has been a time-honored, though hidden, practice of compassionate physicians."[38]

As January 8 grew nearer, the issue of televised Supreme Court sessions arose once again. Would it benefit the public and the Court? The Justices have always vehemently opposed it. Justice David Souter summed up the general sentiment when he said, "The day you see a camera coming into our courtroom, it's going to roll over my dead body."[39]

On Tuesday, January 7, 1997, the evening before oral arguments were presented to the Supreme Court, supporters of PAS gathered for prayer and remembrance at Christ Church Capitol Hill, in Washington, D.C. Two Episcopal ministers—one from New Jersey and the other from California—led the service. Invocations affirmed the beauty of life and the individual nature of every individual's spiritual beliefs. Supporting the diversity of all beings, the "service centered on an ecumenical conceptualization of a supreme being and included the chanting of the Hebrew prayers."[40] The service was held to remember and honor those deaths that have led the right-to-die movement to confront the necessity of ensuring compassion, dignity, and self-determination for all dying people. It also served as a time of support and camaraderie amid the tensions and frantic activities surrounding the next day's arguments.

In an article describing the church service in the nation's capital, *Compassion in Dying's Newsletter* stated the organization's position on the religious issue:

While Compassion in Dying has not pressed arguments of religious liberty in its landmark cases, the point is made that the manner in which one chooses to die arises from deeply held values and convictions related to the meaning of life, God, and eternity. Our attitudes toward suffering, redemption, and compassion are also shaped by our religious beliefs. One can make a rational argument that laws banning aid in dying enforce a particular religious doctrine, while criminalizing other, equally authentic, beliefs.[41]

The following day dawned sunny but bitterly cold. A large and vocal contingent from Not Dead Yet, a militant disabled group, carried placards proclaiming their opposition to a legalized assisted death. Many of them were in wheelchairs. Presenting the other side to cameras and television were about sixteen members of the National Capitol Area chapter of the Hemlock Society. They carried a huge banner at the bottom of the steps of the Supreme Court building.

Several hundred people had spent a long, frigid night outside the building in hopes of being one of a handful, first in line, to join the few journalists and members of the Supreme Court bar allowed to witness the proceedings on this vital issue. With only fifty seats available to the public, scores of people were turned away before the oral arguments began. Those admitted left their briefcases at the door, and note taking was not allowed, standard practices for those privileged enough to hear oral arguments before the High Court.

Before a packed and engrossed courtroom, the Supreme Court Justices heard attorneys from Washington and New York argue that dying patients have no constitutional right to the assistance of their physicians in ending their lives. Meanwhile, attorneys for physicians and their terminal patients countered that dying adults, still able to make informed, voluntary decisions, possess a constitutionally protected liberty interest in having a doctor prescribe a lethal dose of medicine. And, since those on life support are able to hasten their deaths by withdrawing or withholding treatment, it is discriminatory to force those *not* on life-support to bear protracted pain and suffering. Kathryn Tucker would argue the Washington case and Laurence H. Tribe would present the New York case on behalf of those opposed to the restrictive statutes.

Arguing a case before this Court is a challenge—not only because it is the nation's highest tribunal, but also because it is as vocal and energetic a nine-member bench as any attorney could imagine confronting. The present-day Rehnquist Court is full of aggressive questioners. With infrequent exceptions, each case argued before the Court is allotted one hour, split between both sides. However, an attorney does not have thirty minutes painstakingly to lay out the case. The Justices rarely let an attorney speak for more than a couple of minutes before they begin a barrage of questions, often jumping from topic to topic, for the remaining allocated time. The pummeled and frustrated lawyer tries to pick up where he or she left off, as time runs out.

In order to highlight the arguments on both sides, as well as the concerns of the Court, excerpts from the Supreme Court's oral arguments on doctor-assisted suicide in the twin cases of *Washington v. Glucksberg*[42] and *Quill v. Vacco*[43] follow:

William L. Williams, Washington State senior assistant attorney general:

> We are here today representing the people of the state of Washington to defend their legislative policy judgment to prohibit assisted suicide. . . . The issue here today is whether the Constitution requires that the social policy developed by Washington voters must be supplanted by a far different social policy, a constitutionally recognized right to physician-assisted suicide that is contrary to our traditions and overrides the important state interests that are served by the Washington statute.
>
> There are three important state interests that are involved. The first one is life. . . . And, in the hierarchy of constitutional value, certainly the protection of life is the highest. . . . The second one is to prevent abuse and undue influence, and certainly the risk is higher in the physician-assisted suicide context than it is in the refusal of treatment context.
>
> And thirdly, there is a strong interest in regulating the medical profession. . . . The state has an important interest in maintaining a clear line between physicians as healers and curers and physicians as instruments of death of their patients.

Acting U.S. Solicitor General Dellinger:

> The critical issue is the state's overwhelming interest. States have long had laws that affirm the value of life by prohibiting anyone from promoting or assisting a suicide, and I believe that no one disputes the constitutionality of those laws as a general matter. The actual question before the court is whether the Constitution compels an exception to those laws here. In our view it does not. While the individual stories are heart-rending . . . it's important for this court to recognize that, if you were to affirm the judgments below, lethal medication could be proposed as a treatment, not just to those in severe pain, but to every competent terminally ill person in the country. It would be, I think, a grave mistake for the court to impose on 50 states such a marked transformation that had never been tried on even a single state.

Attorney Tucker, representing doctors and patients who challenged Washington's ban on PAS, told the court:

> This case presents the question whether dying citizens in full possession of their mental faculties at the threshold of death due to terminal

illness have the liberty to choose to cross that threshold in a humane and dignified manner. . . . These dying patients want a peaceful death, they want a humane death and they want a dignified death. And, in order to access that kind of death they need the assistance of their physician.

The terminally ill patient does not have the expectation of a continued life beyond this very short interim before death. Certainly the patient . . . that would choose to endure that period of suffering before death and find it enjoyable and find it fulfilling should be permitted to make that choice, and many will make that choice. . . . But for some patients, based on their values and beliefs formed over a lifetime, that additional quantum of suffering is intolerable to their personhood. . . . What we're dealing with here is simply a liberty interest in avoiding pain and suffering. . . . We have a constellation of interests, each of great constitutional dimension. Yes, there is the interest in avoiding pain and suffering. . . . The second in the constellation of interest is decisional autonomy, and the third in the constellation that has bearing here is the interest in bodily integrity. Each of those separate interests is of constitutional dimension and each has bearing here.

Justice Antonin Scalia: "Why should that decision, if it's competent, reasoned and deliberated, why should it be limited to physical pain? What—what about the patient who has terrible emotional suffering in life and just says life is not worth it anymore? . . . You would not allow assisted suicide in that case, I take it?"

Tucker: "No, Your Honor."

Scalia: "Why is that? Because . . . the government makes the judgment that physical pain is worse than emotional suffering? . . ."

Justice Ruth Bader Ginsburg: "Isn't there the possibility of a person saying, gee, I really thought I wanted it yesterday, but today I don't?"

Tucker: "I think that's possible, Justice Ginsburg. I do think that it would be permissible for the state . . . to impose a waiting period. . . ."

Ginsburg: "That's another thing, too, you're talking about all these regulations. . . . Who is then to make all these regulations? . . ."

Tucker: "We do think it should be left to the states. . . ."

Chief Justice William H. Rehnquist: "You're going to find the same thing I suspect that perhaps has happened with the abortion cases, there are people who are just totally opposed and people who are totally in favor of them. So you're going to have those factions fighting it out in every session of the legislature, how far can we go in regulating this. . . ."

Justice Sandra Day O'Connor: "There is no doubt that . . . if we upheld your position, it would result in a flow of cases through the court system for heaven knows how long. I wanted to ask you whether it should enter the balance of state interests versus the interests of the patient here, that this is an issue that every one of us faces, young or old, male or female, whatever it might be. And all of us who are citizens and authorized to vote can certainly participate through that process in the development of state laws in this area. . . ."

Tucker: "I take your point . . . but I do think that we are dealing with an issue, the literature is extensive on this, that ours is a culture of denial of death. And that people in our society do not deal with their own mortality until confronted with their death and because of that I do think we have some concerns that the political process would not be expected to work in a usual fashion. . . ."

Justice David H. Souter: ". . . If, in fact, you are right about the pervasiveness of the denial of death, that denial simply reflects the way we are. And it seems to me that it's a perfectly legitimate reflection when it finds its way into the legislative process. Is there a flaw in that reasoning?"

Tucker: "Well, I think what I was getting at . . . is that because there's the denial and people do not confront mortality until faced up against it, you do not have an activist component that is able to address that in the legislative process. When a patient is on their deathbed, they don't have the ability to become politically active. . . ."

Justice Anthony M. Kennedy: "This is a question of ethics and of morals and of allocation of resources and of our commitment to treat the elderly and infirmed. And surely legislators have much more flexibility and a much greater capacity to absorb those kinds of arguments and make those decisions than we do. You're asking us in effect to declare unconstitutional the law of 50 states. . . ."

Tucker: "We're asking this court to simply recognize the vital nature of this liberty and to leave to state experimentation the regulatory process. . . ."

Scalia: "Declining medical treatment is something quite different from suicide. . . . Why can't a society simply determine as a matter of public morality that it is wrong to kill yourself just as it is wrong to kill someone else?"

Tucker: "This is a liberty, Your Honor, that involves bodily integrity, decisional autonomy and the right to be free of unwanted pain and suffering, and that that constellation of interests gives rise to a vital liberty. These individuals that are in the process of dying are confronted only with the choice of how to die, they are not confronted with the choice of should I live or should I die. . . ."

Dennis Vacco, attorney general of New York State, seeking reinstatement of his state's law prohibiting assisted suicide, told the judges:

The question in this case is whether the state must remain neutral in the face of a decision of one of its citizens to help another kill herself. The Second Circuit below said yes, as a matter of equal protection. It is New York's view, however, that the Constitution does not require this to be the case. Indeed, equal protection is not implicated at all in this case. Patients who withdraw from life support are not similarly situated to terminally ill people who are seeking physician-assisted suicide.

Ginsburg: ". . . The distinction that the Second Circuit fastened on was the terminally ill person who says no more life supports, I want to die, and the person who wants a pill that will achieve the same end. So let's narrow it to what that court was dealing with and tell us why that court was wrong."

Vacco: "The people . . . are not similarly situated. In the first context the individual[s] who [are] at the . . . end stages of their life as the Second Circuit defined it, are exercising their right . . . to refuse treatment. That right which has been recognized for centuries as springing from the common law, the right of being free from battery, [the] right to be let alone. On the contrary, and in contrast, are those individuals who are not attempting to assert . . . that there is some right to have a third party, in this instance physicians, help kill themselves. And we believe that these two acts are clearly distinguishable. . . ."

Ginsburg: "You say you've distinguished the drugs at the last hour or hours of life. But we're told that this treatment, whatever you want to call it, that inevitably will lead to death, will do so in a matter of days, not hours. And that that goes on. And how is this rationally distinguishable from a pill that will work."

Vacco: ". . . It's rationally distinguishable because it is consistent medical practice . . . Providing drugs specifically and solely for the purpose of killing someone has never been embraced by the medical profession."

Souter: ". . . I take it you mean that, once you accept the right of a patient to withdraw all life support including hydration and feeding, then the only way to prevent excruciating pain as the person nears death is with these extraordinarily high dosages of painkiller that induce coma. . . ."

Vacco: "Yes. And indeed the subsequent administration of the palliative care drugs is consistent with the long-standing notion of the double effect, that the drugs in that instance are not being administered for the purpose of causing the death. . . ."

Scalia: "Can the state, if someone goes on a hunger strike and wants to die to protest something or other, can the state force-feed that person?"

Vacco: "Yes. . . ."

Rehnquist: "It seems odd that your bodily integrity is violated by sticking a needle in your arm but not by sticking a spoon in your mouth. I mean, how would you force-feed these people in a way not to violate their bodily integrity? . . ."

O'Connor: "Well, how about a person with terminal kidney disease who says 'I'm not going on dialysis. I know what the result will be, I'm not doing it.' New York can force that treatment; is that right?"

Vacco: "No. . . . New York cannot. In the context of refusing treatment, whether it's terminally ill or otherwise, whether it's the 16-year-old who has been told to go home and take two aspirin or the 97-year-old who is plugged into various medical devices, we respect in New York state that person's right to refuse treatment. . . ."

Souter: "Is . . . the reason you draw the line ultimately between ending the life support and the affirmative act of giving the pill, is it essentially a line that depends on the argument for risk of abuse?"

Vacco: "The principal . . . justification indeed, one of the most compelling reasons, state interest, is the risk of abuse. . . ."

Souter: "Well, why isn't there a risk of abuse that those who might stand to profit or at least themselves risk further discomfort by an early death for a person on life support will try to coerce or persuade that person to end life support when it really isn't a voluntary decision? Why isn't that a risk?"

Vacco: ". . . There is no question that in certain instances there is an overlapping of the risk of abuse. But we believe in the context of physician-assisted suicide, the risk of abuse is far greater."

Ginsburg: "What about the risks on the other side, that even the American Medical Association recognizes? This gray area in between makes doctors fearful of putting people out of pain because they don't know whether that's going to constitute physician-assisted suicide or accepted relief of pain. Isn't that a real risk?"

Vacco: "It's a minimal risk. . . ."

O'Connor: "What if what's given is some form of sedation and the person has asked to be relieved of life-support systems and so the sure consequence of sedation will be an earlier death?"

Vacco: ". . . If the purposes of that sedation is to bring about the death as opposed to treating the symptoms of the pain—"

O'Connor: "It's to alleviate pain but with the certain knowledge that it will hasten the death."

Vacco: "In the context of treating the pain, even though there is a risk of death, pursuant to the principle of double effect, that is not criminal conduct in the State of New York."

Dellinger, arguing in defense of the New York law that criminalizes assisting in a suicide:

> We do not agree that the states' interest in prohibiting lethal medication is lessened by the fact that the state permits competent terminally ill adults to refuse unwanted medical treatment. There is an important common sense distinction between withdrawing artificial support so that a disease will progress to its inevitable end and providing chemicals to be used to kill someone. . . . The historic distinction between killing someone and letting them die is so powerful that we believe that it fully suffices here. . . .

Ginsburg: ". . . If you could, deal with the argument that's been made about winks and nods, that all of this is really a great sham because physician-assisted suicide goes on for anybody who is sophisticated enough to want it."

Dellinger: ". . . We looked and we don't know what the evidentiary basis is for that. We do not know any basis for the conclusion that pain medication's being deliberately offered in excess of what is necessary to relieve pain in order to cause death."

Laurence H. Tribe speaking on behalf of those seeking to allow PAS in New York:

> I don't think so much the issue is how many people violate the law. Charlatans, doctors of death . . . they operate in the dark and we don't know. The winks and nods, I think, affect the capacity of the system to respond humanely and rationally to what is actually going on rather than just to bright-line hypotheticals. The winks and nods really relate to things that we all accept, the principle of double effect. . . . None of these patients is in a state of nature. They're in a hospital or a hospice. And they're receiving chemotherapy, radiation, bone marrow transplants.

Kennedy: "Yes. But when a person on a life support system wants the systems discontinued, she is not committing suicide, which is what you said earlier. She is not doing that, she's allowing nature to take its course. . . ."

Justice Stephen G. Breyer: "What's your response to the proposition that these different groups, interacting with the legislature, are far more suited . . . to come up with an answer than a court writing a Constitutional provision?"

Tribe: ". . . In a sense there are 50 laboratories out there. . . . These laboratories, however, are now operating largely with the lights out. They're operating with the lights out because it's not just New York. What I've described is as far as I've been able to determine through research of the law of at least 35 or maybe 40 states. . . ."

Souter: ". . . Isn't it fair to say that . . . the lights have been out, but the effort to put the lights on is fairly recent? . . ."

Tribe: "When I say the dark, I mean this: Doctors . . . when doctors do a lot of what they do in upping the level of the morphine and actually using more benzodiazepine than is needed to make sure the person is comfortable, but to make sure the person dies sooner, they're not going to talk to others about it because they might be prosecuted because of the lines that are drawn. . . ."

Justice John Paul Stevens: "Tell us what you think the liberty interest is?"

Tribe: "The liberty interest in this case is . . . when facing imminent and inevitable death, not to be forced by the government to endure a degree of

pain and suffering that one can relieve only by being completely unconscious. Not to be forced into that choice, that the liberty is the freedom, at
this threshold at the end of life, not to be a creature of the state but to have
some voice in the question of how much pain one is really going through."

Souter: "Why does the voice just arrive when death is imminent?"

Tribe: "The Court's jurisprudence has identified, I think for good reason,
that life, though it feels continuous to many of us, has certain critical thresholds: Birth, marriage, childbearing. I think death is one of those thresholds.
That is, it is the last chapter of one's life after all. . . ."

Scalia: "All of this is in the Constitution? . . . You see, this is lovely
philosophy. But you want us to frame a Constitutional rule on the basis of
that? Life has various stages: Birth, death . . ."

The two-hour hearing contained more than just confrontation on a particular legal question. The justices addressed changing societal attitudes, the
role of the medical profession, the interests of the individual versus the
interests of the government, economic and moral considerations, the separation of church and state and the impact of modern technology on all of
our lives. Perhaps reflecting the magnitude of the issues and the intensity
of the surroundings, Professor Tribe, making his twenty-third appearance
before the Court, committed the capital sin of male lawyers who argue
before the Supreme Court. He mixed up the two female justices, mistakenly
referring to Ginsburg as O'Connor. Needless to say he quickly apologized.

At the end of two hours of intense debate, it was clear that the Justices
were fascinated by the issues and deeply engaged by the arguments. At the
same time, however, their eagerness to keep the Court out of yet another
momentous question of life and death was apparent. No one on the bench
spoke in favor of a change in the laws. Greenhouse, writing for the *New
York Times*, summed up the tenor of the courtroom:

> Although the doctrinal jargon of due process and equal protection was
> sprinkled throughout the argument, this was a Supreme Court session
> notable for the proportion of plain English that was spoken. The Justices
> wanted theory, but they were also hungry for facts. They sat as judges
> but appeared to feel themselves very much participants, on a human
> level, in a far-reaching societal debate. "This is an issue every one of us
> faces, young and old, male and female, whatever it might be," Justice
> Sandra Day O'Connor said at one point. And Justice Ginsburg, whose
> mother died of cervical cancer at the age of 47, said, "Most of us have
> parents and other loved ones who have been through the dying process,
> and we've thought about these things."

Justice O'Connor experienced a personal brush with death in her fight
against breast cancer. Also, Chief Justice Rehnquist confronted terminal

illness and death himself when his wife, Natalie, died in 1991 after a long battle with ovarian cancer.

Regardless of its members' familiarity with dying, this is not the High Court of the past, the one that placed itself at the frontier of constitutional law. This is not the same Court that found a right to an abortion within the Fourteenth Amendment's right to privacy. That Court has been chastised for not leaving the issue to the states ever since *Roe v. Wade* in 1973, and the 1997 Court did not want to invoke the same criticism.

The reaction to the Justices, by those who heard the arguments, was almost unanimous. Virtually all the Justices expressed at least some skepticism over the idea of establishing a right to physician aid in dying. They each showed a reluctance to intercede in the far-reaching issues of life and death until more information became available through experimentation at the state level.

Early into Tucker's arguments, the Justices signaled that they were not buying her approach. They were not finding her legal arguments persuasive or her interpretation of *Cruzan* correct. Rehnquist and Scalia began a barrage of challenging and sometimes hostile questions. David J. Garrow described it this way in *George* magazine:

> Ruth Ginsburg joined in, criticizing the application of Tucker's liberty argument, and Scalia peppered Tucker with acerbic contentions about how that argument could not be meaningfully restricted to only the terminally ill. Anthony Kennedy and David Souter each suggested likewise, and it rapidly became clear that a decisive majority of the Rehnquist Court had no appetite whatsoever for the Constitutional argument Tucker was giving them. First Rehnquist and then Justice Sandra Day O'Connor voiced additional worries about how an endless slew of additional cases would follow from even partial vindication of Tucker's claims. The atmosphere within the august but always intimate courtroom took on an increasingly chilly air.[44]

The second hour's argument of the New York case featured the state's attorney general, Dennis Vacco, against Harvard law professor Tribe. Garrow continued:

> "When Larry got up, he realized it was all over," explained University of Michigan law professor Yale Kamisar, an outspoken right-to-die opponent. Tribe gamely attempted to defend, and improve upon, the appellate court's conclusion that the distinctions New York's laws imposed upon similarly terminal patients were irrational, but the Justices weren't buying that argument either. As Tribe's thirty minutes expired, what little sense of high drama still remained quickly evaporated from the courtroom.[45]

This climate seems to have affected Justice Souter, one of the Justices most inclined to protect issues of personal privacy. Even he expressed apprehension that providing constitutional protection to an assisted suicide would be difficult to restrain and "will gravitate . . . into euthanasia" before pain might possibly be ameliorated with further time and treatment. Souter noted that only "fairly recently" had the question surfaced as a "serious legislative issue." And he suggested that it might be premature for the Court to assess the risks of making assisted suicide legal. Both Justices O'Connor and Kennedy suggested that the issue be left to the state legislatures to resolve. O'Connor speculated that if the High Court were to legalize the practice, the court system would be jammed with litigation for years to come. Better that the legislatures establish state guidelines to regulate the practice, she believed.

Some Justices asserted that the Supreme Court's prior decisions did not lead logically to a right to assisted suicide. Some asked Tucker and Tribe why only the terminally ill should have such a right. They also asked how legislatures and lower courts would work out the circumstances and conditions of the right. Rehnquist feared the Court could be headed toward legal and legislative turmoil not unlike that surrounding abortion.

All accounts of the session predicted that the Court would overrule the two lower courts and that assisted death would remain illegal. The legal authority for the *New York Times* was no exception, as she sensed the reluctance of the Court to step in and change the rules on dying. Greenhouse continued her assessment of the nine Justices' reactions on that historic day: "The lawyers asked the Justices to weigh terminally ill patients' interest in avoiding uncontrollable pain against the states' interest in protecting life. But the Justices' concern often appeared to be the Court's own interest in avoiding the vulnerability that comes from folding into the Constitution a claimed right that society has not fully embraced."[46]

At a closed-door meeting two days following oral arguments, the Court's nine members took their first vote on whether states may ban physicians from prescribing lethal medication for their terminally ill patients. The nation, however, would probably have to wait until June or July to hear the decision. Once argued in open court, cases disappear for months.

Chief Justice William H. Rehnquist presides over this first vote, taken after each member of the court has had the opportunity to address his or her fellow Justices at a meeting that only they can attend. Justice Breyer, the junior Justice, acts as gatekeeper—making sure that no law clerk, secretary, or other court employee gains entrance. Rehnquist, if he is voting with the majority, assigns who will write the opinion for the Court. If he is voting with the minority, the most senior Justice voting with the majority gets the assigning power. All Justices, however, are free to write a concurring or dissenting opinion.

With all the people involved in the smooth operation of the Supreme

Court, one has to wonder about security and possible leaks to the press. After all, this is Washington, D.C., hardly known for keeping secrets. The Supreme Court, however, is an exception. Unlike most of Washington, Supreme Court leaks almost never occur. "It just never was an issue," says Judge Ruth McGregor of the Arizona Court of Appeals, who clerked for Justice Sandra Day O'Connor in 1981. "Confidentiality was a given." "Court spokeswoman Toni House said the Court 'is a small institution with a traditional high degree of loyalty among the people who work for it. There's a long tradition of keeping its internal workings to itself,' " writes a member of the Associated Press.[47]

June is a frantic time in the marble-pillared Supreme Court building. It looks so calm and collected from the outside, but inside, the "last great decision-writing rush of the season is underway. The Justices are frantically circulating draft opinions, trying to corral votes on their side, firing off dissents when necessary and, with both the stakes and tension rising, firming up what will become the law of the land," writes Joan Biskupic of the *Washington Post*.[48]

Opinions are issued in batches, usually on Mondays. No one outside a tight circle knows when, or which, rulings will be handed down. Journalists "are told only whether an opinion day will be 'regular' (meaning from one to four rulings) or 'heavy' (five or more). At 10 A.M., the nine Justices take their seats on the bench, and the author of the majority opinion reads a brief statement. Shortly after that, the news spreads through radio, television and wire services," says Biskupic.[49]

Based on the conservative sentiments of the Court and on their reactions during oral arguments, the conventional view among legal experts was that the Court would reverse both lower rulings. By the end of the oral arguments, it appeared that the Justices were reluctant to overturn the laws of forty-nine states—Oregon had already voted to legalize the practice, although the implementation was still blocked in another court. Both cases presented the same two issues: does a mentally competent, terminally ill adult have a constitutional right to the assistance of a physician in committing suicide to avoid a prolonged dying process? If so, does the state nevertheless have a sufficient interest in prohibiting the exercise of this right? When the decisions came down, there were both victory and defeat for the right-to-die movement.

The Supreme Court
Leaves the Door Open

The most significant right-to-die decision to date was rendered on June 26, 1997, when the Supreme Court ruled that states might continue to ban the practice of physician-assisted suicide. In a pair of 9–0 decisions, the Court rejected the constitutional challenges to laws in New York and Washington that make assisted suicide a crime. "Our decisions lead us to conclude that the asserted 'right' to assistance in committing suicide is not a fundamental liberty interest protected by the Due Process Clause," said Chief Justice William H. Rehnquist in the Court's majority opinion.[1] Moreover, he wrote, the state interests are so significant that they outweigh any possible liberty defined for dying patients and physicians. In addition, prohibiting the practice does not violate the equal protection clause, because groups of terminally ill individuals *are* treated similarly.

The cases raise a fundamental constitutional question that goes far beyond these decisions. They provide a window into how the Court views individual rights and liberties in general. The crux of the matter is the interpretation of the due process clause of the Fourteenth Amendment, which declares that states may not "deprive any person of life, liberty or property, without due process of law." It is this clause, more than any other constitutional provision, which offers protection to the liberty and freedom of each individual citizen.

The due process clause prohibits laws limiting liberties that are "deeply rooted in this Nation's history and tradition." It is abstract language and open to interpretation by the Justices. The protection it offers depends on whether the Justices read it narrowly or expansively. In order to understand the decisions, and how the Justices could reach different conclusions, it is necessary to understand the two ways of interpreting the due process clause.

A narrow, or strictly construed, reading of the "Nation's history and tradition" test says that the due process clause protects only those specific liberties that have historically been respected by American states. As a result, the clause protects citizens from unwanted and invasive medical treatment, because the common law of most states has, for a long time, granted that protection in the form of laws prohibiting battery and assault. On the other hand, since common law has always *prohibited* an assisted death, it is *not* rooted in our history and tradition, and therefore the practice is not protected by the Constitution. Generally, conservative judges, as well as High Court Justices, interpret the clause narrowly.

By contrast, liberal judges tend to read the clause expansively. An expansive, or broadly construed, reading protects not only the specific liberties that have been recognized in the past, but also those basic values that underlie those specific rights. For example, an expansive interpretation of the clause in relation to assisted suicide would say:

> Yes, there have been laws throughout our nation's history prohibiting assisting in a suicide. The Founding Fathers, however, could not possibly have foreseen how technology would prolong the dying process. The Constitution is a flexible document that must grow and bend under changing circumstances. That's its beauty and why it has lasted for so long. So, even though assisted suicide is not technically part of our "nation's history and tradition," an individual's dignity, self-determination, and freedom of religious beliefs *are the very bedrock of our nation's history.* Therefore, the freedom to end the sufferings and indignities at the end of life is a natural extension of these core values and beliefs and must be protected by the Constitution.

William Rehnquist, Antonin Scalia, and Clarence Thomas, the three most conservative members of the Court, were the only ones adhering to a narrow interpretation of the Fourteenth Amendment's due process clause. Explaining why the Court would not create a new right at the present time, Rehnquist said that many of the laws against suicide and assisted suicide had been formulated in the nineteenth century. As early as 1874 the California legislature made it a crime for any person to "deliberately aid or advise or encourage another to commit suicide," he pointed out. (In fact, Anglo-American common law has punished or otherwise disapproved of assisting in a suicide for more than seven hundred years. It has never been part of our nation's history and tradition.) "The states are currently engaged in serious, thoughtful examinations of physician-assisted suicide and other issues," said the Chief Justice. For the Court now to rule that there is a "fundamental right" to an assisted death, "we would have to reverse centuries of legal doctrine and practice, and strike down the considered policy choice of almost every state," he continued.

It is encouraging news that only three of the sitting Justices see it this way; not only for the right-to-die movement but for all citizens who favor the protection of a broader spectrum of individual rights and liberties. So, even though all nine members of the Supreme Court failed to recognize a right to an assisted suicide in these particular two cases, five Justices, a majority, carefully left open the possibility of a constitutional debate over such a right in the future.

Moreover, although the Justices unanimously rejected the notion of a fundamental "generalized" right to assisted suicide, Rehnquist and the other conservative members of the Court would probably support PAS if the right were grounded in a state legislative enactment, a voter initiative or referendum, or a decision of a state court grounded in that state's constitution rather than in the U.S. Constitution. Should a reversal of policy eventually take place, a decision of this magnitude would take place at the hands of the people and their representatives, not by unelected judges.

In his ruling, Chief Justice Rehnquist encouraged states to explore different approaches and possibilities, in an open debate, as they contemplate the relatively new issue of assisted dying. "Throughout the nation, Americans are engaged in an earnest and profound debate about the morality, legality and practicality of physician-assisted suicide," he wrote in validating state criminal laws against the practice. By declining to find any federal Constitutional barriers to such laws, Rehnquist went on, "our holding permits this debate to continue, as it should in a democratic society."[2]

Rehnquist expressed concern that legalization would have unfortunate and unforeseen consequences for society's most vulnerable, in that "the poor, the elderly and disabled persons" could become victims of "abuse, neglect and mistakes" by doctors, hospital personnel or relatives: "The state's assisted suicide ban reflects and reinforces its policy that the lives of terminally ill, disabled, and elderly people must be no less valued than the lives of the young and healthy."[3]

Two lines of legal reasoning support the Rehnquist majority opinion. In order to reach the conclusion that assisted suicide does not have the stature of a fundamental right deeply rooted in this nation's history and tradition, Chief Justice Rehnquist interpreted two major Supreme Court cases of this decade. The *Cruzan* case is not what the right-to-die movement thought it was. The High Court, in *Cruzan*, had concluded that "the principle that a competent person has a Constitutionally protected liberty interest in refusing unwanted medical treatment may be inferred from our prior decisions."[4] For Rehnquist, *Cruzan* only affirmed the right to refuse treatment, based on a tradition of protecting the patient against being touched without consent (that is, battery), not a more expansive right to hasten one's own death.

Rehnquist sought to clarify the misunderstanding about *Cruzan* by writing in *Quill*: "We assumed the existence of such a right for purposes of that case. But our assumption of a right to refuse treatment was grounded not, as the Court of Appeals supposed, on the proposition that patients have a general and abstract 'right to hasten death,' but on well established, traditional rights to bodily integrity and freedom from unwanted touching."[5]

Secondly, *Planned Parenthood* v. *Casey*, the most recent major abortion case, also does not apply, according to the Rehnquist majority opinion. *Casey* may protect the autonomous rights of the pregnant woman to obtain an abortion, but the Court *failed to extend that right* to all important intimate and personal decisions: "That many of the rights and liberties protected . . . sound in personal autonomy does not warrant the sweeping conclusion that any and all important, intimate, and personal decisions are so protected."[6]

The second line of reasoning focuses on those interests of the state that the state feels obligated to protect. Contrary to the findings of the Ninth and Second Circuits, Rehnquist and his cosigners identified six significant state interests: preservation of life; prevention of suicide as a public health problem; difficulty in evaluating mental depression; protecting the "integrity and ethics" of the physician—specifically the role as "healer"; protecting vulnerable groups from abuse, neglect, mistakes, and financial pressures; and avoiding the "slippery slope"—that is, progressing from assisted suicide to voluntary euthanasia to involuntary euthanasia. Consequently, even if the Court *had* found a constitutionally protected right in physician aid in dying, the state interests are great enough so as to continue the prohibition of the practice.

It is not unusual for the High Court to reverse rulings from the Ninth Circuit. In 1996 "10 of 12 Ninth Circuit cases were reversed (Reinhardt was involved in 8 of the 10). In 1995, the reversal rate was 14 of 17. Not since 1983, when the Supreme Court famously reversed 24 of 27 Ninth Circuit rulings, has the rate been so high."[7] Most of the reversals involved Ninth Circuit expansions of civil liberties, not a popular concept with the current Supreme Court.

Jesse Choper, dean of the University of California Law School, Berkeley, believes that the Ninth Circuit appropriately applies Supreme Court precedents in many of the cases that are reversed. "This is not a renegade court," says Choper. "These aren't sloppy opinions that are being reversed. They are legitimate."[8] They are also more liberal than the Justices in Washington. "You have a group of independent judges in the Western States that don't just go along with the Supreme Court. They are willing to read the law more generously than judges in other circuits. It is forcing the Supreme Court to think harder. That's important," believes Ninth Circuit expert Arthur Hellman, of the University of Pittsburgh Law School.[9]

In reversing the Second Circuit's ruling, the Supreme Court stated that New York's laws draw no distinctions among people, but instead treat all New York citizens the same: "Everyone, regardless of physical condition, is entitled, if competent, to refuse unwanted lifesaving medical treatment; no one is permitted to assist a suicide."[10]

This determination rested on the differentiation between assisting a competent patient to end his or her life, and withdrawing life-sustaining treatment from a competent patient who refuses to consent to its continuation. "The distinction between letting a patient and making that patient die" is understood in the fields of medicine and law. The distinction is certainly not so "arbitrary and irrational" as to be unconstitutional, said Rehnquist. "Logic and contemporary practice support New York's judgment that the two acts are different, and New York may therefore, consistent with the Constitution, treat them differently. By permitting everyone to refuse unwanted medical treatment while prohibiting anyone from assisting a suicide, New York law follows a long-standing and rational distinction."[11]

The distinction between the two practices lies in the different *intents* of the physician. "When a patient refuses life-sustaining medical treatment, he dies from an underlying fatal disease or pathology," Rehnquist wrote. "But if a patient ingests lethal medication prescribed by a physician, he is killed by that medication." The Chief Justice added that a physician who withdraws life-sustaining treatment probably does not want the patient to die, but is simply respecting and following the patient's wishes to avoid futile care. On the other hand, a physician who writes a prescription for lethal medication and thereby assists in a suicide *wants* the patient to die.

The Court supported the principle of the "double effect," favored by the Roman Catholic Church and the AMA. Increasing pain medication is ethically, medically, and legally acceptable even when the treatment may hasten the patient's death, if the medication is *intended* to alleviate pain and suffering, and *not* to cause death.

Proponents of voluntary assisted death argue that the state irrationally distinguishes between PAS and the "double effect." Right-to-die advocates insist that terminal sedation is covert PAS or euthanasia. Not so, say the opponents: "The concept of sedating pharmacotherapy is based on informed consent and the principle of double effect."[12]

The majority opinion, however, failed to see the hypocrisy of permitting terminal sedation and the double effect, and forbidding an assisted death. In all three situations the patient is seeking to hasten a certain, impending death. The result of endorsing palliative care while opposing physician-assisted suicide is "paradoxical," believes law professor and social philosopher Dworkin. "The administration of very high levels of morphine . . . is not regulated in the way any permitted suicide would be, and is therefore much more open to abuse, particularly in the case of the poor and vulnerable patients whose safety has been cited as a main reason for refusing any right to assisted suicide."[13]

An immediate and enormously positive consequence of the Court's decision, however, was its apparent readiness to recognize that dying patients have a right to pain relief. The rulings left room for doctors to give dying patients large amounts of painkillers, even in doses high enough to cause death. Since this practice "happens all the time"[14] anyway, "the effect of the present decisions may well be not only to confirm but to extend that practice." While Chief Justice Rehnquist indicated the acceptability of large doses of painkillers, even if they cause death, other Justices in concurring opinions went even further to disapprove of states' efforts to limit the administration of painkillers.

The unanimous vote to reverse the two lower court decisions left assisted suicide illegal in those states that choose to prohibit it. The Justices also gave the states the power to legalize the practice. The unanimity is deceptive, however, and the "Court's tone was that of a tentative first step rather than a definitive final ruling on the issue," says the *New York Times's* Greenhouse.[15] While the rulings make clear that states may ban assisted suicide, "In reality the decisions were more nuanced," said *Time* magazine. "The right Rehnquist denied was so broadly stated that more modest constitutional claims may someday be affirmed. And five Justices, a majority, wrote concurring opinions that further qualified his meaning."[16]

There were six opinions in the twin right-to-die cases. Rehnquist was only able to garner five votes for an absolute ban on any rights for assisted suicide. Four Justices, led by Sandra Day O'Connor, agreed about the difficulty of deciding the issue. "Beneath both sets of opinions are concurrences about how hard this question is, and about not foreclosing challenges that individuals may make," says Mark Tushnet, a scholar at Georgetown University Law School in Washington, D.C.[17]

The Justices suggested that some terminally ill people in the future might be able successfully to claim a constitutionally protected right to obtain lethal medications from their physicians for the purposes of hastening their deaths. "Our opinion does not absolutely foreclose such a claim," Rehnquist said in the Court's principal opinion, which was signed by four other Justices—Scalia, Kennedy, Thomas, and O'Connor.

While five Justices signed on to Chief Justice Rehnquist's majority opinion, five others wrote separate concurring decisions, resulting in ambiguous rulings. Concurring opinions accounted for a majority of the Court. Justice O'Connor, Rehnquist's crucial fifth vote, also wrote a *separate* opinion that endorsed a limited right-to-die for people in tremendous pain. She made it clear that she did not accept Rehnquist's narrow interpretation of the due process clause, favoring instead a more encompassing view of maintaining the nation's core values rather than only specific past rights. While she agreed that "there is no generalized right to commit suicide," she viewed as still open the question of whether "a mentally competent person who is experiencing great suffering" that cannot otherwise be controlled has a constitutionally based "interest in controlling the circumstances of his or her imminent death." She also left open the possibility of supporting a dying person's right to "obtain relief from the suffering that they may experience in the last days of their lives."[18]

Justice O'Connor emphasized that the Court's rulings do not preclude states from passing assisted-suicide laws that will survive constitutional challenges: "There is no reason to think the democratic process will not strike the proper balance between the interests of terminally ill, mentally competent individuals who would seek to end their suffering and the state's interest in protecting those who might seek to end life mistakenly or under pressure."[19]

Justices Ginsburg and Breyer, neither of whom signed Rehnquist's opinion, but agreed with his ultimate decision to uphold the state bans, endorsed Justice O'Connor's stance. Writing for the *New York Times*, David J. Garrow commented: "The Supreme Court's fractured opinions resolved little. Its apparent unanimity belied the diversity of views visible in concurring opinions by Justices John Paul Stevens, David H. Souter and Stephen G. Breyer."[20] Separately, Stevens and Souter claimed that it was too early to say whether there could ever be a right to assisted suicide. Justice Ginsburg simply said that she agreed with O'Connor.

Souter also reached a different conclusion about an assisted death from Rehnquist's, based on a different perception of the due process clause. If reasoned judgment were applied to the assisted-suicide issue, he believed arguments could be identified of what he called "increasing forcefulness for recognizing some right to a doctor's help in suicide."[21] Breyer also differed from Rehnquist, noting that he would formulate the patient's claim in these cases not as Rehnquist had, but rather in "words roughly like a 'right to die with dignity,' " and he said that "our legal tradition may provide greater support" for such a right. He concluded with the observation that if states did interfere with the "administration of drugs as needed to avoid pain at the end of life," then, "as Justice O'Connor suggests, the Court might have to revisit its conclusions in these cases."[22]

In another concurring opinion, Justice John Paul Stevens, the most liberal member of the Court, characteristically interpreted the Fourteenth Amendment in a broader fashion. Dworkin explains how Stevens's concurring opinion gave the right-to-die movement exactly what it wanted, and that his reversal of the lower court decisions was based on procedural rather than substantive grounds:

> His opinion left little doubt, however, that in what he deemed an appropriate case he would vote to overrule a statute that prevented doctors from helping competent and informed dying patients—not just those whose pain could not otherwise be relieved—to die sooner. He emphasized, as the Philosophers' Brief had, that different people have different religious and ethical convictions about what kind of death most respects the value of their life, and that individual freedom demands that dying patients be permitted to die according to their own convictions. He ended with the uncompromising statement that, "In my judgment . . . it is clear that [the states'] so-called unqualified interest in the preservation

of life . . . is not itself sufficient to outweigh the interest in liberty that may justify the only possible means of preserving a dying patient's dignity and alleviating her intolerable suffering."[23]

Kennedy did not write a separate opinion. Yet it is fair to assume that, based on his opinion in *Casey*, he would construe broadly the range of constitutional protections. *Casey* speaks to that "realm of personal liberty which the government may not enter." O'Connor, Souter, and Kennedy had written a joint opinion in that 1992 abortion decision, endorsing a broad interpretation of the due process clause in favor of abortion. It would be difficult to envision a Justice's interpretation of the due process clause that would allow abortion and not physician-assisted death.

All concurring opinions agreed on the need for state legislatures to explore the issue. The debate must continue—but in the states. Said *Time*: "The Court would rather not see such an explosive issue redeposited in its lap. The Justices palpably yearn for a probing debate in the statehouses."[24]

Justice O'Connor, aware of the state venue's importance for continuing the issue, declared that "the . . . challenging task of crafting appropriate procedures for safeguarding . . . liberty interest is entrusted to the 'laboratory' of the States . . . in the first instance."[25] Justice Souter concurred, saying, "Legislatures . . . have superior opportunities to obtain the facts necessary for a judgment about the present controversy. Not only do they have more flexible mechanisms for fact-finding than the Judiciary, but their mechanisms include the power to experiment, moving forward and pulling back as facts emerge within their own jurisdictions. There is, indeed, good reason to suppose that in the absence of a judgment for respondents here, just such experimentation will be attempted in some of the States."[26]

These four opinions, and particularly Justice O'Connor's, leave open the possibility of constitutional exceptions to state bans against assisted dying. Stuart Taylor, correspondent for the *American Lawyer* and *Legal Times*, speaking as a guest on *NewsHour with Jim Lehrer,* said that these opinions go

"some distance in various ways towards saying, well, we do think there might be some kind of a right in a particular case for an individual suffering patient to die with dignity or at least not to be forced to continue suffering, but the way the broad sweeping decisions of the lower courts striking down these laws as applied to broad groups of undefined people went too far. So there's a mix—there's something for both sides in this decision, but bottom line, both lower courts reversed both of these laws against an assisted-suicide stand. The possibility that some individual patient might be able to get the Court to say this law doesn't—is unconstitutional as applied to me, is left open by—at least Justice O'Connor and four others."[27]

Michael S. Evans J.D., M.S.W., deserves credit for breaking down the information as to what the nine Justices agree on, and how the five concurring Justices differ with the lead opinion. The concurring Justices agreed with the *result* of the lead opinion—that is, to return the subject of assisted suicide to a democratic debate in the states. They did not necessarily agree, however, with the reasoning. Nonetheless, there are four points of total agreement: the states have not had enough time to deal with dying patients' issues, so the two cases before the Court are premature; full pain control is available under state law; "double effect" and terminal sedation are universally used and legally and ethically allowed; and the failure to relieve a dying person's pain and suffering is a deficient aspect of health care, not a legal problem.

As to how the five concurring Justices differed from the opinion written by Chief Justice Rehnquist, there are four categories:

1. They differed on what the issue really was.
   REHNQUIST: "The right to commit suicide with another's assistance."
   BREYER: "[A] right to die with dignity. . . . [A]t its core would lie personal control over the manner of death, professional medical assistance, and the avoidance of unnecessary and severe physical suffering—combined."
   SOUTER: "[Freedom to make] personal decisions regarding their own bodies, medical care, and . . . the brief and anguished remainders of their lives. . . ."
   STEVENS: "Nancy Cruzan's interests were not limited to refusal of unwanted treatment. That refusal was incidental to her deeper interest in 'choosing the manner and timing of her death, . . . [including] her interest in dignity and in determining the character of the memories that will survive long after her death.' "
2. They differed on their views of the "double effect" and access to terminal sedation.
   REHNQUIST: Adopts the standard legal and medical rationale (casuistry) for double effect and terminal sedation—that is, the doctor really does not intend the death, but instead, the *intent* is to relieve pain. The death is the unintended consequence, and therefore, all right. Also, the physician does not cause the death, but rather is following the patient's instructions, which are uttered solely for the purpose of relieving pain.
   O'CONNOR: Accepts the assurances that are contained in the medical amicus briefs—that all patients can obtain medication to alleviate suffering, even though it may cause death.
   BREYER: Says the Court has been told that palliative care is available "in principle." He adds that where comfort care is lacking, it is the responsibility of the medical profession, not the legal profession, to take care of the problem, "which would seem possible to overcome." He also con-

cludes that any future individual case might warrant Constitutional protection if severe pain goes untreated because of state laws that prevent the alleviation of that suffering.

STEVENS: Addresses the "double effect" rationale with five criticisms: Contrary to Rehnquist's findings, removal of life-support *does*, in fact hasten death and may be the doctor's intent to do so; a doctor may write a prescription for lethal medication with the intent to cause death, whether it be used for terminal sedation, the double effect, or assisted suicide; conversely, lethal medication may be prescribed, at the request of the patient, with no intent to cause death, but only to reduce suffering; failure to treat a dying person can be done with the intent to harm or even kill the patient; and many patients prescribed lethal medications never actually take them. Some patients fear death less when they feel they have the option of physician-assisted suicide. They acquire some sense of control in the process of dying, provided by the availability of those medications.

3. They differed on how to draw the line between categories of people who should and should not have an assisted death available to them.

REHNQUIST: Feels that the line cannot be drawn. The borders between terminal and nonterminal, competent and incompetent, etc. are so imprecise that it would be impossible to determine who is and who is not qualified for a hastened death.

STEVENS: Is satisfied that constitutional protection can be limited to qualified cases. He urges that any future case brought before the Court, to be valid, should clearly show that the dying individual is not the victim of abuse, is not suffering from depression, and has made a rational and voluntary decision to seek assistance in dying. Facts about the person would dispel any concerns over the qualifications.

SOUTER: Identifies five different qualifying issues that should be addressed by state legislation: terminal illness; mental competence; whether and to what extent a surrogate may participate; means to assure that the patient's choice is voluntary; and limiting the participation of nonphysicians.

4. Two opinions differ as to the physician's role as healer.

REHNQUIST: Is completely agreeable with the AMA's and the two states' claims that assisting in a suicide is "fundamentally incompatible with the physician's role as healer."

STEVENS: Says that there is already tension between the traditional view of the physician's role and the actual practice of physicians: It is a physician's refusal to administer medication to ease a patient's suffering and make their death dignified that would be inconsistent with the "healer" role; a doctor's refusal to hasten death may be seen by patient and relatives as an abandonment, a rejection, or an expression of paternalistic authority—all inconsistent with the "healing" role; a long-standing doctor-patient relationship will not be harmed if the physician provides the patient with choices other then a tortured death; and physicians are already making decisions that hasten the death of terminally ill patients—by terminating life-support, withholding treatment, or administering terminal sedation.

The Washington and New York rulings left the debate to the states to work out in their state legislatures, and the Court thereby resisted the path it took in the landmark abortion ruling that is still being criticized. *Roe* "began a long debate over whether the judicial or the political branches of the government should decide controversial questions of social policy. . . . After *Roe*, many liberal and conservative scholars criticized the Court for having short-circuited the national debate about abortion at a time when the country was deeply divided and consensus had yet to emerge," wrote Jeffrey Rosen for the *New York Times*.[28]

As states were beginning to develop regulations on abortion in the early 1970s, the Court, in what many people felt was an overstepping of its bounds, took the abortion matter into its own hands by finding a fundamental constitutional right to end a pregnancy. That decision has loomed over the Court ever since. The right-to-die cases, however, represent a different consensus about judicial restraint and a shift toward a deference to the democratic process on assisted suicide. "By extending Constitutional protection to an asserted right or liberty interest," Rehnquist wrote, "we would, to a great extent, place the matter outside the arena of public debate and legislative action."[29] The Court had done just that with abortion. Were the Court to define a new right at a time when states were themselves examining PAS and other end-of-life issues, "We would have to reverse centuries of legal doctrine and practice, and strike down the considered policy choice of almost every state," wrote Rehnquist.[30] And the Court was not prepared to make the same mistake twice.

The "assisted suicide decision reflects the U.S. Supreme Court's restored commitment to decentralized democracy," wrote Michael W. McConnell in the *Wall Street Journal*:

Rather than attempting to impose its own nationwide solution to difficult and contentious questions of moral and social policy (as it did in the abortion cases), the Court seems to have realized that in the absence of clear direction in our constitutional text or history, it is better to allow the people and their elected representatives to wrestle with these problems. . . . The Court's majority says that "in every due process case" where our constitutional text and history are silent and our national experience provides no clear answer, it intends to allow the democratic processes of the 50 states to prevail.[31]

McConnell agreed with the Court's decision to narrowly construe the due process clause. He mentioned four characteristics of the federal judiciary that make it a poor—and in his mind, a dangerous—social policy maker: Any answer imposed by the Court in the name of the Constitution will apply across the nation; constitutional decisions are difficult to change, even when mistaken; because any lines drawn by courts must be based on constitutional principle and not on prudential compromise, it is difficult to limit a new right once it has been recognized; and the Supreme Court is the most unrepresentative body in our governing structure.

Reactions to the Supreme Court's decisions were predictable. Leaders of the AMA, the Roman Catholic Church, and the Clinton administration, were among those quick to praise the Court's rulings. Doctors attending an annual meeting of the AMA in Chicago shouted and cheered when the ruling was announced. Chicago's Cardinal Law, a member of the U.S. Catholic Conference, said the Court "displayed wisdom and restraint" in upholding the laws that "recognize that healers must not be agents of death."[32] And President Clinton hailed it as a "victory for all Americans. It prevents us from going down a very dangerous and troubling path on this difficult and often agonizing issue."[33] The National Right-to-Life Committee vowed action. "We will mobilize in all 50 states to fight efforts to legalize direct killing of the vulnerable through state courts, state legislatures and referenda," said director, David O'Steen.[34]

Harvard law professor Tribe, who represented physicians and patients in the challenge to New York's ban, found it encouraging that five Justices did not foreclose the possibility of an individual's right to an assisted suicide.[35] Doctor Quill guarantees that assisted suicide will continue, "mostly unadvertised and mostly unprosecuted," and predicts that the Court's kind words about painkillers and palliative care will "create quasi-official situations where patients can request sufficient medication to provide a final escape."[36] Private citizen and attorney Robert M. Calica wrote an article for *Newsday* that expressed what many supporters of assisted suicide, including the Ninth and the Second Circuit Courts, believe: "The notion of the state or federal government compelling terminally ill persons to suffer not only intolerable pain, but the personal degradation and imposition of emotional pain upon close family members and friends is clearly repugnant."[37]

As legal scholars across the country analyzed what the Court's decision meant, terminally ill people focused on the reality of their own deteriorating mental and physical faculties and the decision's effect on their own pain and suffering. Judging from the reactions of dying people, although dismayed and disappointed by the Court's rulings, they intend to take control of the last act of their lives—with or without legal sanction.

Dale Gilsdorf, a fifty-eight-year-old psychotherapist diagnosed first with lung cancer and more recently with a brain tumor, intends to swallow a powerful cocktail of drugs. Unfortunately, since the decision still forbids another party from assisting, his final act will probably be executed in a covert fashion, without a doctor at his side to help if something goes wrong. Most important to Gilsdorf is that he will be in control of that ultimate decision. "There's a lot of joy in this," he said. "It's not just doom and gloom at all."[38]

Jeff Fenton is angered by the mistake he feels the Supreme Court made. He is going to end his life at the proper time for him—legally or illegally. "I think my body is my property," says Fenton, forty-four, of San Francisco, living with AIDS yet comforted by a safe deposit box full of life-ending drugs. The decision is "infringing on my rights as a human being. It's none of the Supreme Court's goddamn business what goes on between me and my doctor."[39] His doctor has been writing him prescriptions for sleeping pills, which he hoards for when the time comes. Referring to the common practice of complaining to one's doctor about sleeping problems in order to get barbiturates, Fenton says, "I can have as much insomnia as I want, and he can write as many prescriptions for it as he wants, and there's nothing illegal about it."[40]

Terminal patients are not the only ones ignoring the edict of the Supreme Court. Even though the AMA abhors the thought of legalization, the rank-and-file members of the medical community do not necessarily agree. In fact, a 40 percent showing of physicians who have accommodated the terminally ill and their families' requests for assisted suicide belies the strident approach of the AMA leadership.[41] One such Washington State physician, with a large AIDS practice, who has helped four terminally ill patients to die with the assistance of Valium and a morphine drip, speaks (anonymously) for many physicians who comply with the wishes of their patients. "I don't care what the Court says. If that is what my patient wants and what the family wants and what I want, we are going to do it."[42]

Advocates on both sides of the issue agree about one thing: The Supreme Court's ruling in June 1997 did not settle the controversy and debate over PAS. Certainly the two Circuit Courts of Appeals rulings and that of the Supreme Court have found common ground and focused national attention on improving the care of the dying. The legal battles have spotlighted the failures of the AMA leadership in that department. Our increasing knowledge of the profession's abandonment of patients and its dismissal of patient wishes has pressured it to change. New AMA guidelines outline an intent to elicit better pain medication and urge the nation to expect better compassion and sensitivity from our doctors. A *New York Times* editorial makes the point that a positive result of the assisted-suicide debate thus far "has been to force the medical profession to concede that the inadequate help it now offers patients trying to cope with pain and depression at the end of their lives is not adequate."[43]

However, such uniformity cannot be found on the subject of an assisted death—by the public or by the Supreme Court. The battle now goes to the forty-nine remaining states. Now begins another chapter in a struggle that most assuredly will last for many years. Advocates of physician aid in dying will probable try to develop more legal cases, centered on terminal patients whose physical suffering cannot be relieved by any painkilling medication, no matter how large the dosage. Progress can take place in several ways.

First, appealing an individual conviction is one way. Proponents of legal change sometimes risk their physical liberty in order to effectuate that change. This was the method used in *Roe*, when a criminal conviction was accepted by a doctor for the purpose of forcing a constitutional challenge in the hopes of legalizing abortion.

Second, terminal patients can bring individual cases challenging their state's constitution and laws. They may argue that no pain medication is sufficient to get rid of their pain. They may also say that the laws block their accessibility to palliative care. The Court mentioned the latter two situations as possible winning scenarios. Charles Hall, a terminal AIDS patient in Florida, in 1997 challenged the ban against a death-hastening prescription on the grounds that it violated the right to privacy protected in that state's constitution. He succeeded in Florida's two lower courts but lost in state supreme court.

Third, public opinion also can put pressure on state legislators to lift the bans and allow assisted suicide for a limited group, the terminally ill. Recent polls show that anywhere between two-thirds and three-fourths of the public support legalizing the practice. Legislators, however, motivated by fear as well as pressure from several affluent organizations, are reluctant to stand up and be counted. Even Justice Souter mentioned the possibility of "legislative foot-dragging," and Doctor Quill admitted that he did not have much faith in the legislative process.

Lastly, initiatives and referendums are a possibility for those states that allow them. Patience and perseverance finally paid off in Oregon in 1997, following an initiative three years earlier. A negative to using this approach is the tremendous amount of money it takes to place the issue on the ballot and bring it to fruition. Foes of assisted suicide have virtually unlimited resources for television, radio, and newspaper advertisements, while death with dignity groups are mostly working with ten-to-fifty-dollar donations. It is likely that a combination of these methods will be used. The recent cases are one step in a long process ahead.

In *Washington* v. *Glucksberg* and *Quill* v. *Vacco*, the Supreme Court unanimously held that PAS is not a fundamental liberty interest protected by the Constitution. Notably, five members of the Court wrote or joined in concurring opinions that took a more liberal view. Unexpectedly, the Court unanimously required all states to ensure that their laws do not obstruct the provision of adequate palliative care. These two decisions in no way foreclose the possibility that an individual, as Justice Stevens said, "seeking to hasten her death, or a doctor whose assistance was sought, could prevail in a more particularized challenge." With these words and with the conservative Chief Justice's lack of disagreement with Stevens's assessment, the odds are that the next assisted suicide case will have a positive outcome. The Court left open the distinct possibility that it would uphold the right to an assisted suicide, say, in a case where a physician faced a severe criminal penalty for complying with the request of an unquestionably competent terminally ill patient experiencing intractable pain that even the best palliative care can do nothing to eliminate.

According to David J. Garrow in *George*, the future looks exceedingly bright:

> American public opinion strongly and decisively favors fundamental legal reform, and in time courts or legislatures will bring it about, even if it happens one state at a time. In time, the U.S. Supreme Court very well may accept and endorse the liberty and equality arguments Kathryn Tucker and Laurence Tribe put to the Justices in January, but until that day comes, the right-to-die advocates—perhaps America's next *big* movement—will have to joust in the arena of politics. Keep your eyes peeled, for eventually they're going to win.[44]

PART FIVE

The
View
from
Here

Chapter 21

The Unspoken Argument

The right-to-die is but one element of a larger set of medical, cultural, legal, and economic issues that have converged in response to the extraordinary capability of medical technology to extend life. Similar to other social issues, the right-to-die has not arisen separate and distinct from other concurrent developments of our time. In attempting to answer Why Now?, one must look at the realities of the increasing cost of health care in an aging society, because in the final analysis, economics, not the quest for broadened individual liberties or increased autonomy, will drive assisted suicide to the plateau of acceptable practice. As technology advances, as medical costs skyrocket out of control, as chronic diseases predominate, as the projected rate of the eighty-five-and-older population accelerates, as managed care seeks to cut costs and as Medicare is predicted to go bankrupt by 2007, the pressures of cost containment provide impetus, whether openly acknowledged or not, for the practicalities of an assisted death.

These converging issues should influence our thinking, even though it is politically incorrect to use economics as an argument in favor of the right to choose the time and manner of one's death—for the moment, at least. Even now, however, people are beginning to question the common sense of keeping someone alive, at great societal and personal expense, who prefers to forgo the final hours or weeks of an intolerable existence. To what purpose? Might not money be better spent on preventive treatment, medicine for the young, educating the youth of the nation, or for that matter, the children in the patient's own family. Is there, in fact, a duty to die—a responsibility within the family unit—that should remain voluntary but expected nevertheless? Rationing of health care already exists, but how much limitation on services will the nation tolerate?

Like it or not, the connections between the right-to-die and the cost, value, and allocation of health care resources are part of the political debate, albeit frequently unspoken. Policies are emerging more or less simultaneously; and policies in one arena implicate those in another. Physician-assisted suicide is an idea whose time has come, even if legalization occurs gradually. While government is contemplating these policy issues, the right-to-die movement is gaining momentum in response to a legitimate societal problem—the emotional, physical, and economic toll of the dying experience on not only government, employers, hospitals, and insurance companies, but on families as well.

Medical expenditures used to be small, not because doctors were stingy or inefficient, but because there was very little that medicine could offer—no matter how much the public was willing or able to spend. Since the 1940s, every year has brought new medical advances: new diagnostic techniques to identify problems; new surgical procedures to correct problems that could previously only be allowed to run their course; and new therapies that cure or at the very least alleviate conditions. With the assistance of medical technology, Americans seem able to cheat death in the short term, but the resulting quality of life is often seriously degraded and prohibitively expensive.

In 1970 the U.S. spent 7 percent of its gross domestic product on medical care. National health care spending totaled $949.4 billion or almost 14 percent of the gross domestic product in 1994. Health care spending has increased well over 30 percent since 1990, rising much faster than the economy as a whole. By the year 2000 the amount spent on health care is estimated to be $1.5 *trillion*. Health care is expected to consume 18 percent of the GDP by 2005.

The same underlying factors have increased health care costs since the early 1980s: the aging population, now compounded by middle age baby boomers who require and expect more medical services; expensive medical technology; greed and inefficiency; and new drugs, like those for AIDS, that can cost more than $25,000 a year. Also causing costs to escalate are the cost-blind benefits and insurance systems that exempt most Americans from having to make choices about treatment, and the uniquely American predisposition to believe that everyone is entitled to the best of everything all the time. Traditional medical insurance gives neither doctor nor patient any incentive to think about costs. No other country sends patients to multi-million dollar MRI scanners for mundane complaints, performs open-heart surgery on septuagenarians and even octogenarians, or places terminally ill people in the intensive care unit at anywhere near the rates that we do. The United States, for example, has eight times as many MRI units per capita as Canada. All this costs more money than the nation can afford.

Moreover, spending continues to rise for Medicare, which provides health care for the elderly and disabled, and Medicaid, for low-income families. At age sixty-five, most Americans qualify for Medicare, which is essentially health insurance for the elderly, the best-insured age group in the country. Government programs accounted for 44.3 percent of all health spending in 1994, with a yearly increase of 11.8 percent for Medicare spending. Throughout the 1940s all levels of government spent roughly $1.00 annually on health care for the typical older American. By 1965 the figure had risen to roughly $1,000 and by 1995 to roughly $7,000.

The bitter truth is that by 2003, 75 *percent of the federal budget will be devoted to Medicare, Medicaid, and Social Security. That leaves 25 percent for everything else.* Medicare is facing bankruptcy in 2007. Adding to future problems is that today the cost of caring for each Medicare beneficiary is shared by 3.9 workers who pay into the Medicare Trust Fund. By 2030 the cost will be shared by only 2.2 workers because most of the baby boomers will be over sixty-five and receiving Medicare themselves. Therefore, less money will be going into the fund, yet more money will be paid out. Even now the assets in the Medicare Trust Fund are falling rapidly.

Steve Forbes, editor in chief of *Forbes Magazine* and a guest on ABC's *This Week*, equated the current Medicare program with a ship headed for an iceberg. Politicians, unwilling to make the necessary changes, are counting on someone else being "on the bridge when disaster comes." And disaster is not far off.

Consider the rising cost of health care, skewed in the direction of the seriously ill elderly patient who will die within a short time regardless of the medical intervention implemented. Medical expenditures at the end of life are disproportionately high, while the elderly consume a disproportionate amount of health care resources. These two facts combine to raise serious concerns about our economic future. Health care dollars spent on futile care during the last days and weeks of life are largely responsible for the increasing interest in right-to-die issues. Many are questioning the vast amounts of money spent on temporary rescue services for the dying and the elderly, while health care costs are spiraling out of control and other medical needs, like prenatal care and preventive medicine, are going unaddressed.

Although the precise numbers vary, certain trends and ratios have existed since the early 1960s, say Harvard's Drs. Linda and Ezekiel Emanuel:

> Studies consistently demonstrate that 27% to 30% of Medicare payments each year are for the 5% to 6% of Medicare beneficiaries who die in that year. The latest available figures indicate that in 1988, the mean Medicare payment for the last year of life of a beneficiary who died was $13,316, as compared with $1,924 for *all* Medicare beneficiaries (a ratio of 6.9:1). Payments for dying patients increase exponentially as death approaches, and payments during the last month of life constitute 40% of payments during the last year of life. . . . To many people, reducing expenditures at the end of life seems an easy and readily justifiable way of cutting wasteful spending and freeing resources

to ensure universal access to health care. . . . Many believe . . . that interventions for patients whose death is imminent are inherently wasteful, since they neither cure nor ameliorate disease or disability.[1]

Medicare, therefore, spends almost seven times the amount for the elderly who *die*, as opposed to the elderly who *live*. The largest amounts (over 45 percent) occur within the last sixty days of life.[2]

Indeed, a five-hospital study reveals the exorbitantly high cost of futile care—that is, treatment that has no reasonable probability of providing a quality of life that would be satisfactory to the average patient. Last-minute medical care for patients with near-death diagnosis who died in the hospitals averaged about $10,400 per patient. In the final month of a patient's life, intensive care costs can surpass $100,000. And the total cost to Medicare for medical care provided to patients in their last thirty days came to roughly $20 billion in fiscal year 1995.[3]

The government underwrites only 27 percent of health care costs for those patients *under* sixty-five, yet covers a full 64 percent of costs for those *over* 65. It is this differential in percentages of support that has led policy makers and other interested parties to take a close look at where and how money is being spent on the elderly in the last days and weeks of life. The undeniable truth is that the elderly are putting a strain on the health care system that will only increase and cannot be sustained. It is raising the level of debate over how much health care the elderly are entitled to receive and how much rationing the nation will tolerate. It is safe to say that many unpopular changes will take place over the next several decades. This disproportionate spending is leading some to consider right-to-die possibilities for relief, while others are concerned about possible abuses if the elderly, terminally ill patient feels a "duty to die," allowing resources to fall to the generations next in line.

The U.S. population is aging. The nation is experiencing unprecedented growth in both the numbers and the proportion of the American population that is old, due to trends in longevity and fertility as well as the aging of the large baby boom generation. The proportion of older Americans has tripled in the twentieth century. While only one out of every twenty-five Americans (4 percent) was age sixty-five or older in 1990, as we approach the twenty-first century, one of every eight Americans (13 percent) is at least sixty-five years old. Compare this to the one out of every four or five Americans who will be sixty-five or older by 2030.

America's population is not only aging, but the absolute number of older Americans is increasing exponentially. As the baby boomers enter old age, there will be more than a doubling of the elderly population. The number of people age sixty-five or older is projected to be close to 70 million by the year 2030, twice the number in this age group in 1990. Of particular significance is the fact that *the fastest-growing group in the United States is the oldest of the old,* those age eighty-five and older. Between 1960 and 1994 alone, the number of these oldest old rose 274 percent.

America's population is not as young as it once was. In 1960 more than one of every three Americans (36 percent) was a child under the age of eighteen, and fewer than one in ten (9 percent) was age sixty-five or older. By the year 2030 there will be more Americans over sixty-five than there will be children under eighteen. Medical advances and life-style changes, such as better nutrition and sanitation, have resulted in a remarkable increase in life expectancy. At the time of the nation's founding, the average number of years one could expect to live was 35, compared to 76.1 years for those born in 1996.[4]

A demographic shift will be reshaping the nation over the next several decades, and we must respond intelligently if we are to avoid allowing this shift to bankrupt the country. As the United States is experiencing unprecedented growth in both the numbers of older people and the proportion of the American population that is old, these projected shifts predict disaster if the present system continues unchanged. How severe is the situation expected to be? Jim Towey, former state secretary of health and rehabilitative services and head of the Florida Commission on Aging with Dignity, says Florida must start preparing for the time that the baby boomers begin retiring with the same diligence that the state prepares for a hurricane. But unlike a hurricane, "this is bearing down on us with certainty."[5]

The United States, heretofore a youthful nation, is becoming old, and with it, the cost of health care is staggering. Look at the age composition in Florida today, and you have seen the demographic future of the United States. Nearly one in four to five residents of Florida is now over sixty-five. By early into the twenty-first century, the proportion of all Americans who are elderly will be the same as the proportion of elderly in Florida today. Florida, however, will continue to hold its lead, with one out of four of its residents projected to be sixty-five or older by 2020.

Florida state officials say the elderly bring in about $53 billion in Social Security and other yearly earnings, yet they also pose great fiscal concerns. Reports journalist Mireya Navarro for the *New York Times*:

> The greatest concern, state officials say, is the mounting cost of dealing with disability and chronic illness. Most state spending on the elderly is currently for financing of Medicaid patients in nursing homes and other long-term care facilities, a $1.4 billion cost that is shared with the Federal Government and is growing. . . . Because of the growing need for custodial care of the elderly, Florida is seeking Federal authority to use some Medicaid money to pay for cheaper alternatives to nursing homes, such as houses in which the elderly can live together as a group and services provided by professionals in the individual homes of the elderly on a regular basis.[6]

The extraordinary growth of the oldest old, those over eighty-five, will have an unprecedented impact on the nation's economy. As more Americans live to be octogenarians, large numbers will experience frailty, chronic illness, and mental deterioration, requiring nursing and other long-term and home care—just what Florida is now undergoing. Reporting on research from the National Institute on Aging, demographer James Vaupel suggests that we are on the threshold of a "new paradigm of aging, in which the *average* life expectancy could reach 100 or more."[7]

With the fastest-growing population being those over eighty-five years old, the future toll of aging dementia will reach a new high. These are the ones most likely to suffer from advanced stages of dementia, most often Alzheimer's disease. It is estimated that as many as 50 percent of those eighty-five and older have some signs of the disease.[8] In a recently published academic paper, an American gerontologist, Dr. Robert N. Butler, wrote of dementia: "We will be confronted, indeed, with the 'disease of the twentieth century' being transformed into the epidemic of the twenty-first century."[9] Dementia, increasingly expensive, demanding personal attention, irreversible, debilitating, and dehumanizing, is forcing many to question whether keeping people alive with this chronic illness, against their wishes, makes sense: "Many are beginning to wonder, as America ages and the ranks of the infirmed elderly swell, if this situation does not invite—and even demand—a serious public-policy discussion about life and death, including the right to die," says political scientist Hoefler.[10]

Major changes in the causes, as well as the timing, of death are burdening the nation's economy as never before. Chronic and lingering health conditions have replaced the acute, infectious diseases of the early twentieth century. While less life threatening than infectious diseases, chronic conditions are most often disabling and costly. In 1900 the leading causes of death in the United States, pneumonia and tuberculosis, often struck children and young adults. In the 1990s the leading causes of death are heart disease, cancer, and stroke, and death rates increase with age. The top five chronic conditions for persons aged forty-five and over are, in this order, arthritis, hypertension, impaired hearing, heart disease, and cataracts. People living with chronic illnesses—from ulcers to bad backs to HIV—are living longer than ever before and requiring more care.

Persons with chronic conditions account for a disproportionately large share of health care use, both services and supplies. The average length of hospital stay for such patients—representing 80 percent of all hospital days and 69 percent of all hospital admissions— is 7.8 days, compared with 4.3 for persons without chronic conditions. Surprisingly, almost all (96 percent) of home care visits, 83 percent of prescription drugs used, 66 percent of physician visits, and 55 percent of emergency department visits are made by persons with chronic conditions.

It is not surprising that rates of chronic conditions are highest among the elderly. Medicare and Medicaid play major roles in providing insurance coverage to people with chronic conditions, particularly for those most disabled by them. Medicare provides nearly universal health insurance coverage for the elderly, nearly 90 percent of whom have chronic conditions. In addition, Medicare covers nearly 3.9 million disabled persons and Medicaid pays for services for another 5 million disabled people.

The growth in numbers of elderly people with chronic conditions and dementia produces large numbers of people requiring medical and long-term care. The cost of long-term health care is the fastest growing medical cost in the United States. It is the foremost example of a growing financial problem for the elderly, the disabled, their families, and our nation's bank account. Much of this long-term care takes place in nursing homes, which are staffed and equipped to provide long-term care for the chronically ill, the infirmed, and the disabled. Although people of all ages may sometimes have need for nursing-home care, the vast majority of residents are elderly. The total number of people living in nursing homes in 1990 was 1.8 million, an increase of 24 percent since 1980. Total public outlays for nursing-home care have more than doubled from $11 billion in 1980 to $25 billion in 1990. These outlays are projected to double again in the 1990s, reaching $53 billion annually by the year 2000. Nearly one-half of all nursing-home care is paid for by government funds, a proportion that deeply troubles crafters of public policy.

Surveys have consistently found that most people would rather continue living at home rather than in a nursing home. What has not been known until recently, however, is that the aversion to "such a facility is so strong that a new study of seriously ill people in hospitals found that 30% of those surveyed said they would rather *die* than live permanently in a nursing home."[11] This information begs the question: Why do we, as a nation, not allow these people to die, if they have no alternative to a nursing-home existence and this is what they want? Their lives would conclude with dignity and self-respect, and one measure of cost containment would be in place.

Meanwhile, home health care is the fastest-growing category of Medicare cost. Care that was once limited to hospitals and nursing homes—feeding tubes, IV drips, catheters, even respirators—is now being given at home, partly to reduce health care costs and partially because Americans are increasingly fearful of a hospital's ability to prolong suffering. They opt, if at all possible, to remain at home.

About $20 billion is spent each year on home health care, out of total estimated Medicare outlays of $213.1 billion. The number of home visits virtually exploded from 31 million in 1984 to 209 million in 1994. These beneficiaries are typically stroke and heart disease victims, primarily women eighty-five and over, also the fastest-growing segment of the population.

Demographics and poor hospital care being the norm, long-term and home health care costs are expected to skyrocket out of control in the coming years.

The United States is entering a crisis situation, the kind of emergency we have not dealt with before in this land of plenty. We cannot sustain the unsustainable, nor can we finance the unfinanceable. On our present course we cannot afford to provide for everything to which the elderly have become accustomed. As the baby boomers begin retirement, says economist Peter G. Peterson, in *The Atlantic Monthly*, they will expect the "munificent array of 'entitlements' that were guarantees . . . to every retiring American with no anticipation of the ever-growing length of retirement as life expectancy increases or the ever-rising expectations of independence, affluence, health, and comfort of life in retirement. . . . Neither the founders of Social Security sixty years ago nor the founders of Medicare thirty years ago imagined the demographic shape of America that will unfold over the next several decades."[12]

Increasing numbers of thinking people find it hard to rationalize spending so much to postpone briefly the death of the seriously ill and elderly when so little attention—relative to that in other developed countries—is paid to the prevention of the deaths (and the treatment of the less serious illnesses) of those who are still very much alive. In fact, 30 percent of the population uses more than 90 percent of all health services in any given year.[13]

The United States is embarrassingly weak on preventive medicine for the young. It ranks tenth out of ten Western countries in the percentage of preschool children with full polio, diphtheria-tetanus-pertussis (DTP), and measles immunization. The infant mortality rates top those in any other developed country. The United States also leads the way in the percentage of infants born at low birth weight. Indeed, this country devotes less than 5 percent of health care spending to prevention efforts in any given year, while spending billions on those who, from a medical standpoint, are lost causes.

Peterson highlights the imbalanced spending on young and old:

The United States is the global leader in the life expectancy of 85 year olds but has fallen near the bottom of the industrial world's rankings in rates of infant mortality, marital breakup, child poverty, child suicide, hours of school-assigned homework, and functional illiteracy. Meanwhile, per capita federal spending on the elderly towers *11 to 1* over federal spending on children. The appropriate response to the outra-

geous is to be outraged, yet we seem oblivious to this devastating dis-
proportion.[14]

The perception of the elderly as "greedy geezers" may grow, largely because elderly voters wield enormous political influence, a tribute to their
huge turnout and their determination to keep the public safety net in place.
The American Association of Retired Persons (AARP) embodies the growing
numbers of older citizens and their political strength. Its membership makes
up just over one-half of the total population of the United States aged fifty
or more. AARP's political clout is great at all levels, and from its national
headquarters in Washington, D.C., it wields considerable influence on local,
state, and federal legislation. A strong, effective voice in Washington, AARP
works for public policies on critical issues that affect the economic stability,
health, and social well-being of its current members. The well-being of its
future members does not carry the same weight.

The United States is being forced to consider methods of cost containment. The potential savings to society if advance directives were universally
used are enormous. One method of cost containment, and one that will
eventually become mandatory, will be for insurance companies and Medicare to require that patients execute a Living Will, clearly articulating what
kind of life-sustaining treatment they want and do not want if they become
incompetent and unable to make their own medical decisions.

Information shows that getting people to plan ahead for the medical
care they want as they approach death, can save an average of more than
$60,000 per patient. Dr. Christopher Chambers of Thomas Jefferson Uni-
versity, Philadelphia, reviewed the records of 474 Medicare patients who
died in a hospital. Bills for the 342 patients who had not completed advance
directives were more than three times greater than the bills of the 132
patients who had. The average expense was $95,305 versus $30,478, an
immense difference, especially when multiplied by the approximately two
million people who die every year in the hospital.

Estimates of dollars saved by using advance directives vary according to
who is evaluating the data. Some say that as much as $109 billion might be
saved, overall, "from a policy of asking all patients about their wishes regarding life-sustaining treatment and incorporating those wishes into advance directives."[15] Others say these high figures overestimate savings; that
the execution of advance directives would reduce health care expenditures
by only 3.3 percent. Even this smaller amount, however, would produce
substantial savings.[16]

Regardless of the specific amount, common sense dictates that avoiding
heroic interventions, or even treatment as inconspicuous as antibiotics,
would save the nation money best spent elsewhere. Quite simply, if a
coronary-artery-bypass graft procedure costs $75,000, then avoiding the pro-

cedure saves $75,000. Survey after survey shows that the overwhelming majority of Americans do not want to postpone an inevitable death with futile treatment, yet so few Americans have executed advance directives to forgo such treatment. If more people made their wishes known, and if more physicians paid attention to those wishes and avoided using high-tech intervention for those who do not want it, the medical profession would save money for other public and private health insurers and providers, from Medicare and Medicaid to private HMOs and health insurers. Doctors could contain costs, heighten respect for the patient's self-determination, and instigate a rise in confidence in the medical profession, with new respect for the doctor-patient relationship.

A second method of cost containment is doctor-assisted suicide. While no one is suggesting assisted suicide against the patient's wishes, both advance directives and PAS propose a voluntary shortening of the dying experience and therefore come under the umbrella of the right-to-die. The proposal has been floated that if a mentally competent terminally ill adult wishes to hasten his or her inevitable death with the aid of a physician, then why not allow it? The patient gets what he or she wants, and society saves money that would otherwise be spent on expensive and, most important, *unwanted* end-of-life care. Compassion and dignity are sufficient justifications for its legalization.

By the end of the last decade, American corporations found the cost of insuring their employees unsustainable, and their outrage gave birth to managed care. Managed care is rationing by another name, and rationing of health services will probably not be kind to the elderly in the years ahead. Following World War II, health care was a booming industry with almost unlimited resources for the effort to fight disease. What happened in the intervening years is a dramatic story of national pride, national shame, profit, greed, the medical profession's loss of restraint, and finally, the revolt of the business community. As a result, the cost-conscious dictates of managed care have drastically transformed the health care market, with alarming and uncertain consequences ahead.

Journalist George Anders tells the story of how managed care evolved in his book *Health Against Wealth: HMOs and the Breakdown of Medical Trust.*[17] Researchers at the Rand Corporation, led by Robert Brook, a Johns Hopkins–trained internist, believed that American medicine was riddled with waste: Brook and his colleagues won headlines from the mid-1980s on, with studies reporting that 14 percent of all coronary bypass surgeries in the United States were inappropriate, and that 16 percent of hysterectomies were unnecessary and another 25 percent debatable. Dartmouth physician John Wennberg, in study after study, showed regional discrepancies in how often doctors performed the same procedures. These incidences became powerful ammunition for reformers who argued that American surgeons were operating far too often, treating patients as financial piñatas to be cut open for profit.

Equally repugnant in payers' eyes were doctors who owned their own diagnostic machines and found endless reasons to use them on patients. Congress, in 1989, barred physicians from getting Medicare payments on referrals to diagnostic centers that they owned. The more tests, operations, and patient visits that doctors conducted, the more money they collected. Furthermore, it was the doctors and hospitals that decided what care was appropriate. As a corporate physician admitted later, "We were the ones who created an out-of-control system. . . . Doctors and hospitals were incapable, from an economic standpoint, of governing themselves."[18] The only effective way to change the way medicine was practiced, many employers and insurers came to believe, was to intervene before doctors ever saw a patient. The name for such interventions was managed care.

By the late 1980s medical expenses had been climbing at double-digit annual percentage rates, due to unnecessary testing and surgical procedures carried out to increase billing. Corporations were seething over the fact that employees' health care costs were rising much faster than overall corporate profits. Companies, large and small, saw runaway health costs jeopardizing their businesses. Upon learning one day in 1987 that his company's expenses for employee health care were soaring at a rate of 39 *percent a year*, Edward Hennessy, the longtime chairman of Allied Signal Corporation, literally slammed down his fist and declared, "Enough!"

He invited a dozen big insurers and health plans to compete for the chance to put most of Allied Signal's 76,000 employees and their families into managed care. Workers who chose not to use the cost-effective doctors and hospitals designated by this new system could still see their old physicians. However, those employees would have to pay an uncomfortably large share of the costs themselves. Incentives to stay within the managed-care network would be strong.

The new health plan changed every Allied Signal worker's health coverage in early 1988. Company after company followed suit, and a new approach to medical services was put in place. Holding down expenses became the overriding goal, even if it meant telling employees they could not see certain doctors or go to certain hospitals or have certain costly diagnostic tests. Doctors could no longer boast about how much money they would make, often by relentlessly testing every patient they could, a practice known as "scoping for dollars."

Managed care amounted to a power grab by employers and the insurance industry, whose new approach would be to reward thrift and punish overtreatment. The result was cost-effective and efficient, and employers were delighted. The central tenet was that doctors, hospitals, and patients could not be given free rein any longer to choose whatever course of treatment they wanted. Outside supervision was needed, not only to hold down costs, but also to decide what constituted appropriate care. Managed care experts would decide which doctors and hospitals to include in a treatment network. Outside supervisors could then monitor these medical providers according to standards of cost-effectiveness. Health plans would continue to cover the standard assortment of doctors' visits, tests, and hospital stays. But all the old incentives that encouraged abundant or excessive care would die. Most important, the doctor was no longer in control of the patient's tests and treatments.

Managed care, however, is far from a panacea for the nation's health care woes. With incentives to save money and paying gatekeepers to withhold care, it creates a whole set of new problems. Once managed-care companies entered the for-profit arena of publicly trading on Wall Street, stock prices became the major priority:

> The financial world's values started seeping in. Quarterly earnings mattered much more than before. Executives weren't likely any longer to know many patients or doctors by name. Instead, top managers hovered over computer printouts showing membership growth rates, hospital days per thousand members, and other favorite statistical benchmarks. Cost control became crucial. Security analysts and big investors refused to support a health plan that spent "too much" on members and left too little for shareholders. Thanks to increasingly generous stock-option packages, executives' own fortunes became closely tied to the wiggles of their company's share price.[19]

Editor Kassirer, of the *New England Journal of Medicine*, highlights the inherent conflict within the system in a 1995 essay, "The Morality of Managed Care." Doctors are expected to offer and provide the best quality and quantity of care on the one hand, yet limit the use of time and services to keep expenses down on the other. The result of this dilemma? Physicians will be forced to choose between the best interests of their patients and their own economic survival, predicts Kassirer.[20]

Criticism of managed care may be valid, but the industry developed as a necessary response to outrageous heath costs, inflated by the greed of the medical profession. Restraint in spending has, in fact, stemmed cost increases. In 1991 employers' health care premiums rose 11.5 percent. In 1996 they rose less than 1 percent. Has quality suffered? The answer depends on who you talk to.

Medical cost-cutting is more than just the denial of technology or of treatment. It is more extreme, goes much deeper, and warrants close scrutiny. As hospitals frantically cut costs to survive, they have been reining in one of their biggest expenses—the nursing staff. Many believe that the reduction of nurses has hurt the care patients receive. They complain that the remaining nurses are overworked and spread too thin, that the technicians, hired in place of nurses, are not mentally or educationally up to the task.

In desperate attempts to contain costs, certain practices, unheard of before managed care, are becoming routine. Saving money is serious business. Surgical gear, meant to be used only once, is being resterilized and used again. Medical devices, from arthroscopic knee surgery blades to catheters threaded into patients' hearts, are being recycled, despite microscopic pieces of a previous patient's tissue still being stuck inside. While reactions to microscopic particles left on reused catheters are not life threatening, patients do get fevers, chills, and other uncomfortable symptoms. More serious infections, injuries from chemicals, and mechanical failures from reuse are endangering American lives. However, proponents of this practice contend that reuse is vital in lowering health care costs. A cardiac catheter, for example, selling for three to four hundred dollars can be resterilized for only fifty dollars. Hospitals estimate that reusing catheters can save them ten million dollars a year.[21]

American hospitals, however, are not standing idly by as their profits fall with the advent of managed care. While cutting costs, they are also seeking to increase income. Squeezed financially by cost-cutting HMOs and government programs, they are tapping into a new source of cash—wealthy "foreigners who are willing and able to spend top dollar for care they either can't get at home or prefer to get in the USA."[22] Many of the nation's premier hospitals, including Johns Hopkins Hospital in Baltimore, the Mayo Clinic in Rochester, Minnesota, and Massachusetts General Hospital in Boston are finding ways to compete for this new market of clients. The University of Texas MD Anderson Cancer Center has joined a consortium of eleven other hospitals in the region to cultivate business in the Middle East and Latin America. In 1996, the group went so far as to have a booth at the Arab Health Expo in Dubai, United Arab Emirates. It is too soon to tell what effect this trend will have on Americans' access to first-rate medical care.

As medical dollars become more scarce in the United States, full fees from foreign patients could mean the difference between profitability and loss for those hospitals teetering on the brink of solvency:

On average, foreigners pay full fees for their care, about 10% to 20% higher than HMOs or Medicare will pay. For example, at Baltimore's Johns Hopkins Hospital, a foreign patient typically pays around $28,000 for uncomplicated heart bypass surgery. The managed care rate for the same surgery is $24,000. Medicare reimburses an average $21,000 for bypass surgery. "There's no mystery why we all want foreign patients," says David Jones, an official of the company that owns Massachusetts General Hospital in Boston. "We make more money on them."[23]

No attempt to control the excess increase in health care costs will be successful over the long term unless it addresses the decisions physicians make about treatments, predicts David Eddy, surgeon, writer, professor, and current senior adviser for health policy and management at Kaiser Permanente Southern California:

> The facts are clear. Sooner or later, one way or another, the solution to the cost problem will have to address practitioners' decisions about treatments. Unless physicians can somehow solve the problem on their own, or unless the country makes an about-face and decides to give health care whatever portion of any budget it wants, the forces being reflected in health care reform will inevitably collide with one of the most cherished features of clinical practice—control over day-to-day decisions about how patients should be treated. This collision will not be an unintentional by-product of reform; it will be one of the main instruments of reform.[24]

In the debate over which patients should receive what treatment, the question arises: How much do we want to spend on futile treatment? Futility is defined in various ways. It can be "any effort to provide a benefit to a patient that is highly likely to fail," or another definition: "If a patient lacks the capacity to appreciate the benefit of a treatment, or if the treatment fails to release a patient from total dependence on intensive medical care, that treatment should be regarded as futile."[25]

The main purposes of futile treatment are threefold. It satisfies the family that nothing more can possibly be done, often signifying an inability to let go or to accept that the loved one's life is over. It satisfies a social value that it is unacceptable to give up and that, yes, we may be able to defeat death. That expectation itself is an exercise in futility. It satisfies the belief that everyone is entitled to the fullest of everything, even if it serves no realistic purpose. It is impossible to predict exactly how much money could be saved or reallocated by forgoing futile care and spending the health dollars on those whose lives can be saved or whose quality of life can be enhanced. Conservative estimates, however, place the dollar amount in the tens of billions.

The withholding of futile treatment is not without controversy, however, as physicians and other health care workers begin asserting their rights not to squander money, resources, or attention in situations deemed to be medically futile by everyone except the family. In a case that is the first of its kind (but definitely not the last), the parents of Brianne Rideout, age three, sued Hershey Medical Center in Hershey, Pennsylvania, for turning off the respirator that was enabling Brianne to breathe, against their wishes.[26] It was unprecedented for a hospital to decide discontinuance on its own, without a Living Will, family consent, or a court order. The hospital defended its actions on the basis that the little girl's condition was hopeless and that further medical treatment would be futile. The parents believed that their Christian faith preserved their hope for a miracle. The case was settled out of court.

The case is indicative of the problems confronting health care providers in an era of shrinking budgets and advancing technologies. Who should make the ultimate decision to stop medical care when there is no chance that the patient will improve? The patient or the family has had that prerogative in the past, but what if the family is behaving unreasonably or irrationally in the eyes of the professional? Traditionally the family prevails—but not necessarily with managed care. The hospital said that concerns over resources or the financial cost of caring for Brianne did not factor into the medical center's decision. The Rideouts' attorney, however, reported that the child's medical records showed notations by a social worker that the Rideouts' insurance was running out.

Several hospitals in California have instituted a new policy that would have been unheard of a decade ago. This new policy allows doctors to deny aggressive medical treatment to patients whose cases they consider hopeless, regardless of the families' wishes. This radical innovation is increasingly being considered around the nation as hospitals struggle with the emotionally and financially charged issue of how to care for people at the end of life.

The word "futile" takes on special meaning for the elderly. For example, a treatment that has one chance in ten of helping a patient might be considered worthwhile for a twenty-five-year-old with two small children, yet futile in an eighty-year-old with heart trouble. Society is facing the tough questions that revolve around the effective—although costly—treatments that might give the elderly some added quality years but at the expense of younger, more vital individuals. Fiscal scrutiny is forcing the United States, as well as other technologically advanced nations, to figure out how much they want to spend on the older population.

"Rationing," "resource allocation," and "prioritizing" all essentially describe the same task—that of making choices between priorities when resources are scarce. The possibilities of medical treatments are exceeding available resources. Rationing is part of our system now, and policy leaders agree that further rationing is inevitable. The way forward is to recognize the need for priorities and to develop a consensus. Medical opinion leaders and policy makers are working on establishing a prioritized health system. Resolving conflicts about health care costs will require connecting value to cost. Eddy believes that these decisions would ideally be made through individual decisions at the marketplace: "This would force each of us to weigh the value of those services (their benefits and harms) against the cost we would have to pay and would ensure that, both for the individual and for society as a whole, the value of health care would be worth its cost."[27]

The only state to focus its attention on virtually every aspect of national health policy—access, cost, effectiveness, rationing, and basic care—is

Oregon. The system goes far beyond a concern for *who* should be covered, determining also the content of medical care and *what services* should be covered. A central feature of the plan, the highly controversial feature and the one involving rationing, was to set priorities for Medicaid health services. Although the result is not perfect by any means, Oregon has nevertheless made major contributions to the national debate on the cost, access, and quality of health care and, in so doing, must be congratulated.

Rationing, under consideration in all aspects of medical care, is demanding tough, heartrending choices, and nowhere more so than in neonatal intensive care units. These cases will continue to be aired in the public, as the right-to-die movement moves slowly to the forefront of public thought. Consider the dilemma: Over the last two decades, neonatologists have made remarkable strides in keeping micropreemies alive. Babies born in the twenty-third to twenty-fourth week of the normal forty-week term of pregnancy are known as micropreemies and are extremely fragile. The typical micropreemie weighs slightly more than a pound and can fit into the palm of a hand. One of the biggest problems with these tiny infants is underdevelopment of the lungs. It is only after twenty-three or twenty-four weeks that the infant's capillaries move close enough to the air sacs to carry gases to and from the lungs.

Doctors can now improve the newborn's ability to breathe by administering synthetic lubricants, called surfactants, to help the lungs expand and take in air. Even though this development has resulted in a huge advance in the care of micropreemies, their chances of survival are slim—and expensive. Fewer than 40 percent of infants born between twenty-three and twenty-five weeks of gestation survive, according to the American College of Obstetrics and Gynecology. And that is strictly survival. That's merely leaving the hospital alive, after three months, *at a cost of hundreds of thousands of dollars.* On top of that, nearly 50 percent of those surviving infants experience moderate to severe disabilities, including cerebral palsy and blindness, which continue until death. Policy makers are seriously considering the economic feasibility of treating these infants from the moment of birth onward. Micropreemies are but one example of the growing gap between what is available and what can be provided, as the expenses mount and mount.

Will the infant be allowed to die without treatment or will coverage finance its struggle to survive and its disabilities throughout life? Maybe not. What?! Not cover a treatment that could have some benefit, just because of the cost?! This is America! It's Heresy!! No, it's not. "It is the connection of value to cost. When value and cost are connected, this is the form the connection takes—a conscious comparison of whether some real value offered by an intervention is worth its costs, and a determination to live with the decision. Isn't that rationing? Yes, it is," says Eddy.[28]

Doesn't that sound like managed care? Managed care rules amount to a rationing system, often making it impossible to get as much treatment—from surgery to physical therapy—high-cost medication, experimental therapies, hospital stays or other services as doctor and patient may desire—all in the guise of cost efficiency. "Our core values are threatened by managed care," declared William Speck, the chief executive of Columbia Presbyterian Hospital in New York, in a June 1995 interview. "No one has dared use the rationing word. But this will drive it. We will see denial of expensive technology for elderly people. You survive in managed care by denying or limiting care. That's how you make money," Speck explained.[29] Again, it is the connection of value to cost.

The growing numbers of elderly, particularly those over eighty, and the concomitant growing numbers of patients with dementia, are forcing other unpleasant choices about the future care of this generation. Should taxpayers be subsidizing the knee operation of an eighty-seven-year-old woman who is one hundred pounds overweight, is in the early stages of dementia, and has high cholesterol and heart disease? A growing population, dwindling health care resources, and intense and widespread fear of dementia have forced the uncomfortable question: Should patients with dementia be slated as off-limits for life-sustaining treatment?

Consider the conflicting viewpoints: Some people say that given limited resources, it makes no sense to invest in extended care for demented patients who are a burden to themselves, their families, and society. Others say that demented patients should be treated like all other patients and that no price can be put on any human life. Daniel Callahan weighs the dilemma and comes out on the side of rationing: "If the former view is too crude and insensitive, the latter is increasingly unrealistic and potentially unjust to other sick people who may be deprived of needed resources due to an imbalance of care given to the demented."[30]

Callahan is opposed to physician-assisted suicide and relies heavily on the sanctity of every life. Nevertheless, to control costs, rationing is "inevitable," he says. He believes that the elderly must be valued, but at the same time resources are limited, and as a nation we will have to set fair and compassionate standards. Medicare should establish some real priority system, he says, setting an annual budget and forcing everybody to live within it.

The United Network for Organ Sharing, the group that formulates national rules for allocating organs, set off a storm of protest at the end of 1996 when it imposed the rationing of organs. It proposed giving preference to acute patients whose livers suddenly failed and who would die within days without a transplant. In setting this priority for organ transplants, chronically ill patients who are also on the verge of death would become second in line behind those who suddenly faced liver failure. The purpose is to provide livers to those who are most likely to survive, rather than to those who have been the sickest the longest.

Health care is already rationed in the United States for both the uninsured and the Medicaid populations. In times of budgetary pressure, a typical response by state government is to reduce Medicaid reimbursement to providers or to drop coverage for a portion of poor people already on the Medicaid rolls, rather than to raise taxes or draw funds from other social programs. Such responses ultimately ration care to anonymous people; government need not confront individuals.[31]

As Doctor Speck said, no one has dared to call managed care "rationed care," but that is what it is. Even with managed care and increased competition, in order to control rising costs due to continuing technological innovations and the aging of the population, further rationing of care will be necessary. And the sooner we get our medical costs under control, before the inevitable time of crisis, the easier it will be on the population.

As the cost of health care soars and the population ages, there are equally unsustainable hardships on the family as on the nation's economy and business community. Many dying people report that their one remaining goal in life is to not be a burden on loved ones, yet 7 million Americans, largely women, take care of an ailing or chronically ill parent or spouse.

Dr. Kenneth E. Covinsky, assistant professor of medicine at Case Western Reserve University Medical Center in Cleveland, worries about the family. "We talk a good deal about the financial costs of dying for hospitals, for government, and for insurance companies. But what about the cost of the families? The cost of serious illness we are not measuring is the cost and the burden of suffering to the patient's family," he cautions.[32]

The lives of loved ones are usually seriously compromised by having to care for the ill. The ramifications are physical, emotional, and financial. The burdens of providing constant care, twenty-four hours a day, seven days a week, are overwhelming. When this kind of caregiving goes on for years, with no life or time for herself, the caregiver becomes exhausted and her health is often destroyed. It can also be emotionally devastating to live with a spouse who is increasingly unresponsive and unreachable. The needs of the caregiver suffer. The needs of other family members go unmet. Social life evaporates. Support systems vanish. It becomes impossible to leave home and see friends, while the caregiver's home ceases to be a welcome place to visit.

The financial burdens can be devastating. While most discussions focus solely on the needs of the patient, to the exclusion of the caregiver's concerns and difficulties, John Hardwig, professor of ethical and social/political philosophy, and medical ethics at East Tennessee State University, points to the caregiver's situation:

We must also acknowledge that the lives of our loved ones can be devastated just by having to pay for health care for us. One part of the recent SUPPORT study documented the financial aspects of caring for a dying member of a family. Only those who had illnesses severe enough to give them less than a 50% chance to live six more months were included in this study. When these patients survived their initial hospitalization and were discharged, about one-third required considerable caregiving from their families; in 20% of cases a family member had to quit work or make some other major lifestyle change; *almost one-third of these families lost all of their savings; and just under 30% lost a major source of income.* If talking about money sounds venal or trivial, remember that much more than money is normally at stake here. When someone has to quit work, she may well lose her career. Savings decimated late in life cannot be recouped in the few remaining years of employability, so the loss compromises the quality of the rest of the caregiver's life. For a young person, the chance to go to college may be lost to the attempt to pay debts due to an illness in the family, and this decisively shapes an entire life.[33]

Long-term medical care can wipe out the savings of the elderly and the children of the elderly in no time at all, causing severe economic hardship to the entire family. The cost of long-term care insurance is prohibitive for most people. The average nursing-home bill nationwide is more than $100 a day, with New York State averaging $130 to $230 a day and a nursing home in Manhattan or on Long Island exceeding $100,000 per year.

Not everyone is willing to burden his or her family with futile treatment. Many patients show enormous compassion for their survivors. When faced with economic hardship, patients and family members often opt against certain kinds of care—the kind of care that costs more money. Professor Covinsky, the lead author of a study on the impact of financial hardship on the decision to forgo life-sustaining treatment, found that the likelihood of seriously ill patients deciding against life-prolonging care was 30 percent greater for those whose illnesses caused them great financial hardship—by depleting their savings, for example, or forcing them to postpone education plans for family members—than for similar patients whose family finances were relatively untouched.[34]

The study found that family members' decisions are related to financial experiences to the same degree that patients' decisions are. In 73 percent of the cases, patients and their relatives or health care proxies chose the same course of treatment. In cases where they disagreed, family finances did not seem to be a factor. Covinsky said:

Some have suggested that in some situations family surrogates (health care proxies) may not always be appropriate decision-makers because of the possibility that the decisions they express for the patient might affect them financially. Our data suggests that economic hardship on the family influences surrogates' expressed preferences to the same degree that it affects patients' expressed preferences. We should probably assume that family members are acting in the best interest of the patient.[35]

Until recently, the notion of forgoing treatment or actively seeking a physician's help in dying, motivated by a duty to die, was rarely considered, and certainly not voiced aloud. The unmentionable is unmistakably on the table for discussion as we approach the end of this century. The normally conservative *Hastings Center Report* asked, in its cover story in the spring of 1997, "Is There A Duty To Die?" Hardwig, the author, answered in the affirmative:

> Many people were outraged when Richard Lamm (the former Governor of Colorado) claimed that old people had a duty to die. As modern medicine continues to save more of us from acute illness, it also delivers more of us over to chronic illnesses, allowing us to survive far longer than we can take care of ourselves. It may be that our technological sophistication coupled with a commitment to our loved ones generates a fairly widespread duty to die.[36]

Hardwig, like a growing number of other people, believes there is a duty to refuse life-sustaining treatment if there is no hope of recovery, and also a duty to complete advance directives requesting others to refuse it for you. However, it is not to this group that the author is writing. He is addressing the person who may want to live, even though debilitated, facing dementia, or undergoing treatment that is futile. It is directed to the patient who has bought "the individual fantasy"; that fantasy that leads one to imagine that lives are separate and unconnected, the fantasy that assumes the ailing patient is the only one affected by his or her health care decision. Most discussions of an illness in the family sound as though responsibility is a one-way street. Not so, writes Hardwig. Illness is a two-way street with obligations and responsibilities going both ways.

Hardwig asks his readers:

> Which is the greater burden? (1) To lose a 50 percent chance of six more months of life at age 87? Or (2) To lose all your savings, your home, and your career at age 55? I cannot imagine it would be morally permissible for me to ruin the rest of my partner's life to sustain mine or to cut off my sons' careers, impoverish them, or compromise the quality of their children's lives simply because I wish to live a little longer. This is what leads me to believe in a duty to die.

A rational argument can be made for allowing PAS in order to offset the amount society and family spend on the ill, *as long as it is the voluntary wish* of the mentally competent terminally and incurable ill adult. There will likely come a time when PAS becomes a commonplace occurrence for individuals who *want* to die and feel is it the right thing to do by their loved ones. There is no contradicting the fact that since the largest medical expenses are incurred in the final days and weeks of life, the hastened demise of people with only a short time left would free resources for others. Hundreds of billions of dollars could benefit those patients who not only *can* be cured but who also *want* to live. What possible sense does it make to use limited resources on people who *cannot* be helped and who *do not want* to be helped, either because they themselves have had "enough" or because they believe it is the morally correct thing to do for their family?

It is this kind of thinking that concerns critics of an assisted death. Opponents of the practice are repelled by the thought of assisted suicide as an answer to shrinking health care resources. Supporters of the practice respond that no one is forcing, coercing, or encouraging anyone to do anything. Assisted death is totally *voluntary*—a matter to be decided with the family and with the patient's conscience. The debate goes round and round, and few, if any, change their minds.

Whether one approves or not, however, American society is inching toward allowing the elderly and infirmed to make choices about curtailing life. Economic necessity is forcing us to evaluate medical services in a cost effective manner. This is not a unique concept. Cross-cultural studies reveal patterns of full support and respect for elders until such time as they become dependent on others for survival and perceived as a burden by society. In the past, Japanese elders, ordinarily highly respected by the community, had an obligation to commit suicide when they became a burden, frequently with the assistance of a relative. It is virtually only in those cultures where the Judeo-Christian sanctity-of-life and redemption-in-suffering arguments predominate that behavior like this is prohibited.

Research shows that in many "primitive" societies, once an elder's life has no further economic value to the community and may indeed be an economic liability, the community hastens death by refusing financial and other support to the dependent elder. Eskimo elders are highly revered and nurtured by the community as long as they can contribute to the general good of the group and add to its resources. Once they are no longer productive, however, they are abandoned by the community or assisted in their death. Necessity, rather than indifference or animosity, motivates this behavior.[37]

Elderly, or otherwise incurably ill people, are often aware of the burdens—financial and otherwise—of their care. The government provides no long-term care, and the elderly are often unable to care for themselves, so they turn to family for assistance—families who cannot afford the cost of medical services or the cost of a full-time caretaker. Life consists of waiting for the end to come. Sociologist Harriet Tillick raises an interesting point:

> Does the society have the right to demand that individuals continue an existence which may be filled with actual physical as well as psychic pain? If the society does have the right, then does it also have the responsibility to provide the economic and health support systems needed to keep the elder alive? If the society is not willing (or able) to pay, are we putting elders at risk of abuse by family members who are burdened with the expense (or actual work) of the elder's care? Also, those most at risk would be low income elders whose families may not have the economic resources to put them in a nursing home, nor the ability to care for them in their own homes.[38]

The American public is uncomfortable talking about the money connection, focusing instead on the right of the patient to a dignified death. Herein lies the unspoken argument for physician aid in dying. The rising cost of health care is a societal reality that has promoted a rush of populist interest in constructing a new culture of dying in the United States, focusing on shortening the dying process for those who want it. It is the unspoken connection of value to cost—for the nation, business, and the family unit. In advocating for an assisted death, one is beginning to hear the argument that says: "Look, let's face facts. The nation's economy is about to break under the growing cost of health care and the situation will get markedly worse as baby boomers become elderly and infirmed patients eating at the subsidized table. Families are suffering. Even if reform takes place, how comprehensive will it be? Politicians know it's a losing issue at the ballot box. If someone wants to bail out a little early, why should we stop them? Let's put our energies toward guidelines that will enable the practice to go as smoothly as possible. We certainly won't encourage people to hasten their death, but why should we stop them? Physician-assisted suicide is a win-win situation." Spend some time on the subject, and this unspoken argument will surface—on an ever more frequent basis. It is a pragmatic argument and one that deserves an answer.

Economic necessity is causing massive changes in the future content of our health care, as well as how and when we die—changes that will continue to drive the right-to-die movement largely because of its appeal to common sense. Forces whose existence were unpredictable when our current system was established have combined to necessitate adapting to new demographics, cultural, and social changes. Economic reality, therefore, is the main answer to the question, Why Now?

C h a p t e r   2 2

The Road Ahead

While not reaching anything near the same state of progress as the Netherlands, for the reasons explained in chapter 10, the United States nevertheless has, in its typically erratic fashion, made huge strides toward achieving the rights of individuals to die in a manner, and at a time, of their choosing. Through a series of court cases, elections, and legislative actions over nearly a quarter of a century, at last a roadway through the gothic barricades of religious and legal conservatism is being chiseled out.

Advance directives such as the Living Will, the Health Care Proxy, and Do-Not-Resuscitate orders are now available to all. Yet it is disappointing that so few people—about 15 percent—have taken the trouble to sign them. Oscar Wilde remarked that the prospect of biography considerably heightened his fear of death, and the same dread seems to apply with today's advance directives stating the terms on which a person would like to die. Doing without these documents in this age of medical supertechnology is the most dangerous form of the denial-of-death syndrome.

The day may be not too distant when government, with its eye on soaring medical costs depleting the gross national income, may make it mandatory for every person over fifty years old to sign an advance directive expressing his or her final medical wishes. Obligatory decision making would at least reduce wasteful expenditures on the medical care of those people who have no wish to continue living.

It has taken Oregon, that lovely wooded state with little more than three million latter-day pioneers, to lay the foundations for the other half of the right-to-choose-to-die issue: PAS. While always supportive of advance medical directives, the Hemlock Society served as the persistent voice in the wilderness of the 1980s, speaking out for those patients for whom the document is pointless simply because there is no "plug" to pull. After three failed initiative elections, the breakthrough on PAS came in 1994 in Oregon. Now doctors can, if they wish, write prescriptions for lethal drugs with which a dying patient may kill her or himself. It took another three years of fighting religious-right opponents in the courts before the law was implemented, but succeed it did, becoming the harbinger of a persistent legislative state in the United States.

Which bold state will be next? Maine, Michigan, Arizona, and California are vying to be the next to follow Oregon's model. Reasonable people might think that decisions about dying would be a nonparty political affair, but that is not so, if the Oregon experience is any guide. The state's voters decided they wanted a PAS law, but opponents persuaded the legislature to get involved. When decisions were made in the two chambers to try and get the law repealed, the vote pitted Republicans against Democrats, and only a couple of standout politicians crossed over. In 1996–97 many legislatures were controlled by Republicans, who have strong allies among the Roman Catholic Church and the Christian right. Republicans generally prefer the status quo, and until there is a swing back to Democratic control in more states, legislative reform for PAS has only a slender chance of succeeding.

In these four states, too, a law for PAS only is being sought; voluntary euthanasia has been quietly dropped. "Prescribing-only" bills are softer options in the political arena than are lethal injections, and we all know how politicians love compromises. But can there truthfully be compromise where such a serious subject as dying is concerned? PAS is fine so far as it goes, enabling those patients who can ingest a huge overdose to have a happy release. But it excludes those patients who literally cannot "lift hand to mouth" (end-stage ALS cases are the prime examples), or for those who have had surgery to remove the swallowing and digestive organs, or for those who cannot keep down liquids and solids. Thus, those who most need assisted death cannot receive it under today's compromise PAS laws.

As a group of six physicians, ethicists, and lawyers wrote in the *New England Journal of Medicine*: "To confine legalized physician-assisted death to assisted suicide unfairly discriminates against patients with unrelievable suffering who resolve to end their lives but are physically unable to do so. The method chosen is less important than the careful assessment that precedes assisted death."[1]

Still far from unresolved in the assisted-death issue is the dilemma of depression. When does sadness about the end, leaving every loved person and everything one has achieved, cross over to become clinical depression? Can mental health experts really tell serious depression from minor? Are we not all entitled to a bit of depression if the outlook is appallingly bleak? This is an area that will challenge the best and the brightest in the mental health professions over coming years.

Also troubling is the matter of whether, when a patient asks for a hastened death, a mental health evaluation should be optional or mandatory. The Oregon law makes it a matter of choice; a proposed law in Michigan would make it absolutely mandatory. Opponents of PAS clamor for mental health testing to be obligatory, showing yet again their taste for a reduction in individual freedoms. It was the hateful Soviet regime in Russia, not so long ago, that used psychiatry as a way of incarcerating its dissidents; and the Nazis who used psychiatrists to judge some people as unworthy of life. How quickly we forget the lessons of modern history when it suits us!

The Oregon law, we think, has it just right. The physician must discuss depression with the patient, and if the possibility of it exists, ask the patient to see a psychiatric worker. If the patient refuses, then the physician can decline to help.

If there is one crucial point to be made about assisted death it is this: Now is the time to investigate, formulate, and legislate—for this is a social issue that is here to stay.

A Twentieth-Century Chronology of Voluntary Euthanasia and Physician-Assisted Suicide

1906 First euthanasia bill drafted in Ohio. It does not succeed.

1935 World's first euthanasia society is founded in London, England.

1938 The Euthanasia Society of America is founded by the Rev. Charles Potter in New York.

1954 Joseph Fletcher publishes *Morals and Medicine*, predicting the coming controversy over the right to die.

1957 Pope Pius XII issues Catholic doctrine distinguishing ordinary from extraordinary means of life-support.

1958 Oxford law professor Glanville Williams publishes *The Sanctity of Life and the Criminal Law*, proposing that voluntary euthanasia be allowed for competent, terminally ill patients.

1958 Lael Wertenbaker publishes *Death of a Man*, describing how she helped her husband commit suicide. It is the first book of its genre.

1967 A right-to-die bill is introduced by Dr. Walter W. Sackett in Florida's legislature. It arouses extensive debate but is unsuccessful.

1968 Doctors at Harvard Medical School propose redefining death to include brain death as well as heart-lung death. Gradually this definition is accepted.

1969 The first Living Will is written by attorney Louis Kutner, and his arguments for it appear in the *Indiana Law Journal*.

1969 Voluntary euthanasia bill introduced in the Idaho legislation. It fails.

1969 Elisabeth Kubler-Ross publishes *On Death and Dying*, opening discussion of the once-taboo subject of death.

1970   The Euthanasia Society (U.S.) finishes distributing 60,000 Living Wills.

1973   American Hospital Association creates Patient Bill of Rights, which includes informed consent and the right to refuse treatment.

1973   Dr. Gertruida Postma, who gave her dying mother a lethal injection, receives light sentence in the Netherlands. The furor launches the euthanasia movement in that country (NVVE).

1974   The Euthanasia Society in New York renamed the Society for the Right to Die. The first American hospice opens in New Haven, Connecticut.

1975   Deeply religious leaders of the Christian ecumenical movement, Henry P. Van Dusen, 77, and his wife, Elizabeth, 80, choose to commit suicide rather than suffer from disabling conditions. Their note reads, "We still feel this is the best way and the right way to go."

1975   Dutch Voluntary Euthanasia Society (NVVE) launches its Members' Aid Service to give advice to the dying. Receives twenty-five requests for aid in the first year.

1976   The New Jersey Supreme Court allows Karen Ann Quinlan's parents to disconnect the respirator that keeps her alive, saying it is affirming the choice Karen herself would have made. *Quinlan* case becomes a legal landmark. But she lives on for another nine years.

1976   California Natural Death Act is passed. The nation's first aid-in-dying statute gives legal standing to Living Wills and protects physicians from being sued for failing to treat incurable illnesses.

1976   Ten more U.S. states pass natural death laws.

1976   First international meeting, in Tokyo, of right-to-die groups. Six organizations are represented.

1978   Doris Portwood publishes the landmark book *Commonsense Suicide: The Final Right*. It argues that old people in poor health might justifiably kill themselves.

1978   *Whose Life Is It Anyway?*, a play about a young artist who becomes quadriplegic, is staged in London and New York City, raising disturbing questions about the right to die. A film version appears in 1982. *Jean's Way* is published in England by Derek Humphry, describing how he helped his terminally ill wife to die.

1979   Artist Jo Roman, dying of cancer, commits suicide at a much-publicized gathering of friends that is later broadcast on public television and reported by *The New York Times*.

1979   Two right-to-die organizations split. The Society for the Right to Die separates from Concern for Dying, a companion group that grew out of the Society's Euthanasia Education Council.

1980   Advice column "Dear Abby" publishes a letter from a reader agonizing over a dying loved one, generating 30,000 advance care directive requests at the Society for the Right to Die.

1980   Pope John Paul II issues *Declaration on Euthanasia*, which opposes mercy killing but permits the greater use of painkillers to ease pain and the right to refuse extraordinary means for sustaining life.

1980   Hemlock Society is founded in Santa Monica, California, by Derek Humphry. It advocates legal change and distributes how-to-die information. This launches the campaign for assisted dying in America. Hemlock's national membership will grow to 50,000 within a decade. Right-to-die societies also formed the same year in Germany and Canada.

1980   World Federation of Right-to-Die Societies is formed in Oxford, England. It comprises twenty-seven groups from eighteen nations.

1981   Hemlock publishes "how-to" suicide guide, *Let Me Die Before I Wake*, the first such book on open sale.

1983   Author Arthur Koestler, terminally ill, commits suicide a year after publishing his reasons. His wife, Cynthia, not terminally ill, chooses to commit suicide with him.

1983   Elizabeth Bouvia, a quadriplegic suffering from cerebral palsy, sues a California hospital to let her die of self-starvation while receiving comfort care. She loses and then files an appeal.

1984   Advance care directives become recognized in twenty-two states and the District of Columbia.

1984   The Netherlands Supreme Court approves voluntary euthanasia under certain conditions.

1985   Karen Ann Quinlan dies.

1985   Betty Rollin publishes *Last Wish*, her account of helping her mother to die after a long losing battle with breast cancer. The book becomes a bestseller.

1986   Roswell Gilbert, 76, sentenced in Florida to twenty-five years without parole for shooting his terminally ill wife. Granted clemency five years later.

1986   Elizabeth Bouvia is granted the right to refuse force feeding by an appeals court. But she declines to take advantage of the permission and is still alive in 1998.

1986   Americans Against Human Suffering is founded in California, launching a campaign for what will become the 1992 California Death With Dignity Act.

1987   The California State Bar Conference passes Resolution #3-4-87 to become the first public body to approve of physician aid in dying.

1988   *Journal of the American Medical Association* prints "It's Over, Debbie," an unsigned article describing a resident doctor giving a lethal injection to a woman dying of ovarian cancer. The public prosecutor makes an intense, unsuccessful effort to identify the physician in the article.

1988   Unitarian Universalist Association of Congregations passes a national resolution favoring aid in dying for the terminally ill, becoming the first religious body to affirm a right to die.

1990   Washington Initiative (119) is filed, the first state voter referendum on the issue of voluntary euthanasia and physician-assisted suicide.

1990   American Medical Association adopts the formal position that with informed consent a physician can withhold or withdraw treatment from a patient who is close to death, and may also discontinue life support of a patient in a permanent coma.

1990   Dr. Jack Kevorkian assists in the death of Janet Adkins, a middle-aged woman with Alzheimer's disease. Kevorkian subsequently defies the Michigan legislature's attempts to stop him from assisting in additional suicides.

1990   Supreme Court decides the *Cruzan* case, its first aid-in-dying ruling. The decision recognizes that competent adults have a constitutionally protected liberty interest that includes a right to refuse medical treatment; the court also allows a state to impose procedural safeguards to protect its interests.

1990   Congress passes the Patient Self-Determination Act, requiring hospitals that receive federal funds to tell patients that they have a right to demand or refuse treatment. It takes effect the next year.

1991   Hemlock of Oregon introduces the Death With Dignity Act into the Oregon legislature, but it fails to get out of committee.

1991   Dr. Timothy Quill writes about "Diane" in the *New England Journal of Medicine*, describing his provision of lethal drugs to a leukemia patient who chose to die at home by her own hand rather than undergo therapy that offered a 25 percent chance of survival.

1991   Nationwide Gallup poll finds that 75 percent of Americans approve of Living Wills.

1991   Derek Humphry publishes *Final Exit*, a "how-to" book on self-deliverance. Within eighteen months the book sells 540,000 copies and tops U.S. bestseller lists. It is translated into twelve other languages. Total sales exceed one million.

1991   Choice in Dying is formed by the merger of two aid-in-dying organizations, Concern for Dying and the Society for the Right to Die. The new organization becomes known for defending patients' rights and promoting Living Wills and will grow in five years to 150,000 members.

1991   Washington State voters reject Ballot Initiative 119, which would have legalized physician-aided suicide and aid in dying. The vote is 54–46 percent.

1992   Americans for Death with Dignity, formerly Americans Against Human Suffering, places the California Death With Dignity Act on the state ballot as Proposition 161.

1992   Health care becomes a major political issue as presidential candidates debate questions of access, rising costs, and the possible need for some form of rationing.

1992   California voters defeat Proposition 161, which would have allowed physicians to hasten death by actively administering or prescribing medications for self-administration by suffering, terminally ill patients. The vote is 54–46 percent.

1993   Advance directive laws are achieved in forty-eight states, with passage imminent in the remaining two.

1993   Compassion in Dying is founded in Washington State to counsel the terminally ill and provide information about how to die without suffering and "with personal assistance, if necessary, to intentionally hasten death." The group sponsors suits challenging state laws against assisted suicide.

1993   President Clinton and Hillary Rodham Clinton publicly support advance directives and sign Living Wills, acting after the death of Hugh Rodham, Hillary's father.

1993   Oregon Right to Die, a political action committee, is founded to write and subsequently to pass the Oregon Death With Dignity Act.

1994   The Death With Dignity National Center is founded in California as a national nonprofit organization that works to promote a comprehensive, humane, responsive system of care for terminally ill patients.

1994   More presidential Living Wills are revealed. After the deaths of former President Richard Nixon and former first lady Jacqueline Kennedy Onassis, it is reported that both had signed advance directives.

1994   The California Bar approves physician-assisted suicide. With an 85 percent majority and no active opposition, the Conference of Delegates says physicians should be allowed to prescribe medication to terminally ill, competent adults for self-administration in order to hasten death.

1994   All states and the District of Columbia now recognize some type of advance directive procedure.

1994   Washington State's anti-suicide law is overturned. In *Compassion v. Washington,* a district court finds that a law outlawing assisted suicide violates the Fourteenth Amendment. Judge Rothstein writes, "The court does not believe that a distinction can be drawn between refusing life-sustaining medical treatment and physician-assisted suicide by an uncoerced, mentally competent, terminally ill adult."

1994   In New York State, the lawsuit *Quill et al.* v. *Koppell* is filed to challenge the New York law prohibiting assisted suicide. Quill loses and files an appeal.

1994   Oregon voters approve Measure 16, a Death With Dignity Act ballot initiative that permits terminally ill patients, under proper safeguards, to obtain a physician's prescription to end life in a humane and dignified manner. The vote is 51–49 percent.

1994   U.S. District Court Judge Hogan issues a temporary restraining order against Oregon's Measure 16, following that with an injunction barring the state from putting the law into effect.

<u>1995</u>   Oregon Death With Dignity Legal Defense and Education Center is founded. Its purpose is to defend Ballot Measure 16, legalizing physician-assisted suicide.

<u>1995</u>   Washington State's *Compassion in Dying* ruling is overturned by the Ninth Circuit Court of Appeals, reinstating the anti-suicide law.

<u>1995</u>   U.S. District Judge Hogan rules that Oregon Measure 16, the Death With Dignity Act, is unconstitutional on the grounds that it violates the Equal Protection clause of the Constitution. His ruling is immediately appealed.

<u>1995</u>   Surveys find that doctors disregard most advance directives. *Journal of the American Medical Association* reports that physicians were unaware of the directives of three-quarters of all elderly patients admitted to a New York hospital; the *California Medical Review* reports that three-quarters of all advance directives were missing from Medicare records in that state.

<u>1995</u>   Oral arguments in the appeal of *Quill* v. *Vacco* contest the legality of New York's anti-suicide law before the Second Circuit Court of Appeals.

<u>1995</u>   *Compassion in Dying* case is reconsidered in Washington State by a Ninth Circuit Court of Appeals panel of eleven judges, the largest panel ever to hear a physician-assisted suicide case.

<u>1996</u>   Northern Territory of Australia passes voluntary euthanasia law. Nine months later the Federal Parliament quashes it.

<u>1996</u>   Ninth Circuit Court of Appeals reverses the *Compassion in Dying* finding in Washington State, holding that "a liberty interest exists in the choice of how and when one dies, and that the provision of the Washington statute banning assisted suicide, as applied to competent, terminally ill adults who wish to hasten their deaths by obtaining medication prescribed by their doctors, violates the Due Process Clause." The ruling affects laws of nine western states. It is stayed pending appeal.

<u>1996</u>   Michigan jury acquits Doctor Kevorkian of violating a state law banning assisted suicides.

<u>1996</u>   Second Circuit Court of Appeals reverses the *Quill* finding, ruling that "The New York statutes criminalizing assisted suicide violate the Equal Protection Clause because, to the extent that they prohibit a physician from prescribing medications to be self-administered by a mentally competent, terminally ill person in the final stages of his terminal illness, they are not rationally related to any legitimate state interest." The ruling affects laws in New York, Vermont and Connecticut. (On 17 April the court stays enforcement of its ruling for thirty days pending an appeal to the U.S. Supreme Court.)

<u>1996</u>   U.S. Supreme Court announces that it will review both cases sponsored by Compassion in Dying, known now as *Washington* v. *Glucksberg* and *Quill* v. *Vacco*.

<u>1997</u>   On 8 January the U.S. Supreme Court hears oral arguments for the New York and Washington cases on physician-assisted dying. The cases were heard in tandem but not combined.

1997   ACLU attorney Robert Rivas files an amended complaint challenging the 128-year-old Florida law banning assisted suicide. Charles E. Hall, who has AIDS, asks court permission for a doctor to assist his suicide. The court refuses.

1997   On 13 May the Oregon House of Representatives votes 32–26 to return Measure 16 to the voters in November for repeal (H.B. 2954). On 10 June the Senate votes 20–10 to pass H.B. 2954 and return Measure 16 to the voters for repeal. No such attempt to overturn the will of the voters has been tried in Oregon since 1908.

1997   On 26 June the U.S. Supreme Court reverses the decisions of the Ninth and Second Circuit Court of Appeals in *Washington* v. *Glucksberg* and *Quill* v. *Vacco*, upholding as constitutional state statutes which bar assisted suicide. However, the court also validated the concept of "double effect," openly acknowledging that death hastened by increased palliative measures does not constitute prohibited conduct so long as the intent is the relief of pain and suffering. The majority opinion ended with the pronouncement that "Throughout the nation, Americans are engaged in an earnest and profound debate about the morality, legality and practicality of physician-assisted suicide. Our holding permits this debate to continue, as it should in a democratic society."

1997   Dutch Voluntary Euthanasia Society (NVVE) reports its membership now more than 90,000, of whom 900 have made requests for help in dying to its Members' Aid Service.

1997   Britain's Parliament rejects by 234 votes to 89 the seventh attempt in sixty years to change the law on assisted suicide, despite polls showing 82 percent of British people want reform.

1997   On 4 November the people of Oregon vote by a margin of 60–40 percent *against* Measure 51, which would have repealed the Oregon Death With Dignity Act, 1994. The law officially takes effect (ORS 127.800-897) on 27 October 1997 when court challenges have been disposed of.

1998   Doctor Kevorkian assists the suicide of his ninetieth patient in eight years. His home state, Michigan, passes new law making such actions a crime but it will not take effect until 1999.

1998   Oregon Health Services Commission decides that payment for physician-assisted suicide can come from state funds under the Oregon Health Plan so that the poor will not be discriminated against.

1998   First two people die by making use of the Oregon Death With Dignity Act, receiving physician-assisted suicide. March: In the first six months of the law, forty other applicants are refused as unqualified or die inside the waiting period.

Source: Euthanasia Research & Guidance Organization (ERGO!)
<Ergo@efn.org>
April 1998

A p p e n d i x   B

Laws on Physician-Assisted Suicide in the United States

One state, Oregon, permits physician-assisted suicide.

Three states have abolished the common law of crimes and do not have statutes criminalizing assisted suicide: North Carolina, Utah, and Wyoming.

In Ohio, the state supreme court ruled in October 1996 that assisted suicide is not a crime.

In Virginia, there is no clear case law on assisted suicide, nor is there a statute criminalizing the act, although there is a statute (1997) that imposes civil sanctions on persons assisting in a suicide.

Nine states criminalize assisted suicide through common law: Alabama, Idaho, Maryland, Massachusetts, Michigan, Nevada, South Carolina, Vermont, and West Virginia.

Thirty-five states have statutes explicitly criminalizing assisted suicide: Alaska, Arizona, Arkansas, California, Colorado, Connecticut, Delaware, Florida, Georgia, Hawaii, Illinois, Indiana, Iowa, Kansas, Kentucky, Louisiana, Maine, Minnesota, Mississippi, Missouri, Montana, Nebraska, New Hampshire, New Jersey, New Mexico, New York, North Dakota, Oklahoma, Pennsylvania, Rhode Island, South Dakota, Tennessee, Texas, Washington, and Wisconsin.

Source: National Conference on State Legislatures, November 1997.

The Oregon Death With Dignity Act

(ORS 127.800-897. Implementation: 27 October 1997)

SECTION I

General Provisions

1.01 Definitions. The following words and phrases, whenever used in this Act, shall have the following meanings:

(1) "Adult" means an individual who is 18 years of age or older.

(2) "Attending physician" means the physician who has primary responsibility for the care of the patient and treatment of the patient's disease.

(3) "Consulting physician" means the physician who is qualified by specialty or experience to make a professional diagnosis and prognosis regarding the patient's disease.

(4) "Counseling" means a consultation between a state licensed psychiatrist or psychologist and a patient for the purpose of determining whether the patient is suffering from a psychiatric or psychological disorder, or depression causing impaired judgment.

(5) "Health care provider" means a person licensed, certified, or otherwise authorized or permitted by the law of this State to administer health care in the ordinary course of business or practice of a profession, and includes a health care facility.

(6) "Incapable" means that in the opinion of a court or in the opinion of the patient's attending physician or consulting physician, a patient lacks the ability to make and communicate health care decisions to health care providers, including

communication through persons familiar with the patient's manner of communicating if those persons are available. "Capable" means not incapable.

(7) "Informed decision" means a decision by a qualified patient, to request and obtain a prescription to end his or her life in a humane and dignified manner, that is based on an appreciation of the relevant facts and after being fully informed by the attending physician of:

(a) his or her medical diagnosis;

(b) his or her prognosis;

(c) the potential risks associated with taking the medication to be prescribed;

(d) the probable result of taking the medication to be prescribed;

(e) the feasible alternatives, including, but not limited to, comfort care, hospice care and pain control.

(8) "Medically confirmed" means the medical opinion of the attending physician has been confirmed by a consulting physician who has examined the patient and the patient's relevant medical records.

(9) "Patient" means a person who is under the care of a physician.

(10) "Physician" means a doctor of medicine or osteopathy licensed to practice medicine by the Board of Medical Examiners for the State of Oregon.

(11) "Qualified patient" means a capable adult who is a resident of Oregon and has satisfied the requirements of this Act in order to obtain a prescription for medication to end his or her life in a humane and dignified manner.

(12) "Terminal disease" means an incurable and irreversible disease that has been medically confirmed and will, within reasonable medical judgment, produce death within six (6) months.

SECTION 2

Written Request for Medication to End One's Life in a Humane and Dignified Manner

2.01 WHO MAY INITIATE A WRITTEN REQUEST FOR MEDICATION
An adult who is capable, is a resident of Oregon, and has been determined by the attending physician and consulting physician to be suffering from a terminal disease, and who has voluntarily expressed his or her wish to die, may make a written request for medication for the purpose of ending his or her life in a humane and dignified manner in accordance with this Act.

2.02 FORM OF THE WRITTEN REQUEST
(1) A valid request for medication under this Act shall be in substantially the form described in Section 6 of this Act, signed and dated by the patient and witnessed by at least two individuals who, in the presence of the patient, attest that to the best of their knowledge and belief the patient is capable, acting voluntarily, and is not being coerced to sign the request.

(2) One of the witnesses shall be a person who is not:

(a) A relative of the patient by blood, marriage or adoption;

(b) A person who at the time the request is signed would be entitled to any portion of the estate of the qualified patient upon death under any will or by operation of law; or

(c) An owner, operator or employee of a health care facility where the qualified patient is receiving medical treatment or is a resident.

(3) The patient's attending physician at the time the request is signed shall not be a witness.

(4) If the patient is a patient in a long term care facility at the time the written request is made, one of the witnesses shall be an individual designated by the facility and having the qualifications specified by the Department of Human Resources by rule.

SECTION 3

Safeguards

3.01 ATTENDING PHYSICIAN RESPONSIBILITIES
The attending physician shall:

(1) Make the initial determination of whether a patient has a terminal disease, is capable, and has made the request voluntarily;

(2) Inform the patient of:

(a) his or her medical diagnosis;

(b) his or her prognosis;

(c) the potential risks associated with taking the medication to be prescribed;

(d) the probable result of taking the medication to be prescribed;

(e) the feasible alternatives, including, but not limited to, comfort care, hospice care and pain control.

(3) Refer the patient to a consulting physician for medical confirmation of the diagnosis, and for determination that the patient is capable and acting voluntarily;

(4) Refer the patient for counseling if appropriate pursuant to Section 3.03;

(5) Request that the patient notify next of kin;

(6) Inform the patient that he or she has an opportunity to rescind the request at any time and in any manner, and offer the patient an opportunity to rescind at the end of the 15 day waiting period pursuant to Section 3.06;

(7) Verify, immediately prior to writing the prescription for medication under this Act, that the patient is making an informed decision;

(8) Fulfill the medical record documentation requirements of Section 3.09;

(9) Ensure that all appropriate steps are carried out in accordance with this Act

prior to writing a prescription for medication to enable a qualified patient to end his or her life in a humane and dignified manner.

3.02 CONSULTING PHYSICIAN CONFIRMATION
Before a patient is qualified under this Act, a consulting physician shall examine the patient and his or her relevant medical records and confirm, in writing, the attending physician's diagnosis that the patient is suffering from a terminal disease, and verify that the patient is capable, is acting voluntarily and has made an informed decision.

3.03 COUNSELING REFERRAL
If in the opinion of the attending physician or the consulting physician a patient may be suffering from a psychiatric or psychological disorder, or depression causing impaired judgment, either physician shall refer the patient for counseling. No medication to end a patient's life in a humane and dignified manner shall be prescribed until the person performing the counseling determines that the person is not suffering from a psychiatric or psychological disorder, or depression causing impaired judgment.

3.04 INFORMED DECISION
No person shall receive a prescription for medication to end his or her life in a humane and dignified manner unless he or she has made an informed decision as defined in Section 1.01(7). Immediately prior to writing a prescription for medication under this Act, the attending physician shall verify that the patient is making an informed decision.

3.05 FAMILY NOTIFICATION
The attending physician shall ask the patient to notify next of kin of his or her request for medication pursuant to this Act. A patient who declines or is unable to notify next of kin shall not have his or her request denied for that reason.

3.06 WRITTEN AND ORAL REQUESTS
In order to receive a prescription for medication to end his or her life in a humane and dignified manner, a qualified patient shall have made an oral request and a written request, and reiterate the oral request to his or her attending physician no less than fifteen (15) days after making the initial oral request. At the time the qualified patient makes his or her second oral request, the attending physician shall offer the patient an opportunity to rescind the request.

3.07 RIGHT TO RESCIND REQUEST
A patient may rescind his or her request at any time and in any manner without regard to his or her mental state. No prescription for medication under this Act may be written without the attending physician offering the qualified patient an opportunity to rescind the request.

3.08 WAITING PERIODS

No less than fifteen (15) days shall elapse between the patient's initial and oral request and the writing of a prescription under this Act. No less than 48 hours shall elapse between the patient's written request and the writing of a prescription under this Act.

3.09 MEDICAL RECORD DOCUMENTATION REQUIREMENTS

The following shall be documented or filed in the patient's medical record:

(1) All oral requests by a patient for medication to end his or her life in a humane and dignified manner;

(2) All written requests by a patient for medication to end his or her life in a humane and dignified manner;

(3) The attending physician's diagnosis and prognosis, determination that the patient is capable, acting voluntarily and has made an informed decision;

(4) The consulting physician's diagnosis and prognosis, and verification that the patient is capable, acting voluntarily and has made an informed decision;

(5) A report of the outcome and determinations made during counseling, if performed;

(6) The attending physician's offer to the patient to rescind his or her request at the time of the patient's second oral request pursuant to Section 3.06; and

(7) A note by the attending physician indicating that all requirements under this Act have been met and indicating the steps taken to carry out the request, including a notation of the medication prescribed.

3.10 RESIDENCY REQUIREMENTS

Only requests made by Oregon residents, under this Act, shall be granted.

3.11 REPORTING REQUIREMENTS

(1) The Health Division shall annually review a sample of records maintained pursuant to this Act.

(2) The Health Division shall make rules to facilitate the collection of information regarding compliance with this Act. The information collected shall not be a public record and may not be made available for inspection by the public.

(3) The Health Division shall generate and make available to the public an annual statistical report of information collected under Section 3.11(2) of this Act.

3.12 EFFECT ON CONSTRUCTION OF WILLS, CONTRACTS AND STATUTES

(1) No provision in a contract, will or other agreement, whether written or oral, to the extent the provision would affect whether a person may make or rescind a request for medication to end his or her life in a humane and dignified manner, shall be valid.

(2) No obligation owing under any currently existing contract shall be conditioned or affected by the making or rescinding of a request, by a person, for medication to end his or her life in a humane and dignified manner.

3.13 INSURANCE OR ANNUITY POLICIES

The sale, procurement, or issuance of any life, health, or accident insurance or annuity policy or the rate charged for any policy shall not be conditioned upon or affected by the making or rescinding of a request, by a person, for medication to end his or her life in a humane and dignified manner. Neither shall a qualified patient's act of ingesting medication to end his or her life in a humane and dignified manner have an effect upon a life, health, or accident insurance or annuity policy.

3.14 CONSTRUCTION OF ACT

Nothing in this Act shall be construed to authorize a physician or any other person to end a patient's life by lethal injection, mercy killing or active euthanasia. Actions taken in accordance with this Act shall not, for any purpose, constitute suicide, assisted suicide, mercy killing or homicide, under the law.

SECTION 4

Immunities and Liabilities

4.01 IMMUNITIES

Except as provided in Section 4.02:

(1) No person shall be subject to civil or criminal liability or professional disciplinary action for participating in good faith compliance with this Act. This includes being present when a qualified patient takes the prescribed medication to end his or her life in a humane and dignified manner.

(2) No professional organization or association, or health care provider, may subject a person to censure, discipline, suspension, loss of license, loss of privileges, loss of membership or other penalty for participating or refusing to participate in good faith compliance with this Act.

(3) No request by a patient for or provision by an attending physician of medication in good faith compliance with the provisions of this Act shall constitute neglect for any purpose of law or provide the sole basis for the appointment of a guardian or conservator.

(4) No health care provider shall be under any duty, whether by contract, by statute or by any other legal requirement to participate in the provision to a qualified patient of medication to end his or her life in a humane and dignified manner. If a health care provider is unable or unwilling to carry out a patient's health care provider shall transfer, upon request, a copy of the patient's relevant medical records to the new health care provider.

4.02 LIABILITIES

(1) A person who without authorization of the patient willfully alters or forges a request for medication or conceals or destroys a rescission of that request with the intent or effect of causing the patient's death shall be guilty of a Class A felony.

(2) A person who coerces or exerts undue influence on a patient to request medication for the purpose of ending the patient's life, or to destroy a rescission of such a request, shall be guilty of a Class A felony.

(3) Nothing in this Act limits further liability for civil damages resulting from other negligent conduct or intentional misconduct by any persons.

(4) The penalties in this Act do not preclude criminal penalties applicable under other law for conduct which is inconsistent with the provisions of this Act.

SECTION 5

Severability

5.01 SEVERABILITY

Any section of this Act being held invalid as to any person or circumstance shall not affect the application of any other section of this Act which can be given full effect without the invalid section or application.

SECTION 6

Form of the Request

6.01 FORM OF THE REQUEST

A request for a medication as authorized by this Act shall be in substantially the following form:

Request for Medication to End My Life in a Humane and Dignified Manner

I, _____, am an adult of sound mind.

I am suffering from _____, which my attending physician has determined is a terminal disease and which has been medically confirmed by a consulting physician.

I have been fully informed of my diagnosis, prognosis, the nature of medication to be prescribed and potential associated risks, the expected result, and the feasible alternatives, including comfort care, hospice care and pain control.

I request that my attending physician prescribe medication that will end my life in a humane and dignified manner.

Initial One:

_____ I have informed my family of my decision and taken their opinion into consideration.

_____ I have decided not to inform my family of my decision.

_____ I have no family to inform of my decision.

I understand that I have the right to rescind this request at any time.

I understand the full import of this request and I expect to die when I take the medication to be prescribed.

I make this request voluntarily and without reservation, and I accept full moral responsibility for my actions.

Signed: _____

Dated: _____

Declaration of Witnesses

We declare that the person signing this request:

(a) Is personally known to us or has provided proof of identity;

(b) Signed this request in our presence;

(c) Appears to be of sound mind and not under duress, fraud or undue influence;

(d) Is not a patient for whom either of us is attending physician.

_____ Witness 1/

Date

_____ Witness 2/

Date

Note: One witness shall not be a relative (by blood, marriage or adoption) of the person signing this request, shall not be entitled to any portion of the person's estate upon death and shall not own, operate or be employed at a health care facility where the person is a patient or resident. If the patient is an inpatient at a health care facility, one of the witnesses shall be an individual designated by the facility.

_____ ORS 127.800-897 implemented as from 27 October 1997.

Notes

INTRODUCTION

1. Harris Poll, 69 percent (August 1997); Field Poll of California, 70 percent (March 1997); Gallup Poll, 75 percent (April 1996).

1: MEDICAL TECHNOLOGY'S ONSLAUGHT

1. James M. Hoefler, *Deathright* (San Francisco: Westview Press, 1994), p. xiii.

2. Ibid., p. 230.

3. Paul Wilkes, "Is There a Right to Die? *Times and Post Intelligencer*, 24 Nov. 1996.

4. Claire Martin, "Choosing Life or Death," *Denver Post*, 18 Feb. 1997.

5. Henry R. Glick, *The Right to Die*, (New York: Columbia University Press, 1992), p. 14.

6. Daniel Callahan, "Ethics and the Medical Ambivalence Towards Death," *Humane Medicine* 10, no. 3 (July 1994), p. 177.

7. Glick, *The Right to Die*, p. 13.

8. Robert J. Samuelson, *The Good Life and Its Discontents* (New York: Times Books, 1995), p. 32.

9. Hoefler, *Deathright*, p. 33.

10. David J. Rothman, *Strangers at the Bedside* (New York: Basic Books, 1991), p. 51.

11. Ibid., pp. 53–54.

12. Stanley J. Reiser, "The Birth of Bioethics," Special Supplement, *Hastings Center Report* 23, no. 6 (1993).

13. Ibid.

14. Sherwin B. Nuland, *How We Die* (New York: Alfred A. Knopf, Inc., 1994), p. 254.

15. Joseph Fennelly, "The Gift of Karen Ann Quinlan: The Healing of the Art," *Quinlan: A Twenty Year Retrospective*, Princeton, N.J., 12–13 Apr. 1996.

16. Callahan, "Ethics and the Medical Ambivalence Towards Death."

17. George Soros, "Reflections on Dying" Alexander Ming Fisher Lecture Series at Columbia Presbyterian Medical Center, 30 November 1994.

18. Hoefler, *Deathright*, p. 19.

19. Ibid., p. 236 (no. 20).

20. *In re Jobes*, 108 N.J. 394, 529 A.2d 434 (1987).

21. Hoefler, *Deathright*, p. 19.

22. *Quill v. Vacco*, 80 F. 3d 716 (2d Cir. 1996).

23. Callahan, "Ethics and the Medical Ambivalence Towards Death," p. 183.

2: THE RIGHTS CULTURE'S IMPACT

1. Paul Berman, *A Tale of Two Utopias* (New York: W. W. Norton & Company, 1996), p. 21.

2. Ibid., p. 22.

3. Ibid., pp. 186–87.

4. Ibid., p. 51.

5. Ibid., p. 123.

6. Hoefler, *Deathright*, p. 29.

7. Ibid., p. 95.

8. Arthur S. Berger, *Dying and Death in Law and Medicine* (Westport, Conn.: Praeger Publishers, 1993), p. 84.

9. *Union Pacific Railroad Co. v. Botsford*, 141 U.S. 250 (1891).

10. *Schloendorff v. Society of New York Hospital*, 105 N.E. 92 (N.Y. 1914).

11. *Planned Parenthood of Southeastern Pennsylvania v. Casey*, 505 U.S. 833 (1992).

12. Henry K. Beecher, "Ethics and Clinical Research," *New England Journal of Medicine* 274 (1966): pp. 1354–60.

13. Glick, *The Right to Die*, p. 76.

14. Louis Kutner, *Indiana Law Review* (Summer 1969).

15. Ibid.

16. George J. Annas, *The Rights of Patients* (Carbondale: Southern Illinois University Press, 1989), p. 259.

17. Ibid., p. 240.

18. Rothman, *Strangers at the Bedside*, p. 245.

19. *Bouvia v. Superior Court*, 179 Cal. App. 3rd 1127, 225 Cal. Rptr. 297 (Ct. App. Dist., Div. 2), rev. den. 5 June 1986.

20. Kirk Cheyfitz, "Medicine Fails the Dying," *Detroit Free Press*, 20 June 1996.

21. Burt Herman, "Authorities Ignore," *The Oregonian*, 17 Oct. 1997.

22. "Dr. Kevorkian Says His Trial Is a Lynching," *New York Times*, 7 May 1996.

23. Ibid.

3: THE DECLINE OF THE DOCTOR-PATIENT RELATIONSHIP

1. Robert J. Samuelson, *The Good Life and Its Discontents* (New York: Times Books, 1995), p. 51.

2. Edwin Chen, "Distress Over Health System Seen Growing," *Los Angeles Times*, 24 Jan. 1997.

3. Ibid.

4. Associated Press, *The Register Guard*, 23 April 1998.

5. Rothman, *Strangers at the Bedside*, pp. 129–30.

6. Leslie Papp, "Don't Go to Hospital Alone, MD Warns," *Toronto Star*, 26 Jan. 1997.

7. Rothman, *Strangers at the Bedside*, p. 79.

8. Henry K. Beecher, "Ethics And Clinical Research," *NEJM* 274 (1966): 1354–60.

9. Rothman, *Strangers at the Bedside*, p. 64.

10. Hearing on Human Experimentation, 23 Feb. 1973, pp. 378–79.

11. Arnold Relman, "The *Saikewicz* Decision: Judges as Physicians," *NEJM* 298 (1978):508–9.

12. Paul Ramsey, *The Patient as Person* (New Haven, Conn.:1970).

13. Rothman, *Strangers at the Bedside*, p. 12.

14. Ibid., p. 108.

15. "Informed Consent Rule Draws Differing Reactions," Reuters, 23 Dec. 1996.

16. Lauren Neergaard, "Experiments on the Dying," Associated Press, 23 December 1996.

17. David J. Rothman, Book Review of *The Ethics of Research Involving Human Subjects: Facing the 21st Century*, *NEJM* 336, no. 12 (Mar. 20, 1997).

18. Jack Kevorkian, "Perspective on Medical Ethics; At Least My Patients Gave Consent," *Los Angeles Times*, 12 Feb. 1997.

19. George J. Annas, "Law, Medicine and Ethics: 20 Years After *Quinlan*," *Quinlan: A Twenty Year Retrospective*, Princeton, N.J. 12–13 April 1996.

20. Christine Gorman, "Doctors Dilemma," *Time*, Aug. 25, 1997.

21. Jerome P. Kassirer and Marcia Angell, editorial, "The High Price of Endorsement," *NEJM* 337, no. 10 (4 Sept. 1997).

22. Bernard Lo, "End-of-Life Care After Termination of SUPPORT," Special Supplement, *Hastings Center Report* 25, no. 6 (1995): S6–S8.

23. Marcia Angell, "The Supreme Court And Physician-Assisted Suicide," Editorial, *NEJM* 336, no. 1 (2 Jan. 1997).

24. Stephen Jamison, "Final Acts of Love: Families, Friends, and Assisted Dying," *Noetic Sciences Review* (Summer 1996), p. 16.

25. Hoefler, *Deathright*, p. 67.

4: POOR END-OF-LIFE CARE

1. Ira Byock, "Dying: After the Court Ruling," *Wall Street Journal*, 27 June 1997.

2. Christine K. Cassel, "Overview on Attitudes of Physicians Toward Caring for the Dying Patient," *ABIM End-of-Life Patient Care Project*, Distributed at the Conference on Care Near the End-of-Life, June 1995, Harvard Medical School, Division of Continuing Medical Education, Boston, Mass., pp. 1–6.

3. Cindy Schreuder and Ronald Kotulak, "The Quality of Death," *Chicago Tribune*, 29 June 1997.

4. Mark O' Keefe, "A New Way of Dying," *Oregonian*, 28 Sept. 1997.

5. Shannon Brownlee and Joannie M. Schrof, "The Quality of Mercy," *U.S. News & World Report*, 17 Mar. 1997, pp. 54–67.

6. Wesley J. Smith, *Forced Exit: The Slippery Slope from Assisted Suicide to Legalized Murder* (New York: Times Books, 1997).

7. B. Schoenberg and A. C. Carr, "Educating the Health Professional in the Psycho-Social Care of the Terminally Ill," *Psycho-Social Aspects of Terminal Care.* (New York, N.Y.: Columbia University Press, 1972).

8. Kathleen M. Foley, "Competent Care for the Dying Instead of Physician-Assisted Suicide," *NEJM* 336, no. 1 (2 Jan. 1997).

9. *Cancer Pain Relief and Palliative Care*, Report of a WHO Expert Committee (Technical Report Series 804, World Health Organization, Geneva, 1990).

10. Ibid.

11. Richard L. Worsnop, "Oregon Residents to Vote Again on 'Right to Die' Law," *San Diego Union-Tribune*, 22 Sept. 1997.

12. Ezekiel J. Emanuel, "The Painful Truth About Euthanasia," *Wall Street Journal*, 7 Jan. 1997.

13. Paul J. Van Der Maas, Johannes J. M. Van Delden, Loes Looman Pij-nennborg, "Euthanasia and Other Medical Decisions Concerning the End of Life," *Lancet* 338 (14 Sept. 1991).

14. Marcia Angell, "The Supreme Court and Physician-Assisted Suicide," *NEJM* 336, no. 1, 2 Jan. 1997.

15. George J. Annas, "How We Lie," Special Supplement, *Hastings Center Report* 25, no. 6 (1995): S12–S14.

16. Cassel, "Overview on Attitudes of Physicians Towards Caring for the Dying Patient."

17. C. S. Cleeland, R. Gonin, A. K. Hatfield, et al, "Pain and Its Treatment in Patients with Metastatic Cancer," *New England Journal of Medicine*, 1994; 330:592–6.

18. W. Breitbart, B. D. Rosenfeld, S. D. Passik, M. V. McDonald, H. Thaler, Portenoy, "The Undertreatment of Pain in Ambulatory AIDS Patients," *Pain,* 1996; 65:243–9.

19. The SUPPORT Principal Investigators, "A Controlled Trial to Improve Care for Seriously Ill Hospitalized Patients," *Journal of the American Medical Associations*, 1995; 274:1591–8.

20. C. Seale, A. Cartwright, *The Year Before Death*, (Hants, England: Avebury, 1994).

21. Tracy L. Pipp, "Conquering Pain," *Detroit News*, 1 August 1997.

22. "Committee on End-of-Life Care Calls for Narcotics Reform," Reuters, 5 June 1997.

23. M. D. Steinberg, M. F. Morrison, E. M. Rothchild, S/D/ Block, E/H. Cassem, M. D. Sulliven, S. Younger, "The Role of the Psychiatrist in End-Of-Life Treatment Decisions," Subcommittee on Psychiatric Aspects of Life-Sustaining Technology, American Psychiatric Association, 1995.

24. E. S. Shneidman, "Nation Survey of Attitudes Toward Death," *Death and Dying*, edited by R. Freelton, E. Markessen, G. Owen, T. J. Schecher (Reading, Mass.: Heldson Wesley Publishing Co., 1978), 23.

25. Carol M. Ostrom, "How Doctors Learn How to Handle Death," *Seattle Times*, 19 May 1997.

26. M. Z. Solomon, "Seizing the Moment: How Academic Health Centers Can Improve End of Life Care," *Academic Health Centers in the Managed Care Environment*, (edited by D. Korn, C. J. McLaughlin, and M. Osterrweis (Washington D.C.: Association of Academic Health Centers, 1995).

27. Ibid.

28. George Soros, "Reflections on Dying," Alexander Ming Fisher Lecture Series at Columbia Presbyterian Medical Center, 30 Nov. 1994.

29. Brownlee and Schrof, "The Quality of Mercy."

30. Susan Hattis Rolef, "Ending the Pain," *Jerusalem Post*, 9 Dec. 1996.

31. Andrew A. Skolnick, "End of Life Care Movement Growing," *JAMA* 278 (1997), 967–69.

32. Andi Rierden, "A Doctor's Look at Life and Death," *New York Times*, 16 Nov. 1997.

33. C. Richard Chapman and Jonathan Gavrin, "Suffering and the Dying Patient," *Drug Use in Assisted Suicide and Euthanasia*, edited by Margaret P. Battin and Arthur G. Lipman (New York: Pharmaceutical Products Press, an imprint of Haworth Press, Inc., 1996), pp. 67–90.

34. Thomas Maier, "Dr. Death Legacy: New Drug Laws, Suicide Issue Spurs Ways to Manage," *Newsday*, 15 June 1997.

35. Christine Gorman, "Medicine: The Case for Morphine," *Time*, 28 Apr. 1997, p. 64.

36. "Committee on End-of-Life Care Calls for Narcotics Reform," Reuters, 5 June 1997.

37. Brownlee and Schrof, "The Quality of Mercy."

38. CBS *60 Minutes*, 8 Dec. 1996.

39. Ibid.

40. "Florida Doctor Is Charged with Murder," *New York Times*, 5 Dec. 1996.

41. "Dr. Pinzon Acquitted in Florida," *Hemlock's TimeLines*, July, Aug., Sept. 1997.

42. Robert A. Burt, "The Supreme Court Speaks–Not Assisted Suicide but a Constitutional Right to Palliative Care," *NEJM* 337, no. 1 (23 Oct. 1997).

43. Tracy L. Pipp, "Conquering Pain," *Detroit News*, 1 Aug. 1997.

44. Ambrose Evans-Pritchard, "California Goes to Pot While Washington's Drug Cops Fume," *Telegraph* (United Kingdom), 22 Dec. 1996.

45. Daniel Q. Haney, "Medical Journal Backs Marijuana," Associated Press, 29 Jan. 1997.

46. Warren E. Leary, "U.S. Panel Urges Study of Medical Marijuana," *New York Times*, 21 Feb. 1997.

47. Jerome P. Kassirer, "Federal Foolishness and Marijuana," *NEJM* 336, no. 5 (Jan. 20, 1997).

48. Editorial, "Reefer Madness," *Boston Globe*, 7 Jan. 1997.

49. Christopher Wren, "Doctors Criticize Move by Clinton," *New York Times*, 31 Dec. 1996.

50. "Federal Plan Gives Patients Marijuana," *Oregonian*, 1 Dec. 1996.

51. Brownlee and Schrof, "The Quality of Mercy."

52. O'Keefe, "A New Way of Dying."

53. Editorial, "Life's Final Days Get Better," *Oregonian*, 8 June 1995.

54. O'Keefe, "A New Way of Dying."

55. Ibid.

5: THE IMPACT OF AIDS

1. Jeremy A. Sitcoff, "Death With Dignity: AIDS & A Call for Legislation," *John Marshall Law Review* 29, no. 3, (Spring 1996), pp. 677–710.

2. Russel Ogden, *Euthanasia, Assisted Suicide & AIDS* (New Westminster, B. C., Canada: Peroglyphics Publishing, 1994), p. 57.

3. Van der Maas et al., "Euthanasia and Other Medical Decisions Concerning the End of Life," *Lancet* 338 (1991) p. 669.

4. Jody B. Gable, "Release from Terminal Suffering? The Impact of AIDS on Medically Assisted Suicide Legislation," *Florida State University Law Review* 22, no. 2 (Fall 1994).

5. Ogden, *Euthanasia, Assisted Suicide & AIDS*, p. 102.

6. F. Larue, A. Fontaine, S. M. Collaau, "Underestimation and Undertreatment of Pain in HIV Disease: Multicentre Study," *British Medical Journal* 314, no. 7073 (4 Jan. 1997).

7. Steven D. Passik, Margaret V. McDonald, Barry D. Rosenfeld, William S. Breitbart, "End of Life Issues in Patients with AIDS: Clinical and Research Considerations," *Drug Use in Assisted Suicide and Euthanasia*, ed. Margaret P. Battin and Arthur G. Lipman (Pharmaceutical Products Press, an imprint of Haworth Press, Inc., 1996), pp. 91–111.

8. Daniel Golden, "A Time to Die," *Boston Globe*, 7 Oct. 1990.

9. Ogden *Euthanasia, Assisted Suicide & AIDS*. p. 61.

10. Ibid., p. 58.

11. Peter M. Marzuk, "Increased Risk of Suicide in Persons with AIDS," *JAMA* 259 (1988), p. 1333.

12. James L. Werth, *Rational Suicide?* (Washington, D.C.: Taylor & Francis, 1996).

13. Ibid.

14. Ibid.

15. Gina Kolata, "AIDS Patients Turning More Often to Suicide," *New Orleans Times-Picayune*, 14 June 1994.

16. Ibid.

17. Nina Clark, *The Politics of Physician-Assisted Suicide* (New York: Garland Publishing, 1997), pp. 83–84.

6: AT LAST, NEW RIGHTS FOR PATIENTS

1. Arthur S. Berger, *Dying and Death in Law & Medicine* (Westport, Conn.: Praeger Press, 1993), pp. 45–46.

2. *In re Quinlan*, 137 NJ Super. 227, 348 A.2d 801 (Ch. Div. 1975), *rev'd*, 70 NJ 10, 355 A.2d 647, *cert. denied*, 429 U.S. 922 (1976).

3. M. L. Tina Stevens, "What Quinlan Can Tell Kevorkian About the Right to Die," *The Humanist*, 13 March 1997.

4. *Cruzan v. Director, Missouri Dept. of Health*, 497 U.S. 261 (1990).

5. Joseph and Julia Quinlan with Phyllis Battelle, *Karen Ann: The Quinlans Tell Their Story*, (Garden City, N.Y.: Doubleday & Co., Inc. 1977).

6. Ronald E. Cranford, "Termination of Treatment in the Persistent Vegetative State," *Seminars in Neurology* 4:1 (March 1984), pp. 36–44.

7. Ronald E. Cranford, "The Persistent Vegetative State: The Medical Reality (Getting the Facts Straight)," *Hastings Center Report*, Feb./Mar. 1988.

8. Ibid.

9. Richard A. McCormick, " 'Moral Considerations' Ill Considered," *America*, 14 Mar. 1992, p. 211.

10. Quinlan, In re, supra.

11. Norman L. Cantor, "Sanctity of Life and Dignity in Dying," *Quinlan: A Twenty Year Retrospective*, Princeton, New Jersey, April 12–13, 1996.

12. Glick, *The Right To Die*, p. 61.

13. Ibid., p. 159.

14. Ibid., p. 159.

15. Rothman, *Strangers at the Bedside*, pp. 1–2.

16. Ibid., p. 238.

17. Hoefler, *Deathright*, p. 91.

18. Paul W. Armstrong, Introduction, *Quinlan: A Twenty Year Retrospective*, Princeton, N.J. 12–13 April 1996.

7: THE BIRTH OF THE HEMLOCK SOCIETY

1. Derek Humphry, *Jean's Way* (London: Quartet Books, 1978), chap. 6.
2. Derek Humphry, "The Right to Die with Dignity", London *Evening Standard*, 24 Apr. 1978.
3. Jeffrey J. Kamakahi, Ph.D., and Elaine Fox, Ph.D., "Who's Fighting to Die, A Look at Hemlock Society Membership," *Timelines*, July 1996.
4. Meg Cox, "Suicide Manual for Terminally Ill Stirs Heated Debate", *Wall Street Journal*, "Marketplace," 12 July 1991.

8: STEP FORWARD, STEP BACKWARD

1. *Cruzan v. Director, Missouri Dept. of Health*, 497 U.S. 261 (1990).
2. William Colby, "Christmas, 1990," *Quinlan: A Twenty Year Retrospective*, Princeton, New Jersey, April 12–13, 1996.
3. Ibid.
4. "Deaths Elsewhere," *Detroit Free Press*, August 21, 1996.
5. Paul W. Armstrong, "Of Counsel" *Quinlan: A Twenty Year Retrospective*, Princeton, New Jersey, April, 12–13, 1996.
6. George J. Annas, "At Law: Nancy Cruzan In China," *Hastings Center Report*, Sept./Oct., 1990, pp. 39–41.
7. Richard A. Knox, "Patients' Last Wishes Found Often Overlooked," *Boston Globe*, 17 April 1998.
8. Diane M. Gianelli, "Karen Ann Quinlan's Family Remembers," *Quinlan: A Twenty Year Retrospective"* Princeton, N.J., April 12–13, 1996.

9: A TALE OF TWO DOCTORS

1. Derek Humphry, "Dr. Kevorkian's Assisted Suicide Tactics Could Derail Law Reform," *Hemlock Quarterly* 47 (Apr. 1992).
2. Speech to the National Press Club, 27 Oct. 1992.
3. "Polls Show Growing Support for Kevorkian, Euthanasia," Eugene, *Register-Guard*, 6 Dec. 1997.
4. Jack Kevorkian, "A Comprehensive Bioethical Code for Medical Exploitation of Humans Facing Imminent and Unavoidable Death," *Med. Law* (1986), pp. 181–97.
5. "Death by Appointment Only," *Healthcare Weekly Review* 3, no. 23 (24 Aug. 1987).
6. Jack Lessenbury, "Death and the Matron", *Esquire*, Apr. 1997.
7. "Prosecutor Will Try to Ban 'Suicide Machine,'" *Detroit News*, 6 June 1990.
8. Ibid.
9. Michael Betzold, *Appointment with Doctor Death* (Momentum Books, Troy, Mich., 1993), p. 52.

10. Ibid. p. 63.

11. Ibid.

12. Speech to the National Press Club, 27 Oct. 1992.

13. "Four People Kevorkian Helped Weren't Sick," *Beacon Journal*, (Akron, Ohio), 19 Oct. 1997.

14. Speech to the National Press Club, 29 July 1996.

15. Ibid.

16. Speech to the National Press Club, 27 Oct. 1992.

17. George Kovanis, "Kevorkian Enables People to Take Command," *Detroit Free Press*, 4 Mar. 1997.

18. "Authorities Ignore Kevorkian's Aid in Suicides," Associated Press report in *The Oregonian*, 17 Oct. 1997.

19. Ibid.

20. *New England Journal of Medicine*, 7 Mar. 1991.

21. Ibid.

22. Ibid.

23. Ibid.

24. Ibid.

25. *New York Times*, 22 July 1991.

26. Ibid. 27 Sept. 1993.

27. Ibid.

26. *Newsday*, 11 Aug. 1991.

27. *New England Journal of Medicine*, 5 Nov. 1992.

28. Ibid.

29. *New York Times*, 29 Aug. 1996.

30. Ibid.

31. Ibid.

32. Ibid.

10: THE DUTCH EXPERIMENT

1. *Journal of the American Medical Association* 272, no. 4 (25 Jan. 1995), p. 323.

2. *New England Journal of Medicine*, 335 (1996), pp. 1706–11.

3. Ibid.

4. Gerrit van der Wal et al., "Evaluation of the Notification Procedure for Physician-assisted Suicide Death in the Netherlands," *New England Journal of Medicine*, 335 (1996), pp. 1706–11.

5. "Life-terminating Acts Without Explicit Request of Patient," *Lancet* 341 (1993), pp. 1196–99.

6. *New England Journal of Medicine* 335 (1996), pp. 1699–705.

7. Ibid.

8. *The Right to Die*, "Euthanasia in the Netherlands," p. 177.

9. *Lawful Exit*, by Derek Humphry, p. 47.

10. "Assisted Suicide Among Psychiatric Patients in the Netherlands," by

J. F. M. Kerkhof, *Journal of Crisis Intervention and Suicide Prevention*, 15, no. 2. (1994).

11. "*State* v. *Chabot,* A Euthanasia Case from the Netherlands," *Ohio Northern University Law Review* 20, no. 3 (1994).

12. Ibid.

13. Letter in *Newsletter of the American Society of Law, Medicine and Ethics,* 11 (Fall 1994).

14. "Killing the Psychic Pain," *Time,* 4 July 1994, p. 61.

15. "Dutch Psychiatrists OK Suicide," Associated Press report, 19 June 1997.

11: THE WORLD'S PROBLEM

1. Prof. Meinrad Schar, "*Assisted Suicide in Switzerland: When Is It Permitted?*" Unpublished essay, 1996.

2. Speech by Prof. Shinichi Fujita to the Ninth International Conference of the World Federation of Right to Die Societies, Kyoto, Oct. 1992.

3. Former Judge Narita's Speech to the world conference is reprinted in "*Participants' Lectures,*" published in English as a booklet by the Japan Society for Dying with Dignity, 1993.

4. Dr. Helga Kuhse, "*Morality, Public Policy and Medically Assisted Dying for Now-Competent Patients,*" delivered to the Australian Medical Association Forum, Canberra, 11 Aug. 1996.

6. Ibid.

7. *The Age,* Melbourne, 22 Feb. 1997.

8. ABC News, 16 Dec. 1996.

9. Ibid.

10. *Hansard,* 9 Sept. 1996.

11. *The Age,* 10 Dec. 1996.

12. ABC News, 16 Dec. 1996.

13. *Medical Journal of Australia* (1997), pp. 166–91.

14. ABC News, 14 Feb. 1997.

15. Ibid.

16. E-mail to Derek Humphry, 23 Nov. 1997.

12: RELIGION RESISTS CHANGE

1. Hoefler, *Deathright.*

2. John E. Nowak, Ronald D. Rotunda, Nelson J. Young, *Constitutional Law* (St. Paul, Minn.: West Publishing Co., 1986), p. 1032.

3. Berger, *Dying and Death in Law and Medicine,* p. 80.

4. Nowak, et al, *Constitutional Law,* p. 1032.

5. Pope John Paul II, *Evangelium Vitae on the Value and Inviolability of Human Life,* Rome, 25 March 1995, p. 51.

6. *The Vatican's Declaration on Euthanasia,* Rome, 5 March 1980.

7. Immanuel Jacobovits, *Jewish Medical Ethics* (New York: Block 1959), pp. 123–4.

8. Pope Paul II, *Evangelium Vitae*, p. 37.

9. Andy Carvin, "Words to Live By, Words to Die By: Rhetorical Discourse and the Euthanasia Debate," Graduate School Northwestern University, 1 June 1994, p. 5 (obtained on Internet).

10. Pope Paul II, *Evangelium Vitae*, p. 42.

11. Peter Singer, *Rethinking Life and Death* (New York: St. Martin's Press, 1994), p. 197.

12. Ronald B. Miller, "Assisted Suicide and Euthanasia: Arguments For and Against Practice, Legalization and Participation," in *Drug Use in Assisted Suicide and Euthanasia*, (edited by Margaret P. Battin and Arthur G. Lipman, Pharmaceutical Products Press, an imprint of Haworth Press, Inc. 1996), pp. 11–41.

13. *The Vatican's Declaration on Euthanasia*

14. Thomas B. Koetting, "When Do You Say Enough is Enough?" *Wichita Eagle*, 2 March 1997.

15. "Some Catholics in Nebraska Face Excommunication Order," *New York Times*, 17 May 1997.

16. Vincent Stuart, "Blessed Relief," *Newsday*, 21 Feb. 1997.

17. Pope John Paul II, *Evangelium Vitae*, p. 51.

18. Alan Meisel, *The Right To Die* (New York: John Wiley & Sons, Inc., 1989), pp. 80–81.

19. Barbara J. McGuire, Commentary #1, Case #6, "Assisted Suicide and Euthanasia: Cases and Commentaries," edited by Sharon M. Valente and Judith M. Saunders in *Drug Use in Assisted Suicide and Euthanasia* (ed: Margaret P. Battin and Arthur G. Lipman) (New York: Pharmeceutical Products Press, an imprint of the Haworth Press, Inc., 1996), p. 344.

20. Peter Singer, *Rethinking Life and Death* (New York: St. Martin's Press, 1994), p. 221.

21. Thomas A. Preston, "Killing Pain, Ending Life," *New York Times*, 1 Nov. 1994.

22. Ibid.

23. Rabbi Immanuel Jakobovits, *Jewish Medical Ethics: A Comparative and Historical Study of the Jewish Religious Attitudes to Medicine and Its Practice* (New York: Philosophical Library, 1959), p. 345.

24. Ellen Debenport, "What Does God Say to the Dying About Prolonging Life?" *St. Petersburg Times,* 10 Feb. 1997.

25. Peter Steinfels, "Briefs," *New York Times*, 20 May 1996.

26. Ibid.

27. Gerald Larue, *Playing God: Fifty Religious Views on Your Right to Die*, (Wakefield, Rhode Island: Moyer Bell, 1996), p. 8.

28. Ibid., p. 7.

29. Henry Weinstein and Larry Stammer, "High Court Test of Assisted Suicide Ruling Sought," *Los Angeles Times*, 26 March 1996.

30. David Crumm, "Catholics, Muslims Unite in Court to Fight Suicide," *Detroit Free Press*, 12 Nov. 1996.

31. Peter Steinfels, "U.S. Catholic Bishops Open Drive on Doctor-Assisted Suicide," *New York Times*, 21 March 1996.

32. Frank Bruni, "Cardinal's Easter Joy is Tempered by Court Rulings on Assisted Suicide," *New York Times*, 8 April 1996.

33. Jacob Heilbrunn, "Neocon v. Theocon," *New Republic*, 30 Dec. 1996.

34. Ibid.

35. Ibid.

36. Richard L. Berke, "Taped Speech Discloses Robertson's Political Goals," *New York Times*, 18 Sept. 1997.

13: MEDICAL HIERARCHY OPPOSES REFORM

1. *Hemlock News of Washington State*, April 1992.

2. Hoefler, *Deathright*, p. 108.

3. Arnold Relman, "The Saikewicz Decision: Judges as Physicians," *New England Journal of Medicine* 298 (1978), pp. 508–9.

4. American Medical Association and Council of Education and Judicial Affairs, Withholding or Withdrawing Life Prolonging Medical Treatment (Dearborn, Michigan: American Medical Association, 1986).

5. Ruth L. Fischbach, Conference on "Care Near the End of Life," sponsored by the Harvard Medical School, Division of Medical Ethics, June 1995.

6. Christine Mitchell, Conference on "Care Near the End of Life," sponsored by the Harvard Medical School, Division of Medical Ethics, June 1995.

7. Anthony L. Back et al., "Physician-Assisted Suicide and Euthanasia in Washington State," *Journal of the American Medical Association*, 1996, 275:918–925.

8. Diane M. Gianelli, "Euthanasia Groups Wooing Doctors," *American Medical News*, 14 Feb. 1994.

9. Diane M. Gianelli, "Doctors Get No Clear Legal Message in Suicide Ruling," *American Medical News*, 23 May 1994.

10. Oz Hopkins Koglin, "Oregon Doctors Agree to Disagree on Measure 16," *Oregonian*, 30 October 1994.

11. C. T. Revere, "State Medical Society Stays Neutral on Assisted Suicide," *Ann Arbor News*, 9 May 1994.

12. Koglin, "Oregon Doctors Agree to Disagree on Measure 16."

13. Diane M. Gianelli, "AMA Steps Up Efforts Against Assisted Suicide," *American Medical News*, 4 May 1996.

14. Amicus Brief of the American Medical Association, the American Nurses Association, and the American Psychiatric Association, et al., in support of petitioners, 12 Nov. 1996.

15. Amicus Brief of the American Medical Student Association and a Coalition of Distinguished Medical Professionals, in support of respondents, 10 Dec. 1996.

16. Ibid.

17. Lori Montgomery, "Medical Student Group Backs Assisted Suicide," *Detroit Free Press*, 11 Dec. 1996.

18. Brenda C. Coleman, "Doctors Discuss Suicide Policy," *Seattle Post Intelligencer*, 24 June 1996.

19. Ibid.

20. Ibid.

21. George M. Burnell, *Final Choices* (New York: Plenum Press, 1993), p. 80.

22. A. Buchman et al., "Attitudes of Michigan Physicians and the Public Towards Legalizing Physician-Assisted Suicide and Voluntary Euthanasia," 334 *New England Journal of Medicine* 3303–3309 (1996).

23. A. Lee et al., "Legalizing Assisted Suicide—Views of Physicians in Oregon," 335 *New England Journal of Medicine* 310–315 (1996).

24. B. T. Scott, "Physicians' Attitude Survey: Doctors and Dying: Is Euthanasia Becoming Accepted?" *Medical Opinion* 3 (1974): 31–34.

25. "NTN Communications Survey Shows 78 Percent Believe That Assisted Suicide Should Be Legalized By the Federal Government," Business Wire, 20 Jan. 1997.

26. Charles Laurence, "An Appointment With Dr. Death," *Daily Telegraph* (U.K.), 22 April 1997.

27. Lee et al., "Legalizing Assisted Suicide—Views of Physicians in Oregon."

28. "Doctors Split Over Legalizing Assisted Suicide," *Reuters News Report*, 13 July 1994.

29. Ibid.

30. Sheri Fink, "Half of U.S. Neurologists Support Assisted Suicide for the Terminally Ill," *Oregonian*, 29 April 1998.

31. Back et al., "Physician-Assisted Suicide and Euthanasia in Washington State: Patient Requests and Physician Responses," *Journal of the American Medical Association* 27, (1996), pp. 918–25.

32. Doukas et al., "Attitudes and Behaviors on Physician-Assisted Death: A Study of Michigan Oncologists," *Journal of Clinical Oncologists* 13, no. 5 (1995), pp. 1055–61.

33. Elisabeth Rosenthal, "Doctors Face Tough Decisions on Assisted Suicide," *New York Times*, 13 Mar. 1997.

34. Daniel Q. Haney, "More Doctors Willing to Help AIDS Patients Die," *Detroit Free Press*, 11 July 1996.

35. Editorial, "Competent Care for the Dying Instead of Physician-Assisted Suicide," 336 *New England Journal of Medicine*, no. 1, 2 Jan. 1997.

36. Statement Issued by the American Association of Critical Care Nurses, 22 May 1996.

37. Jonathan D. Moreno, *Arguing Euthanasia: The Controversy over Mercy Killing, Assisted Suicide, and the Right to Die*, (New York: Simon & Schuster, 1995) p. 14.

38. Derek Humphry, *Let Me Die Before I Wake* (Los Angeles: Hemlock Society, 1982), p. 25.

39. Mary Chris Jaklevic, "The Hidden Debate: Providers Fear Impact of Regulations on Assisted Suicide," *Modern Healthcare*, 17 Feb. 1997.

40. American Medical Association, 17 Jan. 1997.

41. Lori Montgomery, "Care Providers Discuss Assisted Suicide Guidelines," *Long Beach Press-Telegram*, 26 Sept. 1996.

42. Ibid.

43. *Oxford English Dictionary*, 2nd ed., S.V. "hero."

44. Editorial, *British Medical Journal*, 8 June 1996.

14: PRESIDENT AND GOVERNMENT RESIST REFORM

1. Joan Biskupic, "Administration Opposes Physician-Assisted Suicide," *Washington Post*, 13 Nov. 1996.

2. Ibid.

3. Ibid.

4. Jim Abram, "House Bars Assisted Suicide Funding," Associated Press, 10 April 1997.

5. Ibid.

6. William J. Clinton, "Clinton Statement on Assisted Suicide," The White House, 30 Apr. 1997.

7. William J. Clinton, "Statement by the President on Court Decision on Physician-Assisted Suicide," The White House, 27 June 1997.

8. *Coalition for Economic Equity* v. *Wilson*, 110 F.3d 1431 (1996).

9. Tony Mauro, "Judges Taking Heat for Overturning Initiatives," *USA Today*, 12 May 1997.

10. Michelle Rushlo, "Pols Nix Arizona Marijuana Referendum," Associated Press, 15 April 1997.

11. Ibid.

12. "Oregon Beats Political Machine," *Long Beach Press-Telegram*, 10 Dec. 1997.

13. Diane M. Gianelli, "Oregon Assisted-Suicide Vote Still Raising Questions, Obstacles," *American Medical News*, 24 Nov. 1997.

15: THE WEST COAST RESORTS TO THE POLLS

1. *The Oregonian*, 6 Nov. 1997.

2. *Register-Guard*, Eugene, 5 Nov. 1997.

3. Ibid.

4. Ibid.

5. *The Oregonian*, 8 Nov. 1997.

6. *Register-Guard*, Eugene, 9 Nov. 1997.

7. *Register-Guard*, Eugene, 6 Nov. 1997.

8. *The Oregonian*, 5 Nov. 1997.

9. "The Humane and Dignified Death Act," *Hemlock Quarterly* 22 (Jan. 1986).

10. Derek Humphry, *Lawful Exit* (Junction City, Ore.: Norris Lane Press, 1993), p. 56.

11. *Final Exit* (New York: Dell) p. 199.

12. *Lawful Exit*, pp. 107–8.

13. Ibid.

16: OREGON BREAKS THROUGH

1. "The Roper Poll of the West Coast, 1991," Hemlock Society pamphlet, 1991.

2. "What's in a Word?" Roper Poll, ERGO! pamphlet, 1993.

3. *American Medical News*, 8 Nov. 1993.

4. *The Oregonian*, 11 Oct. 1994.

5. *Sunday Oregonian*, 30 Oct. 1994.

6. *American Medical News*, 25 Apr. 1994.

7. *The Oregonian*, 11 Nov. 1994.

8. *American Medical News*, 7 Nov. 1994.

9. *Register-Guard*, Eugene, 11 Oct. 1994.

17: OREGON GIVES A SECOND MANDATE

1. Derek Humphry attended the meetings of all committees, plus the House and the Senate, during April, May, and June 1997. This and other following quotes are from his notebook.

2. "Legalizing Assisted Suicide—View of Physicians in Oregon," NEJM, 1 Feb. 1996 (275–12. 310).

3. *The Oregonian*, 3 Oct. 1997.

4. Russell Sadler, *Register-Guard*, Eugene, 2 Nov. 1997.

5. *The Oregonian*, 28 Apr. 1997.

6. Ibid.

7. Linda Ganzini, M.D., et al., "Attitudes of Oregon Psychiatrists Towards PAS," *American Psychiatry Journal* 153, no. 11 Nov. 1996, pp. 1469–75.

8. "A Survey of Voters in Oregon on Issues Related to Measure 16," Feb. 1997, GLS Research, Santa Monica, Calif.

9. *Sunday Oregonian*, 11 Sept. 1997.

10. Ibid.

11. *Wall Street Journal*, 4 Nov. 1997.

12. *Register-Guard*, Eugene, 8 Oct. 1997.

13. *The Oregonian*, 15 Oct. 1997.

14. *Register-Guard*, Eugene, 16 Oct. 1997.

15. Center for Responsive Politics, *New York Times News Service*, 28 Nov. 1997.

16. *Register-Guard*, Eugene, 26 Oct. 1997.

17. *The Oregonian*, 16 Nov. 1997.

18. *Register-Guard*, Eugene, 19 Nov. 1997.

19. *Washington Post*, 15 Nov. 1997.

20. *The Oregonian*, 9 Nov. 1997.

21. Ibid.

22. *The Oregonian*, 6 Nov. 1997.

23. *Life at Risk* 7, no. 9 (Nov. 1997).

18: HOW THE OREGON LAW WORKS

1. Oregon Death with Dignity Act, ballot measure 16. Nov. 8, 1994, general election.

2. Steve Woodward, "The Suicide Equation," *Oregonian*, 7 Dec. 1997.

3. "Advocates Say Assisted Suicide Requests Number at Least 42," Associated Press, 24 April 1998.

4. "Third Person Uses Assisted Suicide Law, Newspaper Says," Associated Press, 9 May 1998.

5. Roth, Meisel, and Lidz, "Tests of Competency to Consent to Treatment" *134 Am.J. Psychiatry* 279 (1977).

6. Alan Meisel, *The Right to Die* (New York: John Wiley, 1989), p. 183.

7. B. R. Furrow. S. H. Johnson, T. S. Jost, R. L. Schwartz, *Health Law* (St. Paul, Minn: West Publishing, 1991), p. 1104.

8. *Satz v. Perlmutter*, 362 So. 2d 160 (Fla. Dist. Ct. App. 1978), aff'd, 379 So. 2d 359.

9. Meisel, op. cit., pp. 192–3.

10. *In re Ingram*, 102 Wash. 2d 827, 689 P.2d 1363 (1984).

11. Ann Alpers, and Bernard Lo, "Physician-Assisted Suicide in Oregon: A Bold Experiment," *Journal of the American Medical Association*, 274, 9 Aug. 1995, No. 6, pp. 483–87.

12. President's Commission for the Study of Ethical Problems in Medicine and Biomedical and Behavioral Research, *Deciding to Forgo Life-Sustaining Treatment* (1983), p. 47.

13. Alpers, and Lo, "Physician-Assisted Suicide in Oregon," pp. 485–7.

14. Ibid, p. 485.

15. "The Death with Dignity Act Finally Reaches Implementation," *The Oregon Report*, published by the Oregon Death with Dignity Legal Defense and Education Center, Volume IV, Number 1, Winter/Spring, 1998. For further information, write Compassion in Dying Federation of America at 6312 Southwest Capitol Highway, Suite 415, Portland, Oregon 97201. The Internet address is: http://www.compassionindying.org

16. Steve Woodward, "Oregon Will Cover Assisted Suicide," *Oregonian*, 27 Feb. 1998.

19: ON THE WAY TO THE SUPREME COURT

1. Washington Rev. Code, RCW 9A36.060 (1) (1994).

2. *Compassion in Dying Newsletter*, Winter, 1998.

3. *Washington* v. *Glucksberg*, 117 S. Ct. 2258 (1997).

4. *Planned Parenthood* v. *Casey*, 505 U.S. 833 (1992).

5. *Compassion in Dying* v. *Washington*, 850 F. Supp. 1454 (1994).

6. Ibid.

7. *Compassion in Dying Newsletter* 4, p. 1.

8. *Compassion in Dying* v. *Washington*, 79 F.3d 790 (9th Cir. 1996).

9. Id.

10. Id.

11. Id.

12. Id.

13. Lori Montgomery, "Death's Other Image," *Detroit Free Press*, 16 Dec. 1996.

14. *Quill* v. *Koppell*, 870 F. Supp. 78 (S.D.N.Y. 1994).

15. *Quill* v. *Vacco*, 80 F.3d 716 (2d Cir. 1996).

16. Id.

17. Id.

18. Id.

19. Frank Bruni, "Court Overturns Ban in New York on Aided Suicides," *New York Times*, 3 April 1996.

20. "Leave It to the States," *The Economist*, 12 Oct. 1996, p. 19.

21. Ibid.

22. Linda Greenhouse, "An Issue for a Reluctant High Court," *New York Times*, 6 Oct. 1996.

23. Amicus Brief of the Catholic Medical Association, in support of petitioners, 12 Nov. 1996.

24. Amicus Brief of the Evangelical Lutheran Church in America in support of petitioners, 12 Nov. 1996.

25. Amicus Brief for the Institute for Public Affairs of the Union of Orthodox Jewish Congregations of America ("UOJCA") and the Rabbinical Council of America, in support of petitioners, 12 Nov. 1996.

26. Amicus Brief of 36 Religious Organizations, Leaders and Scholars, in support of respondents, 10 Dec. 1996.

27. Amicus Brief of the American Medical Association, et al., in support of petitioners, 12 Nov. 1996.

28. Amicus Brief of the American Association of Homes and Services for the Aging, et al., in support of petitioners, 12 Nov. 1996.

29. Amicus Brief of the American Medical Students Association and a Coalition of Distinguished Medical Professionals, in support of respondents, 10 Dec. 1996.

30. Ibid.

31. Amicus Brief for the National Hospice Organization, in support of petitioners, 12 Nov. 1996.

32. Amicus Brief of the Coalition of Hospice Professionals, for affirmance of the judgments below, 10 Dec. 1996.

33. Amicus Brief of Senate Judiciary Committee Chairman Sen. Orrin G. Hatch (R., Utah); House Judiciary Committee Chairman Rep. Henry J. Hyde (R., Ill.); and Chairman of the House Judiciary Subcommittee on the Constitution Charles T. Canady (R. Fla.) in support of petitioners, 12 Nov. 1996.

34. Amicus Brief of Legislators, in support of respondents, 10 Dec. 1996.

35. Amicus Brief of Surviving Family Members in Support of PAS, in support of respondents, 9 Dec. 1996.

36. Petitioners' Brief of Vacco and Pataki and of State of Washington.

37. Amicus Brief for Ronald Dworkin, et al., in support of respondents, 10 Dec. 1996.

38. Amicus Brief of the ACLU et al., supporting respondents, 10 Dec. 1996.

39. Tim O'Brien, "High Court T.V.," *New York Times*, 6 Jan. 1997.

40. *Compassion in Dying Newsletter*, Winter 1997.

41. Ibid.

42. *Washington* v. *Glucksberg*, 117 S.Ct. 2258 (1997).

43. *Quill* v. *Vacco*, 117 S.Ct. 2293 (1997).

44. David J. Garrow, "Nine Justices & A Funeral," *George*, June 1997, pp. 56–63.

45. Ibid.

46. Linda Greenhouse, "High Court Hears 2 Cases Involving Assisted Suicide," *New York Times*, 9 Jan. 1997.

47. Richard Carelli, "Supreme Court Keeps Secrets Well," Associated Press, 10 Jan. 1997.

48. Joan Biskupic, "In Supreme Court's Deadline Season, Tensions Rise and Some Votes Shift," *Washington Post*, 9 June 1997.

49. Ibid.

20: THE SUPREME COURT LEAVES
THE DOOR OPEN

1. *Washington* v. *Glucksberg*, 117 S.Ct. 2258 (1997). *Quill* v. *Vacco*, 117 S.Ct. 2293 (1997).

2. Id.

3. Id.

4. *Cruzan* v. *Director, Missouri Dept. of Health*, 497 U.S. 261 (1990).

5. *Quill*, supra.

6. Id.

7. Robert Marquand, "Reinhardt versus Rehnquist: A War Between Two Courts," *Christian Science Monitor*, 6 Mar. 1997.

8. Ibid.

9. Ibid.

10. *Quill*, supra.

11. Id.

12. Reply Brief for Petitioners (quoting P. Rousseau, "Terminal Sedation in the Care of Dying Patients," 156 *Archives Internal Medicine* 1785, (1996)).

13. Ronald Dworkin, "Assisted Suicide: What The Court Really Said," *New York Review of Books*, 25 Sept. 1997.

14. Gina Kolata, "When Morphine Fails to Kill," *New York Times*, 23 July 1997.

15. Linda Greenhouse, "No Help for Dying," *New York Times*, 27 June 1997.

16. David Van Biema, "Death's Door Left Ajar," *Time*, 7 July 1997, p. 30.

17. Robert Marquand, "Ruling Banning Assisted Suicide Will Slow, But Not End Right to Die Trend," *Christian Science Monitor*, 27 June 1997.

18. *Quill*, supra.

19. Id.

20. David J. Garrow, "Letting the Public Debate About Assisted Suicide," *New York Times*, 29 June 1997.

21. *Glucksberg*, supra.

22. Id.

23. Dworkin, "Assisted Suicide."

24. Van Biema, "Death's Door Left Ajar," p. 30.

25. *Quill*, supra.

26. *Glucksberg*, supra.

27. PBS *NewsHour* interview by Margaret Warner of Stuart Taylor, 26 June 1997.

28. Jeffrey Rosen, "Nine Votes for Judicial Restraint," op-ed article in *New York Times*, 29 June 1997.

29. *Glucksberg*, supra.

30. Id.

31. Michael W. McConnell, "Supreme Humility," *Wall Street Journal*, 2 July 1997.

32. David G. Savage, "Hight Court Refuses To Grant Constitutional 'Right To Die,'" *Los Angeles Times*, 27 June 1997.

33. Ibid.

34. Terence Monmaney, "Suicide Issue Now in Court of Public Opinion," *Los Angeles Times,* 27 June 1997.

35. Joan Biskupic, "Unanimous Decision Points to Tradition of Valuing Life," *Washington Post*, 27 June 1997.

36. Van Biema, "Death's Door Left Ajar."

37. Robert M. Calica, "Assisted-Suicide Edict Denies Us a Right," *Newsday*, 30 June 1997.

38. Kim Murphy and Maria La Ganga, "Terminally Ill Are Determined to Make Their Own Judgments," *Los Angeles Times*, 27 June 1997.

39. Ibid.

40. Ibid.

41. Calica, "Assisted-Suicide Edict Denies Us a Right."

42. Amy Goldstein, "High Court's Decision on Suicide Leaves Doctors in a Gray Zone," *Washington Post*, 27 June 1997.

43. Editorial, *New York Times*, 28 June 1997.

44. Garrow, "Nine Justices & A Funeral," pp. 57–63.

21: THE UNSPOKEN ARGUMENT

1. E. J. Emanuel and L. L. Emanuel, "The Economics of Dying," *New England Journal of Medicine* 330: 24 Feb. 1994, pp. 540–544.

2. Robert F. Weir, *Abating Treatment with Critically Ill Patients* (New York: Oxford University Press, 1989), pp. 21–22.

3. Eric Lindblom, "Where There's a Living Will," *Washington Monthly*, Nov. 1995, p. 11.

4. Urie Bronfenbrenner, Peter McClelland, Elaine Wethington, Phyllis Moen, and Stephen Ceci, with Helene Hembrooke, Pamela Morris, and Tara White, *The State of Americans*, (New York: Free Press, 1996), pp. 211–16.

5. Mireya Navarro, "Florida Is Cutting-Edge Lab for Big Generational Shifts," *New York Times*, 7 Aug. 1996.

6. Ibid.

7. Bronfenbrenner, *The State of Americans*, p. 58.

8. Ibid., p. 221.

9. Nicholas D. Kristof, "Aging World, New Wrinkles," *New York Times*, 22 Sept. 1996.

10. Hoefler, *Deathright*, p. 60.

11. Susan Gilbert, "Study Shows Many Prefer Not to Live in Nursing Homes," *New York Times*, 6 Aug. 1997.

12. Peter G. Peterson, "Will America Grow Up Before It Grows Old?" *The Atlantic Monthly*, May 1996, pp. 57–58.

13. Larry R. Churchill, "Market Meditopia: A Glance at American Health Care in 2005," *Hastings Center Report* 27, no. 1 (1997), pp. 5–6.

14. Peterson, "Will America Up Before It Grows Old?"

15. P. A. Singer and F. H. Lowy, "Rationing, Patient Preferences and Cost of Care at the End of Life," *Arch Intern Med*, 152 (1992), pp. 478–80.

16. Emanuel and Emanuel, "The Economics of Dying," p. 542.

17. George Anders, *Health Against Wealth: HMOs and the Breakdown of Medical Trust* (New York: Houghton-Mifflin, 1996).

18. Ibid., p. 25.

19. Ibid., p. 61.

20. Jerome Kassirer, "Managed Care and the Morality of the Marketplace," *New England Journal of Medicine*, 6 July 1995.

21. Lauren Neergaard, "Hospitals Reusing Surgical Gear," Associated Press, 11 Jan. 1997.

22. Steven Findlay, "U.S. Hospitals Attracting Patients from Abroad," *USA Today*, 22 July 1997.

23. Ibid.

24. D. M. Eddy, "Three Battles To Watch in the 1990s," *Journal of the American Medical Association* 270 (1993), pp. 520–526.

25. Lawrence J. Schneiderman and Nancy S. Jecker, *Wrong Medicine*, (Baltimore: Johns Hopkins University Press, 1995).

26. Frank Bruni, "A Fight Over Baby's Death and Dignity," *New York Times*, 9 Mar., pp. 1996.

27. D. M. Eddy, "Rationing by Patient Choice," *Journal of the American Medical Association*, 265 (1991); pp. 105–8.

28. D. M. Eddy, "Connecting Value and Cost," *Journal of the American Medical Association*, 264 (1990), pp. 1737–39.

29. Anders, *Health Against Wealth*, interview with William Speck, p. 47, 12 May 1995.

30. Daniel Callahan, "Terminating Life-Sustaining Treatment of the Demented," *Hastings Center Report* 25, no. 6 (1995), pp. 25–31.

31. Martin A. Strosberg, "The Oregon Plan And Health Care Rationing," Lecture at Union College Schenectady, N.Y., 28 May 1989.

32. "Burden of Suffering Engulfs Family Finances," *Medical Ethics Advisor* 12, no. 9 (Sept. 1996), p. 100.

33. John Hardwig, "Is There a Duty to Die?" *Hastings Center Report* 27, no. 2 (1997), pp. 34–42.

34. K. E. Covinsky, C. S. Landefeld, T. Teno et al. "Is Economic Hardship on the Families of the Seriously Ill Associated with Patient and Surrogate Care Preferences?" *Archives of Internal Medicine* 156 (1996), pp. 1737–41.

35. "Study Suggests Finances Weigh Heavy on the Dying," *Medical Ethics Advisor* 12, no. 9 (Sept. 1996), p. 99.

36. Hardwig, "Is There a Duty to Die?"

37. Harriet E. Tillock, Paper Presented at the Annual Meeting of the American Sociological Association in Cincinnati, Ohio, Aug. 1991.

38. Ibid.

22: THE ROAD AHEAD

1. Miller, Quill, Brody, Fletcher, Gostin and Meier, "Sounding Board: Regulating physician-assisted death", *New England Journal of Medicine* 331, no. 2, 14 July 1994.

Index

About the Authors

DEREK HUMPHRY is an international journalist and author who has been campaigning for the right to choose to die for more than twenty years. He began this fight soon after his first wife, Jean, dying of cancer, asked him to help her commit suicide to escape further suffering. The incongruity of risking imprisonment for a crime that he considered a necessary act of love was the spur to fight for law reform.

He has written six books on the subject of euthanasia—assisted good death. Of these *Jean's Way* was a best-seller in Britain and Australia, while *Final Exit* was a *New York Times* best-seller for eighteen weeks in 1991. *Final Exit* has been translated into twelve languages, selling more than a million copies worldwide. With a new edition published in 1997, it remains today the top-selling book on the subject.

He founded the Hemlock Society in 1980, built it into a nationally known organization with eighty chapters, relinquishing the reins in 1992 to concentrate on writing and lecturing on euthanasia. He is president of the Euthanasia Research & Guidance Organization and a director of the World Federation of Right to Die Societies. He appears regularly on television and radio discussion programs.

The British-born Humphry, sixty-eight, has worked as a staff writer for the London *Daily Mail*, the London *Sunday Times*, and the *Los Angeles Times*. He won the 1972 Martin Luther King Memorial Prize for the contribution of his book *Because They're Black* to racial harmony and the 1997 Socrates Award for *Final Exit*. He is married and lives near Eugene, Oregon.
<dhumphry@efn.org>

MARY CLEMENT, attorney and expert on right-to-die issues, is an outspoken advocate of protecting self-determination and autonomy in matters of personal health. She is the attorney for Derek Humphry's organization, ERGO!, and in this capacity contributed to amicus briefs for the Ninth and Second

Circuit Courts of Appeals and the United States Supreme Court cases on physician-assisted suicide.

She is also President of Gentle Closure, Inc., an organization that helps people address end-of-life concerns, including living wills, health care proxies, nonhospital do-not-resuscitate orders, anatomical gifts, and consultations for the removal of unwanted medical treatment. Detailed question and answer booklets prepared by Ms. Clement accompany customized documents.

She is a member of the Board of Directors of the Hemlock Society and its sister organization, PRO USA. Ms. Clement has also written articles for *The New York Times* and the *World Federation of Right-to-Die Societies Newsletter* and other publications and has appeared on radio and television as an expert supporter of physician aid-in-dying for the terminally ill. Television appearances include *Court TV* and CNBC's *Equal Time*. She is a frequent lecturer on end-of-life issues at such places as the Association of the Bar of the City of New York.

Ms. Clement started law school twenty-four years after graduating from college, thereby fulfilling a long-held dream. She was admitted to the New York State Bar in 1993, the same month she turned fifty. She lived all of her life in Manhattan until she moved to Sedona, Arizona, in 1996. She has two grown sons.

<Marydclem@aol.com>